# EXAM ESSENTIALS PRACTICE TESTS

# Cambridge English: Advanced (CAE)

# 2

**Tom Bradbury**
**Eunice Yeates**

NATIONAL
GEOGRAPHIC
LEARNING

Australia · Brazil · Mexico · Singapore · United Kingdom · United States

**NATIONAL GEOGRAPHIC**
**L E A R N I N G**

**Exam Essentials Practice Tests 2**
**Cambridge English: Advanced (CAE)**
**(with key)**

**Tom Bradbury and Eunice Yeates**

Publisher: Gavin McLean

Publishing Consultant: Karen Spiller

Editorial Project Manager: Stephanie Parker

Development Editor: Diane Hall

Strategic Marketing Manager: Charlotte Ellis

Project Editor: Tom Relf

Manufacturing Buyer: Eyvett Davis

Cover design: Oliver Hutton

Compositor: Cenveo® Publisher Services

National Geographic Liaison:
    Wesley Della Volla

Audio: Martin Williamson,
    Prolingua Productions

DVD-ROM: Tom, Dick and Debbie Ltd

Contributing writer: Susan Yokes
    (video materials)

For product information and technology assistance, contact us at
**Cengage Learning Customer & Sales Support, cengage.com/contact**

For permission to use material from this text or product,
submit all requests online at **cengage.com/permissions**
Further permissions questions can be emailed to
**permissionrequest@cengage.com**

ISBN: 978-1-285-74507-7

**National Geographic Learning**
Cheriton House, North Way, Andover, Hampshire, SP10 5BE
United Kingdom

National Geographic Learning, a Cengage Learning Company, has a mission to bring the world to the classroom and the classroom to life. With our English language programs, students learn about their world by experiencing it. Through our partnerships with National Geographic and TED Talks, they develop the language and skills they need to be successful global citizens and leaders.

Locate your local office at **international.cengage.com/region**

Visit National Geographic Learning online at **NGL.Cengage.com/ELT**
Visit our corporate website at **www.cengage.com**

**Photos**
169 t (Radius Images/Alamy), 169 c (1bestofphoto/Alamy), 169 b (Chris Whitehead/Getty Images), 170 t (Bambu Productions/Getty Images), 170 b (Ryan McVay/Getty Images), 170 c (RioPatuca Images/Fotolia), 172 t (Oleksandr Rupeta/Alamy), 172 c (dbimages/Alamy), 172 c (Ocean/Corbis UK Ltd), 172 b (Marka/Superstock Ltd.), 173 b (Deyan Georgiev/Alamy), 173 t (Richard Freeda/Getty Images), 175 c (Chris Ryan/Getty Images), 175 t (Pavel Losevsky/Fotolia), 175 b (Moodboard/Corbis UK Ltd), 176 c (BRIAN ANTHONY/Alamy), 176 t (Helen King/Corbis UK Ltd), 176 b (Jose Luis Pelaez Inc/Blend Ima/Corbis UK Ltd), 178 b (Denkou Images/Alamy), 178 c (SelectStock/Getty Images), 178 t (JGI/Jamie Grill/Blend Images/C/Corbis UK Ltd), 179 t (iMate/Fotolia), 179 c (Ghislain & Marie David de Lossy/Getty Images), 179 b (John Cumming/Getty Images), 181 t (Gijsbert Hanekroot/Alamy), 181 c (Carolyn Clarke/Alamy), 181 b (Ariel Skelley/Getty Images), 182 t (Marco Simoni/Robert Harding/Getty Images), 182 c (Cultura/Henn Photography/Getty Images), 182 b (Oliver Furrer/Getty Images), 184 c (Eric Nathan/Alamy), 184 t (Martin Barraud/Getty Images), 184 b (Bruce Ayres/Getty Images), 185 b (Mike Goldwater/Alamy), 185 t (Thomas Imo/Alamy), 185 c (Yoram Lehmann/Getty Images), 187 t (Christian Mueller/Shutterstock), 187 b (JMiks/Shutterstock), 187 c (Education Images/UIG/Getty Images), 188 b (Angela Hampton Picture Library/Alamy), 188 c (Hero Images/Hero Images/Corbis UK Ltd), 188 t (Rainer Elstermann/Getty Images), 190 c (Blend Images/Alamy), 190 b (Bubbles Photolibrary/Alamy), 190 c (Chabruken/Getty Images), 191 t (Dragon Images/Shutterstock), 191 c (imtmphoto/Shutterstock), 191 b (Voyagerix/Shutterstock)

**Texts**
Adapted from 'Caveman café brings Stone Age diet to the Berlin masses' by Tony Paterson, The Independent, 27 October 2011, copyright The Independent. Adapted from 'Birdwatching is the best training for animal behaviour' by Tim Birkhead, The Guardian, 24 February 2012, Copyright Guardian News & Media Ltd 2012. Adapted from 'Why the Maya Fell: Climate Change, Conflict - And a Trip to the Beach?' by Nicholas Mott, http://news.nationalgeographic.com/news/2012/11/121109-maya-civilization-climate-change-belize-science/, 9 November 2012. Adapted from Student Entrepreneurs by Laura Bridgestock, 27 March 2012, http://www.topuniversities.com/student-info/student-stories/student-entrepreneurs. Adapted from OSU Student Entrepreneur Talks Taking Risk, Embracing Failure, and Tasting the Business Life by OSU Startup Crew, http://oregonstate.startupweekend.org/2013/05/08/osu-student-entrepreneur-talks-taking-risk-embracing-failure-and-tasting-the-business-life/, with permission from Oregon State University Startup Crew. Adapted from 'The seductive phrase every publisher craves' by Robert McCrum, The Observer, 10 April 2011, Copyright Guardian News & Media Ltd 2011. Adapted from 'Ice Water Diver', Rhian Waller, National Geographic Magazine, http://ngm.nationalgeographic.com/125-exploration/risk-takers-gallery#/8, July 2013. Adapted from 'The long and short of what makes a leader' by Roger Dobson, The Independent, 10 February 2013, copyright The Independent. Adapted from 'The cycle path to happiness' by Simon Usborne, The Independent, 18 December 2012, copyright The Independent. Adapted from 'Care farms help people recover their better nature' by Bibi van der Zee, http://www.guardian.co.uk/society/2011/aug/02/care-farms-young-people-nature-benefit, Copyright Guardian News & Media Ltd 2011. Adapted from 'Why we build by Rowan Moore' review by Philippa Sockley, The Telegraph, 26 September 2012, © Telegraph Media Group Limited 2012. Adapted from 'The Architect's Home by Peter Gossel' review by Rowan Moore, The Observer, 21 April 2013, Copyright Guardian News & Media Ltd 2013. Adapted from '20th-Century World Architecture: The Phaidon Atlas by Phaidon editors; The Future of Architecture Since 1889 by Jean-Louis Cohen' review by Rowan Moore, The Observer, 28 October 2012, Copyright Guardian News & Media Ltd 2012. Adapted from 'Species Hunt' by A. R. Williams, National Geographic Magazine, http://ngm.nationalgeographic.com/2013/04/125-explore/seeking-new-species, April 2013. Adapted from 'The heart of Hemingway' by Sam Leith, The Spectator, 7 January 2012, http://www.spectator.co.uk/books/7545693/the-heart-of-hemingway/. Adapted from 'Have you got what it takes to be an Olympic athlete?' by Kate Carter, The Guardian, 28 January 2013, Copyright Guardian News & Media Ltd 2013. Adapted from 'What does it take to run a record label?' by Jack Oughton, http://careers.guardian.co.uk/what-does-it-take-to-run-a-record-label, Copyright Guardian News & Media Ltd 2013. Adapted from 'The Hook: Is it a good or bad time to start an indie label?' by Lars Brandle, http://www.themusicnetwork.com/music-features/industry/2013/04/02/the-hook-is-it-a-good-or-bad-time-to-start-an-indie-label/, 2 April 2013, with permission from The Music Network. Adapted from 'Celebrating Baby's 60th birthday and the start of the computer age' by Pat Hurst, Newsdesk, September 2013, with permission from The Press Association. Adapted from 'Hold the line - overheard phone calls more distracting than room full of people chatting' by Steve Connor, The Independent, 13 March 2013, copyright The Independent. Adapted from 'Australia's lost giants' by Joel Achenbach, National Geographic Magazine, http://ngm.nationalgeographic.com/2010/10/dreamtime-animals/achenbach-text, October 2010. Adapted from 'The artists' artist: modern composers' by Anna Tims, The Guardian, 4 August 2011, Copyright Guardian News & Media Ltd 2011. Adapted from 'Relics to Reefs' by Stephen Harrigan, National Geographic Magazine, http://ngm.nationalgeographic.com/2011/02/artificial-reefs/harrigan-text, February 2011. Adapted from 'Have you considered History of Art?' by Laura Shand, The Independent, 1 October 2102, copyright The Independent. Adapted from Museum careers, http://www.museumsassociation.org/careers -nos 9921/9922/9924/9929, with permission from Museums Association, www.museumsassociation.org. Adapted from 'Forest Giant' by David Quammen, National Geographic Magazine, http://ngm.nationalgeographic.com/2012/12/sequoias/quammen-text, December 2012. Adapted from http://www.spiked-online.com/index.php?/inspired/ articles 1386/1398/1458/1384, with permission from spiked Ltd. Adapted from 'Why you will never sleep on a plane if a baby is crying' by Nick Collins, The Telegraph, 17 October 2012, © Telegraph Media Group Limited 2012. Adapted from 'The enduring myth of music and maths' by Tim Gowers, The Independent, 6 July 2011, copyright The Independent. Adapted from 'The Truth About Chimps' by Joshu

Although every effort has been made to contact copyright holders before publication, this has not always been possible. If notified, the publisher will undertake to rectify any errors or omissions at the earliest opportunity. Note that the sample answer sheets in the Practice tests are not the updated official answer sheets provided by Cambridge as these were not available at the time of publication.

Printed in China by RR Donnelley
Print Number: 06      Print Year: 2018

# Contents

| Section | | Page |
|---|---|---|
| Exam overview | ▶ ▶ | 4 |
| Introduction | ▶ ▶ | 6 |
| DVD-ROM introduction | ▶ ▶ | 10 |
| Test 1 with guidance | ▶ ▶ | 12 |
| Test 2 with guidance | ▶ ▶ | 32 |
| Test 3 with guidance | ▶ ▶ | 52 |
| Test 4 | ▶ ▶ | 71 |
| Test 5 | ▶ ▶ | 90 |
| Test 6 | ▶ ▶ | 109 |
| Test 7 | ▶ ▶ | 128 |
| Test 8 | ▶ ▶ | 147 |
| Sample answer sheets | ▶ ▶ | 166 |
| Materials for Paper 4 | ▶ ▶ | 169 |
| Writing bank | ▶ ▶ | 193 |
| Glossary | ▶ ▶ | 206 |
| Audio scripts | ▶ ▶ | 217 |
| Answer key | ▶ ▶ | 233 |

**CAMBRIDGE ENGLISH: ADVANCED**

**Paper 1: READING AND USE OF ENGLISH** (1 hour 30 minutes)

| Part | Task type and focus | Number of questions | Task format |
|------|---------------------|:---:|-------------|
| 1 | **Multiple-choice cloze**<br>Task focus: vocabulary | 8 | A multiple-choice cloze text with eight gaps, followed by eight four-option questions. |
| 2 | **Open cloze**<br>Task focus: grammar and some vocabulary | 8 | A modified cloze text with eight gaps which you fill with the appropriate word. |
| 3 | **Word formation**<br>Task focus: vocabulary | 8 | A text with eight gaps. You are asked to complete the text by making an appropriate word from the word prompt you are given for each gap. |
| 4 | **Key word transformations**<br>Task focus: grammar and vocabulary | 6 | This task consists of six discrete key word transformations. You are asked to complete a sentence which means the same as the given sentence using the key word. |
| 5 | **Multiple choice**<br>Task focus: reading for detailed understanding of a text, gist, opinion, attitude, tone, purpose, main idea, meaning from context, implication, text organisation features | 6 | You answer six four-option multiple-choice questions on a text. |
| 6 | **Short texts**<br>Task focus: reading to understand meaning across different texts. | 4 | You read four short texts by different writers on a similar topic, and with a similar purpose. Reading across the texts, you identify similarities and differences in the themes and opinions of the writers. |
| 7 | **Missing paragraphs**<br>Task focus: close reading of a text, identifying references and meanings across discourse. | 6 | You read a text from which six paragraphs have been removed. There is one extra paragraph. You decide which paragraphs complete each gap in the text. |
| 8 | **Multiple matching**<br>Task focus: reading for specific information in a text, detail, opinion, attitude | 10 | You match ten questions to different texts or different sections of a text. |

**Paper 2: WRITING** (1 hour 30 minutes)

| Part | Task type and focus | Number of questions | Task format |
|------|---------------------|------------------|-------------|
| 1 | **Question 1**<br>Essay | Part 1 is compulsory.<br>220–260 words | You write an essay based on a given title and accompanying ideas, including one of your own. |
| 2 | **Questions 2–4** may include an email/a letter, a report, a review or a proposal | You have a choice from three tasks.<br>220–260 words | You carry out a writing task, using the appropriate style and format. |

**Paper 3: LISTENING** (40 minutes approximately)

| Part | Task type and focus | Number of questions | Task format |
|------|---------------------|---------------------|-------------|
| 1 | **Multiple choice**<br>Task focus: understanding gist, detail, function, purpose, feeling, attitude, opinion, genre, agreement, etc. | 6 | A series of short unrelated extracts, from monologues or exchanges between interacting speakers. There is one three-option question for each extract. |
| 2 | **Sentence completion**<br>Task focus: detail, specific information, stated opinion | 8 | A monologue. The task consists of eight gapped sentences. |
| 3 | **Multiple choice**<br>Task focus: understanding attitude and opinion, main idea, specific information and gist | 6 | A listening text involving interacting speakers. You have six four-option multiple-choice questions, and need to decide what the correct answer is. |
| 4 | **Multiple matching**<br>Task focus: understanding mood and attitude, main ideas, specific information and context | 10 | Five short monologues, all on a similar theme. You listen once and match each speaker to information from two separate lists. |

**Paper 4: SPEAKING** (15 minutes approximately)

| Part | Task type and focus | Input | Task format |
|------|---------------------|-------|-------------|
| **1**<br>**Interview**<br>(2 mins) | The interlocutor asks each candidate to say a little about themselves. | Verbal questions | You must be able to<br>• give personal information.<br>• talk about present circumstances / past experiences.<br>• talk about future plans. |
| **2**<br>**Individual long turn**<br>(4 mins) | Each candidate talks about a pair of photographs for 1 minute, followed by a 30-second response from the second candidate. | Visual stimuli, with verbal and written instructions | You must be able to<br>• give information.<br>• express your opinions.<br>• relate photos to yourself and your own experience. |
| **3**<br>**Two-way collaborative task**<br>(4 mins) | The interlocutor asks candidates to carry out a task based on written prompts. | A written question with written stimuli and verbal instructions | You must be able to<br>• exchange information and opinions.<br>• express and justify opinions.<br>• agree, disagree or partly agree.<br>• suggest and speculate. |
| **4**<br>**Discussion**<br>(5 mins) | The interlocutor asks candidates general opinion questions related to the topic covered in Part 3. | Verbal prompts | You must be able to<br>• exchange information and opinions.<br>• express and justify opinions.<br>• agree, disagree or partly agree. |

*Exam Essentials Practice Tests* is a series of materials published by National Geographic Learning for students preparing for the major EFL/ESL examinations: Cambridge English: First (FCE); Cambridge English: Advanced (CAE); and International English Language Testing System (IELTS). The series is characterised by the close attention each component pays to developing a detailed knowledge of the skills and strategies needed for success in each paper or part of the exams.

*Cambridge English: Advanced (CAE) Practice Tests* helps learners become aware of the Cambridge English: Advanced (CAE) exam requirements, offers details about the format and language in the exam, and helps learners develop exam skills necessary for success. The book also provides extensive practice in all parts of the exam, using the actual test format.

## Taking the Exam

Cambridge English: Advanced is one of a series of five Cambridge English exams corresponding to different levels of the Common European Framework of Reference for Languages (CEFR):

- Cambridge English: Key (KET) CEFR Level A2
- Cambridge English: Preliminary (PET) CEFR Level B1
- Cambridge English: First (FCE) CEFR Level B2
- Cambridge English: Advanced (CAE) CEFR Level C1
- Cambridge English: Proficiency (CPE) CEFR Level C2

Cambridge English: Advanced is widely recognised by universities and similar educational institutions, and in commerce and industry, as proof that the holder of this qualification can take a course of study in English at university level, and also carry out managerial and professional work effectively. It can also be used as proof of English skills when applying for employment in English-speaking environments.

The exam can be taken on many dates during a year, and can be taken on paper or on a computer. It consists of four Papers.

## Paper 1 Reading and Use of English (1 hour 30 minutes)

- Part 1 is a multiple-choice cloze task. You read a text with eight gaps. This is followed by eight four-option multiple-choice questions. You need to complete each gap with the correct option. Part 1 tests your knowledge of vocabulary, including idioms, fixed phrases, phrasal verbs, collocations and shades of meaning.

- Part 2 is an open cloze task. You read a text with eight gaps. You need to complete each gap with an appropriate word. Part 2 tests your knowledge of the structure of the language – grammar and some vocabulary.

- Part 3 is a word formation task. You read a short text with eight gaps. You need to complete each gap with an appropriate word formed from a prompt word in capitals that appears to the right of the text on the same line as the gap. Part 3 tests your knowledge of how words are formed from other words.

- Part 4 consists of six sentences, each of which is followed by a word and a gapped sentence. You need to complete the gapped sentence so that its meaning is the same as the first sentence using three to six words, including the word given. Part 4 tests your knowledge of vocabulary and grammar.

- Part 5 consists of a long text with six four-option multiple-choice questions. Part 5 tests your ability to read for detail, gist, opinion, attitude, purpose, implication and text organisation features such as reference and comparison.

- Part 6 consists of four short texts written by four different people about the same subject, together with four questions. The questions test your ability to understand the opinions and attitudes expressed in the texts and to identify when writers agree and disagree with each other.

- Part 7 consists of a long text from which six paragraphs have been removed and placed in jumbled order after the text. You have to decide from where in the text the paragraphs have been removed. Part 7 tests your understanding of how a text is structured.

- Part 8 consists of a long text with several sections or several short texts. There are 10 questions which require you to decide which section of the long text or which short text each one refers to. Part 8 tests your ability to read for specific information, detail, opinion and attitude.

**Paper 2 Writing (1 hour 30 minutes)**

- Part 1 is compulsory. You are required to write an essay in 220–260 words. Before you write your answer, you must read the instructions as well as an input text or texts. Part 1 focuses on your ability to evaluate, express opinions, hypothesise, etc. Persuasion is always an important element in your writing in Part 1.

- There are three questions to choose from in Part 2. For questions 2–4, you are required to write an email/letter, a proposal, a report or a review in 220–260 words. Part 2 focuses on your ability to give opinions, persuade, justify, give advice, compare, etc.

- Both parts of the Writing Paper test your ability to write a text according to instructions in an appropriate style and register for a given purpose and target reader. Effective text organisation, accuracy and a good range of vocabulary are also important.

**Paper 3 Listening (approximately 40 minutes)**

- Part 1 consists of three short monologues or texts involving interacting speakers. You are required to answer two three-option multiple-choice questions for each extract. Part 1 tests your ability to understand feeling, attitude, opinion, purpose, function, agreement, course of action, general gist, detail, etc.

- Part 2 consists of a long monologue. You are required to complete eight gapped sentences with information you hear on the recording. Each gap is completed by one, two or three words or a number. Part 2 tests your ability to understand specific information and stated opinion.

- Part 3 consists of a text involving interacting speakers. You are required to answer six four-option multiple-choice questions. Part 3 tests your ability to understand attitude and opinion.

- Part 4 consists of five short monologues on a related theme. There are two tasks in this part. Both tasks require you choose from a list of options the opinion that each speaker expresses. Part 4 tests your ability to understand gist, attitude and main point and to interpret context.

**Paper 4 Speaking (approximately 15 minutes)**

The Speaking Paper generally involves two candidates and two examiners.

- In Part 1 you have a brief conversation with the examiner. Part 1 tests your ability to give personal information and use social and interactional language.

- In Part 2 the examiner gives you and the other candidate visual and written prompts. Each candidate is required to use the prompts he/she is given to talk for a minute. He/She is also required to answer a question based on the other candidate's prompts in 30 seconds. Part 2 tests your ability to organise a larger unit of discourse to compare, describe, express opinions and speculate.

- In Part 3 the examiner gives you and the other candidate visual and written prompts. You are required to use the prompts to have a conversation with the other candidate. Part 3 tests your ability to sustain an interaction, exchange ideas, express and justify opinions, agree and/or disagree, suggest, evaluate, reach a decision through negotiation, etc.

- In Part 4 the examiner asks you questions based on the topics you talked about in Part 3. You are required to have a three-way discussion with the examiner and the other candidate. Part 4 tests your ability to exchange information, express and justify opinions, agree and/or disagree.

## Preparing for the exam

In preparing for the four Papers, the following points should be taken into account.

### Reading and Use of English

To prepare for the **Use of English** (Parts 1, 2, 3 and 4), you need to develop your awareness and use of both grammatical structures and vocabulary. You need to know how structures such as verb forms, modal and auxiliary verbs, pronouns, prepositions, conjunctions, modifiers and determiners are used correctly in a variety of different types of text. You also need a good knowledge of vocabulary, so learn whole phrases rather than single words in isolation, how words and phrases are used in combination with other words, how words can have different meanings and uses, and how different words can be formed from a root. It helps to read widely and to pay attention to grammar and vocabulary as you read. Make use of dictionaries and grammar books (except when doing the tests), and develop an efficient system for recording the new vocabulary and grammar you encounter.

To prepare for the **Reading** (Parts 5, 6, 7 and 8), you should read from a range of material: newspapers, magazines, journals, novels, leaflets, brochures, etc. When you read, pay attention to text organisation features, train yourself to recognise the author's purpose in writing and his or her tone, and learn to read between the lines for what is implied rather than stated explicitly. It is important to practise different reading strategies that can be used for different parts of the Reading Paper, for example skimming for the main idea and gist, scanning to locate specific information or reading closely to determine the writer's precise meaning.

## Writing

You need to be familiar with all the text types you may be required to write in the exam. You should also be aware of the criteria that will be used in marking your texts.

- Has the candidate achieved the purpose stated in the instructions?
- Does the text have a positive general effect on the target reader?
- Does the text cover all the content points?
- Is the text organised effectively and are ideas linked appropriately?
- Has language been used accurately?
- Does the text have a good range of vocabulary and grammatical features?
- Is the register appropriate for the task?
- Is the layout appropriate?

## Listening

You should practise listening to a wide variety of spoken English: announcements, speeches, lectures, talks, radio broadcasts, anecdotes, radio interviews, discussions, etc. You should also practise listening for different purposes: to understand gist, identify context or attitude or find specific information.

## Speaking

You should practise speaking English as much as possible. It is important to master conversational skills such as turn taking and the appropriate way to participate in a discussion, giving full but natural answers to questions and requesting clarification.

Further information can be obtained from the Cambridge English website: www.cambridgeenglish.org

## *Practice Tests*: contents

*Cambridge English: Advanced (CAE)* in the *Exam Essentials Practice Tests* series prepares candidates for the Cambridge English: Advanced examination by providing **eight full practice tests,** which accurately reflect the latest exam specifications.

There are **three guided tests** at the beginning, which feature **essential tips** to practise exam strategy. These tips offer guidance and general strategies for approaching each task. Other tips offer advice relevant to specific questions in the guided tests. These guided tests will help students prepare for each paper, while the following five **tests (without guidance)** will offer students thorough practice at a realistic exam level.

The **DVD-ROM** accompanying the book includes the audio materials for all the Listening Papers. These accurately reflect the exam in both style and content. Moreover, the audio materials for Tests 1 and 2 have been recorded with the repetitions and full pauses, exactly as in the exam itself.

A **writing bank** includes **sample answers** for the kinds of tasks that occur in Paper 2 (Writing), writing tips in the form of notes and **useful phrases** for the different task types. Varied **visual materials** for Paper 4 (Speaking) have also been included, while a **language bank** supplies useful phrases and expressions for use in the Speaking Paper.

There is also a **glossary** for each test, explaining vocabulary that is likely to be unfamiliar to students.

Clear and straightforward design simplifies use of the book. **Exam overview** tables ensure that key information is readily accessible, while a specially designed menu makes it easy to navigate through the different parts and papers of each practice test.

You will find **sample exam answer sheets** on pages 166–168 which you can photocopy and use to note down your answers. These will help you practise using the answer sheets you will be given in the real exam.

For more practice, there is also an additional book of tests for this exam: *Exam Essentials Practice Tests 1 Cambridge English: Advanced (CAE)*.

## *Practice Tests*: principles

In writing this book, three guiding principles have been observed.

Firstly, that it should be useful for teachers, students sitting the Cambridge English: Advanced exam for the first time or re-sitting the exam, whether they are working alone or in a class. Students approaching the exam for the first time would be best advised to work through the book linearly, developing their skills and confidence; those re-sitting the exam can consult the Exam overview tables to concentrate on particular areas for targeted revision. The **without key** edition can be used by students working in a class, while the **with key** edition includes a detailed **answer key and all the audio scripts,** ensuring that students working alone can benefit from support while attempting these tests.

The second principle is that the questions should accurately reflect the range of questions found in the Cambridge English: Advanced exam. Thus students obtain guidance concerning the general content and the best way of approaching the tasks from the questions themselves. Seeing the questions in this light – as instructions to the candidate from the examiner rather than intimidating challenges – also helps students feel less daunted by the whole experience of sitting a major exam like this.

The third principle is that the texts used in the practice tests should be not only representative of those used in the exam, but also varied and interesting. Everyone finds it easier to learn if the subject matter is relevant to his or her lifestyle and interests. In choosing, editing and creating the texts here, we have done our utmost to ensure that the experience of working with this book is as stimulating and rewarding as possible.

This edition of *Exam Essentials* for students of Cambridge English: Advanced (CAE) includes a brand new DVD-ROM which focuses on the Speaking test component of the Cambridge English: Advanced examination. The DVD-ROM includes two videos:

- a complete Cambridge English: Advanced Speaking test.
- a short clip giving valuable advice about the Cambridge English: Advanced Speaking test.

To maximise learning from the complete Cambridge English: Advanced Speaking test, the following PDFs are also available on the DVD-ROM:

- a worksheet for individual or class use.
- an answer key for the worksheet.
- the complete script of the Speaking test.

## A complete Speaking test

A full Cambridge English: Advanced Speaking test interview is approximately 15 minutes in length. Please note that the interview shown on this DVD-ROM is a slightly extended version of the Speaking test. This allows for a wide range of language and types of response to be included. This interview also features high-level candidates whose performance would achieve a good pass in the exam. The video therefore provides a good model to follow. Don't worry if you feel you may not perform to this high standard in every area of the test. You will need to demonstrate a good level, but you will not need to use every structure or item of vocabulary perfectly in order to pass the test.

The video clearly details:

- the role of the examiners.
- the timings of the test.
- the four parts of the test and what is involved in each one.

### The role of the examiners

There are two examiners in the test room. Examiner 1 (the interlocutor) asks the candidates questions and handles the tasks. He or she has to keep to very strict timings and has a script to follow. Unscripted conversation or questions are therefore not possible. This is to ensure that each candidate receives equal treatment. Examiner 2 (the assessor) does not usually speak in the test, except to greet the candidates. However, Examiner 2 will make notes. Both examiners give marks to the candidates.

### The timings of the test

Part 1: Interview – 2 minutes (3 minutes for groups of three)

Part 2: Individual long turn – 4 minutes (6 minutes for groups of three)

Part 3: Collaborative task – 4 minutes (6 minutes for groups of three)

Part 4: Discussion – 5 minutes (8 minutes for groups of three)

### The four parts of the test

Part 1: Interview – this includes greeting the candidates, introducing the examiners and general questions about yourself.

Part 2: Individual long turn – this involves talking about two out of three pictures and briefly answering a question about your partner's pictures after he/she has spoken.

Part 3: Collaborative task – this is where both candidates talk about prompts on a diagram, and reach a decision through negotiation.

Part 4: Discussion – the interlocutor leads a discussion by asking candidates questions. Candidates exchange information and opinions related to the topic in Part 3.

### How each part of the test should be answered

The video offers tips for improving candidates' performance in each of the four parts. In Part 1, candidates need to give personal information, talk about their present circumstances, talk about past experiences and future plans as well as express opinions. In Part 2, candidates need to express their opinions through comparing, hypothesising and speculating on the pictures given. In Part 3, candidates need to work together to exchange ideas and opinions, agree or disagree, suggest, speculate, evaluate and reach a decision through negotiation. In Part 4, candidates express and justify their opinions and agree and disagree.

## Tips and advice

Following the Speaking test, there is a short clip to supplement the speaking tips given in the book. In this section, which is about five minutes long, an examiner gives some tips and advice about how to do well in the Cambridge English: Advanced Speaking test.

## The worksheet

This printable worksheet accompanies the complete Cambridge English: Advanced Speaking test. Although primarily designed for self-study, the worksheet can also be used in the classroom. It provides in-depth information about the Speaking test and focuses on the language each candidate uses in the video.

The worksheet is divided into four sections which relate to each part of the Speaking test. It includes activities which:

- draw students' attention to key features of the candidate's response.
- relate these features to the marking criteria used by the examiners.
- give the student practice in developing their own answers for similar questions.

A separate answer key and a full video script are also provided.

PAPER 1  Reading and ▸  Part 1
          Use of English      Part 2
                              Part 3
PAPER 2  Writing              Part 4
                              Part 5
PAPER 3  Listening            Part 6
                              Part 7
PAPER 4  Speaking             Part 8

For questions **1–8**, read the text below and decide which answer (**A, B, C** or **D**) best fits each gap. There is an example at the beginning (**0**).

Mark your answers **on the separate answer sheet**.

**Example:**

**0**   **A**   scan        **B**   glance        **C**   view        **D**   spot

```
0 | A   B   C   D
    ‾‾  ▬▬  ‾‾  ‾‾
```

## Essential tips

- Part 1 of the Reading and Use of English paper tests your awareness of vocabulary.

- Read the whole text to get a general idea of the subject.

- There is only one correct answer for each question, and it must fit in the sentence and also the meaning of the whole text.

- The gapped word may be part of a collocation (two words that are frequently combined – e.g. *make progress*), a phrasal verb or an expression, or it may just be the only suitable word for the specific context.

- Look carefully at the words before and after each gap. For example, sometimes only one option is correct because of a preposition that follows the gap.

**Question 2:** All four options fit the gap in terms of their meaning but only one option is followed by the preposition *on*.

**Question 4:** This is an example of a collocation. Only one option goes with *forbidden*.

**Question 5:** Which of these phrasal verbs means 'to cause something new to happen'?

**Question 8:** This is an example of an item where the answer depends on the grammatical structure that comes after. Only one of the options can be followed by an infinitive – *to have lost* – in this sentence.

## A Stone-Age restaurant

At first (**0**) …….., Berlin's Sauvage restaurant looks much like many other fashionable eateries. But look closely and you'll discover that it offers an unusual experience (**1**) …….. Paleolithic (or Stone-Age) food.

Diners sit at candle-lit tables and eat meals (**2**) …….. on the dietary habits of our prehistoric (**3**) …….. who lived between two million and 200,000 years ago. The food includes unprocessed fruit, vegetables, meat, fish, eggs, nuts and seeds, but sugar, bread, rice and dairy products are (**4**) …….. forbidden, as they were unavailable to Stone Age hunter-gatherers.

The restaurant's owners insist that the 'Paleo diet' (**5**) …….. greater energy levels, increased muscle mass and clearer skin. 'Many people think this diet is just a passing fashion, but it's a world-wide (**6**) ……..,' says one. It is probably strongest in the USA where thousands of people have apparently gone 'Paleo'. One of the best-known people to (**7**) …….. the caveman cuisine is the veteran pop singer, Tom Jones, who (**8**) …….. to have lost more than ten kilos after switching to it.

| | | | | |
|---|---|---|---|---|
| **1** | **A** consisting | **B** starring | **C** highlighting | **D** featuring |
| **2** | **A** based | **B** linked | **C** derived | **D** inspired |
| **3** | **A** founders | **B** originators | **C** ancestors | **D** pioneers |
| **4** | **A** tightly | **B** precisely | **C** extremely | **D** strictly |
| **5** | **A** brings about | **B** sets up | **C** pulls out | **D** follows with |
| **6** | **A** situation | **B** phenomenon | **C** circumstance | **D** incident |
| **7** | **A** enter | **B** adopt | **C** assume | **D** exert |
| **8** | **A** asserts | **B** maintains | **C** claims | **D** states |

| PAPER 1 | Reading and Use of English | ▸ | Part 1 |
|---|---|---|---|
| | | | Part 2 |
| PAPER 2 | Writing | | Part 3 |
| | | | Part 4 |
| PAPER 3 | Listening | | Part 5 |
| PAPER 4 | Speaking | | Part 6 |
| | | | Part 7 |
| | | | Part 8 |

For questions **9–16**, read the text below and think of the word which best fits each gap. Use only one word in each gap. There is an example at the beginning (**0**).

Write your answers **IN CAPITAL LETTERS on the separate answer sheet**.

Example: | 0 | O | F | | | | | | | | | | | | | | | | | | | |

## Body language – do we really understand it?

Newspapers accuse a well-known footballer (**0**) …….. anti-social behaviour in a night club. His manager makes a public statement in (**9**) …….. he asserts that the young man is innocent. When asked (**10**) …….. makes him so sure, the manager says 'he looked me straight in the eye when he told me.'

Can we really know (**11**) …….. or not someone is telling the truth just by looking in their eyes? Psychologist Robert James is far (**12**) …….. convinced. '(**13**) …….. and large, maintaining eye contact is something liars do because eye movements are fairly easy to control.'

Communications expert Becky Rhodes shares his scepticism. 'Body language clues are never precise (**14**) …….. to rely on with absolute confidence,' she says. She illustrates this by describing the 'Othello error', named (**15**) …….. Shakespeare's tragic character who claims his wife has been deceiving him and then interprets her shocked reaction (**16**) …….. guilt. 'Personally, the minute I see a security guard watching me in a shop, I start looking guilty, so my body language definitely doesn't reflect the truth about me.'

## Essential tips

▸ Part 2 of the Reading and Use of English paper tests your awareness of grammar and common expressions, and your ability to use these words correctly.

▸ Read the whole text to get a general idea of the subject.

▸ Most of the gaps need grammatical words. Decide which type of word each gap needs. These could include: prepositions (e.g. *of*, *in*), articles (*a*, *the*), pronouns (*they*, *it*, *them*), relative pronouns (*who*, *which*), conjunctions (*and*, *so*), parts of verbs (*be*, *been*), modal verbs (*might*, *must*), particles of phrasal verbs (*look* **through**, *look* **into**), parts of phrases (*in* **order** to).

▸ The gap will probably not need a topic word. For example, in the phrase *she might have known*, *known* would not be gapped, but *she* or *might* or *have* could be.

▸ Sometimes more than one answer is possible. For example, if *may* is possible, *might* and *could* are often possible too. So, don't worry if you can think of more than one answer, just choose one.

▸ The word you choose must fit the meaning of the text as a whole. So, when you complete the task, read the whole text to see if it all makes sense.

**Question 9:** A relative pronoun is needed here. Which one can follow a preposition?

**Question 11:** Look at the whole sentence, and particularly at this part of the question: *can we know … or not someone is telling the truth?* Which word often follows *know* in questions?

**Question 12:** Look at the whole of the second paragraph. The psychologist does not believe the manager was right. Which word fits *far … convinced* to express this idea?

**Question 13:** This is a linking phrase which means 'in general'. You need a preposition to complete it.

PAPER 1   Reading and ▶
Use of English

PAPER 2   Writing

PAPER 3   Listening

PAPER 4   Speaking

Part 1
Part 2
Part 3
Part 4
Part 5
Part 6
Part 7
Part 8

For questions **17–24**, read the text below. Use the word given in capitals at the end of some of the lines to form a word that fits in the gap **in the same line**. There is an example at the beginning (**0**).

Write your answers **IN CAPITAL LETTERS on the separate answer sheet**.

**Example:** | 0 | S | H | O | R | T | A | G | E | S | | | | | | | | |

## Fog catchers – a way of getting water into the desert

In the Atacama Desert of northern Chile, water (**0**) ........   **SHORT**
are nothing new. In one of the driest places on earth,
some local (**17**) ........ have never seen a drop of rain.   **RESIDE**
(**18**) ........, water supplies for the few remote settlements   **HISTORY**
have been trucked in. In the last 20 years, however,
some communities have turned to 'fog catchers' as an
alternative source of water and a means of (**19**) ........ the   **VITAL**
arid land.

Although it never rains, a heavy (**20**) ........ fog often rolls off   **COAST**
the Pacific Ocean and across the desert. As it reaches the rocky
foothills of the Andes mountains, (**21**) ........ is captured in large,   **MOIST**
specially designed nets. Droplets run down the nets into pipes,
and then into (**22**) ........ tanks. This water is fresh enough to drink,   **STORE**
but enough is also collected for other uses like washing
and farming.

This simple and (**23**) ........ technology is relatively cheap and easy   **INVENT**
to manage, which is why 'fog catchers' are now being tried out in
other parts of the world where (**24**) ........ of desertification is   **REVERSE**
a high priority.

## Essential tips

▶ Part 3 of the Reading and Use of English paper tests your knowledge of vocabulary, in particular your ability to build words from a basic root using prefixes and suffixes and making other kinds of changes.

▶ Read the whole text to get a general idea of the subject.

▶ Think about which type of word is needed for each gap. Is it a verb, noun, adjective or adverb? Try writing V (for verb), N (for noun), ADJ (for adjective) or ADV (for adverb) by the gaps to remind yourself of the word type required.

▶ Look at the whole sentence, not just the line with the gap in it.

▶ Look at the word in capital letters to the right of the gap. You will need to alter the form of this word by adding a prefix or suffix or by making some other change.

▶ Some words will need more than one change.

▶ When you've finished the task, read through it again and check that it all makes sense.

▶ As you read it again, check the spelling, and, also, whether words should be singular or plural.

**Question 17:** Look at the words before and after the gap to check whether the word should be singular or plural.

**Question 18:** An adverb is often needed at the start of a sentence. First, think about how to form an adjective from *history*. Then, think how this adjective can become an adverb. Also, check the spelling.

**Question 19:** A verb meaning 'giving new life to' is needed here. You will need to add a prefix and a suffix.

**Question 20:** Sometimes you may think that no change is needed. Here, for example, you may think that *coast fog* is possible. However, you will always need to make some change to the word in capital letters. In this case, you need to change *coast* in some way to make it an adjective.

PAPER 1 Reading and
Use of English

PAPER 2 Writing

PAPER 3 Listening

PAPER 4 Speaking

Part 1
Part 2
Part 3
**Part 4**
Part 5
Part 6
Part 7
Part 8

## Essential tips

▸ Part 4 of the Reading and Use of English paper tests your knowledge of grammar, vocabulary and sentence structure, and your ability to use these in an accurate way.

▸ For each question, read both sentences carefully. The second sentence must have the same meaning as the first, but in different words.

▸ You must not change the key word in any way.

▸ You may need to change the word order. Think about words that may need to change, for example, an adjective to an adverb, or the other way round.

▸ You may need to change the sentence from negative to positive or from active to passive, or the other way round.

▸ You must use between three and six words. Contracted words count as two words, e.g. *don't = do not*.

**Question 25:** Which phrase means 'knew nothing at all'? How can *whose* be used to mean 'who the folder belonged to'?

**Question 26:** What pattern of words comes after *encourage*? What phrase beginning *make a ...* means the same as *complain*? How should *formally* be changed?

**Question 27:** Can you change *demolish* to make a noun? Can you think of a phrase including *place* that means 'happened'?

**Question 30:** What passive structure beginning with *have* means 'get someone to service your car'? If the structure is passive, you do not need to mention who serviced the car – i.e. the mechanic. Notice that the first sentence begins with *wanted* in the past; make sure the changes you make express this meaning.

For questions **25–30**, complete the second sentence so that it has a similar meaning to the first sentence, using the word given. **Do not change the word given.** You must use between **three** and **six** words, including the word given. Here is an example (**0**).

**Example:**

**0**  Chloe would only eat a pizza if she could have a mushroom topping.

**ON**

Chloe .......................................... a mushroom topping when she had a pizza.

The gap can be filled with the words 'insisted on having', so you write:

**Example:** | **0** | INSISTED ON HAVING |

Write **only** the missing words **IN CAPITAL LETTERS on the separate answer sheet.**

---

**25**  Paula knew nothing at all about who the folder belonged to and why it appeared on her desk.

**WHOSE**

Paula had absolutely .......................................... and why it appeared on her desk.

**26**  Naomi said Michael should formally complain about the service they'd had at the hotel.

**MAKE**

Naomi encouraged .......................................... about the service they'd had at the hotel.

**27**  The stadium was demolished in 2003, and there are still no plans to build a new one.

**PLACE**

The .......................................... in 2003, and there are still no plans to build a new one.

**28**  Jenny's achievements impress me much less than her sister's do.

**NEARLY**

I don't think Jenny's achievements are .......................................... her sister.

**29**  Unless someone comes late, we should be able to get through all the points in today's meeting.

**TURNS**

As .......................................... on time, we should be able to get through all the points in today's meeting.

**30**  I wanted to get a mechanic to service my car before I went on holiday, but I didn't have time.

**HAVE**

I would like .......................................... before I went on holiday, but I didn't have time.

| PAPER 1 | Reading and ▶ | Part 1 |
|---|---|---|
| | Use of English | Part 2 |
| PAPER 2 | Writing | Part 3 |
| | | Part 4 |
| PAPER 3 | Listening | **Part 5** |
| PAPER 4 | Speaking | Part 6 |
| | | Part 7 |
| | | Part 8 |

You are going to read a newspaper article. For questions **31–36**, choose the answer (**A, B, C** or **D**) which you think fits best according to the text.

Mark your answers **on the separate answer sheet**.

# Birdwatching

*Bird expert Tim Birkhead looks at the fascinating subject of what we know or can know about birds.*

The sight of two lovebirds nibbling each other's necks is enough of a cliché that we barely give it a second thought. These small parrots are called lovebirds because their closeness and mutual preening resemble human affection. But what do they feel when they behave like that? Indeed, do they feel anything at all? Even asking the question seems wrong somehow, especially if you consider yourself an ethologist, a student of animal behaviour. The Nobel Prize winner, Niko Tinbergen, warned fellow ethologists to steer well clear of feelings. 'This is not the method we shall follow in our study of animal behaviour,' he announced in 1951. Like most ethologists, through much of my career I have hardly deviated from this hard-nosed approach. But every so often, I have seen something that simply wouldn't sit easily with it.

When my boyhood birdwatching became an obsession rather than simply a hobby, my despairing father warned me that I'd never make a career out of it, but luckily I did. Birdwatching is the best possible training for studying animal behaviour; to study birds well, you have to almost think like a bird. I spent years on various remote islands watching those great seabirds, guillemots. Intensely social, guillemots live shoulder-to-shoulder in huge city-like colonies. Like us they form friendships and long-term pair bonds and, like lovebirds, they show their affection for their partners through mutual preening and striking greeting ceremonies.

Once as I watched, an incubating guillemot stood up from its egg and roared out its greeting – apparently to no one. I was perplexed, but on looking out to sea – hundreds of metres away – there was a guillemot flying towards the colony. A few seconds later, it landed beside its partner. Guillemots were never quite the same for me after this. They can see so much better than I can, and they have some kind of guillemot-recognition system in their brain. The moment eventually inspired me to explore and write about the way birds use vision, hearing, touch, smell, taste and feelings to experience the world.

While it was relatively straightforward to describe how much better or worse a bird sees, hears, smells or touches than we do, trying to understand – scientifically – how a bird feels is fraught with difficulties. As the philosopher Thomas Nagel pointed out in his 1974 essay 'What is it like to be a bat?', we cannot know what it is like to be another person, let alone another species. He chose bats because they are mammals and we share a lot of physiology and neurobiology with them, and because bats possess a sense most of us don't have: echolocation (listening for echoes to locate things). I suspect Nagel thought that no human can echolocate, but in fact some blind people do so extremely well. Nagel's point, however, is this: because it is impossible to know what it is like to be another person, trying to imagine what non-humans feel is a waste of time.

It isn't. The behavioural thinking that I have followed all these years has served me, and other scientists like me, well. But it's also a kind of trap. Anything that doesn't fit gets ignored because the intellectual framework doesn't permit one to say something different for fear of being labelled unprofessional. But ways of thinking come and go. As our knowledge of animal behaviour has increased, and with it the realisation that so many behaviours we once considered uniquely human, like tool use and language, aren't, the boundaries are changing.

It's all very well to study the survival value of long-term pair bonds or mutual preening, but without knowing anything about the sensory bases for these behaviours, our understanding is always going to be incomplete. A few years ago, behaviourial zoologists discovered 'symmetry', and assumed that symmetry (for example, in a perfectly proportioned human face or a peacock's tail) constituted beauty and quality, and was therefore the basis for the selection of partners. Few researchers bothered to test whether animals could assess symmetry in the same way as we can. One who did checked whether female starlings could distinguish males based on the symmetry of their feathers. These highly social birds couldn't. Their senses weren't up to it. Any study that had assessed starling partner choice on the basis of symmetry without knowing this would have reached false conclusions. In contrast, the sense of vision in starlings (and most other birds) is far better than our own: they can discriminate many more colours than we can, and they use this to assess potential partners.

31  What does the writer suggest about birds in the first paragraph?

   **A**   The names commonly given to them can be inappropriate.

   **B**   People are often too subjective in the way they think about them.

   **C**   Insufficient attention is paid to the way they behave towards each other.

   **D**   Most serious research on them ignores the idea they might have emotions.

32  What does the writer say about himself in the second paragraph?

   **A**   His personal sympathies lie with particular species of birds.

   **B**   He has managed to achieve what was expected of him.

   **C**   He recognised early on how unusual his interests were.

   **D**   His understanding of birds stems from lengthy observation.

33  The writer describes a particular incident in the third paragraph to explain

   **A**   what originally attracted him to guillemots.

   **B**   what led him to investigate birds' senses.

   **C**   the challenges that birdwatchers encounter.

   **D**   the sophistication of guillemot communication.

34  Why does the writer refer to an idea put forward by Thomas Nagel?

   **A**   to underline the differences between birds and mammals

   **B**   to explain scientists' neglect of an aspect of animal research

   **C**   to emphasise the significance of the subject he is studying

   **D**   to draw attention to advances in scientific knowledge

35  What point does the writer make in the fifth paragraph?

   **A**   The way animals behave may have changed over time.

   **B**   Scientific debate has become more and more competitive.

   **C**   Research has shown the limitations of certain ideas about animals.

   **D**   The cautious approach he adopted in his work is a source of regret to him.

36  The writer discusses the study of 'symmetry' to illustrate

   **A**   the danger of ignoring birds' senses as a subject of study.

   **B**   the fact that birds tend to have better eyesight than humans.

   **C**   the idea that theories in science are disproved on a regular basis.

   **D**   the error in regarding beauty as a key factor in birds' choice of partners.

PAPER 1 Reading and ▸ Part 1
         Use of English   Part 2
                          Part 3
PAPER 2 Writing          Part 4
                          Part 5
PAPER 3 Listening        **Part 6**
                          Part 7
PAPER 4 Speaking         Part 8

You are going to read four contributions to a debate on whether entry to museums should be free of charge. For questions **37–40**, choose from the contributions **A–D**. The contributions may be chosen more than once.

Mark your answers **on the separate answer sheet**.

# Should entry to museums be free of charge?

*The views of four speakers at a conference on museum funding are summarised here.*

**A**

In the late 1990s, the then UK government decided to end admission charges to a number of leading museums and art galleries in the country, and within a few years visitor numbers to these institutions had almost doubled; one report estimated an increase from 27 to 42 million visitors within a year. This is the clearest possible evidence for the popularity of free museum admission, with both local citizens and tourists. It is no coincidence that the UK saw an impressive growth in tourism to the country in the same period, and there is no need to go into detail here about the implications of this for employment and general prosperity. Add to this the contribution that museums make in communicating culture, knowledge and inspiration to visitors, particularly younger ones, and it becomes obvious that the state investment required to fund free entry to museums pays off handsomely.

**B**

It is hardly surprising that surveys show most people favour free museum admission. Why would anyone spurn a free chance to see a collection of beautiful paintings or some fascinating historical objects? The fact is, however, that although visitor numbers generally go up when admission is free, more detailed analysis of the figures reveals some complex issues. For example, it is far from certain that free museum access automatically brings in the tourists. Most market research indicates that they want quality and will pay for it if necessary. Moreover, the evidence suggests that people who run museums which rely on the state for their funding have little incentive to make their collections more exciting and imaginatively displayed in order to boost visitor numbers; the fee, or absence of one, does their work for them. The need to attract paying customers, on the other hand, tends to concentrate the minds of museum and gallery directors.

**C**

Free admission to museums and galleries usually causes attendance to rise and, with effective marketing, stimulates growth in the tourist industry. However, studies have also found that, by and large, increased entries are accounted for by tourists, who do not pay local income taxes, and more frequent visits by local people who already go to museums, rather than a wider spread of the population. In other words, all taxpayers subsidise museum access for tourists and a limited local largely middle-class demographic who could afford to pay for museum admission. Therefore, the claim that free museums make the wider population more knowledgeable and cultured is questionable at best. The fact is, the majority have little interest in museums and are resentful when they learn how much they are paying for them. They would be even more perturbed to hear that state-funded museums, free of the need to compete to survive, tend to be complacent and unenterprising.

**D**

Museums have a crucial role to play in preserving and transmitting a nation's history and heritage, and in broadening intellectual and cultural horizons, among the younger generation in particular. Opinion polls show that most people understand this and, for this reason, favour free access. They also show people understand that free museum admission requires state funding, which in turn depends on taxation. While most of us dislike paying taxes, we know what they are for. People can also appreciate that government funding gives those who run museums a certain level of security which allows them to plan for the longer-term. This tends to lift the quality of museum collections and the way they are displayed and explained to visitors. Great museums which have free access also help to boost tourism, which is so central to the economic well-being of many countries nowadays.

## Which contributor

shares A's view regarding the role of museums in education?    **37** [ ]

has a different opinion from the others about the possible impact of the cost of entry to museums on tourism?    **38** [ ]

has the same opinion as C on the way state funding affects the development of museums?    **39** [ ]

takes a different view from the others regarding public attitudes towards the cost of entry to museums?    **40** [ ]

# Essential tips

- Part 6 of the Reading and Use of English paper tests your ability to understand opinions and attitudes expressed in different texts and to decide whether different writers have similar or different opinions. There are always four short texts by different writers about the same subject.

- Read the title and the texts quickly to get a general idea of what they are about. Don't worry if there are words or phrases you don't understand.

- Look carefully at the four questions and highlight the key words relating to the topic in each.

- Read the first text and highlight the parts of the text that refer to each of the questions. Write the relevant question numbers next to the text. Then do the same for the other three texts.

- Go through the questions again and highlight the part asking you to differentiate somehow between texts (usually at the beginning of the question).

- Then look at the parts of each text that are relevant to Question 37. Compare them carefully and decide which have similar views and which have different views.

**Question 37:** The key words in this question are *role of museums in education*. The relevant part of text A is '... the contribution that museums make in communicating culture, knowledge and inspiration to visitors, particularly younger ones ...' Now look at the other three texts and highlight references to education. As in text A, the word *education* may be paraphrased. The question asks which contributor shares A's view, so you need to work out which text expresses a similar view to A's.

**Question 38:** The key words in this sentence are *impact of the cost of entry ... on tourism* and you are asked to find a different opinion from the others, so you need to find three views that are similar and one that is different. The relevant part of text A is '... the clearest possible evidence for the popularity of free museum admission, with both local citizens and tourists. It is no coincidence that the UK saw an impressive growth in tourism.' So, writer A says free museum entry increased tourism. The relevant part of text B is 'It is far from certain that free museum access automatically brings in the tourists.' Is this similar or different from the view expressed in A? Now, go through the same process with texts C and D.

PAPER 1  Reading and ▶
          Use of English

PAPER 2  Writing

PAPER 3  Listening

PAPER 4  Speaking

Part 1
Part 2
Part 3
Part 4
Part 5
Part 6
**Part 7**
Part 8

You are going to read a magazine article about the ancient Maya civilisation in Central America. Six paragraphs have been removed from the article. Choose from the paragraphs **A–G** the one which fits each gap (**41–46**). There is one extra paragraph which you do not need to use.

Mark your answers **on the separate answer sheet**.

# The rise and fall of the ancient Maya civilisation

No civilisation has fallen quite like the Maya, seemingly swallowed by the jungle after centuries of urban, cultural and agricultural evolution. What went wrong? Recent discoveries point not to a cataclysmic eruption, earthquake or plague but rather to climate change. But first came the boom years, roughly AD300 to 660. At the beginning of the so-called Classic Maya period, some 60 Maya cities sprang up across much of modern-day Guatemala, Belize and Mexico's Yucatán Peninsula.

**41**

But then came the bust, a decline that lasted at least two centuries. By 1100, the residents of once thriving Maya cities seem to have just disappeared. In the nineteenth century, when explorers began discovering the overgrown ruins of 'lost cities', theorists imagined an immense volcanic eruption or earthquake — or maybe an empire-wide pandemic.

**42**

One study of stalagmites in a cavern in Belize links swings in weather patterns to both the rise and fall of the empire. Formed by water and minerals dripping from above, stalagmites grow more quickly in rainier years, giving scientists a reliable record of historical rainfall trends. 'The early Classic Maya period was unusually wet,' according to lead researcher Douglas Kennett. And during this time, he says, 'the population proliferated, aided by a surge in agriculture.'

**43**

But the long wet spell turned out to be an anomaly. When the climate pendulum swung back, hard times followed. 'Mayan systems were founded on those high rainfall patterns,' Kennett said. 'They could not support themselves when patterns changed.'

The following centuries were characterised by repeated and, at times extreme, drought. Agriculture declined and, not coincidentally, social conflict rose.

**44**

But times would get even harder. The stalagmite record suggests that between 1020 and 1100 the region suffered its longest dry spell of the last 2,000 years. With it, the study suggests, came crop failure, famine, mass migration and death. By the time Spanish conquistadors arrived in the sixteenth century, inland Maya populations had decreased by 90 per cent, and urban centres and farms had been abandoned and reclaimed by forest.

**45**

According to climate scientist, Benjamin Cook, this widespread deforestation reduced the flow of moisture from the ground to the atmosphere, interrupting the natural rain cycle and in turn reducing rainfall. Computer simulations that Cook ran for one study show that localised drying decreased atmospheric moisture by five to 15 per cent annually. 'Even a ten per cent decrease is considered an environmental catastrophe,' he says.

**46**

But, according to Professor of Environment and Society B.L. Turner, 'that's the kind of oversimplification we're trying to get away from. The Mayan situation is not applicable today — our society is just so radically different.' In his own study, Turner concludes that the natural environment recovered rather quickly after the dry centuries. What happened to the Maya, he suggests, is that in order to escape starvation and wars inland, many moved to coastal areas where life was comparatively easier. And once there, they may simply have forgotten their great cities.

**A** To some extent, however, the Maya may have shaped their own decline. At the height of the civilisation, the area had a population of tens of millions, and vast numbers of trees would have been cut down to make space for cities and farms, and to provide fuel.

**B** Indeed, it was during the rainiest decades of this era, from AD440 to 660, that the cities sprouted. In fact, all the hallmarks of Maya civilisation — sophisticated political systems, monumental architecture, complex religion — came into full flower during this era.

**C** One common misconception is that the Maya completely vanished after the arrival of the Spanish in the sixteenth century. There are, in fact, Mayan people still in the area today, with their own culture and traditions. The mystery, historically, is why their cities were abandoned and never reclaimed.

**D** With their pyramids, squares, ball courts and government buildings, they were where the urban Maya discussed philosophy, developed an accurate solar-year calendar and relished the world's first hot chocolate. Farmers, too, were riding high, turning hillsides into terraced fields to feed the fast-growing population.

**E** Add this to the broader trend and the situation becomes dire — a cautionary tale for the modern world, some warn. The fear is that, as more and more forestland is turned into farms and cities, and as global temperatures continue to rise, we may risk the same fate that befell the Maya.

**F** The Maya religious and political system was based on the belief that rulers were in direct communication with the gods. When these divine connections failed to produce rainfall and good harvests, tensions probably developed. In only 25 years between 750 and 775, for example, 39 rulers commissioned the same number of stone monuments — evidence of 'rivalry, war, and strategic alliances,' according to Kennett's study.

**G** Today, however, scientists generally agree that the Maya collapse has many roots, all intertwined — overpopulation, warfare, famine, drought. And one of the hottest fields of inquiry in recent years has centred on climate change, perhaps of the Maya's own doing.

# Essential tips

- Part 7 of the Cambridge English: Advanced Reading and Use of English exam tests your understanding of the organisation of a text, in particular the way paragraphs are connected with each other.

- Read the main text quickly to get a general idea of what it is about and how it is organised. Do not worry about the gaps or any words you do not know at this point.

- Then, carefully read each paragraph in the main text. Make sure you know what the main idea in each paragraph is.

- Read the gapped paragraphs **A–G**, and make sure you know what the main idea in each is.

- Look for links between the main text and the gapped paragraph. The gapped paragraph may have links to the paragraph before it, or the paragraph after it, or to both.

- The links between paragraphs might be: connected ideas; related vocabulary – e.g. *wolves and bears* in one paragraph and *these animals* in the other; reference words like *this, there, she, her*; linking words and phrases such as *firstly, secondly, however, that's why, on the other hand*.

- There is one extra gapped paragraph which will not fit any gap.

- Once you have finished, re-read the completed text and make sure that it makes sense.

**Question 41:** The last sentence in the previous paragraph is about the growth of the Mayan cities. Several gapped paragraphs refer to the cities. Look for one that gives some extra details about the cities, and which contains pronouns referring to the cities.

**Question 42:** The last sentence of the previous paragraph refers to nineteenth-century theories about the disappearance of the Maya civilisation. Look for a gapped paragraph which contrasts this with more modern theories.

**Question 43:** The following paragraph starts 'But the long wet spell turned out to be an anomaly.' Can you find a gapped paragraph which refers to a 'wet spell'?

**Question 45:** The following paragraph starts with a sentence about the effect of 'this deforestation'. Which gapped paragraph refers to deforestation?

PAPER 1 Reading and ▶ Part 1
        Use of English    Part 2
                          Part 3
PAPER 2 Writing           Part 4
                          Part 5
PAPER 3 Listening         Part 6
                          Part 7
PAPER 4 Speaking          Part 8

You are going to read a magazine article about four students who have started their own businesses. For questions **47–56**, choose from the students (**A–D**). The students may be chosen more than once.

Mark your answers **on the separate answer sheet.**

## Which student

| | |
|---|---|
| acknowledges the value of taking expert advice? | **47** |
| is unconcerned about the possibility of failure? | **48** |
| is surprised at the lack of competition for her business? | **49** |
| has established a precedent in her university? | **50** |
| accepts that her business may have had a negative impact on her studies? | **51** |
| has created a business which has exceeded her expectations? | **52** |
| believes her personality has changed through working on her business? | **53** |
| regrets missing out on certain aspects of student life? | **54** |
| thinks that entrepreneurs like her should follow their instincts? | **55** |
| claims to have benefited from skills acquired while taking part in an unrelated activity? | **56** |

# Essential tips

▶ In this part of the exam you are required to read one text or a number of short texts to find specific information, which may include an opinion or the expression of an attitude.

▶ Read the instructions, the title and the questions.

▶ Skim through the texts quickly to get a general idea of what they are about. Don't worry if there are words or phrases you don't understand.

▶ Read each question again and make sure you understand what it is asking. Underline the key words in the question (the words that show you what you should look for in the text).

▶ Scan the text for ideas or words that relate to the question. Read the relevant part of the text carefully.

▶ Remember that the part of the text that gives the answer for each question will almost certainly not use the same words; instead, it will express the idea in a different way.

▶ All the texts are about the same topic, so similar points may be made in two or three texts. When you match a question with a text, make sure it reflects exactly what is in that text.

**Question 47:** The word *expert* is in the question. Look for other words in the texts that express a similar idea. Then check that the part of the text you find also expresses the idea of acknowledging the value of taking advice.

**Question 48:** Think of other words or phrases that express the same idea as 'failure'. Then scan the texts for references to this. Make sure the one you choose contains the idea that the writer is unconcerned about the possibility of failure.

**Question 49:** What other words or phrases could express the idea of 'competition' for a business? Look through the texts quickly to see if you can find an expression of surprise with regard to competition.

# Students who start businesses

*Meet some enterprising students who have started their own businesses while at university.*

## A  Lisa James

As she's doing business studies, it may not be surprising that Lisa James has set up her own company, but it's happened on a much greater scale than she'd envisaged. The idea for Carefree Flowers came from a visit to a friend who was in hospital. Real flowers were banned, so instead, Lisa created an arrangement of origami paper ones, each containing an individualised message. Before long, Lisa and her mother, Maria, had set up Carefree Flowers to cater for the demand.

Lisa handles the marketing and design. 'Mum does the rest, so I can do my coursework, though not much else – I don't go to parties, for example.' She's also good at managing her time. 'It's something I got used to at school – I did competitive athletics and had to fit it around schoolwork.'

Lisa plans to continue developing the business, but she can't look too far ahead. 'Someone else might see the potential in it and take our trade away. That'd hurt, but if it happened, I guess I'd start another business.'

## B  Joanna Payne

Joanna Payne is in her final year of a computer science degree. Her university offers 'sandwich' courses, meaning that students can spend year three of a four-year degree working for a business. When Joanna proposed devoting the year to setting up her own business, her lecturers were hesitant but agreed. Joanna launched Buccaneer Productions, specialising in creating games for smart phones. The three games she's released so far have impressed the university so much that it's now policy to encourage sandwich-year entrepreneurship. Joanna's sandwich year was busy, but her life is even more hectic now as she has to juggle lectures and a dissertation with running the business. 'I'd love to go out at weekends like my course mates do, but I can't afford the time,' she says. 'The apps market is really fast-moving and tough, and you've got to keep on top of it, otherwise it can all come crashing down.' The upside, of course, is that Joanna now has a pretty good idea of what it takes to set up an apps business.

## C  Alexis Taylor

When Alexis Taylor graduates in psychology, she will leave university with a well-established business, Taylor Tutors. The company offers one-to-one tutoring for high school students. All the tutors are students with recent experience of school. Alexis came up with the idea in her first year. 'It seemed an obvious way to earn some money,' says Alexis. 'I set up a database of students from my university, did some marketing in local schools, and it pretty much evolved as I'd imagined. I don't know why no one else has done it. I worry they might do actually.' She thinks she was fortunate to have chanced upon a mentor, John Martino, an older businessman who kept her on track at times.

Her business and the degree are both relatively flexible, but Alexis admits to having missed classes and deadlines in her hectic lifestyle. 'Also, I probably haven't done as much reading as I should've – psychology's a heavy subject in that sense.' But she's convinced she's done enough, and her entrepreneurial experience will stand her in good stead.

## D  Zoe Roberts

Two months after Zoe started her art degree, her bicycle was stolen. 'It was a real shock and I immediately wanted to do something,' she says. With the help of a lecturer, she designed a 'cycle wrapper', a cover to reduce bike theft and protect bikes from the weather.

Eighteen months later, it's still just a prototype. Zoe has set up a company, filed a patent, talked to potential investors and manufacturers, and even persuaded the university authorities that the 'wrapper' could bear the university name. But a product launch still seems a distant concept. 'I had no idea it would take so long,' she says. 'I've spent as much time on this project as on my degree. Sometimes I wonder whether it's been worth it. But it's transformed me. I'm much tougher than I used to be. People have told me to give up. They say the 'wrapper' will never work. But a gut feeling tells me it'll come good and I need to stick with it. As a poor student, I've got nothing to lose really, so that's what I'll do.'

PAPER 1  Reading and
Use of English

**PAPER 2  Writing**  ▶

PAPER 3  Listening

PAPER 4  Speaking

# Essential tips

▶ Paper 2 consists of two parts. Part 1 of the Writing paper is compulsory for everyone. You will be asked to produce an essay in which you must develop and support an argument on a supplied topic. The essay should always be between 220 and 260 words.

▶ In Part 2 there are three writing tasks. You must choose one of the three to answer. The types of text you can choose to write will include: an email or letter (formal or informal), a proposal, a report or a review.

▶ You should practise producing each text type that appears in the test.

▶ The information you will need in order to plan and produce each written piece in the test is called the input text. This input text might take the form of a bulleted list, an advertisement, a notice, an announcement, etc. Always read the input text carefully to make sure you understand exactly what you are being asked to write.

▶ Pay particular attention to the purpose of each written piece and its target reader.

▶ It is very important to write each item in the appropriate register. Think about whether the language you use should be formal or informal. Ask yourself whether you need to sound neutral or persuasive.

▶ Be aware of the structure you will need to use for each item you write. For example, how should you organise the paragraphs in your essay and what must each one contain? In your report, should you use headings and lists?

▶ Plan before you write, but don't spend too much time drafting a rough version; you won't have time to rewrite it properly. Use your own words as far as possible.

▶ Get into the habit of learning what 220–260 words look like in the various forms required for the test. Try to ensure that your handwriting is clear. You may lose points if the examiner cannot read what you have written.

▶ Allow a few minutes before the end of the test to quickly read through your work, checking your spelling and punctuation.

▶ See the Writing bank on pp. 193–205 for examples of the different types of writing required for this test.

PAPER 1 Reading and
        Use of English

**PAPER 2 Writing** ▶ **Part 1**
                      Part 2

PAPER 3 Listening

PAPER 4 Speaking

You **must** answer this question. Write your answer in **220–260** words in an appropriate style on the separate answer sheet.

1   Your class has attended a public meeting on a proposal to build a bypass around your town (a road that avoids the town). You have made the notes below.

---

> **Local politicians point out the following benefits of the bypass:**
>
> - a welcome reduction in pollution and noise
> - improved transport links
> - less traffic congestion in the town centre

> **Some opinions expressed in the meeting:**
>
> "Traders in the town will suffer economically."
>
> "Land will have to be cleared, and we are concerned about the impact on the environment."
>
> "What about loss of revenue when tourists no longer visit sites of historical interest in the town?"

Write an essay for your tutor discussing **two** of the benefits in your notes. You should **explain whether you think the advantages of the bypass outweigh the disadvantages** and **provide reasons** to support your opinion.

You may, if you wish, make use of the opinions expressed in the meeting, but you should use your own words as far as possible.

## Essential tips

▶ Read the instructions carefully. Note how many benefits you are asked to address.

▶ What can you learn from the input text? Does everyone who attended the public meeting feel the same about the proposal?

▶ When referring to the points made at the meeting, try to use your own words. Don't copy the information from the input text.

▶ What is the standard structure of an essay? What should you include in each part of it?

▶ Who is going to read the essay? What is the appropriate register you should use here?

▶ Are you required to simply report what happened at the meeting, or are you being asked to express your own opinion?

PAPER 1 Reading and
          Use of English

PAPER 2 Writing          ▶  Part 1
                            Part 2

PAPER 3 Listening

PAPER 4 Speaking

# Essential tips

▶ In this part of the test, you
  will have the opportunity
  to express yourself more
  imaginatively and creatively.

▶ Remember, you only need to
  choose one task in Part 2 of
  the Writing paper.

▶ Read each of the three
  questions carefully. Choose
  the one that you are most
  comfortable with.

**Question 2**

▶ Read the input text carefully.
  Who is the email from?

▶ How will you organise and
  structure your proposal?
  Remember, it is important
  to show that you have
  understood what you need to
  do here, and to present your
  proposal in a clear way.

▶ What idea could you
  propose? Don't spend too
  much time trying to think
  of the best possible idea.
  However, make sure that
  your idea directly relates to
  improving the employees'
  working experience.

▶ What is the appropriate
  register to use here?

▶ Plan before you begin writing.
  Do you have enough points
  to make in order to meet
  the required word count of
  220–260?

**Question 3**

▶ What sort of letter do you
  think is called for here:
  formal, semi-formal or
  informal?

▶ Check that you remember
  how to set out a letter in
  English.

▶ As always, pay attention to
  the instructions and don't
  leave anything out. Note, for

Write an answer to **one** of the questions **2–4** in this part. Write your answer in **220–260** words in an appropriate style on the separate answer sheet. Put the question number in the box at the top of the page.

2  You have received the following email from the Managing Director at your place of work.

---

Dear Colleagues,

I am pleased to announce that a generous budget of £3,000 has been set aside to improve the working experience of everyone at the company. I invite all employees to submit a proposal outlining how they feel this money would best be spent. Please illustrate exactly how you believe your proposal will positively impact everyday life at the company. The most popular proposal will be implemented.

Good luck!

Margaret Wheeler

CEO

---

Write your **proposal**.

3  In your local newspaper, you have just read an article heavily criticising students' behaviour in the town, outside of school hours. Write a letter to the editor and include the following information:

  • your overall reaction to the article
  • specific points that you agree or disagree with, and why
  • a suggestion for a follow-up article.

Write your **letter**.

4  You see this ad on a community noticeboard.

---

New Book Group

We need your help to compile a reading list of book titles for our new book group! So far, we have 20 members; men and women ranging in age from 17 to 58. Please send us your review of a novel that you think will appeal to our group members, giving reasons for your choice. Thank you.

---

Write your **review**.

example, that one of the bullet points asks you to mention specific points which you agree or disagree with, giving your reasons why.

▶ What key phrases are you likely to need for expressing agreement, disagreement and opinions?

**Question 4**

▶ Read the ad carefully. Who is the book review for?

▶ Note that you are not necessarily required to write about a book that you like; the objective is to recommend

a novel that will appeal to the group members.

▶ Mention the genre of the novel. For example, is it crime fiction, a romantic novel, a thriller, etc.?

▶ Stick to the structure of a book review, outlining the plot and demonstrating a clear understanding of the themes and the main characters.

▶ Balanced book reviews tend to be more effective than reviews which are entirely positive or entirely negative.

PAPER 1  Reading and
          Use of English

PAPER 2  Writing

**PAPER 3  Listening** ▶ **Part 1**
                        Part 2
                        Part 3
                        Part 4

PAPER 4  Speaking

## Track 1

You will hear three different extracts. For questions **1–6**, choose the answer (**A**, **B** or **C**) which fits best according to what you hear. There are two questions for each extract.

**Extract One**

You overhear two friends discussing an incident that happened with another friend.

1   The woman did not challenge the friend because she
    **A**   feels her friend is aggressive.
    **B**   doesn't believe it would help.
    **C**   thinks her friend would be hurt.

2   What does the man think the woman should do?
    **A**   Say something immediately.
    **B**   Back down and just let it go.
    **C**   Discuss the issue rationally.

**Extract Two**

You hear two people discussing the British winter.

3   The woman says she dislikes the British winter because she
    **A**   comes from the Mediterranean.
    **B**   doesn't have the right clothes.
    **C**   finds it much too cold and dark.

4   From the man's point of view, the British winter is
    **A**   just long enough.
    **B**   not long enough.
    **C**   a little too long.

**Extract Three**

You hear a couple disagreeing about Valentine's Day.

5   What is the man's main complaint about the event?
    **A**   He is upset because he can't afford it.
    **B**   He is annoyed by the selfishness of it all.
    **C**   He hates champagne and chocolates.

6   What point are the couple in agreement on?
    **A**   that Valentine's Day is really a money-making scheme
    **B**   that they should go to a restaurant on Valentine's Day
    **C**   that Valentine's Day is an important, romantic occasion

# Essential tips

▶ Read carefully through each question before the recording is played. Think about what you are going to hear. Practising the strategy of prediction will increase your chances of successful listening.

▶ One of the objectives in this part of the test is identifying how the speaker feels. Remember to listen for adjectives that describe feelings and attitudes. You should also pay attention to the speaker's tone of voice, which will provide you with clues as to how he or she feels.

▶ Remember that the questions and answer options may be paraphrased, that is, they may use different words from the ones used by the speakers. Pay close attention to the meaning expressed rather than waiting to hear the same words and expressions in the recording.

**Question 1:** It is clear that the woman did not challenge her friend, but what was the reason for this? How would you describe her attitude to the whole situation?

**Question 2:** Pay close attention to the language used in the answer options. Can you find the same meaning, perhaps expressed using different words, anywhere in the recording?

**Question 6:** Note that you need to look for a point of agreement here. Does the man or woman mention anything about agreeing with the other one?

PAPER 1  Reading and
          Use of English

PAPER 2  Writing

**PAPER 3  Listening**  ▶  | Part 1 |
                          | **Part 2** |
                          | Part 3 |
                          | Part 4 |

PAPER 4  Speaking

🎧 **Track 2**

You will hear a radio producer describing how she got into her career. For questions **7–14**, complete the sentences with a word or short phrase.

## Essential tips

▸ Always read the instructions carefully.

▸ One focus of this part of the test is listening for specific information. Look at the sentences and pay attention to their structure. This will help you to identify the parts of speech you may need to complete each one.

▸ Remember that each gap may be completed by a number, a word, or a phrase.

▸ The subject of the recording is provided in a heading at the top of the page. By reading it, you can make predictions about what you are going to hear, and begin to think about all the vocabulary you know related to that topic.

▸ The recording will be played twice. Try to complete each sentence the first time, and confirm your answers the second time.

**Question 8:** What does Tara say about her own experience of studying media or journalism at university?

**Question 10:** The word *to* appears before the gap. What part of speech do you need here? Don't forget that you may need more than one word. Pay attention to see if a phrasal verb is used by the speaker.

**Question 11:** What could, potentially, have been a discouraging aspect of the work experience programme at the radio station (but wasn't for Tara)?

**Question 13:** What does Tara say about moving to London and the job she is in now?

## BECOMING A RADIO PRODUCER

Tara Blackshaw was asked to talk to the audience about her

(**7**) ..................................................... .

Tara explains that studying media or journalism at university

was not (**8**) ....................................................... she took.

She doesn't necessarily think it's a bad idea to do a

(**9**) ......................................................., but it's not a requirement.

Finding and pursuing a career in an area they are passionate about

is the one thing Tara wants the audience members to

(**10**) ....................................................... from the talk.

Tara was not discouraged by the fact that the training programme at her local radio

station was (**11**) ....................................................... .

She describes how certain she was that she had found her ideal job as soon as she

(**12**) ....................................................... in the studio.

Fifteen years before, Tara had relocated to London and was

(**13**) ....................................................... for her current job.

Tara describes the work as a (**14**) .......................................................

because it can be challenging and difficult, but also very rewarding.

PAPER 1 Reading and
Use of English

PAPER 2 Writing

PAPER 3 Listening ▶

PAPER 4 Speaking

Part 1
Part 2
Part 3
Part 4

## Essential tips

▶ One of the things you will be asked in this part of the exam is to identify attitude and opinion. As always, listen carefully to what the speakers say, but pay attention to how they say it as well.

▶ The questions here are multiple-choice with four answer options. Remember, you may hear items from all four options mentioned in the recording, but listen carefully to identify the one that answers the question correctly.

▶ The instructions will tell you the topic of the recording. Take a minute to think about any vocabulary you know related to that topic.

**Question 16**: This question asks you about Fiona's attitude at the beginning of the conversation. How does she sound to you? Which of the options best matches her tone of voice?

**Question 18**: Without listening to the recording, any of these options could be possible, but remember to listen for what the speaker specifically states.

**Question 20**: You already know from the question that Nick describes how making ski films affects him. Only one of the options is correct, and he may express this idea using different words. What does he say about how the process makes him feel?

🎧 **Track 3**

You will hear two friends, Fiona and Matthew, discussing an interview which featured an American skier and filmmaker called Nick Waggoner. For questions **15–20**, choose the answer (**A**, **B**, **C** or **D**) which fits best according to what you hear.

15 What is Matthew doing when Fiona arrives at the coffee shop?
   A   He has started reading the interview.
   B   He is in the middle of reading the interview.
   C   He has finished reading the interview.
   D   He is thinking about reading the interview.

16 What is Fiona's reaction to the topic, at first?
   A   genuinely curious about it
   B   completely bored with it
   C   totally fascinated by it
   D   not that interested in it

17 What made Nick Waggoner choose the location for his film *Solitaire*?
   A   It was suitable for using a helicopter.
   B   He liked the challenge it would provide.
   C   It had the most dramatic landscapes.
   D   The snow conditions were perfect there.

18 What was the impact of Arne Backstrom's death on Nick and Zac?
   A   It was OK as they didn't know Arne well.
   B   It affected Nick and Zac very deeply.
   C   They decided to abandon the project.
   D   They were not entirely surprised by it.

19 What did Nick and Zac do after Arne's death?
   A   They learned how to fly a plane.
   B   They connected with other colleagues.
   C   They moved the film dates forward.
   D   They learned how to paraglide.

20 How does Nick describe the effect that making ski films has on him?
   A   He says it energises him.
   B   He says it bores him.
   C   He says he doesn't like it.
   D   He says it frightens him.

PAPER 1   Reading and
               Use of English

PAPER 2   Writing

**PAPER 3   Listening**          ▶
                                        Part 1
                                        Part 2
PAPER 4   Speaking                Part 3
                                        **Part 4**

## Essential tips

▶ Part 4 of the Listening paper is a matching exercise. There are three additional options that you will not need.

▶ You are required to do two tasks at the same time in this part of the test. Read the instructions and make sure you understand exactly what you will need to listen for in each task.

▶ The five speakers will speak on the same theme. Pay attention to the main points and attitudes they express.

▶ Remember, the options do not appear in the order in which they are heard on the recording.

**Questions 21–25:**

**Option A:** If someone avoids writing, what kinds of words might they use to express this?

**Option D:** Who, if anyone, mentions their own opinion of their writing?

**Option H:** For this option to be correct, someone must mention how often they write. What sorts of words should you listen for here?

**Questions 26–30:**

**Option B:** This option mentions 'enthusiasm', which may or may not be the exact word used in the recording. Does any speaker use words or phrases with the same meaning to describe their experience in the writers' group?

**Option F:** What kind of tone of voice do you think someone would use if they felt the writing group members were 'harsh critics'?

**Option G:** This option provides you with two clues before you listen. You know you need to identify a speaker who mentions the feedback they get in the writers' group and the amount they get. What does 'constructive' mean? Does anyone express this idea?

### Track 4

You will hear five short extracts in which people talk about being in writers' groups.

**While you listen you must complete both tasks.**

---

### TASK ONE

For questions **21–25**, choose from the list (**A–H**) what each speaker says about their own writing.

| | | | |
|---|---|---|---|
| **A** | tends to avoid writing | | |
| **B** | panics under pressure | Speaker 1 | **21** |
| **C** | finds the process isolating | Speaker 2 | **22** |
| **D** | is satisfied with their own work | Speaker 3 | **23** |
| **E** | feels it's a waste of time | Speaker 4 | **24** |
| **F** | had been out of practice | Speaker 5 | **25** |
| **G** | never finishes anything | | |
| **H** | writes every day | | |

### TASK TWO

For questions **26–30**, choose from the list (**A–H**) what each speaker says about their experience of being in a writer's group.

| | | | |
|---|---|---|---|
| **A** | enjoys the positive feedback | | |
| **B** | gets the enthusiasm they need | Speaker 1 | **26** |
| **C** | looks forward to the social aspect | Speaker 2 | **27** |
| **D** | doesn't like the group leader | Speaker 3 | **28** |
| **E** | finds the motivation to keep writing | Speaker 4 | **29** |
| **F** | thinks the members are harsh critics | Speaker 5 | **30** |
| **G** | minds the lack of constructive feedback | | |
| **H** | struggles to find time to attend | | |

PAPER 1 Reading and
Use of English

PAPER 2 Writing

PAPER 3 Listening

**PAPER 4 Speaking**

# Essential tips

### Part 1

▶ This part of the test has two phases. In the first phase, the examiner will ask you a couple of basic things about yourself. In the second phase, you will be asked broader types of questions about your life and your opinions.

▶ Listen carefully to what you are being asked. If you didn't understand or hear the question clearly, don't be afraid to ask the examiner to repeat it.

▶ The objective of Part 1 is to show that you can interact socially. Don't go off the point in order to talk about something you have already prepared. Keep your answers relevant to the questions.

▶ Don't panic if you are caught off guard by a question and find it difficult to think of the answer, e.g. 'What is your happiest memory?' You can supply any happy memory, or you can even make one up.

### Part 4

▶ This focus here is on expressing and justifying opinions. Remember, you can hold any opinion you want, but you must support your ideas with examples.

▶ Be respectful of your partner's views and remember to be polite.

▶ You can practise using appropriate expressions, such as *I see what you're saying, but ...*, *That's an interesting point; however, ...*, *From my own point of view ...* and so on.

## Part 1 (2 minutes)

The examiner will ask you a few questions about yourself and about a general topic. For example, the examiner may ask you:

- **How long have you been studying English?**
- **What do you enjoy most about learning English?**
- **What is your happiest memory?**

## Part 2 (4 minutes)

You will each be asked to talk on your own for about a minute. You will each be given three different pictures to talk about. After your partner has finished speaking, you will be asked a brief question connected with your partner's photographs.

| **Audiences** (compare, contrast and speculate) |
|---|

Turn to pictures 1–3 on page **169**, which show people in different audiences.

(*Candidate A*), it's your turn first. Here are your pictures. They show **audiences in different situations**.

I'd like you to compare **two** of the pictures and say **what kind of event the people are attending, and describe how they appear to be responding to it**.

(*Candidate B*), **which of these audiences do you relate to the most? Why?**

| **Job types** (compare, contrast and speculate) |
|---|

Turn to pictures 1–3 on page **170**, which show people doing different jobs.

Now, (*Candidate B*), here are your pictures. They show **people doing different jobs**.

I'd like you to compare two of the pictures and say **what kind of person would choose this job type and what challenges the job might present**.

(*Candidate A*), **which of these jobs would you least like to do? Why?**

## Part 3 (4 minutes)

Look at page **171,** which shows some potential benefits of teenagers learning to save money.

| **Teenage savings** (discuss, evaluate and negotiate) |
|---|

**Here are some ways in which teenagers might benefit from developing the habit of saving money** and a question for you to discuss. First, you have some time to look at the task.

(*Pause 15 seconds*)

Now talk to each other about **how important these benefits may or may not be.**

Now you have a minute to decide **which benefit is the most important for teenagers.**

## Part 4 (5 minutes)

The examiner will encourage you to develop the topic of your discussion in Part 3 by asking questions such as:

- Is it more important for teenagers to save money or just to enjoy 'the best years of their lives'? Why?
- Do you think that financial responsibility should be limited to adults? Why (not)?
- It has been said that setting and managing a budget can be of benefit to a teenager. Do you agree?

PAPER 1  Reading and ▸
         Use of English

PAPER 2  Writing

PAPER 3  Listening

PAPER 4  Speaking

Part 1
Part 2
Part 3
Part 4
Part 5
Part 6
Part 7
Part 8

For questions **1–8**, read the text below and decide which answer (**A, B, C** or **D**) best fits each gap. There is an example at the beginning (**0**).

Mark your answers **on the separate answer sheet**.

**Example:**

| **0** | **A** presents | **B** appears | **C** springs | **D** lands |

```
0 | A   B   C   D
    ⎯   ▬   ⎯   ⎯
```

## **Essential tips**

▸ Read through the text first for general understanding.

▸ Remember that the gapped word or words will often be part of a collocation or a fixed phrase.

▸ Check the words on each side of the gap carefully. Often, the options have very similar meanings but only one is correct because of a word (e.g. a particular verb) before the gap or another word (e.g. a preposition) after it.

▸ Remember to read the whole text through again when you have completed the task to check whether it makes sense.

**Question 1:** Which verb often goes with *it* to mean 'be successful'?

**Question 3:** The idiom *to go to any ... to do something* means to make a big effort to achieve something, including taking extreme or unusual steps. Which word completes the idiom?

**Question 5:** All four words can form phrases with *in*. However, three of them express the idea of a series of things, but only one expresses the idea of the result of a series of things. The result here is boosted sales.

**Question 7:** We often use one of these adjectives to describe something abstract like an aim or an idea which is difficult to define or achieve. This is the meaning here. The other words are used to describe places that are hard to reach or things that are hard to see.

# **Word-of-mouth success – what publishers dream of**

'Word of mouth', a phrase that first (**0**) …….. in Shakespeare's play *Twelfth Night*, is the kind of publicity all publishers want for their books. Positive reviews are useful, but it's only when lots of people start talking about a book that it really (**1**) …….. it sales-wise. Word of mouth is what (**2**) …….. behind the initial success of JK Rowling's Harry Potter books, for example.

Some publishers will go to any (**3**) …….. to stimulate the phenomenon. Years ago, one company paid its own staff to read books published by the company whenever they travelled on public transport. The thinking was that the bright yellow covers would (**4**) …….. and become the subject of casual conversations among passengers, which would in (**5**) …….. boost sales.

With the (**6**) …….. of social networking, creating word of mouth has almost become a science. However, despite Twitter, Facebook and the rest, publishers still find it as difficult as ever to generate that (**7**) …….. thing, a viral conversation about a new book that persuades lots of people to buy it. It still seems to be unclear what the (**8**) …….. to achieving word of mouth is.

| | | | | |
|---|---|---|---|---|
| **1** | **A** pushes | **B** hits | **C** makes | **D** gets |
| **2** | **A** formed | **B** ran | **C** rested | **D** lay |
| **3** | **A** lengths | **B** extents | **C** terms | **D** measures |
| **4** | **A** show off | **B** stick up | **C** stand out | **D** shine on |
| **5** | **A** order | **B** turn | **C** line | **D** sequence |
| **6** | **A** advent | **B** entrance | **C** outset | **D** opening |
| **7** | **A** remote | **B** isolated | **C** hidden | **D** elusive |
| **8** | **A** root | **B** key | **C** base | **D** guide |

| PAPER 1 Reading and Use of English ▶ | Part 1 |
| --- | --- |
| | **Part 2** |
| PAPER 2 Writing | Part 3 |
| | Part 4 |
| PAPER 3 Listening | Part 5 |
| PAPER 4 Speaking | Part 6 |
| | Part 7 |
| | Part 8 |

# Essential tips

▶ Read the text quickly for general meaning.

▶ Remember that the gapped words will be structural items like articles, pronouns, prepositions and linkers. A few may form part of common expressions.

▶ Read the whole sentence to see whether the word you need is part of a longer or parallel structure like *either … or* or *on the one hand … on the other hand*.

▶ Remember that there could be more than one correct answer. But you should write one word only in the gap.

**Question 9:** From the whole text, we learn that our knowledge of deep-sea corals is still limited, but scientists are trying to find out more about them. Can you think of a two-word phrase *as …*, which means 'so far' or 'up to this point in time'?

**Question 11:** Gaps at the beginning of sentences can often look difficult to fill. The best approach is to look carefully at the previous sentence or the whole sentence that follows the gap, or both. In this case, look carefully at what comes after it. The text tells us that previously Rhian could only study the corals using robotic submarines, but now she is able to dive in the Alaskan fjords. Which word can go with *recently* to give the idea of 'previously'?

**Question 13:** This is an example of a longer, parallel structure: *… only, … but …*

**Question 16:** Can you think of a common structural word to complete an expression that means 'almost impossible'?

For questions **9–16**, read the text below and think of the word which best fits each gap. Use only one word in each gap. There is an example at the beginning (**0**).

Write your answers **IN CAPITAL LETTERS on the separate answer sheet**.

**Example:** `0` `I` `N` ☐☐☐☐☐☐☐☐☐☐☐☐☐☐☐☐☐☐☐☐☐

## Ice water diver

Rhian Waller is a marine biologist with a special interest (**0**) …….. deep-sea corals. She admits that, as (**9**) …….., little is known about these corals because they are very hard to reach, 1000 metres below the ocean's surface. However, (**10**) …….. is known is that they are being damaged by fishing nets, and research is needed to support conservation work.

(**11**) …….. recently, Rhian had only been able to study the corals through film sent from robotic submarines, but then some were discovered in Alaskan fjords that were shallow (**12**) …….. to dive in. This was a wonderful opportunity, but two problems faced Rhian initially: (**13**) …….. only was the water in the fjords scarcely above freezing, but she had never actually dived before.

She describes the experience as 'intense'. Within five minutes (**14**) …….. being in the water, her head and hands were completely numb, and she often had (**15**) …….. poor visibility she couldn't even see her own elbow. Despite the extreme conditions, however, Rhian's team were able to gather data on the corals of a kind that is (**16**) …….. but impossible in the deep ocean.

PAPER 1  Reading and ▸  Part 1
         Use of English    Part 2
                           **Part 3**
PAPER 2  Writing          Part 4
                           Part 5
PAPER 3  Listening        Part 6
                           Part 7
PAPER 4  Speaking         Part 8

For questions **17–24**, read the text below. Use the word given in capitals at the end of some of the lines to form a word that fits in the gap **in the same line**. There is an example at the beginning (**0**).

Write your answers **IN CAPITAL LETTERS on the separate answer sheet**.

**Example:** | 0 | P | R | E | S | I | D | E | N | T | I | A | L | | | | | | |

## Essential tips

▸ Read through the text for general understanding.

▸ Remember to think about the type of word that should go in each gap – a verb, noun, adjective or adverb?

▸ Remember that some words will need more than one change – a prefix and a suffix.

▸ If the word needed is a noun, check whether it should be singular or plural.

▸ When you've finished the task, read through it again and check that it all makes sense.

**Question 17:** A noun is needed here. Be careful with the spelling.

**Question 18:** If the gap is the first word in a sentence and it is followed by a comma, what type of word is it likely to be?

**Question 19:** *Facial* is an adjective, so the gapped word here will be a noun. Should it be singular or plural?

**Question 20:** The word needed here is a noun. But does it refer to people or a more abstract idea? Read the whole paragraph before deciding.

## Leaders with long faces

In most (**0**) …….. elections in the USA in the twentieth century, the taller of the two candidates won. This association of (**17**) …….. with success is something that has been widely accepted. (**18**) …….., some recent research suggests that people's confidence in a potential leader can also be influenced by how long that person's face is.

According to Daniel Re, one of the main researchers, our natural attraction to facial (**19**) …….. that suggest tallness, as long faces do, is thought to have evolved long ago when the (**20**) …….. of a community depended on choosing the right leader. 'Especially when we're faced with a (**21**) …….. situation, we seem to prefer the most dominant-looking people for leadership,' he says.

In the study, (**22**) …….. were asked to manipulate faces on a computer screen in order to make them look like people they would want as national leaders. A significant number chose to (**23**) …….. the faces, particularly for male leaders in difficult times.

As Dr Re noted, the implication is that 'leadership choices are affected by physical features that are (**24**) …….. to political expertise.'

**PRESIDENT**

**HIGH**

**INTEREST**

**CHARACTER**

**SURVIVE**

**THREAT**

**VOLUNTARY**

**LONG**

**RELEVANT**

| PAPER 1 | Reading and Use of English | ▶ | Part 1 |
| | | | Part 2 |
| PAPER 2 | Writing | | Part 3 |
| PAPER 3 | Listening | | **Part 4** |
| PAPER 4 | Speaking | | Part 5 |
| | | | Part 6 |
| | | | Part 7 |
| | | | Part 8 |

## Essential tips

▶ Remember to read both sentences carefully in each question. The second sentence must have the same meaning as the first.

▶ Remember that you must not change the key word in any way, and that you must use between three and six words.

▶ You can use contractions, e.g. *can't*, *wouldn't*, but remember that they count as two words. Make sure you count the number of words you write in the gap carefully.

▶ When you have completed a question, read through it again and check that the meaning is the same and the spelling is correct.

**Question 25:** The first sentence is all in the past simple. Is the second sentence also past simple? What structure is needed in the second sentence?

**Question 26:** Be careful with the tense. Also, you need to change *misunderstood* to a noun.

**Question 27:** Which phrase with the word *stand* means 'no way' or 'no possibility'?

**Question 29:** You need a passive structure to introduce the information here. Also, *handed* in this context needs a preposition after it.

For questions **25–30**, complete the second sentence so that it has a similar meaning to the first sentence, using the word given. **Do not change the word given.** You must use between **three** and **six** words, including the word given. Here is an example (**0**).

**Example:**

**0**   Chloe would only eat a pizza if she could have a mushroom topping.

**ON**

Chloe ........................................... a mushroom topping when she had a pizza.

The gap can be filled with the words 'insisted on having', so you write:

**Example:** | **0** | INSISTED ON HAVING |

Write **only** the missing words **IN CAPITAL LETTERS on the separate answer sheet**.

---

**25**   I only watched that film because you recommended it to me.

**NEVER**

I would ........................................... you hadn't recommended it to me.

**26**   It seems as if we misunderstood what the aims of the course were.

**BEEN**

There seems ........................................... what the aims of the course were.

**27**   The traffic was so bad that there was obviously no way we would get to the theatre on time, so we went home.

**STAND**

The traffic was so bad that we obviously didn't ........................................... to the theatre on time, so we went home.

**28**   Michelle's brother talks a lot more than she does.

**NOWHERE**

Michelle is ........................................... her brother.

**29**   There's a rumour that Jordi Marse, the Barcelona manager, has resigned this morning.

**HANDED**

Jordi Marse, the Barcelona manager, ........................................... his resignation this morning.

**30**   I'm sure people will object to the idea of building a new runway at the city airport.

**BOUND**

There ........................................... the idea of building a new runway at the city airport.

| PAPER 1 | Reading and ▸ | Part 1 |
| | Use of English | Part 2 |
| PAPER 2 | Writing | Part 3 |
| | | Part 4 |
| PAPER 3 | Listening | **Part 5** |
| PAPER 4 | Speaking | Part 6 |
| | | Part 7 |
| | | Part 8 |

You are going to read a newspaper article. For questions **31–36**, choose the answer (**A**, **B**, **C** or **D**) which you think fits best according to the text.

Mark your answers **on the separate answer sheet**.

# Cycling

### *Keen cyclist Simon Usborne looks at some research on cycling.*

You need only look at a professional cyclist to appreciate the potential effects of cycling on the body. But what about the mind? It's a question that has long challenged psychologists, neurologists and anyone who has wondered how, sometimes, riding a bike can induce what feels close to a state of meditation.

I'm usually incapable of emptying my mind but there have been occasions on my bike when I realise I have no recollection of the preceding kilometres. Whether riding along country lanes in spring, or doing city commutes, time can pass unnoticed in a blissful blur of rhythm and rolling, and I'm not alone in feeling this.

But what do we really know about how cycling affects us? Danish scientists who set out to measure the benefits of breakfast and lunch for academic achievement among children found diet helped, but that the way pupils travelled to school was far more significant. Those who cycled or walked did better than those who travelled by car or public transport. Another study by the University of California showed that old people who were most active, including those who cycled, had five per cent more grey matter than those who were least active.

But what is it about cycling that makes us believe it has a special effect? Psychiatrist John Ratey thinks cycling increases 'the chemistry in your brain that makes you feel calm,' but also that carrying out multiple operations, like negotiating a junction or jostling for space in a race, can be an effective therapy. He is currently leading a study in which more than 20 pupils with attention deficit hyperactivity disorder (ADHD), a condition affecting the ability to apply one's mind to something, are expected to show improved symptoms after a course of cycling. The link between cycling and ADHD is well-established. It's 'like taking a little bit of Ritalin,' Dr Ratey says, Ritalin being a stimulant commonly used to treat ADHD. Exercise can achieve the same effect as prescribed medicine, but not all exercise is equal, as shown in a German study involving 115 students, half of whom did activities such as cycling that involved complex coordinated movements, while the rest performed more straightforward exercises with the same aerobic demands. Both groups did better than they previously had in concentration tests, but the 'complex' group did a lot better.

There have been other interesting findings too. In 2003, neuroscientist Dr Jay Alberts rode a tandem bicycle across the American state of Ohio with a friend who has Parkinson's disease (a condition affecting the nervous system). The idea was to raise awareness of the disease, but to the surprise of both riders, the patient showed significant improvements. Dr Alberts then scanned the brains of 26 Parkinson's patients during and after an eight-week exercise programme using stationary bikes. Half the patients were allowed to ride at their own pace, while the others were pushed incrementally harder, just as the scientist's tandem companion had been. All patients improved, and the 'tandem' group showed particularly significant increases in connectivity between areas of grey matter responsible for functions such as walking and picking things up. Cycling, and cycling harder, was helping to heal their brains.

We don't know how this happens, but there is more startling evidence of the link between Parkinson's and cycling. A video on the internet features a 58-year-old Dutchman with severe Parkinson's. At first, we watch the patient trying to walk along a hospital ward. He can barely stand and his hands shake uncontrollably. Cut to the car park, where we find the man on a bicycle being supported by staff. With a push, he's off, cycling past cars with perfect balance and coordination. After a loop, he comes to a stop and hops to the ground, where *line 37* he is immediately immobile again. Doctors don't fully understand this discrepancy either, but say the bicycle's rotating pedals may act as some sort of visual cue that aided the patient's brain.

The science of cycling is evidently incomplete, but perhaps the most remarkable thing about it for the everyday rider, its effects on hyperactive children notwithstanding, is that it can require no conscious focus at all. The apparent mindlessness of pedalling can not only make us happier, but also leave room for other thoughts. On the seat of my bike, I've solved problems at work, made life decisions and reflected usefully on emotional troubles, as, I'm sure, have countless others.

▶ Remember that in this part of the test, you need to understand various things about a text: detailed meaning, the writer's opinions and attitudes, the purpose of the whole text or of one paragraph, how the text is organised and how different words and phrases relate to each other. Sometimes the meaning is suggested or implied rather than stated explicitly, and you need to understand this.

▶ Read through the text for overall understanding and to see how it is organised. Don't worry if there are words or phrases you don't understand.

▶ Read each question and highlight the key words. Highlight the piece of text where this question is answered.

▶ Look in the text for the answer to the question. One of the options will express the same idea, but probably not in the same words as in the text.

▶ Check that the three other options are definitely incorrect. Sometimes you will be able to find the answer by eliminating each wrong option in turn.

**Question 31:** This is an example of a question about the writer's 'purpose'. What is the main point of the second paragraph? Read the paragraph again and also look at what comes before and after the paragraph. Then go through each option carefully. Option A: he gives some personal information but is that the point of this paragraph? Option B: is he introducing a new subject here? Option C: is he expressing an opinion in this paragraph? Option D: is he illustrating a point? If so, what is the point?

31 What is the writer's main intention in the second paragraph?
   A to give some personal information
   B to introduce a new subject
   C to express his opinion
   D to illustrate a point

32 According to the third paragraph, what do certain studies show?
   A Cyclists tend to live longer than non-cyclists.
   B Cycling seems to be the healthiest form of exercise.
   C Intellectual performance appears to be boosted by cycling.
   D Older people appreciate the value of exercise more than young people do.

33 What do the studies described in the fourth paragraph suggest?
   A Cycling has as much impact on physical fitness as simpler physical activities.
   B The variety of tasks involved in cycling can be hard for some children to cope with.
   C Children suffer from ADHD because they are deprived of physical exercise like cycling.
   D The act of cycling can improve the ability to focus attention on a task.

34 Studies of people with Parkinson's disease reveal that
   A cycling on ordinary bikes is better than cycling on stationary bikes.
   B the social aspects of cycling are important for people with Parkinson's.
   C the more effort Parkinson's sufferers put into cycling the more good it does them.
   D not every person who suffers from Parkinson's will benefit from cycling.

35 What does 'this discrepancy' in line 37 refer to?
   A how cycling could be incorporated into treatment for Parkinson's
   B why someone with Parkinson's can cycle but not walk
   C why Parkinson's affects some people and not others
   D how a link between cycling and Parkinson's was discovered

36 With the phrase 'its effects on hyperactive children notwithstanding', the writer is referring to the fact that cycling
   A is more life-enhancing to adults than younger people.
   B enables people to think more effectively.
   C can be both complex and mindless.
   D is not yet fully understood.

**Question 35:** Even if you are not sure what the word *discrepancy* means, you should be able to work out the answer here. The word *either* just after *discrepancy* refers back to the beginning of the paragraph – 'we don't know how this happens' – which is about what's described in the previous paragraph. This tells you that 'this discrepancy' is about something said in this paragraph. What is the main topic of this paragraph?

**Question 36:** Even if you are not sure about the meaning of the word *notwithstanding*, you can still work out what is meant here. Look back at the part of the text which mentions 'hyperactive children'. According to the text, what makes cycling good for 'hyperactive' children? According to the final paragraph, what makes cycling good for people referred to here?

| PAPER 1 | Reading and | ▶ | Part 1 |
| | Use of English | | Part 2 |
| PAPER 2 | Writing | | Part 3 |
| | | | Part 4 |
| PAPER 3 | Listening | | Part 5 |
| PAPER 4 | Speaking | | **Part 6** |
| | | | Part 7 |
| | | | Part 8 |

You are going to read four comments in a debate about zoos. For questions **37–40**, choose from the comments **A–D**. The comments may be chosen more than once.

Mark your answers **on the separate answer sheet**.

# Zoos

*Zoos are notable tourist attractions as well as being centres of research and conservation. However, there is a long-running debate about whether it is right to keep wild animals in captivity, particularly in urban locations. Here are four contributions to a recent online discussion about the subject.*

**A**

With the destruction of natural habitats in so many parts of the world, zoos play an increasingly important role in conservation. Without their intervention, many more of the world's surviving species would become extinct. Zoos are able to intervene because of their expertise, which is developed through long-term, sustained studies at the zoos themselves, but also in support of field work in the wild. One advantage of having this scientific work done in zoos is that it becomes more easily accessible to the wider public. Zoos are great vehicles for informing people of all ages, though particularly younger ones, in a direct and memorable way, about the proper treatment of animals, and how crucial they are to the world's different ecosystems. This has not always been the case, but modern zoos look after animals well and, as such, present a valuable model to the wider population.

**B**

There have been many bad zoos in the past, but zoo animals today are well-fed and cared for in spacious surroundings. Zoologists and animal psychologists are brought in to design species-appropriate enclosures and activities. Studies of animals in zoos provide information that would be very hard to obtain in the wild. A study of gorillas at zoos in the UK and the USA, for example, discovered that happiness can increase the primates' lives by up to 11 years, and findings of this kind are useful for zoologists in both zoos and the wild. Sadly, zoos' efforts to breed animals that are close to extinction have mostly failed. The issue here is that the odds against reviving a species from a tiny captive community are very high. But generally, as institutions of scientific endeavour, zoos are crucial in the wider dissemination of knowledge, skills and values with regard to wildlife.

**C**

Care of wild animals in captivity tends to be much more humane than it was in the past, but the fact is that zoos are for commerce and entertainment. Most visitors go to zoos to be diverted by weird and wonderful creatures rather than to learn. One zoo study found that visitors spent less than eight seconds per snake and one minute per lion. What could possibly be learned from that? It is also widely acknowledged that, despite the best intentions of scientists, most zoo-based attempts to breed species in order to stave off extinction have been strikingly unsuccessful. Captive breeding programmes will only ever work in large nature reserves. Moreover, claims that zoos are ideal locations for studying animal behaviour conveniently ignore the point that environments affect behaviour, and so studies of animals in zoos may only tell us about captive populations and provide little data about animals in their natural habitats.

**D**

However well intentioned zoo-keepers may be, zoos can never replicate the natural habitats of most wild animals. As a result, zoo animals are psychologically affected and often display abnormal, even self-destructive, behaviour. Attempts to use zoos for breeding threatened species are also well intentioned, but, with rare exceptions, they fail to bear fruit. The key factor again is probably that zoos are nothing like nature, and wild animals simply do not breed well in confinement. The notion that zoos can be places of learning, enlightening the population about wildlife, is also well meant, but how much can visitors really discover about wild animals from seeing them in cages and small enclosures? The only way to understand an animal properly is to see it in its natural environment, and, if that is not possible, then film and books will give a more accurate picture than the artificial and misleading context of a zoo.

## Which writer

takes a similar view to D regarding the role zoos play in educating the public?

| 37 |    |
|----|----|

has a different opinion from the others about the well-being of animals kept in zoos?

| 38 |    |
|----|----|

takes a different view from the others regarding zoos and endangered species in zoos?

| 39 |    |
|----|----|

shares A's opinion of zoos as centres of research?

| 40 |    |
|----|----|

# Essential tips

- Remember: in this part of the exam you have to decide whether four different writers have similar or different opinions about a particular subject.

- Read the title and the texts quickly for general understanding.

- Highlight the key words in each question.

- Read the first text and highlight the sections that relate to each question. Remember to write the question numbers in the relevant places. Do the same for each text.

- Then look across the four texts and compare the parts of the texts that refer to each question. Read the opinions carefully and decide which ones are similar and which are different.

**Question 37:** The key words here are *the role zoos play in educating the public.* Look at this part of text D: 'The notion that zoos can be places of learning, enlightening the population about wildlife, is also well-meant, but how much can visitors really discover about wild animals from seeing them in cages and small enclosures?' In D's view, are zoos effective at educating the public or not? When you have decided what D thinks, look through the other texts for a similar view.

**Question 38:** The key words here are *the well-being of animals kept in zoos. Well-being* can refer to both physical and mental health. You are asked to find one writer expressing a different opinion on this point from the other three. A says this: 'This has not always been the case, but modern zoos look after animals well and, as such, present a valuable model to the wider population.' So A says zoo animals are well cared for and implies that, as a result, their health is good. B says 'zoo animals today are well-fed and cared for in spacious surroundings. Zoologists and animal psychologists are brought in to design species-appropriate enclosures and activities.' So, B also says the care is good and the implication is that the animals are healthy. So, now we know that either C or D expresses a different view. Which one is it?

PAPER 1 Reading and
Use of English

PAPER 2 Writing

PAPER 3 Listening

PAPER 4 Speaking

Part 1
Part 2
Part 3
Part 4
Part 5
Part 6
**Part 7**
Part 8

You are going to read a newspaper article about a special farm which provides help to teenagers with behavioural problems. Six paragraphs have been removed from the article. Choose from the paragraphs **A–G** the one which fits each gap (**41–46**). There is one extra paragraph which you do not need to use.

Mark your answers **on the separate answer sheet**.

# Care farms

Before breakfast, two young people head down to the woods, struggling a little with the heavy bag of food for the pigs. 'Scatter them in different piles,' says the farm staff member. 'If you put them in one place, the smaller pigs won't be able to get anything.' The pigs, which are enormous, surge towards us, and their new feeders step backwards. 'I'm not doing that,' says 15-year-old Daniel firmly.

**41**

The teenagers are part of a group from a London secondary school who are staying at Jamie Fielden's farm, one of a number of 'care farms' providing a type of eco-therapy. The pupils brought here have been chosen by their teachers: 14 year-old Sofia, for example, has a difficult home life, Georgia, 14, is extremely quiet, and Sam, 13, has challenging behaviour.

**42**

Besides farmwork, the young people have group sessions with the farm psychotherapist who teaches them techniques for calming down, or for dealing with difficult situations. They can do 'horse-whispering' with her, one-to-one therapy making use of one of the farm horses. Phones and sweets are banned, as part of the focus on creating a calm, supportive atmosphere and reducing over-stimulation.

**43**

And the young people seem to be thriving. Aaron, a 12-year-old with serious attendance issues, is clearly taken with the horse whispering: 'I feel as though the horse is calm and I'm calm. I had to work out how to speak calmly to make her do what I wanted.'

**44**

And this is what Fielden aims to provide. Trained as a teacher, he wants to 'give young people a chance to have the experiences that I had as a kid growing up on a farm'. He set up the farm with a couple of other teachers and his mother, a psychotherapist, a few years ago. The farm's main source of income is the fees schools pay to send pupils there, and since opening, more than 700 children have attended.

**45**

Care farms first appeared over a decade ago in the UK. Now, there are more than 80, and they have their own association called Care Farm UK. Founder member Ian Egginton-Metters says: 'There is evidence that 'green care' works. Charities give funding for our eco-therapy projects, which are focused around taking people out of institutions and putting them in the natural environment.'

**46**

Whatever the reasons, however, there is clearly an impact. A week after the pupils arrive back at school in west London from Jamie's Farm, teachers report on a difference in behaviour. Georgia gave a talk to her class about her experiences, Sofia's participation in class is better than it has ever been, and Sam says he wants to go back to the farm next year. There is no doubt amongst the teachers that they will continue to send troubled pupils to the farm in years to come.

**A** A classmate, Hasan, describes a similar sense of tranquillity. 'I expected to be really annoyed and bored here, but as soon as we arrived it was fantastic. There's so much space. You don't get stressed out. There's time to think.' Like his peers, he has a complicated home life and needs support.

**B** Along with this, the teachers accompanying them are encouraged to form closer bonds with their charges and to observe the way that farm staff interact with the young people, and the methods they use to get the behaviour they want.

**C** This expansion of the sector is evident, but there are differing explanations as to why care farming makes a difference, ranging from those pointing to the therapeutic aspect of the physical labour and the contact with plants and animals, to others claiming it is all to do with taking people away from their problems at home.

**D** Before coming here he was sceptical, but no longer. 'There's something about coming here, from very chaotic environments, as most of

these young people do, that does them good. You have to work hard, take responsibility, and you're a valued member of the community.'

**E** Sofia, however, who is a good head shorter than her fellow pupil, moves forward, methodically pouring out a dozen small heaps under the trees. 'She's a natural,' says her supervisor admiringly. Sofia does not look up, but a little smile flickers across her young face.

**F** An impressive figure, but isn't it an expensive option for schools? Fielden believes the results justify the cost. Eight out of ten children who stay at the farm show a persistent improvement in behaviour. 'Head teachers tell me they're rebooking because they're no longer seeing those children in trouble. That's what we want.'

**G** Most of them, they soon tell me, have never been to the countryside before. For five days, they get up early, eat wholesome food and do various chores dependent on the season. It is summer and they are pulling up coriander from the vegetable beds, feeding animals and helping with the harvest.

# Essential tips

▶ Remember that in this part of the test you need to understand the organisation of a text – how the paragraphs work together.

▶ Read through the main text first for a general understanding of its subject and organisation.

▶ Then read the gapped paragraphs A–G, and make sure you know what each one is about.

▶ Look for links between the main text and the gapped paragraphs. Remember that a gapped paragraph may have links to the paragraph before it, or the paragraph after it, or both.

▶ The links may be connected ideas, related vocabulary, pronouns, linking adverbs and expressions and so on.

▶ Sometimes more than one of the paragraphs A–G look possible for a gap, but there is only one correct answer. If you look carefully, you will find reasons to exclude all attractive-looking paragraphs except the correct one.

▶ Don't forget to read through the completed text to check that it makes sense.

**Question 41:** The first main text paragraph mentions two young people, a member of the farm staff, pigs and Daniel who is one of the two young people. If you look quickly these gapped paragraphs all look possible: A, D, E and G. In paragraph A, Hasan could be Daniel's classmate, but does the rest of the first sentence in A fit? In paragraph D, the first sentence seems to follow from the previous paragraph, but does the rest of D follow? In paragraph E, Sofia could be Daniel's fellow pupil – does the rest of E fit? In paragraph G, *they* could refer to Sofia and Daniel, but does *most of them* make sense after the first main paragraph?

**Question 42:** The previous paragraph refers to a group of children from a school in London. Which gapped paragraph could also refer to this group?

**Question 43:** The previous paragraph describes what the therapy for the young people consists of. Which paragraph gives more information about what happens to this group?

**Question 44:** The first sentence of the following paragraph is: 'And this is what Fielden aims to provide.' What could *this* refer to?

PAPER 1 Reading and ▸ | Part 1
Use of English | Part 2

PAPER 2 Writing | Part 3
Part 4
PAPER 3 Listening | Part 5

PAPER 4 Speaking | Part 6
Part 7
**Part 8**

You are going to read reviews of books about architecture. For questions **47–56**, choose from the reviews (**A–D**). The reviews may be chosen more than once.

Mark your answers **on the separate answer sheet**.

## About which book is the following stated?

| | |
|---|---|
| The exact function of the book is difficult to determine. | **47** |
| Sometimes the style of writing can be difficult to read. | **48** |
| Very few architects or buildings of note are left out of it. | **49** |
| It contains examples of well-directed humour. | **50** |
| Useful references to little-known architectural work are included. | **51** |
| It is based on other writing by the same author. | **52** |
| It provides evidence that one view of architects is false. | **53** |
| It gives a more accurate account than previous books on the same subject. | **54** |
| The size of it is misleading. | **55** |
| The author is rightly critical of architecture from a particular period. | **56** |

## Essential tips

▸ Remember that in this part of the test you read one long text or a few short texts to find specific information, which may include an opinion or the expression of an attitude.

▸ Read the instructions and the title.

▸ Then, either skim read the text first before you read the questions, or read the questions first before you skim read the text. Experiment and see which way works better for you.

▸ When you read the questions, highlight the key words that show you what you should look for in the text.

▸ Remember that the part of the text that gives the answer to a question will almost certainly not use the same words, and the meaning may be implied rather than stated clearly.

▸ Also, similar points may be made in two or three texts, so when you match a question with a text, make sure they have exactly the same meaning.

**Question 47:** A key word here is *function*. Which review refers to what the book might be used for?

**Question 48:** The key ideas here are *the style of writing* and *difficult to read*. You are unlikely to find these exact words in the reviews, but can you find any paraphrases of them?

**Question 49:** The expression *of note* means important or well known. Two of the reviews refer to architects or buildings that have been left out of the books. Which review says that very few important ones have been left out?

# Reviews of books about architecture

## A   *The Meaning of Home* by Edwin Heathcote

This book is so slim and whimsical-looking you could easily mistake it for 'bookshop candy' – those cute, little tomes perched around cash registers – but don't be fooled. While entertaining enough, it also draws on the work of such heavy-hitting intellectuals as Ludwig Wittgenstein, Walter Benjamin and Carl Jung. It grew from Heathcote's popular series of newspaper columns but here he expands on those pieces with each of the 34 chapters focussing on an individual household room or a discrete building component (floor, ceiling, roof, etc.). Each chapter is a densely packed mixture of observations and curiosities, delivered in an almost stream-of-consciousness narrative, drawing on tidbits of history, folklore, mythology, philosophy, architectural innovation, scientific research, symbols, rituals and literature, plus cinema and other areas of popular culture.

Many of the ideas are fascinating, though some rooms get far more interesting treatment than others – and certain observations (such as the notion that traditional cellars in legend, movies, and real life are often dark, creepy places, harbouring unknowns) state the obvious. Nonetheless, what comes across overall is how passionately Heathcote has reconsidered the home and how broadly he has read and observed.

## B   *Why We Build* by Rowan Moore

Rowan Moore, a trained architect and architecture critic for *The Observer* newspaper, has produced a thought-provoking, philosophical look at the relationship between people and buildings, from the often power-crazed planners and architects to those who come later, and work and live in them. One could say there are almost two books here: partly a biography of the brilliant Brazilian architect, Lina Bo Bardi, it is also a much wider exploration of the impetuses behind modern architecture. Moore takes us from the extraordinary artificial Palm Islands in Dubai to the Dome in London, via many buildings, periodically returning to descriptions of Bo Bardi's poetic and humane work. Justifiably hard-hitting in his treatment of many of the skyscrapers that have gone up in London in the last two decades, his elegant, sharp wit is regularly put to good use, revealing the waste, vanity and muddled-thinking associated with many of the larger construction projects.

## C   *The Architect's Home* by Peter Gossel

A favourite fiction about modern architects is that they don't live in their own creations but favour elegant historical houses while condemning others to their concrete monstrosities. The 480 pages devoted to 100 projects by European architects, mostly from the past 100 years, in Peter Gossel's book amply refute this charge. Beautifully produced, with well-chosen images and prose that is informative if not always very digestible, *The Architect's Home* shows how absolutely wonderful modern architecture can be.

We have the fabulous creations of some of the twentieth century architectural greats such as Le Corbusier, Gropius and Aalto, but alongside them Gossel has unearthed a number of unfamiliar gems such as Charlotte Perriand's house in the Savoie mountains of France and the black-painted studio of the Swede, Sigurd Lewerentz. There are a fair number of strange omissions such as Konstantin Melnikov's amazing house in Moscow, but, on the whole, the demonstration that, when given the chance, modern architects do in fact build adventurous and imaginative homes for themselves is very welcome.

## D   *20th Century World Architecture* by Phaidon editors

In the middle of the last century, writers such as Nikolaus Pevsner tried to define the architecture of their epoch. It was about the inevitable progression to an architecture suitable to the machine age. This so-called 'modern movement' was led by a small number of masters – Walter Gropius, Le Corbusier and Mies van der Rohe – and its advance was marked out by a few canonical works, such as villas, exhibition pavilions and factories. When the inevitable reaction came, and traditionalists called for a return of decoration and historical styles, the distilled version of modern architecture promoted by Pevsner and others became a useful caricature.

The reality was more complicated, and now the publishers Phaidon have produced this huge book to put the record straight. They have largely succeeded. Setting architecture in wider geographical and cultural contexts, the book's range is highly impressive. It is hard to quibble with any inclusions or exclusions of either people or their constructions. My only reservation is that it suffers from some uncertainty of purpose. Clearly not a guidebook – with 3800 photographs of 757 buildings it is almost too heavy to lift – it's not quite an encyclopedia either.

PAPER 1 Reading and
        Use of English

PAPER 2 Writing ▶

PAPER 3 Listening

PAPER 4 Speaking

# Essential tips

▶ Part 1 is always an essay in response to a proposition of some kind, made, for example, in a seminar or lecture or panel discussion. Your task is to develop and support an argument on the particular topic supplied. You cannot predict what the topic will be, but you can learn to identify the advantages and disadvantages of various propositions and how to present them in an organised way.

▶ You should practise working on 'for and against' essays and familiarise yourself with the correct structure: an introduction, main body (usually two paragraphs) and a conclusion.

▶ Use formal language in the Part 1 essay and present your argument clearly. State the topic, then provide the key points for and against the proposal, supporting these ideas, where possible, with examples or justifications.

▶ If you happen to feel strongly about the topic, be sure to remain objective. Don't use emotional language and don't express your own opinion until the final paragraph of the essay.

▶ Practise using appropriate linking words and phrases to introduce points, to add points, to contrast points and to conclude the essay.

▶ Read carefully through questions 2, 3 and 4 in Part 2 before deciding which item you will write. Make sure you know how to structure the text type you choose and that you know the appropriate vocabulary to use.

▶ Remember that all questions in Part 2 could require formal or informal writing. The question will not specify which register you should use; you will need to figure this out from the input text. To determine this, pay close attention to the style and tone of the input text, and who the target reader of the piece will be.

▶ Read as many letters, reports, proposals and reviews as possible. You can find a wide range of professional reviews, for example, online. (Ensure these are on reputable and professional websites.) Pay attention to how they are structured and the language that they use.

▶ In the test, there will be blank pages in the question booklet where you can jot down some notes if you wish. Don't spend too long planning at the expense of completing your written piece.

▶ Resist the temptation to reuse any points provided in the input text. You can certainly refer to them, but do so in your own words rather than reproducing them exactly as they appear in the test. It is important to demonstrate your own range of language.

▶ You will not be allowed to use a dictionary during the test.

PAPER 1  Reading and
          Use of English
PAPER 2  Writing  ▶  **Part 1**
                      Part 2
PAPER 3  Listening
PAPER 4  Speaking

You **must** answer this question. Write your answer in **220–260** words in an appropriate style on the separate answer sheet.

1  One of your professors is a committed vegetarian. In a recent lecture, she proposed that all meat dishes be removed from the menu in the cafeteria. You have made the notes below.

> **Why we should ban meat from our cafeteria**
>
> - healthier for everyone
> - what about animals' rights?
> - better environment if no meat consumption

> **Other students expressed these opinions during the lecture:**
>
> "Eating meat is natural and normal and always has been."
>
> "But where does all this stop? Should we also ban milk, cheese and eggs?"
>
> "What about personal choice and people's right to eat whatever they want?"

Write an essay for your professor discussing **two** of the points she made. You should **explain whether or not you think banning meat from the canteen is the best choice for everyone** and **provide reasons** to support your opinions.

You may, if you wish, make use of the opinions expressed in the lecture, but you should use your own words as far as possible.

## Essential tips

▶ Decide which two points you are going to focus on. Then think about how you can expand on and develop each one.

▶ Be sure to stick to the point and keep the essay on track. Avoid repeating yourself.

▶ Remember, this is an academic essay and the register should be formal. Don't use slang or other informal language.

▶ Think about the words and phrases you could use to present each point.

▶ You can argue for or against the proposal, but do so objectively. Try not to let your personal feelings come through as you write the essay. Remember, you may state your own opinion in the conclusion, but it shows skill if you can maintain a distance and present the facts clearly. You can also argue both sides of the proposal and write a balanced, objective argument overall.

▶ Use examples to support each advantage or disadvantage that you mention. Remember, for the purposes of this exercise, the examples do not have to be real or true.

PAPER 1  Reading and
            Use of English
**PAPER 2  Writing**  ▶  Part 1
                          **Part 2**
PAPER 3  Listening
PAPER 4  Speaking

Write an answer to **one** of the questions **2–4** in this part. Write your answer in **220–260** words in an appropriate style on the separate answer sheet. Put the question number in the box at the top of the page.

2   A couple of years ago you did a *Volunteering Abroad* programme in South Africa. Your 17-year-old cousin, Dan, is thinking of doing the same thing and has written to you asking about it.

Read the extract from Dan's email.

> The animal conservation work you did sounds interesting – can you tell me a bit more about it, for example, which animals did you work with? I definitely hope to do a lot of travelling while I'm there too. Can you suggest anywhere I can visit? I suppose what I'm wondering more than anything is whether you think I'll enjoy it.
>
> Thanks, Paul!
>
> Dan

Write your **email**.

3   You see this post on a community website:

Your local council is compiling a web page about public transport options in your town. They would like local people to send in reports about the public transport services they use. In your report, you should:

- mention which services you use and how often you use them
- describe the quality of the service including factors such as cost and reliability
- recommend or suggest any services and facilities that you think are missing.

Write your **report**.

4   You receive this flyer from a local arts group.

> Film Event
>
> On the grounds of City Hall every Friday this summer we will screen a film free of charge. We would like you to suggest suitable titles, but we specifically want films that are socially relevant today. The screenings will begin at 9.00 p.m. each Friday. Please send us your review of a film that you think would be suitable, giving reasons for your choice.

Write your **review**.

## Essential tips

▶ Not all possible Part 2 task types appear on every paper. For example, you could be asked to produce a letter (formal or informal), or you could be asked to write an email.

▶ The review question could be based on a book or a film, but you might also be asked to review a product or service, or an event or performance. You may invent any of these items if you wish.

**Question 2**

▶ What is the style of the input text? What register should you use?

▶ Don't make the mistake of thinking that an email does not require the same attention to detail as a letter; organisation and layout are equally important here.

▶ What can you learn from the instructions and from Dan's email? Underline the information that will be important to consider in your reply.

▶ Remember, you can also come up with other points not featured in the input text.

**Question 3**

▶ As you consider answering this question, ask yourself whether you have an adequate range of vocabulary on the topic of transport.

▶ Structure in all text types is very important, but in a report it is vital that the information is presented in an organised way, making it easy for the reader to follow and understand. It is a good idea to use headings in a report.

▶ Pay attention to the areas mentioned in the input text and don't leave any of them out.

▶ Notice that you are also required to include some suggestions or recommendations in your report.

**Question 4**

▶ Be careful not to rush in and write a review of any film you happen to like very much. In this case, it must be socially relevant.

▶ What does *socially relevant* mean? You need to demonstrate in your review that your chosen film has social relevance.

▶ Bear in mind that this will be a public screening. Will the event mainly be for adults? How can you tell?

▶ The film you write about does not have to be real; you can make one up to suit this purpose. The important thing is that you provide a proper assessment of the film and show how it would be a suitable choice for the event.

PAPER 1 Reading and
Use of English

PAPER 2 Writing

**PAPER 3 Listening** ▶ | Part 1
Part 2
Part 3
Part 4

PAPER 4 Speaking

**Track 5**

You will hear three different extracts. For questions **1–6**, choose the answer (**A, B** or **C**) which fits best according to what you hear. There are two questions for each extract.

**Extract One**

You hear a man making a phone call to deliver some good news.

**1** Is the woman busy when her friend phones her?
   **A** She is very busy.
   **B** She is not busy at all.
   **C** She is a little busy.

**2** What surprised the man?
   **A** that he had actually passed the driving test
   **B** that he had felt so nervous before the test
   **C** that his friend was nervous before her test

**Extract Two**

You hear a woman telling a friend about her experience at a careers fair.

**3** What is the woman's attitude?
   **A** pessimistic
   **B** bored
   **C** angry

**4** What does the man advise the woman to do?
   **A** speak to her parents
   **B** become an accountant
   **C** make a focused plan

**Extract Three**

You hear a woman discussing plans for her cousin's visit with a friend.

**5** What is the man's criticism of the woman's plan?
   **A** There won't be enough time to visit all the places.
   **B** He is concerned that it might be too boring.
   **C** Her cousin doesn't like museums or galleries.

**6** Does the woman agree with the man's suggestion?
   **A** Yes, she does.
   **B** No, she doesn't.
   **C** She is undecided.

# Essential tips

▶ Make sure you listen to the entire extract before choosing your answer.

▶ Always try to choose your answer after the first listening, and confirm it after the second.

▶ Don't panic if you hear any words you don't recognise. Listen carefully and think about the context of what is being said.

▶ Listen for any stressed words. These often contain important information, either for specific details or for letting you know how the speaker feels.

**Question 2:** You need to identify something that surprised the man, something unusual, something he hadn't expected. What word in the extract signals this idea?

**Question 3:** In order to identify the woman's attitude, you need to listen to the points she makes, but also to her tone of voice. Read the answer options carefully. Which one best describes her attitude?

**Question 4:** Don't hurriedly choose an answer option just because you recognise a key word in the extract. Ensure that the full idea expressed in the answer you choose can be heard in the extract.

**Question 6:** You need to find out whether there is agreement between the speakers. Listen for language that indicates agreement or disagreement.

PAPER 1   Reading and
          Use of English

PAPER 2   Writing

PAPER 3   Listening   ▶
          Part 1
          Part 2
          Part 3
          Part 4

PAPER 4   Speaking

## Essential tips

▶ Practise for this part of the test by listening to podcasts of lectures or presentations.

▶ Make the most of the time before the recording is first played by reading carefully through the rubric, the title and the set of statements. These will help you to think about the type of information you need.

▶ In this part of the test, all correct answers are the exact words or phrases as they are used in the recording. The statements may be paraphrased, but the missing words are not.

▶ If you are really not sure, you should make your best guess rather than leaving a blank space. No marks are deducted for getting an answer wrong, and you may have understood more than you realise.

**Question 7:** What does the speaker like doing when she travels? What part of speech follows *for*? What other words can you think of for *sleep*?

**Question 9:** Listen for a reference to the idea of travel being extended or stopping. This is where you will find the missing word or phrase.

**Question 10:** The use of the word *more* suggests that the speaker makes a comparison, and you know from the sentence structure that you need an adjective here. What adjective does she use?

**Question 13:** There is a reference to a trend here. What trend does the woman mention? Remember, she may use a term other than 'trend'.

🎧 **Track 6**

You will hear a travel writer describing her relationship with sleep. For questions **7–14**, complete the sentences with a word or short phrase.

# SLEEP, WONDERFUL SLEEP

The woman's guilty secret is that she schedules time for

(**7**) .......................................................... on her trips.

According to the woman, a (**8**) .........................................................

of travelling is sleeping better.

The woman believes that our travel experience is extended when we sleep; it isn't a

(**9**) .......................................................... from it.

She comments that the sleep we experience when travelling tends to be significantly

more (**10**) .......................................................... .

For the speaker, getting over long-distance travel is particularly affected by

(**11**) .......................................................... adjustments.

She finds that sleep while travelling is more (**12**) ..............................................................

than what we experience at home.

The speaker refers to a trend called (**13**) ........................................................, which

involves not rushing journeys.

In the end the speaker thinks she might (**14**) .......................................................... to her

fellow travellers how much she actually sleeps when she's on the road.

PAPER 1 Reading and
Use of English

PAPER 2 Writing

PAPER 3 Listening ▶

PAPER 4 Speaking

Part 1
Part 2
Part 3
Part 4

## Essential tips

▸ This is the longest part of the Listening paper. Practise listening to recordings of this length so that you don't lose your focus before the end of the recording in the test.

▸ Pay attention to the question stem and listen for 'trigger' words. For example, if the question asks *How long …?* listen for time frames.

▸ Remember, the questions appear in the same order as the information in the recording.

▸ Unlike Part 2, the answers in Part 3 may be paraphrased from the recording, so listen carefully for the key ideas.

**Question 16:** Notice the word *overall* in the question. Martin might mention various difficulties, but this tells you that you need to identify an overall, or main, problem.

**Question 17:** As always, pay close attention to how the question is phrased. Note that it doesn't ask what Martin says to the students, but what he emphasises to them.

**Question 20:** Pay attention to the pronoun *who* and listen for any mention of study groups. What does Martin say about them?

🎧 **Track 7**

You will hear a radio interview about the challenges which first-year college students often face. For questions **15–20**, choose the answer (**A**, **B**, **C** or **D**) which fits best according to what you hear.

15  What does Martin Ferguson say about his job as an Information and Advice Officer?
   A   His professional background is working in customer service.
   B   He recruits students and enrols them at Stanmere College.
   C   He helps students before and after they begin their course.
   D   He works exclusively with the first year university students.

16  Martin says that, overall, the most common difficulty for students starting college is
   A   the new environment.
   B   the volume of work.
   C   too much freedom.
   D   time management.

17  What does Martin emphasise to students?
   A   that there isn't any shame in being weak
   B   that how they're feeling is very common
   C   that all of their friends are struggling too
   D   that it's important to show their feelings

18  Regarding finances, what does Martin give his students?
   A   a course in financial management
   B   tricks for saving their money
   C   a pre-made budget for students
   D   tips on how to spend less money

19  Primarily, according to Martin, additional difficulties include students'
   A   physical and psychological well-being.
   B   concerns about failing their exams.
   C   anxieties about their family back home.
   D   lack of meaningful friendships.

20  Who does Martin recommend study groups to?
   A   students who are worried about exams
   B   students who like clubs and societies
   C   students who are not very outgoing
   D   students who might be depressed

PAPER 1 Reading and
Use of English

PAPER 2 Writing

**PAPER 3 Listening** ▶

PAPER 4 Speaking

Part 1
Part 2
Part 3
**Part 4**

🎧 **Track 8**

You will hear five short extracts in which people talk about the things they do to reduce stress.

**While you listen you must complete both tasks.**

---

**TASK ONE**

For questions **21–25**, choose from the list (**A–H**) what each speaker says about what brought them to this particular practice.

A   was worried about taxes

B   was busy relocating                    Speaker 1 [  **21**  ]

C   takes on too much                      Speaker 2 [  **22**  ]

D   had left a busy job                    Speaker 3 [  **23**  ]

E   lost a family member                   Speaker 4 [  **24**  ]

F   does it for free at the gym            Speaker 5 [  **25**  ]

G   lacked a healthy balance

H   has a very physical job

**TASK TWO**

For questions **26–30**, choose from the list (**A–H**) what each speaker says about the effect the practice has on them.

A   gets a tranquil feeling

B   sleeps more often                       Speaker 1 [  **26**  ]

C   feels a burden lifted                   Speaker 2 [  **27**  ]

D   gained some weight                      Speaker 3 [  **28**  ]

E   feels their mind has cleared           Speaker 4 [  **29**  ]

F   is totally relaxed                      Speaker 5 [  **30**  ]

G   no longer has nightmares

H   thinks life seems less hectic

## Essential tips

▶ As this part of the test focuses on gist and attitude, a good way to practise for it is to study the kind of vocabulary that expresses feelings and attitudes.

▶ The series of five short recordings will be played through once and then replayed. Unlike in Part 1, they will not be played and replayed one at a time.

▶ Practise working on two tasks at once.

▶ The instructions will tell you what the common theme is. Take a moment to try and predict what you might hear in the recording.

▶ Even though the speakers may mention practices you have never heard of before, don't worry. You won't be asked questions about the practices themselves, only how the speaker started doing them and how they feel afterwards.

**Questions 21–25:**

**Option B:** What does *relocating* mean? Do any of the speakers talk about this?

**Option E:** *Lost a family member* is another way of saying what? Does anyone make reference to this?

**Option F:** Does anyone mention the gym and, importantly, do they say anything about not paying fees?

**Questions 26–30:**

**Option A:** What is another way of saying *tranquil*? Who, if anyone, makes specific reference to this?

**Option B:** Be sure to consider the entire phrase in each option. Does anyone mention sleep and, if so, do they say they sleep more often now?

**Option H:** More than one speaker may describe their life as being hectic, but does anyone specifically say the effect of the practice is that their life now feels less crazy?

PAPER 1 Reading and
          Use of English

PAPER 2 Writing

PAPER 3 Listening

PAPER 4 Speaking

## Essential tips

**Part 1**

▶ In this part of the test, the examiner (or interlocutor) will not direct you to interact with your partner, but it's fine if you do.

▶ Remember to speak clearly. It's understandable that you may feel nervous but try not to rush what you are saying.

▶ Always give complete answers rather than a brief *yes* or *no*. Make a habit of repeating part of the question, which will ensure that you address what you are being asked, e.g. *What are your hobbies? My hobbies are …*

▶ Wherever possible, try to offer additional information, for example, include a brief reason for the answer you have just given.

**Part 2**

▶ In this part of the test, you have to talk on a subject for about a minute. This is a long time, so make sure that you prepare for the test by practising talking for this amount of time.

▶ The examiner could ask you to compare or contrast pictures, identify things in them or to speculate about them. You will be given three pictures and you have to talk about two of them.

▶ There will probably be two parts to the question that you are asked about the pictures, so make sure you answer both parts. If you can't think of anything to say, make time to think by using hesitation phrases, e.g. *let me see, I'm not sure about that, let me think about that for a moment.*

▶ Listen carefully while the other candidate is talking as the examiner will ask you an extra question related to what the other candidate has been talking about. You should answer in about 30 seconds.

**Part 1** (2 minutes)

The examiner will ask you a few questions about yourself and about a general topic. For example, the examiner may ask you:

- **What are your hobbies?**
- **Do you like watching films in English?**
- **What kind of career interests you the most?**

**Part 2** (4 minutes)

You will each be asked to talk on your own for about a minute. You will each be given three different pictures to talk about. After your partner has finished speaking, you will be asked a brief question connected with your partner's photographs.

| **Restaurants** (compare, contrast and speculate) |
| --- |

Turn to pictures 1–3 on page **172**, which show different restaurants.

(*Candidate A*), it's your turn first. Here are your pictures. They show **different types of restaurant.**

I'd like you to compare **two** of the pictures and say **what kinds of dishes are probably served in each one and who might typically dine** in these restaurants.

(*Candidate B*), **which of these restaurants appeals to you the most? Why?**

| **Collector items** (compare, contrast and speculate) |
| --- |

Turn to pictures 1–3 on page **173**, which show different collector items.

Now, (*Candidate B*), here are your pictures. They show **various items that people collect.**

I'd like you to compare **two** of the pictures and describe **what kind of person would collect these items and why people collect things.**

(*Candidate A*), **which of these collections do you think is the most interesting? Why?**

**Part 3** (4 minutes)

Look at page **174,** which shows some potential benefits of online learning.

| **Online learning** (discuss, evaluate and negotiate) |
| --- |

**Here are some benefits of online learning** and a question for you to discuss.

First, you have some time to look at the task.

(*Pause 15 seconds*)

Now talk to each other about **ways in which students can benefit from online learning and how relevant you feel these benefits are.**

Now you have a minute to decide **what you feel is the main *disadvantage* of online learning, and why.**

**Part 4** (5 minutes)

The examiner will encourage you to develop the topic of your discussion in Part 3 by asking questions such as:

- Which do you prefer between online learning and learning in the traditional classroom? Why?
- With online learning, is it possible to have interaction with other learners?
- In the near future, do you think people will only study online? Why (not)?

PAPER 1 Reading and  ▶  Part 1
         Use of English     Part 2

PAPER 2 Writing           Part 3
                          Part 4
PAPER 3 Listening         Part 5

PAPER 4 Speaking          Part 6
                          Part 7
                          Part 8

For questions **1–8**, read the text below and decide which answer (**A**, **B**, **C** or **D**) best fits each gap. There is an example at the beginning (**0**).

Mark your answers **on the separate answer sheet**.

**Example:**

**0**   **A**   view          **B**   survey          **C**   outline          **D**   inquiry

| 0 | A | B | C | D |
|---|---|---|---|---|

## Essential tips

▶ Read through the text quickly first.

▶ Remember that only one option is correct for each gap. It needs to fit in the sentence and also with the meaning of the whole text.

▶ Look carefully at the words before and after each gap. For example, sometimes only one option is correct because of a preposition that follows the gap.

▶ When you have completed all the gaps, read through the text again to check that it makes sense.

**Question 1:** This is a phrase which means 'just about to do something'.

**Question 2:** Look at the words following the gap. Which adverb is likely to collocate with *long*?

**Question 3:** Which of these phrasal verbs means 'it was discovered that'?

**Question 4:** All four options could be used to start a sentence. However, three of them either have the wrong meaning or need to be followed by a preposition.

## Finding new species

A group of scientists recently conducted a biodiversity (**0**) ........ of a tropical forest in Suriname, Latin America. One day, a local guide caught a large catfish, and was on the (**1**) ........ of cutting it up for cooking when two of the scientists intervened. They had noticed that the creature had (**2**) ........ long spines, probably to protect it from predators. It (**3**) ........ out to be an undiscovered species. (**4**) ........ any catfish in reference books, the as yet unnamed fish was one of 46 candidates for new species status that the scientists found during their visit.

In the 1730s, Swedish botanist Carl Linnaeus (**5**) ........ rules for classifying species, the most basic biological (**6**) ........: since then, scientists have catalogued more than 1.7 million species, but it is thought that there may be as many as 8.7 million on earth. Figures for different groups of animals have been (**7**) ........ and most mammal, birds and reptiles are believed to have been discovered. Fish, shellfish and spiders, however, are a different story, and literally millions of species of insects (**8**) ........ for future generations to discover.

| # | A | B | C | D |
|---|---|---|---|---|
| 1 | edge | line | verge | border |
| 2 | intensely | utterly | highly | exceptionally |
| 3 | turned | came | carried | gave |
| 4 | Opposite | Unlike | Contrary | Distinct |
| 5 | laid on | set out | fixed up | put through |
| 6 | category | section | department | version |
| 7 | accounted | composed | compiled | joined |
| 8 | stay | endure | persist | remain |

| PAPER 1 | Reading and Use of English ▶ | Part 1 |
| | | Part 2 |
| PAPER 2 | Writing | Part 3 |
| | | Part 4 |
| PAPER 3 | Listening | Part 5 |
| PAPER 4 | Speaking | Part 6 |
| | | Part 7 |
| | | Part 8 |

For questions **9–16**, read the text below and think of the word which best fits each gap. Use only one word in each gap. There is an example at the beginning (**0**).

Write your answers **IN CAPITAL LETTERS on the separate answer sheet**.

**Example:** | 0 | T | H | E | | | | | | | | | | | | | | | | | | |

---

## Why you forgot what you came into the room for

The brain may be (**0**) ........ least understood organ in the human body. It guides everything we do, but every (**9**) ........ often it lets us down. One annoying, if (**10**) ........ exactly life-threatening, example of this is when you walk into a room, (**11**) ........ to realise you have forgotten what your reason for going there was. Why is (**12**) ........ an incredibly powerful organ as the brain unable to remind us of something that simple?

(**13**) ........ spent many years investigating the brain, scientist Gabriel Radvansky thinks he has an answer. He has conducted numerous experiments in (**14**) ........ participants' memories were tested after crossing a room or exiting through a doorway. Invariably, passing through a doorway resulted (**15**) ........ more memory errors. Radvansky refers to what happens as an 'event boundary' in the brain. As (**16**) ........ as the brain is concerned, a doorway is a boundary between one event, or experience, and another. The brain files away all information about the first event, and focuses on the second, the new room; this makes it hard to recall a decision made in a previous room.

# Essential tips

▶ Read the whole text quickly.

▶ Most of the gaps need grammatical words. Decide which type of word each gap needs. These could include: prepositions (e.g. *of*, *in*), articles (e.g. *a*, *the*), pronouns (e.g. *they*, *it*, *them*, *theirs*), relative pronouns (e.g. *who*, *which*), conjunctions (e.g. *and*, *so*), parts of verbs (e.g. *be*, *been*), modal verbs (e.g. *might*, *must*), particles of phrasal verbs (e.g. *look* **through**, *look* **into**), parts of phrases (e.g. *in* **order** *to*).

▶ The gap will probably not need a topic word. For example, in the phrase *if only he had known about*, *known* would not be gapped, but *if*, *only*, *he*, *had* or *about* could be.

▶ Remember that the word you choose must fit the meaning of the whole text, not just a few words before and after a gap. Read the complete text to see if it makes sense.

**Question 10:** Look at the whole sentence here. Is it 'life-threatening' to forget why you have entered a room? Thinking about this question should lead you to the missing word.

**Question 11:** This is a phrase, *... to do something*, used to describe something that happens immediately afterwards and causes surprise or disappointment.

**Question 12:** Look carefully at the structure of the whole sentence following the gap. Why is the word *as* there?

**Question 13:** If you can't think of a suitable word here, it may help to try thinking of a phrase that makes sense. In this case, *Because he has* would fit the sentence. In written English, phrases like *because he has*, *after he had*, *when he had* are often replaced by a particular form of an auxiliary verb before a past participle – auxiliary verb + *spent*.

PAPER 1  Reading and
         Use of English

PAPER 2  Writing

PAPER 3  Listening

PAPER 4  Speaking

Part 1
Part 2
**Part 3**
Part 4
Part 5
Part 6
Part 7
Part 8

For questions **17–24**, read the text below. Use the word given in capitals at the end of some of the lines to form a word that fits in the gap **in the same line**. There is an example at the beginning (**0**).

Write your answers **IN CAPITAL LETTERS on the separate answer sheet**.

**Example:** | 0 | I | N | D | U | S | T | R | I | A | L | | | | | | | | |

## Essential tips

▶ Read the whole text for general understanding first.

▶ When you decide which type of word is needed for a gap, note it down next to the gap – noun, verb, adjective or adverb. Only these four types of word are tested in this part of the exam.

▶ Remember that some words will probably need more than one change.

▶ Be careful with spelling.

▶ Check whether nouns should be singular or plural.

▶ When you complete the task, read through the text again. Does it all make sense?

**Question 18**: What type of word is *advances*? So, what type of word is needed for the gap?

**Question 19**: You need to form a noun here. It can be either singular or plural.

**Question 20**: The noun required here refers to a process of simulating something that happened in the past.

**Question 21**: What kind of word can often come before an adjective, modifying the adjective?

## Early human development and climate change

According to recent research, it was in times of wetter weather that early human beings in southern Africa made the greatest (**0**) ........   **INDUSTRY**
and cultural leaps forward. (**17**) ........ of modern humans is   **EMERGE**
thought to have taken place in Africa over 200,000 years ago,
but two eras of (**18**) ........ advances have been identified in   **INNOVATE**
southern Africa about 71,500 and 64,000 to 59,000 years ago,
which saw the development of personal (**19**) ........ in the form   **ADORN**
of shell jewellery, also of bone tools and probably of language.
In a computer-based (**20**) ........ of climate change over the last   **CONSTRUCT**
100,000 years, scientists discovered that these two periods were
characterised by (**21**) ........ heavy rainfall in southern Africa,   **NOTE**
whilst the rest of the continent experienced long-term drought.
The researchers believe their (**22**) ........ support the view that   **FIND**
there was significant movement of ancient humans to the more
hospitable conditions of southern Africa. This would have
resulted in population (**23**) ........., competition for resources and   **GROW**
exchange of ideas, which in turn fuelled progress. So, these
distant ancestors of ours may well have benefited (**24**) ........   **TECHNOLOGY**
from climate change.

PAPER 1  Reading and
         Use of English    ▸

PAPER 2  Writing

PAPER 3  Listening

PAPER 4  Speaking

| Part 1 |
| Part 2 |
| Part 3 |
| **Part 4** |
| Part 5 |
| Part 6 |
| Part 7 |
| Part 8 |

## Essential tips

▸ Part 4 tests a wide range of grammatical structures and vocabulary items. However, certain things are often required: changing the word order, replacing ordinary verbs with phrasal verbs, changing verbs to nouns and vice versa.

▸ Don't forget: you must not change the key word and you have to use between three and six words. Remember also that contractions count as two words (e.g. *don't* = two words).

▸ Remember that each question usually tests two different points. For example, changing an active to a passive structure, plus changing a verb to a noun.

▸ When you have completed a question, read through it again and make sure that you have not changed the meaning.

**Question 25:** *Must* expresses the idea of 'sure'. Because 'he wasn't lying' is about the past, what structure needs to follow *must*? And which verb collocates with *truth*?

**Question 26:** What phrase including *it* and *long* expresses the idea that something 'soon' happened? Which phrasal verb with *on* means 'acquire' or 'accept'?

**Question 27:** The first part of this question tests a structure used to give emphasis; it means 'although something is / was ...'. In the second part of the question, you will need to change a verb to a noun.

**Question 28:** You need a passive structure here. You also need a phrasal verb meaning 'to challenge someone'.

For questions **25–30**, complete the second sentence so that it has a similar meaning to the first sentence, using the word given. **Do not change the word given.** You must use between **three** and **six** words, including the word given. Here is an example (**0**).

**Example:**

**0**  Chloe would only eat a pizza if she could have a mushroom topping.

**ON**

Chloe .......................................... a mushroom topping when she had a pizza.

The gap can be filled with the words 'insisted on having', so you write:

**Example:** | **0** | INSISTED ON HAVING |

Write **only** the missing words **IN CAPITAL LETTERS on the separate answer sheet**.

---

**25**  We've talked a lot about Peter's description of what happened that day at the beach and I'm sure he wasn't lying.

**MUST**

We've talked a lot about Peter's description of what happened that day at the beach and he ........................................ truth.

**26**  Once Catherine moved to the Finance Department, she soon acquired more responsibilities than she had ever had in her previous job.

**LONG**

Once Catherine moved to the Finance Department, it ........................................ on more responsibilities than she had ever had in her previous job.

**27**  Radford has contributed in a useful way this season but the team would probably be fine without him.

**THOUGH**

Useful ........................................ this season, the team would probably be fine without him.

**28**  We could always rely on Maria to challenge our supervisor whenever he became too bossy and demanding.

**STAND**

Maria could always ........................................ to our supervisor whenever he became too bossy and demanding.

**29**  Everyone in the office was really surprised when the manager decided to cancel the meeting.

**OFF**

The manager's decision to ........................................ as a real surprise to everyone in the office.

**30**  John said that he wouldn't hesitate to recommend Elaine for the coaching job at Darnell Sports Centre.

**HAVE**

John said that he ........................................ Elaine for the coaching job at Darnell Sports Centre.

| PAPER 1 Reading and Use of English ▶ | Part 1 |
| | Part 2 |
| PAPER 2 Writing | Part 3 |
| | Part 4 |
| PAPER 3 Listening | **Part 5** |
| | Part 6 |
| PAPER 4 Speaking | Part 7 |
| | Part 8 |

You are going to read a book review. For questions **31–36**, choose the answer (**A**, **B**, **C** or **D**) which you think fits best according to the text.

Mark your answers **on the separate answer sheet**.

# Hemingway's Boat

*Sam Leith reviews a biography of the great American novelist and short story writer, Ernest Hemingway:*
*Hemingway's Boat: Everything He Loved in Life, And Lost, 1934–1961, by Paul Hendrickson.*

In *Hemingway's Boat*, Hendrickson takes the idea that writing about Hemingway's boat *Pilar* is a way of getting at deep things about the man. *Pilar* was there all the second half of his life and fishing was more than a recreation for Hemingway: it was at the centre, this book plausibly suggests, of his being in the world. Paul Hendrickson duly set about getting to the core of Hemingway's relationship with *Pilar*. And how!

He hasn't just interviewed Hemingway's sons and surviving former friends and helpers. He has investigated the history of the company that built Hemingway's boat, and visited the muddy waterway in which she first floated. If a journalist published a news report on Hemingway's arrival in Cuba, where he lived for many years, Hendrickson will have studied his subsequent career. If Hemingway fished a particular stream on one occasion in his teens, Hendrickson will have fished it too. This is the total immersion school of – well, biography isn't quite the word. It's a sort of mental home invasion.

The narrative loops around in time – describing the acquisition of the boat, and going forward and back to his childhood, zipping into his legacy, and closing in on his death. As well as the *Pilar* story, it describes, at some length, a trio of others. There's Arnold Samuelson, a well-educated wanderer who ended up crewing his boat; there's Walter Houk, a junior diplomat, whose wife worked as Hemingway's secretary and who was similarly taken up; and there's Hemingway's youngest son, Gregory ('Gigi'). The author interviewed the latter two, and extensively researched the first, telling their previously under-examined stories fully and sympathetically in the hope that, in the overlap between them, we'd get somewhere close to Hemingway. It works.

This book places you formidably deep in Hemingway's world and life. It takes you down to the insertions and deletions in manuscripts, and shows you how the sentences were formed; with what agony and then excitement he wrote. Not that it cuts corners on the wild, action-man stuff either. Hemingway was insanely competitive, and behaved with infantile petulance when a guest out-hunted or out-fished him. At one point the author remarks drily, when Hemingway shoots himself in the leg on board *Pilar*: 'Perhaps if the fisherman hadn't been trying to land the fish and gaff it and shoot it in the head all at once, the accident would never have occurred.' And he sure did love shooting. Here we meet Hemingway shooting at bottles, shooting his initials into the top of a shark's head, blowing away seabirds with a shotgun, and so on.

But here, too, is the Hemingway who knew what a monster he could be, and regretted it. This was a man who was capable of great acts of kindness and generosity, and of remorse. There are some killingly poignant quotes – long, wonderful letters written to the sick children of friends, for instance, and the interviews with his beloved but tragic son Gigi. It gathers to a really moving end. There is so much in this long book which is interesting and enlightening that it defies any attempt to reduce it to a neat outline.

So I regret that I do have some reservations. *Hemingway's Boat* has received praise, not only for its research, but for its prose; it's in a style that strikes some people as literary. To my mind, however, it's showily overwritten. Besides the tricksy devices like sudden switches to the present tense, it abounds with pompous turns of phrase – sometimes clumsily repeated, among the crazy level of descriptive detail, with at least three chapters containing the words 'Amid so much ruin, still the beauty'. Which brings to mind all the irritating verbless sentences.

The problem is, he's doing several things: this is not just a book about Hemingway, it's also a memoir of writing a book about Hemingway, and, in some sense, it's a novelisation of the author's worshipful and faintly competitive relationship with his literary master. He bosses the reader about ('take another look at the photograph') and lets what he takes to be Hemingway-style confidence drift into his prose. It's as if someone has told Hendrickson that this is literary writing, and that it will make the difference between a good book and an astonishing one. I don't think Hemingway – who, as Hendrickson admits, is much harder to imitate than he looks – would have agreed. I'm sure it's just Hendrickson. The fact is, though, this book would have been astonishing without it.

**31** The reviewer's main intention in the second paragraph is to illustrate
  A how difficult it was for Hendrickson to write about Hemingway.
  B how detailed Hendrickson's research on Hemingway was.
  C how important boats and fishing were to Hemingway.
  D how much variety there was in Hemingway's life.

**32** According to the reviewer, why did Hendrickson devote so much of his book to Samuelson, Houk and Gregory Hemingway?
  A They had never been written about before by biographers of Hemingway.
  B They were the most important people in Hemingway's life.
  C They provided clues to Hemingway's true character.
  D They all spent time with Hemingway on his boat.

**33** What does the reviewer suggest about Hendrickson's biography in the fourth paragraph?
  A It enhances Hemingway's reputation as a writer.
  B It goes into too much detail about certain aspects of Hemingway's behaviour.
  C It underlines the influence Hemingway's lifestyle had on his writing.
  D It gives a balanced picture of Hemingway as a writer and as a man.

**34** What point does the reviewer make about Hendrickson's biography in the fifth paragraph?
  A It is difficult to summarise.
  B It gets worse as it goes along.
  C It can be too sentimental in places.
  D It is best when showing Hemingway's good side.

**35** The reviewer quotes the words 'Amid so much ruin, still the beauty' to exemplify
  A a tricksy device.
  B a pompous turn of phrase.
  C a crazy level of descriptive detail.
  D a verbless sentence.

**36** What point does the reviewer make in the final paragraph?
  A Hendrickson makes some of the same mistakes as Hemingway did in his writing.
  B Hendrickson's biography would have met Hemingway's approval.
  C Hendrickson's book is excellent in spite of the way he writes.
  D Hendrickson has taken notice of some bad advice.

# Essential tips

▶ Make sure you read the title and the byline just underneath it. This should be a helpful introduction to the subject of the text you are going to read.

▶ Read the text quickly for general understanding. Try to get an idea of the way it is organised.

▶ Read each question and highlight the key words. Find and mark the relevant piece of text for each question.

▶ Look at the options for the first question and highlight the key words in them. Then look at the relevant piece of text and highlight words that relate to each option, before deciding which option best reflects the text.

▶ If you find it difficult to decide which option is best, try eliminating options that you feel confident are wrong. Narrowing your choice down like this should help you find the answer.

**Question 31:** This is an example of a question about the writer's 'purpose' in one part of the text. What is the main point of the second paragraph? Look at the options carefully. Options A and B are about the way Hendrickson worked, while Options C and D are about Hemingway. Is the main focus of the second paragraph on what Hendrickson did or on what Hemingway did? Often with 'purpose' questions, it helps to look at the previous paragraph too.

**Question 32:** Find and mark the section in which Samuelson, Houk and Gregory are mentioned. Then examine each option in turn. Option A: we are told that Hendrickson describes these three people 'at some length', but does the text suggest that biographers had never written about them before? Option B: all three people featured in Hemingway's life, but does the text say they were the most important people in his life? Option C: all three seem to have been close to Hemingway and so would know something about the novelist's character, but does the text suggest they 'provided clues' about it? Option D: the text says that Samuelson and Houk spent time on Hemingway's boat, and we could assume that his son would have done too. But does the text say this is why Hendrickson wrote about them 'at some length'?

**Question 35:** Mark the relevant part of the text. Then highlight or underline in the text where the quote in the question stem and each of the options are referred to. You may not know what every word or phrase in the options means, but by looking carefully at the structure of the sentences in the text, you should be able to work out what the phrase refers to.

| PAPER 1 Reading and Use of English | Part 1 |
| | Part 2 |
| | Part 3 |
| | Part 4 |
| PAPER 2 Writing | Part 5 |
| PAPER 3 Listening | **Part 6** |
| PAPER 4 Speaking | Part 7 |
| | Part 8 |

You are going to read four reviews of a book about maps. For questions **37–40**, choose from the reviews **A–D**. The reviews may be chosen more than once.

Mark your answers **on the separate answer sheet**.

# *On The Map* by Simon Garfield

*Four reviews of Simon Garfield's book about the long and varied history of map-making.*

**A**

*On The Map* offers a chronological history of maps, atlases, charts and globes from Ancient Egypt to contemporary digital cartography, and along the way provides a wealth of facts and anecdotes, all delivered with the expansive liveliness of an expert story-teller. Simon Garfield acknowledges he is neither a cartographer nor a professional historian, but his painstaking research and enthusiasm more than compensate for any omissions – there is very little on maps of Asia, for example – or for the lack of a rigorous guiding principle of the kind expected in books with more academic pretensions. Garfield, justifiably, is as enthralled by the beautiful, often factually erroneous drawings of the distant past as he is by today's GPS, video-game landscapes and social-media-based graphics. Given Garfield's descriptive intensity, it seems particularly strange that the black-and-white map illustrations that feature throughout are often reduced in scale to an extent that they become practically illegible.

**B**

Perhaps because Simon Garfield is a journalist rather than a historian, his understanding of the average reader's attention span is mercifully realistic. In this eminently readable history of map-making, Garfield rarely offers a train of thought that is not rounded off with a fascinating anecdote or neat piece of cartographic trivia. The fact that the book, which covers a lot of ground in over 400 pages, tends to wander unpredictably or gloss over certain important subjects, only adds to its appeal for the non-specialist. Regrettably, the visual presentation of maps – too many compressed, hard to decipher images – fails to match the standard of the text. Also, some of Garfield's observations on contemporary achievements in map-making like GPS – 'a loss to geography, history, navigation … and the sense of being connected to the world around us' – seem overly critical. On the whole, however, this is a fine introduction to the subject.

**C**

Simon Garfield clearly has a gift for digging up intriguing facts and stories, and this wide-ranging history of map-making, from Ptolemy in Ancient Alexandria to the interactive, digital images of today, generously illustrated with well-chosen historical treasures, is entertaining in many respects. Its best chapters tend to be those built around controversies such as the debate over the authenticity of a map claimed to depict sea voyages to America by the Norse hundreds of years before Columbus, but, overall, it suffers from a lack of a clear focus. Ironically, for a book about maps, the reader all too easily gets lost in all the vivid detail and anecdotes. One is also distracted by some awkward phrasing and surprisingly imprecise language. On the whole, however, the book does the job as a lively guide for those who are interested in maps but do not necessarily know much about them.

**D**

All surveys are, by nature, selective, and it is hardly surprising that a book such as *On The Map*, which attempts to cover over 2,000 years of map-making in an accessible way for readers who know little about the field, should skip or just sample certain subjects – for example, the methods and tools map-makers have used through history are barely touched on. Harder to accept or rationalise is the apparent lack of a guiding principle, besides that of cramming in as many fascinating facts as possible, and making it all fun. Garfield has a talent for communicating a telling detail or a curious turn of events, and he is particularly strong on certain periods of history, including the modern era. His chapter on such achievements as satellite navigation systems and mapping structures in computer games shows an admirably open-minded curiosity.

## Which reviewer

shares C's opinion about the way the book is organised?

37

has a different opinion from the others about the quality of writing in the book?

38

takes a similar view to A regarding the reproduction of maps in the book?

39

shares D's view on the way the book's author deals with recent developments in map-making?

40

# Essential tips

- Remember that you need to decide whether four different writers have similar or different views on the same subject.

- Read the title and the texts quickly to familiarise yourself with the subject.

- Highlight the key words in the questions.

- Go through each text carefully in turn, highlighting the sections relating to each question. Write the question numbers next to parts you highlight. Remember that the ideas in the question may be expressed differently in the texts, for example by using synonyms or changing the way a concept is expressed grammatically, e.g. *education* could be expressed as 'the way people learn'.

- Remember that a question will ask you to identify a writer's view on a subject and compare it with other people's views. The question tells you what the subject is, but not what any of the writers' views are. For example, if you are asked who shares writer A's view on the 'significance of something', you are not told whether A thinks it is significant or not – that is for you to work out.

**Question 37:** The key words here are *the way the book is organised*. You are asked who shares C's opinion about this. C says that 'overall, it suffers from a lack of a clear focus. Ironically, for a book about maps, the reader all too easily gets lost in all the vivid detail and anecdotes.' So, C thinks the 'lack of clear focus' is a problem with the way the book is organised. B's view of the book is that 'The fact that the book, which covers a lot of ground in over 400 pages, tends to wander unpredictably ... only adds to its appeal for the non-specialist.' 'Tends to wander unpredictably' tells us that B also thinks the book lacks a 'clear focus', but B regards this as positive – it 'only adds to its appeal for the non-specialist.' So, B does not fully share C's opinion. Now look at what A and D say. Which one, like C, has a critical view of the book's organisation?

**Question 38:** The key words here are *the quality of writing in the book*, and you are asked to identify which reviewer has *a different opinion* from the other three about this. A says the books is 'all delivered with the expansive liveliness of an expert story-teller.' So, A thinks the writing is very good. B refers to 'this eminently readable history of map-making.' So, B thinks the writing is of high quality too. Now we know that either C or D must have a different opinion about the quality of the writing. Which one is it?

| PAPER 1 | Reading and | ▶ | Part 1 |
| | Use of English | | Part 2 |
| PAPER 2 | Writing | | Part 3 |
| | | | Part 4 |
| PAPER 3 | Listening | | Part 5 |
| | | | Part 6 |
| PAPER 4 | Speaking | | **Part 7** |
| | | | Part 8 |

You are going to read a newspaper article about fitness tests for athletes. Six paragraphs have been removed from the article. Choose from the paragraphs **A–G** the one which fits each gap (**41–46**). There is one extra paragraph which you do not need to use.

Mark your answers **on the separate answer sheet**.

# Have you got what it takes to be a top athlete?

*Journalist Kate Carter tries out some advanced tests for sports people at Loughborough University's Sports Science Institute*

Not so long ago, identifying a potential sports star was a matter of seeing how well they could sprint around a track, or kick a football. Now, sports scientists use advanced tests to determine fitness, agility, body composition, reaction times and much more. But how does an average recreational athlete compare? A recent convert to running, I'm at the Sports Science Institute lab at Loughborough University, which gathers statistics on athletes from a range of sports, to find out my potential. Dr James Carter, head of the institute, starts by getting my standard physical measurements.

| 41 | |

I am made to sit in a device called a BodPod, and given a scan to examine bone density and create a picture of my internal body fat. After that, it's on to the treadmill for the VO2 max test, which measures fitness. This consists of running at increasing speed on an ever steeper incline while puffing into a large mask, a disconcerting experience as it reduces your vision to virtually nothing.

| 42 | |

An average woman has a VO2 max of around 35 ml/kg/min, while an elite athlete might be as high as 70 ml/kg/min (for men the range is around 40–85). Mine is 54, which is respectable for a recreational runner. I also turn out to be a carb burner rather than a fat burner, which I'm taking as licence to eat more. Next up are a couple of cognitive tests to assess my reactions.

| 43 | |

I don't do so well at the whole-body agility test – a frame with 12 lights at varying heights you have to leap or duck to extinguish – but Dr Carter reassures me that this matters less for endurance than for other sports.

| 44 | |

You just pedal on a stationary bike, then accelerate madly for ten seconds, before trying to sustain that power for 30 seconds. Just? Add in increasing resistance and it feels as if you are cycling through treacle on a bike with two flat tyres into a headwind. And it hurts.

| 45 | |

As I start to recover from this final challenge, it occurs to me that it's easy to imagine a future in which babies are screened at birth to join a super breed – or at least an elite training programme. Dr Carter mentions the film *Rocky IV* which has something similar in it. He is joking – but in truth, it's not so implausible.

| 46 | |

There are, of course, things the tests can't show yet: the psychology of the athlete, tactics, nutrition. But the scientific data that can be recorded is very useful, and not just for professional athletes. I personally have learned a huge amount about what I could feasibly achieve in my next race, as well as specific steps to move up to my goal of a full marathon. And next time I come back, I'm determined to conquer that bike.

**A** The first of these uses a large board full of bulbs, which light up in a random sequence. You hit them to turn them off, while simultaneously shouting out the numbers that appear on a small screen. I do better than the average, which I put down to being used to dealing with two small children.

**B** For all the cutting edge equipment and carefully designed assessments, what Dr Carter is unable to evaluate, as he readily admits, are such crucial factors as 'pain tolerance, doing the training day in, day out and self-belief.'

**C** Looking at someone's genome to determine whether they're suited to team sports or individual endurance may be 'accessible in the next decade,' Dr Carter says. 'Say we've got a group of 15-year-olds who are genetically suited to certain sports, are we going to put them through special regimes for the next decade? That's where some of the research is going.'

**D** After measuring my handgrip strength (I'm delighted to be 'average', given my arms are like spaghetti), it's time for the final hurdle: the Wingate test. Or as I shall always think of it, the longest half minute of my life. It sounds relatively easy.

**E** Disappointingly, it turns out I've been kidding myself about my height for years. Weight, though, is less important than body composition and it's the latter that the first of a series of hi-tech tests will assess.

**F** So much so that hours later I can still feel the lactic acid, brought on by the extreme pedalling, burning in my legs. 'Sprinters, cyclists – this is their test,' explains Dr Carter. Top athletes 'need to be performing well on this or there's something wrong.'

**G** While I am doing this, Dr Carter records my data. One of the key indicators, he explains, is 'the respiratory exchange ratio, which is the combination or the ratio of oxygen consumed and carbon dioxide produced. When that ratio goes over one, that's when we know to increase the gradient.'

# Essential tips

- ▶ Read through the main part of the text so that you know what it is generally about and how it is organised.

- ▶ Then look through the gapped paragraphs to see what the topic of each one is.

- ▶ Look for links between the main text and the gapped paragraphs. A gapped paragraph can have links with the previous paragraph, the following one, or both.

- ▶ Don't spend too long deciding which paragraph fits one of the gaps. If you have difficulty, move on to the next gap. You may be able to identify the solution for the problem gap by a process of elimination.

- ▶ Remember to check that the completed text makes sense by reading through it one final time.

**Question 41:** Look at the last sentence in the first paragraph of the main text. What are 'standard physical measurements' likely to be?

**Question 42:** In the last sentence of the second paragraph, the journalist describes running on a treadmill 'at increasing speed on an ever steeper incline'. An *incline* is a slope. Which gapped paragraph contains a phrase which has a similar meaning to 'ever steeper incline'? You may need to look at more than just the first sentence of each gapped paragraph.

**Question 43:** The last sentence of the paragraph before gap 43 tells us that the next tests she is going to take will assess her 'reactions'. Which gapped paragraph describes a test of reactions, rather than strength or stamina?

PAPER 1  Reading and ▶
          Use of English

PAPER 2  Writing

PAPER 3  Listening

PAPER 4  Speaking

Part 1
Part 2
Part 3
Part 4
Part 5
Part 6
Part 7
Part 8

# Essential tips

▸ Read the instructions and the title. If there is an introductory comment under the title, read this because it will give you an idea about the subject of the article.

▸ If you want to get faster at this task, try reading the questions first. As you read them, highlight the key words that indicate what to look for in the text.

▸ Then read the first section of the text. Each section is likely to have at least one and no more than four related questions.

▸ When you identify a sentence or phrase that you think answers one of the questions, highlight it and write the question number at the side of the text. This may save you time later if you find part of another section that you think may also answer the same question.

▸ Remember that similar points may be made in two or three sections, but there is only one correct answer. So, when you match a question with a section, make sure it says precisely what is in that section.

**Question 47:** First, find the sections that refer to the 'current economic climate'. Then, identify which of these refer to 'innovative approaches'.

**Question 48:** What is 'time away from business' likely to involve? Who is it likely to be spent with? Which of the sections referring to 'time away from work' includes a point about 'decision-making'? Remember that while the idea may be the same in the question and text, the words used in each are likely to be different.

You are going to read four people's thoughts about running your own record label. For questions **47–56**, choose from the people (**A–D**). The people may be chosen more than once.

Mark your answers **on the separate answer sheet**.

## Which person

| | |
|---|---|
| feels innovative approaches make sense in the current economic climate? | 47 |
| thinks time away from business is required to ensure good decision-making? | 48 |
| believes that making and selling music involves less risk than it used to? | 49 |
| values working with people who have different skills? | 50 |
| believes record labels should take on traditionally unfamiliar functions? | 51 |
| welcomes the variety of work that running a record label entails? | 52 |
| believes in delegating certain aspects of business to outside organisations? | 53 |
| thinks the future of the music industry is uncertain? | 54 |
| emphasises the importance of understanding consumers? | 55 |
| rejects the idea of producing music with commercial success as the main objective? | 56 |

**Question 51:** *Take on* here means 'start to do', and *functions* here are 'business activities'. Which section refers to business activities which may not 'traditionally' have been carried out by record labels?

# What does it take to run a record label?

*The internet and other developments in technology have had a major impact on the music industry. What are the implications for those wanting to run their own record label? Four people who have set up small, independent record labels share their insights.*

## A  Ben Wolf

Fundamentally, I'm a music enthusiast. I started off as a DJ in dance clubs, and setting up a record label seemed like the logical next step. There are always unknown factors, but in my experience, the key to success in this business is putting yourself in the position of the other person involved and anticipating their needs or what makes them tick. Why does a DJ want to play a certain record? Who would sell or buy a record? With digital technology, establishing an independent label has become more manageable. The industry has a tendency to bemoan the fact that sales and income are massively down, but what is equally true is that the costs of producing, manufacturing and promoting music have been reduced, so if you're sensible, there's less to lose these days. Two other crucial points: you need to be a team player because no single person could handle everything, and while you need a balance between your professional and your family life, you need to be ready to dedicate yourself to the job 100% when necessary.

## B  Henry Stone

I'm co-founder of an independent record label. We've discovered some great musical artists, a few of whom have become very popular and have more than paid back what we invested in them, but we don't play the game of predicting which artists will fly or flop in the market. Our focus is on working with creative, inspiring songwriters or musicians, and how to further their message. The mutually supportive relationship I have with my co-founder, Mark, is fundamental to what we've achieved; neither of us could have survived on our own. We've been going for some years but it still doesn't feel like a job. No two days are the same, whether we're promoting an event, filming a documentary, releasing a record, or checking out a band in the studio. You have to be careful with burn-out, though. I'm often up at 7.00 a.m. and still emailing beyond midnight, but I ensure that when I'm with family and friends, work is blocked out entirely. Without perspective and space, your judgement can go to pieces.

## C  Kerry Murphy

If I was 21 years old, just out of college, and with the understanding of the music industry that I have now, I'm not sure I'd set up a record label. I can think of less time-consuming and more straightforward and lucrative businesses to get into, and it's not going to get any easier. But, if you feel compelled to do it – some of us do – then I would consider a partnership with somebody who has strengths in areas where you are weak, and vice-versa. That's worked for me. Also, I wouldn't get too enamoured with the things that others already do well. We're associated with distributors around the world that are just great at what they do, and we've learned not to interfere. We have even given up having an in-house sales team; outsourcing works fine. Our primary concern now is with the music; making sure our artists are on time, look great and are well funded.

## D  Riz Amal

I think now is a great time to start a label if that's your thing. With everything changing so rapidly, no one really knows what the landscape will be in two years' time, let alone 20. The old-school record label model has been dying out for years, and with sales and income falling, as they have been virtually everywhere, the smart thing to do is to try to break the mould. Being a pioneer always brings with it the danger of failure, and it's likely to require all-consuming commitment in terms of time and energy, but there may be no alternative. The lines between what an independent record label does and what the manager of a musician or band does will continue to blur. Labels will need to get involved in artists' tours, in their merchandising and even publishing – activities they have tended to stay away from. As long as the numbers balance, and the budgets and forecasts are realistic, then there's no reason why a new independent label can't work.

PAPER 1 Reading and
        Use of English

PAPER 2 Writing ▶ ‖ Part 1
                    Part 2

PAPER 3 Listening

PAPER 4 Speaking

# Essential tips

### Question 1

▶ Remember the structure of a
  'for and against' essay, and
  take a few minutes to plan
  your points and examples
  before you begin writing.

▶ The examiner wants to see
  that you can clearly present
  and support an argument. Try
  to consider arguments *both*
  for and against the proposal.

▶ It's not a good idea to bring
  your personal experience into
  the essay unless it's directly
  relevant and will usefully
  support a specific point.

▶ Because of the word limit,
  you need to make sure that
  your points are concise.
  Develop the habit of
  reducing long sentences so
  that they only include the
  key information. However,
  ensure that your sentences
  don't become too short; if
  they seem to be short, try
  to combine a couple. Try
  not to repeat yourself or use
  unnecessary words.

▶ When you reread your essay,
  check that it has a logical
  flow of ideas. Make sure it is
  not vague. Remember, the
  reader is unable to ask for
  clarification on any points, so
  ensure that you have been
  precise.

You **must** answer this question. Write your answer in **220–260** words in an appropriate style on the separate answer sheet.

**1** Your class was in the audience of a panel discussion for a current affairs television programme, discussing a government proposal to make physical education and sport compulsory for five hours per week in all UK secondary schools, and for all year groups. You have made the notes below.

---

**PE and sports in schools – 5-hour weekly minimum**

- Sport and PE give students the opportunity to develop important skills outside the classroom, such as commitment and teamwork.
- Physical activity promotes overall well-being, and choices such as walking or cycling are also better for the environment.
- The number of overweight and obese young people has become alarming.

---

**Various audience members expressed these opinions during the discussion:**

"This may be OK for primary school, but students in secondary should be allowed to choose."

"Unfair; not everyone likes sport."

"How can we fit this into the school week? Will academic work suffer as a result?"

---

Write an essay for your tutor discussing **two** of the points in your notes. You should explain **how you think the government should proceed** and **provide reasons** to support your opinions.

You may, if you wish, make use of the opinions expressed in the discussion, but you should use your own words as far as possible.

PAPER 1  Reading and
            Use of English

**PAPER 2  Writing** ▶ | Part 1
PAPER 3  Listening          | **Part 2**
PAPER 4  Speaking

Write an answer to **one** of the questions **2–4** in this part. Write your answer in **220–260** words in an appropriate style on the separate answer sheet. Put the question number in the box at the top of the page.

**2** You recently took a domestic flight which was badly delayed, and service from the crew was poor. Write a letter to the customer services manager and include the following information:

- plane sat on the runway for over two hours with no information from the crew
- one member of staff was particularly rude when two passengers asked if they could switch seats
- after take-off, it was announced that no food or drinks would be served, not even mineral water.

Write your **letter**.

**3** Every student at your university received this email from the Vice Chancellor.

Dear Student,

We are deeply grateful to Mrs Iris Kerr, who has generously donated the sum of £20,000 to the university. Mrs Kerr specifically requested that the students be consulted on how these funds should be used. Please put your ideas into a proposal and submit it to my office by 15 March. Be sure to indicate why you believe your suggestion would be the very best use of this money.

Yours sincerely,

Dr Walter Greenleigh

Vice Chancellor, Offords University

Write your **proposal**.

**4** You have attended the first music festival ever held in your region, which ran for ten days with various events in different parts of the area. Write a review for your local newspaper. Be sure to say whether you felt the festival was a success and what, if anything, might be done differently next year.

Write your **review**.

# Essential tips

**Question 2:**

▶ What kind of letter do you need to produce here? What register should you use?

▶ In letters of complaint it is acceptable to use strong words to convey your dissatisfaction but remain polite and avoid making accusations. You should never be rude.

▶ State the facts clearly and firmly.

▶ It is not explicitly stated in the instruction, but you should tell the Customer Services Manager what you expect from them. You can also state a time frame in which you require any follow-up or action.

▶ Remember to end the letter with a respectful closing phrase.

**Question 3:**

▶ Ask yourself if you have a solid proposal for how this money could be spent. You need to begin writing as quickly as possible so don't spend too long trying to think of ideas. Remember, however, that your idea does not have to be an excellent one. What is important to the examiner is how you present it in the proposal.

▶ The objective of a proposal is to convince somebody of something. Practise using persuasive language for this part of the test.

▶ You don't have to use headings when you write this piece, but include them if they will make your proposal clearer. You can also use numbered or bulleted lists.

▶ Remember to finish with a solid conclusion summarising the main points of your proposal.

**Question 4:**

▶ You have some scope in this task type. The input text does not give a great deal of information about the music festival, which means that you are free to invent your own details.

▶ Decide how you want to approach the task. Will you indicate that the event was mainly a big success or a complete failure, or somewhere in between?

▶ What kind of adjectives could you use? Try to avoid very general adjectives such as *good* or *nice*.

▶ Bear in mind that your review will be published in a newspaper. What register should you use?

▶ While a review is essentially an opinion piece, and your opinion needs to be stated, don't lose sight of providing facts and clear examples with each point.

▶ Note the final part of the instruction. Do you have a suggestion for the next music festival?

PAPER 1  Reading and
         Use of English

PAPER 2  Writing

PAPER 3  Listening  ▶  | Part 1 |
                        | Part 2 |
                        | Part 3 |
                        | Part 4 |

PAPER 4  Speaking

## Essential tips

**Question 1:** Read the three answer options carefully. Does the man say anything about money or expenses? Does he mention dirt or filth, or any similar terms? Does he talk about the pace of life? What does *pace* mean?

**Question 4:** A very important listening skill is identifying feelings and attitudes, which you are required to do in this question. What does the woman actually say? How does she *sound*? Which adjective best describes how she feels? If you are not familiar with one of the words provided, focus on the ones you do understand and decide whether they answer the question correctly or not. Through a process of elimination, you can still arrive at the correct answer.

**Question 5:** In this part of the test, you may find that all of the answer options are items you have heard in the extract. It is vital that you pay close attention to the question and focus on what you are specifically asked.

**Question 6:** Listen carefully for a phrase of disagreement. What, specifically, is it in relation to?

🎧 **Track 9**

You will hear three different extracts. For questions **1–6**, choose the answer (**A, B** or **C**) which fits best according to what you hear. There are two questions for each extract.

**Extract One**

You hear two former college friends who bump into each other in London.

1  What did the man not like about London when he lived there?
   A   the pace of the life
   B   the dirt of the city
   C   the cost of living

2  To make the man feel better, the woman says that
   A   she really loves the countryside too.
   B   she is also quite a boring person.
   C   her feelings about London might change.

**Extract Two**

You hear a new employee chatting with a colleague about her first week at the company.

3  Why does the woman have to go to so many meetings?
   A   Because it's her first week at the company.
   B   It's a particularly busy time at the company.
   C   It's a normal part of that company's culture.

4  How does the woman seem at the end of the conversation?
   A   outraged
   B   alarmed
   C   reassured

**Extract Three**

You hear two friends discussing college applications.

5  Where will the woman go to university?
   A   She's going to the college best known for her subject.
   B   She is still trying to make her mind up about it.
   C   She's going to a university which is very far away.

6  The woman doesn't agree that a bigger university would mean
   A   better faculty members.
   B   a better campus life.
   C   a more fun experience.

PAPER 1 Reading and
Use of English

PAPER 2 Writing

PAPER 3 Listening ▶
Part 1
**Part 2**
Part 3
Part 4

PAPER 4 Speaking

## Essential tips

**Question 8:** From the sentence structure, you should be able to identify what part of speech is missing here. What adjective does Conor use about his friend?

**Question 10:** Remember that the statement may paraphrase what was said by the speaker, but the missing information will always be the exact word or words they used. What does Conor describe as being 'limited'? He may have used another word with a similar meaning to *limited*.

**Question 11:** Food items are mentioned with regard to the garden project but, remember, the question is about a project Conor was involved in himself. Does he mention anything related to food? You have an additional clue in the statement: it was the project that meant the most to him.

**Question 13:** What verb is missing here? What does Conor say about other people getting involved in projects?

🎧 **Track 10**

You will hear a community volunteer called Conor McManus talking about how he first got involved in this area, and describing the kind of projects he has worked on. For questions **7–14**, complete the sentences with a word or a short phrase.

# COMMUNITY AWARENESS

Conor's first community involvement was with a group that effectively stopped the building of a big (**7**) ......................................................... in the town centre.

Conor admits that, at first, he wasn't keen to get involved, but his friend was very (**8**) ......................................................... .

He describes his original impression of community volunteers as (**9**) ......................................................... people.

Later, he explains, he realised that his (**10**) ......................................................... was quite limited.

Conor says the project that meant the most to him was providing food for (**11**) ......................................................... .

Conor's friend told him about her community garden project in which (**12**) ......................................................... were given by an experienced gardener.

He mentions that anyone interested could contribute their talents to projects, or just (**13**) ......................................................... their time.

Conor finishes by pointing out that, for some people, this area could become their (**14**) ......................................................... .

PAPER 1  Reading and
         Use of English

PAPER 2  Writing

PAPER 3  Listening ▶
                        Part 1
                        Part 2
PAPER 4  Speaking       **Part 3**
                        Part 4

🎧 **Track 11**

You will hear a public meeting in which Dr Freya Davidson, the Dean of Studies of Caledonia College, is interviewing Malcolm Meade, the Administrative Officer from the Consulate-General of Japan, about the Japan Exchange and Teaching Programme. For questions **15–20**, choose the answer (**A**, **B**, **C** or **D**) which fits best according to what you hear.

## Essential tips

**Question 17:** What does the word *obligatory* mean? If you are not sure, what do you think it could mean, given that only one answer option is correct?

**Question 18:** In his answer about the Councillor for International Relations role, Mr Meade also talks about the Sports Exchange Advisors. Listen carefully so that you do not confuse the information about each one. You need to identify what he says about the CIR role.

**Question 19:** Regarding the application process, Mr Meade mentions several phases and the periods in which they take place. What is another way of saying 'successful candidates'?

15  The number of participants in the first JET Programme was around
    **A**  25.
    **B**  50.
    **C**  1,000.
    **D**  50,000.

16  What, according to Mr Meade, is 'team-teaching'?
    **A**  sharing cultural information about one's home country
    **B**  supporting students with language skills like pronunciation
    **C**  preparing materials and teaching with Japanese teachers
    **D**  joining students in after-school activities like English club

17  Which of the following is obligatory in order to apply for the JET Programme?
    **A**  Japanese language ability
    **B**  an undergraduate degree
    **C**  knowledge of Japanese culture
    **D**  previous teaching experience

18  What does Mr Meade say about the Councillor for International Relations (CIR) role?
    **A**  Only seven people are hired each year.
    **B**  Applications for it are not accepted.
    **C**  A good level of Japanese is required.
    **D**  Candidates must be nominated for it.

19  When are successful candidates informed that they've been accepted to the JET Programme?
    **A**  January
    **B**  April
    **C**  July
    **D**  October

20  Mr Meade says that some JET participants feel lonely because
    **A**  they didn't think very carefully about the commitment.
    **B**  they find that one year is a long time away from home.
    **C**  the placements are usually in fairly rural communities.
    **D**  they tend to find it difficult to adjust to Japanese culture.

PAPER 1  Reading and
          Use of English

PAPER 2  Writing

**PAPER 3  Listening** ▶

PAPER 4  Speaking

Part 1
Part 2
Part 3
**Part 4**

## Essential tips

**Questions 21–25:**

**Option A:** What do we mean when we say 'a trade'? Is it different from a profession? Do any of the speakers talk about this?

**Option C:** Does anyone speak about expectations and a family business?

**Option D:** What relevance does *justice* have to a chosen career path? Does this fit with any of the extracts?

**Option E:** Don't lose sight of the original question which is about the specific reason they are in their careers. Does anyone say they chose that line of work *because of* the salary?

**Questions 26–30:**

**Option A:** Who, if anyone, makes reference to art or creativity or artistic interests?

**Option D:** What is another way of saying *early retirement*? Does anyone mention this idea?

**Option E:** Does anyone talk about starting their own business? They may not have used this exact term.

**Option F:** What is typically involved in publishing? Does anyone talk about their hopes for the future in this regard?

🎧 **Track 12**

You will hear five short extracts in which people talk about their careers.

**While you listen you must complete both tasks.**

---

**TASK ONE**

For questions **21–25**, choose from the list (**A–H**) what each speaker says about how they came to be in this career.

A  had a preference to work in a trade

B  wanted to have a challenging career          Speaker 1 [ **21** ]

C  was expected to join the family business      Speaker 2 [ **22** ]

D  has always had a strong sense of justice      Speaker 3 [ **23** ]

E  was motivated by a high salary and prestige   Speaker 4 [ **24** ]

F  came to this industry by chance               Speaker 5 [ **25** ]

G  never had particularly high ambitions

H  started at the bottom, climbed the ranks

**TASK TWO**

For questions **26–30**, choose from the list (**A–H**) what each speaker says about their plans or hopes for the future.

A  would like to be an artist

B  has an opportunity to teach                   Speaker 1 [ **26** ]

C  wants to be a big executive                   Speaker 2 [ **27** ]

D  plans to take early retirement                Speaker 3 [ **28** ]

E  hopes to start their own business             Speaker 4 [ **29** ]

F  would like to be in publishing                Speaker 5 [ **30** ]

G  wants to work for a big charity

H  dreams of being famous one day

PAPER 1  Reading and
           Use of English

PAPER 2  Writing

PAPER 3  Listening

PAPER 4  Speaking

# Essential tips

**Part 3**

▶ In Part 3 of the Speaking paper you have to work with the other candidate to discuss an issue and reach a decision.

▶ The examiner will give you a mind map containing the issue for discussion and a few key points to help you. You have three minutes for the main discussion, so there is time to really explore the issue in detail. As well as giving your own opinion, you need to involve and interact with the other candidate.

▶ After the discussion, the examiner will ask you to reach a decision together about an aspect of the topic. Remember that there is no correct answer here, and that it is acceptable to disagree.

▶ Remember that this part of the test is for you to show the examiner how well you can express your views, discuss an issue, negotiate and come to an agreement with another person.

**Part 4**

▶ In this section you will need vocabulary related to careers. If you can't think of the name of a particular profession, don't worry, you can always describe that job instead.

▶ When you are asked how you might feel about something, remember to use speculative phrases such as, *I imagine I might feel ...* or *For me, I suppose it could be ...*

▶ If a question asks you to address a preference, try to comment on both options before stating which one you prefer, and why.

**Part 1** (2 minutes)

The examiner will ask you a few questions about yourself and about a general topic. For example, the examiner may ask you:

- **How many people are there in your immediate family?**
- **What quality do you most like in other people?**
- **Do you think people should continue to study new things throughout their lives?**

**Part 2** (4 minutes)

You will each be asked to talk on your own for about a minute. You will each be given three different pictures to talk about. After your partner has finished speaking, you will be asked a brief question connected with your partner's photographs.

> **Important occasions** (compare, contrast and speculate)

Turn to pictures 1–3 on page **175**, which show different occasions.

(*Candidate A*), it's your turn first. Here are your pictures. They show **various important occasions**.

I'd like you to compare **two** of the pictures and say **how the people appear to be feeling and why**. They could also be experiencing some **negative emotions. What might these be?**

(*Candidate B*), **which of these do you think is the most important occasion? Why?**

> **Shopping experiences** (compare, contrast and speculate)

Turn to pictures 1–3 on page **176**, which show different shopping experiences.

Now, (*Candidate B*), here are your pictures. They show **different shopping experiences.**

I'd like you to compare **two** of the pictures. Describe **how these shopping experiences differ and whether each method of shopping is suited to a different type of person. Why (not)?**

(*Candidate A*), **which method of shopping do you personally prefer? Why?**

**Part 3** (4 minutes)

Look at page **177**, which shows some general points about employment status.

> **Employment categories** (discuss, evaluate and negotiate)

**Here are some points about working full-time for a company versus working for yourself** for you to discuss. First, you have some time to look at the task.

(*Pause 15 seconds*)

Now talk to each other about **the benefits of each employment category and whether you think one is better than the other. Why?**

Now you have a minute to decide **what qualities a person would need in order to be successfully self-employed**.

**Part 4** (5 minutes)

The examiner will encourage you to develop the topic of your discussion in Part 3 by asking questions such as:

- What kind of careers do you think are best suited to self-employment?
- There has been a growing trend of self-employment in the past ten years. Why do you think that is?

| PAPER 1 | Reading and Use of English ▶ | Part 1 |
|---------|------|--------|
| | | Part 2 |
| PAPER 2 | Writing | Part 3 |
| | | Part 4 |
| PAPER 3 | Listening | Part 5 |
| | | Part 6 |
| PAPER 4 | Speaking | Part 7 |
| | | Part 8 |

For questions **1–8**, read the text below and decide which answer (**A, B, C** or **D**) best fits each gap. There is an example at the beginning (**0**).

Mark your answers **on the separate answer sheet**.

**Example:**

**0** **A** uncovering **B** excavating **C** unearthing **D** exposing

| 0 | A | B | C | D |
|---|---|---|---|---|

# The world's oldest pots

While (**0**) …….. in Xianrendong Cave in south-east China recently, archaeologists discovered the oldest fragments of pottery ever found. These pieces of clay pots have been (**1**) …….. back 20,000 years to a time when many parts of the earth were covered by huge ice sheets. At this time, food was relatively (**2**) ……… Fat, an important (**3**) …….. of energy was hard to (**4**) …….. by, so cooking was essential to (**5**) …….. energy from various food sources such as potatoes and meat. Marrow found in animal bones is very (**6**) …….. in fat, and archaeologists believe the cave dwellers may have cooked bones to obtain it. There is also some evidence that they cooked other food items like shellfish.

One important (**7**) …….. of the pottery found in Xianrendong Cave is that it was made several thousand years before the birth of agriculture. This discovery, along with other recent ones in east Asia, (**8**) …….. the long-held conventional theory that farming and permanent settlements had to be established before people could begin to make pottery.

| 1 | **A** referred | **B** counted | **C** chased | **D** traced |
|---|---|---|---|---|
| 2 | **A** faint | **B** scarce | **C** seldom | **D** bare |
| 3 | **A** source | **B** cause | **C** base | **D** root |
| 4 | **A** stand | **B** go | **C** come | **D** get |
| 5 | **A** relieve | **B** release | **C** restore | **D** retain |
| 6 | **A** lavish | **B** ample | **C** deep | **D** rich |
| 7 | **A** outlook | **B** factor | **C** aspect | **D** form |
| 8 | **A** disproves | **B** denies | **C** defeats | **D** disposes |

| PAPER 1 | Reading and | ▸ | Part 1 |
| | Use of English | | Part 2 |
| PAPER 2 | Writing | | Part 3 |
| | | | Part 4 |
| PAPER 3 | Listening | | Part 5 |
| PAPER 4 | Speaking | | Part 6 |
| | | | Part 7 |
| | | | Part 8 |

For questions **9–16**, read the text below and think of the word which best fits each gap. Use only one word in each gap. There is an example at the beginning (**0**).

Write your answers **IN CAPITAL LETTERS on the separate answer sheet**.

**Example:** 0 | I | N | T | O

---

# A computer called Baby

When the machine jokingly named Baby whirred (**0**) ........ life on 21 June 1948, it became the world's first modern computer. And nothing (**9**) ........ ever be the same again. Developed by Tom Kilburn and Freddie Williams, two scientists at Manchester University in the UK, Baby was the first device to have all the components now regarded (**10**) ........ characteristic of the basic computer. It could store (**11**) ........ only data, but also a short user programme in electronic memory and process it at electronic speed. In many respects, Baby, which was big enough to fill a room, was completely (**12**) ........ today's small, powerful computers. A smartphone can store several hundred million (**13**) ........ more bytes of data than Baby could. But it was a key breakthrough.

(**14**) ........ being a British invention, however, the original research was not fully exploited in the UK, and other countries soon raced ahead in harnessing the new technology. Both inventors had successful academic careers, but (**15**) ........ ever made the money of people like Bill Gates, the billionaire founder of Microsoft, who was as (**16**) ........ unborn when Baby first came to life.

PAPER 1 Reading and ▶
          Use of English

PAPER 2 Writing

PAPER 3 Listening

PAPER 4 Speaking

Part 1
Part 2
**Part 3**
Part 4
Part 5
Part 6
Part 7
Part 8

For questions **17–24**, read the text below. Use the word given in capitals at the end of some of the lines to form a word that fits in the gap **in the same line**. There is an example at the beginning (**0**).

Write your answers **IN CAPITAL LETTERS on the separate answer sheet.**

**Example:** | 0 | A | N | N | O | Y | A | N | C | E | | | | | | | | |

# Overhearing mobile phone conversations

For many people, unintentionally hearing a mobile phone
conversation causes more (**0**) …….. and frustration than the                **ANNOY**
general background noise of people talking to each other.
Scientists from the University of San Diego recently carried out
an interesting study with a group of (**17**) …….. to investigate          **VOLUNTARY**
this phenomenon in a controlled way. The (**18**) …….. were               **PARTICIPATE**
asked to solve a series of anagram puzzles while, (**19**) ……..           **KNOW**
to them, researchers conducted a scripted conversation in
the background, either between two people in the room or
between someone on a phone and a caller not in the room.
(**20**) …….., subjects found the one-sided phone conversation         **OVERWHELM**
more (**21**) …….. and distracting than the two-sided interaction.       **MEMORY**
One of the researchers, Dr Rosa Vessal, suggested that two-way
conversations are less distracting because they are easier to
follow. 'The content of a phone conversation is (**22**) …….. ,' she       **PREDICT**
said. 'Not knowing where it's heading is distracting.' What are
the (**23**) …….. of the research? One might be that we should not        **IMPLY**
(**24**) …….. how distracting overheard phone conversations can          **ESTIMATE**
be for drivers.

| PAPER 1 | Reading and ▶ | Part 1 |
| | Use of English | Part 2 |
| PAPER 2 | Writing | Part 3 |
| | | **Part 4** |
| PAPER 3 | Listening | Part 5 |
| PAPER 4 | Speaking | Part 6 |
| | | Part 7 |
| | | Part 8 |

For questions **25–30**, complete the second sentence so that it has a similar meaning to the first sentence, using the word given. **Do not change the word given.** You must use between **three** and **six** words, including the word given. Here is an example (**0**).

**Example:**

**0**  Chloe would only eat a pizza if she could have a mushroom topping.

**ON**

Chloe .......................................... a mushroom topping when she had a pizza.

The gap can be filled with the words 'insisted on having', so you write:

**Example:** | **0** | INSISTED ON HAVING |

Write **only** the missing words **IN CAPITAL LETTERS on the separate answer sheet.**

---

**25**  I was really surprised to bump into Marianne at the airport.

**LAST**

Marianne ......................................... to bump into at the airport.

**26**  I was amazed that John stopped eating meat completely in an attempt to improve his health.

**GAVE**

Much ......................................... eating meat completely in an attempt to improve his health.

**27**  Like many students, Joe would find it very difficult to pay for everything he needs if his parents didn't help him.

**ENDS**

Like many students, Joe would have great ......................................... the help of his parents.

**28**  My tutor says she's been too busy to read my essay, but she'll mark it by the end of the week.

**ROUND**

My tutor says she ......................................... my essay yet, but she'll mark it by the end of the week.

**29**  You can understand why Andrew's comments upset Sofia so much.

**BLAMED**

Sofia can't ......................................... at Andrew's comments.

**30**  'I promise I will never tell anyone about the missing files,' said Jenny.

**WORD**

Jenny ......................................... never tell anyone about the missing files.

PAPER 1  Reading and
          Use of English  ▶
PAPER 2  Writing
PAPER 3  Listening
PAPER 4  Speaking

Part 1
Part 2
Part 3
Part 4
**Part 5**
Part 6
Part 7
Part 8

You are going to read a magazine article. For questions **31–36**, choose the answer (**A**, **B**, **C** or **D**) which you think fits best according to the text.

Mark your answers **on the separate answer sheet**.

# Australia's lost giants

*Thousands of years ago, Australia had large populations of huge animals. What happened to them?*

Across Australia, scientists have discovered thousands of fossils of ancient megafauna, huge animals that lived 100,000 to 40,000 years ago, during the Pleistocene era. The remains include those of giant snakes, huge flightless birds, two-and-a-half-metre-tall kangaroos, hippo-like beasts and six-metre-long lizards. These animals dominated their ecosystems, and then were gone in an extinction spasm that swept away nearly every animal weighing 50 kilogrammes or more. What happened exactly? Given how much ink has been spilled on the extinction of the dinosaurs 65 million years ago, it's a wonder that more hasn't been devoted to the fate of the Pleistocene megafauna, creatures that were both dramatically large and, for some time, co-existent with humans.

In the Americas, native megafauna died out relatively soon after the arrival of humans, about 13,000 years ago. In the 1960s, scientist Paul Martin developed what became known as the 'blitzkrieg hypothesis' to explain the extinction process: humans created havoc as they spread through the Americas, wielding stone-tipped spears *11* to annihilate animal populations. But it wasn't comprehensive; North America kept its deer, bears, bison and moose, while South America retained jaguars and llamas.

What happened to Australia's megafauna is one of the planet's most baffling paleontological mysteries. Kangaroos – hardly giants – are the largest indigenous land animals to have survived on the continent. For years, scientists blamed climate change. Indeed, Australia has been drying out for a million years or more, and megafauna were faced with a continent that became increasingly parched and denuded of vegetation. Paleontologist Tim Flannery suggests, somewhat differently, that humans, who arrived on the continent around 50,000 years ago, used fire to hunt, which led to deforestation and a dramatic disruption of the water cycle. What's certain, Flannery says, is that something dramatic happened to Australia's large creatures – abruptly (how abruptly is a matter of debate) – around 46,000 years ago, strikingly soon after the invasion of a tool-wielding, intelligent predator. There does appear to be more than mere coincidence here.

Flannery advanced the Australian version of Martin's 'blitzkrieg hypothesis' in a book called *The Future Eaters*. He also put forward an even more ambitious thesis that human beings, generally, are prone to ruining ecosystems and destroying their own futures. The book proved highly controversial. Some viewed it as critical of the Aborigines, the first Australians, who pride themselves on living in harmony with nature. The more basic problem is that nothing has been found to prove that humans killed any megafauna – not one animal skeleton with a spear tip in it, for example. Such kill sites have been found in the Americas, but there's no archaeological *28* analog in Australia. One scientist said: "If this were a murder trial, it wouldn't get past first base."

The debate about megafauna pivots, substantially, on dating old bones and sediments. If scientists can show that the animals disappeared within a few hundred years, or even a couple of thousand years, of the arrival of humans, there's a strong case that one thing was the direct result of the other. Flannery contends that islands hold another clue to the mystery. Some species of megafauna survived on Tasmania and other islands until 40,000 years ago, when falling sea levels allowed humans to finally reach them, Flannery says. This argument relies on the lack of fossil evidence for a prolonged human-megafauna overlap. If, however, we find evidence that human beings and megafauna co-existed for thousands of years, then the role of humans in the extinctions would become blurry at best. Certainly it would rule out a rapid, Martin-Flannery-style blitzkrieg.

Although the data currently available is limited and inconclusive, there would seem to be great value in investigating what happened. The blitzkrieg hypothesis paints an alarming picture of human beings rapidly wiping out a great number of animals. But there's an even more ominous scenario: the extinctions didn't happen because of overkill but rather through an incremental sequence of events, including climate change, during which the people involved could not fully discern what was happening to their environment. This brings us to today. 'The way we've lived and are living is destroying our future,' Flannery says. Yet we're only gradually figuring out how we're changing our world and the extent to which we're harming or even driving to extinction countless species.

**31** What does the reviewer suggest in the first paragraph about the large animals of the Pleistocene period?

- **A** They were historically less important than the dinosaurs.
- **B** More is known about them than about dinosaurs.
- **C** Relatively little has been written about them.
- **D** They were larger than is often thought.

**32** What does the word 'it' in line 11 refer to?

- **A** the spread of humans in the Americas
- **B** the disappearance of megafauna
- **C** the human practice of hunting
- **D** the theory Martin put forward

**33** What point does the writer make about the extinction of ancient Australian megafauna in the third paragraph?

- **A** The idea that humans contributed to it is plausible.
- **B** It is likely to have been more gradual than previously thought.
- **C** The theory that it resulted from climate change has been disproved.
- **D** It is hard to understand why kangaroos survived while other species didn't.

**34** The writer quotes a scientist in line 28 in order to emphasise that

- **A** it is a mistake to compare different continents.
- **B** humans are being unfairly characterised as criminals.
- **C** there is no real evidence to support Flannery's theory.
- **D** Australian Aborigines should be allowed to defend themselves.

**35** According to the fifth paragraph, what is the key information dating techniques need to provide?

- **A** how long humans have lived on various islands
- **B** when humans became capable of long sea journeys
- **C** when megafauna first appeared in a certain locations
- **D** how long humans and megafauna lived alongside each other

**36** What is the writer doing in the final paragraph?

- **A** anticipating further research developments
- **B** introducing an opposing point of view
- **C** illustrating a point made previously
- **D** raising some wider concerns

| PAPER 1 | Reading and ▶ | Part 1 |
| | Use of English | Part 2 |
| | | Part 3 |
| PAPER 2 | Writing | Part 4 |
| PAPER 3 | Listening | Part 5 |
| | | **Part 6** |
| PAPER 4 | Speaking | Part 7 |
| | | Part 8 |

You are going to read four comments by media analysts about the future of printed newspapers. For questions **37–40**, choose from the comments **A–D**. The comments may be chosen more than once.

Mark your answers **on the separate answer sheet**.

# Does the printed newspaper have a future?

*As more and more people use TV, the internet and various forms of social media as sources of news and information, the future of the traditional newspaper is the subject of much debate. Can the printed format survive? Four media analysts offer their thoughts.*

**A**

The traditional newspaper clearly faces stiff competition from television and the internet, but reports of its terminal decline are greatly exaggerated. In China, India and much of Latin America, newspaper sales have actually risen in recent years, and if news organisations work in an intelligent way – combining print and digital operations as many already do – then the future of news on paper should be assured. The format has a lot going for it, not least that people generally trust newspapers as sources of reliable, detailed information. Print journalists have time to check facts carefully and are able to present stories in well-written, coherent forms. So much reporting on TV and online, on the other hand, is instant, speculative and lacks the bigger picture. The other key factor is that people like to touch and hold paper, and newsprint tends to be much easier on the eyes than text on a screen.

**B**

There is something very satisfying about turning the pages of a newspaper, glancing across the headlines, then settling down to read an article that catches your eye. It is a feeling many people miss when accessing news in a digital format, but for the generations who have grown up reading electronic media, it is not something they will have any great attachment to. For most younger people, printed newspapers make little sense. The entire contents of a newspaper, and so much more, can be found on the website of the same title. Some people have welcomed the replacement of newspapers with digital media for environmental reasons – fewer newspapers mean fewer trees cut down – but this is not a real issue as most newspapers nowadays are printed on recycled paper. The key point is that, with rapidly declining readership, printed newspapers represent an increasingly antiquated business model, which is unlikely ever to recover.

**C**

A respected media analyst recently looked at current trends in the American printed newspaper industry and calculated that within 30 years it would be extinct. And there is no reason to believe that the fate of newspapers elsewhere in the world would be very different. Those who champion the traditional format have some strong arguments to make: that newspapers are friendlier objects to handle than electronic gadgets, that forestry and paper production are no less sustainable as industries than those which manufacture and power digital technology, and that the content of newspapers tends to be of greater depth, accuracy and trustworthiness than in any other form of media. These are all fine points worth making, but the bottom line is that the traditional newspaper is an obsolete format and, as such, is destined to perish sooner or later.

**D**

The printed newspaper has had a long life: over 500 years since the invention of the printing press. Fundamentally, however, it is just a piece of technology, a device now approaching the end of its natural lifespan. Its successor, digital technology, can do everything the newspaper does and much more. The vastness of the internet means it can provide information in a great variety of ways. Long, detailed investigations can be found as easily as brief, ephemeral updates. Technological developments mean that digital devices are as easy to handle and read as newspapers, and give far wider and more flexible access to information. In terms of energy and material resources, digital technology is much more efficient, as you only use it when content is actually required, whereas newspapers are printed whether they are read or not. The demise of a historically significant piece of technology is bound to cause distress but it will happen, whether we like it or not.

## Which analyst

has a different opinion from the others about the
physical experience of reading printed newspapers?

37 ☐

takes a similar view to C regarding the quality of news
reporting in printed newspapers as compared with digital media?

38 ☐

shares B's opinion about the environmental impact of
printed newspapers?

39 ☐

takes a different view from the others regarding the long-term
viability of printed newspapers?

40 ☐

| PAPER 1 | Reading and Use of English ▸ | Part 1 |
| PAPER 2 | Writing | Part 2 |
| | | Part 3 |
| PAPER 3 | Listening | Part 4 |
| PAPER 4 | Speaking | Part 5 |
| | | Part 6 |
| | | **Part 7** |
| | | Part 8 |

You are going to read a magazine article about wildlife reserves in Kenya. Six paragraphs have been removed from the article. Choose from the paragraphs **A–G** the one which fits each gap (**41–46**). There is one extra paragraph which you do not need to use.

Mark your answers **on the separate answer sheet**.

# Kenya's great wildlife – exploring two nature reserves in east Africa

'Is that a black or white rhino?' Our guide Joseph tested how much attention we had been paying. We had seen a white rhino first, extremely close up, casually grazing while we took pictures. That's the first clue. Black rhino are much more nervous and aggressive, and you shouldn't get close. Second clue, the shape of its back. Finally, look at the mouth. It turns out 'white' was coined by happy accident many years ago, when the Afrikaans word for 'wide' was mistaken and the name stuck; in contrast, the black rhino has a thinner, beak-like lip.

| **41** | |

Our trip was organised by an organisation called Farside Africa, whose passionate support for conservation efforts enabled us to get right to the heart of projects in Kenya. First stop was Lewa House, part of Lewa Wildlife Conservancy, a private reserve north of Nairobi, with a small airstrip a short drive away.

| **42** | |

At the forefront of rhino conservation in Kenya, Lewa currently has 71 black and 56 white rhino, more than ten per cent of Kenya's total rhino population – counted daily by a team of rangers. Huge resources have been channelled into their protection, but unfortunately the illegal hunters still sometimes win the day, their reward guaranteed by a buoyant black market in which the price of black rhino horn exceeds that of gold.

| **43** | |

Lewa House itself is perched on a hill, secluded cottages with dramatic vistas across the rolling landscape:

mighty elephants trundling along the horizon, a zebra wandering through your garden. Guests gather for lunch by the pool or dinner in the house, where Calum and Sophie welcome them like extended family.

| **44** | |

The second half of our trip was a couple of hours' drive away, in Laikipia, at Ol Pejeta Conservancy, another reserve dedicated to the protection of rhino and the development of local communities. While Lewa relies heavily on donors, Ol Pejeta is striving to create a sustainable project and, together with revenue from tourism, uses innovative ventures in combining livestock and arable farming with wildlife.

| **45** | |

In Ol Pejeta Conservancy, we were hosted at Kicheche Camp by Andy and Sonja. By 'camp' you may read 'canvas', but the comparison with traditional camping ends there; they have designed a cosy retreat with all creature comforts and personal touches. The only reminder we were in a tent came from our obvious proximity to a variety of animal calls that pierced the night.

| **46** | |

Oh, and we ticked the big cat box too. Both by day and by night, we encountered lion, witnessing what incredible beasts they are as they sauntered majestically through their kingdom. Somewhat lazily, they gave chase to some baby warthog and resting ostriches, and came away without a catch, but our immediate proximity to each event was exhilarating.

**A**  They have steadily built a fine base for exploring, and we saw more than we could have hoped: graceful giraffe, endangered Grevy's zebra, large families of elephant, no less than four species of eagle and, of course, the rhino. Alas, we were not to see a big cat as the grass was high after the rains, and they proved elusive.

**B**  As the sun dipped behind the hills at the end of each fantastic day, however, we were able to enjoy the serenity of the wilderness, along with enthralling conversation about Kenyan wildlife and culture.

**C**  It's so disturbing it hardly bears thinking about, but when we were offered the chance to talk to the security team about their work, we took it. They treated us to a demonstration: from the scent of a single footprint, a specially trained dog expertly tracked a 'poacher' through the scrub, an exercise that has helped the team make hundreds of arrests.

**D**  We steadily approached, and as the animal treated our arrival calmly, we could work out which it was. Sadly, the few of these remarkable creatures we were lucky enough to see are part of a declining population – though, fortunately, there are many people battling to save them.

**E**  Perhaps because the landscape was drier and flatter, we saw even more wildlife here than in the previous reserve, more than making up for the interrupted sleep. Swathes of warthog were an obvious addition, along with many jackal and a solitary hyena.

**F**  Joseph came to collect us there, and needlessly explained that we would see much more than rhino; either side of the runway gathered zebra, a couple of giraffe and an ostrich before our very eyes.

**G**  Besides this income diversification, there is a successful campaign to demonstrate that grazing cattle can regenerate grasslands and give back to the wildlife. Among the animals here are four of only seven remaining northern white rhino worldwide. They are in an enclosed reserve with added security, their horns trimmed to be less enticing to poachers.

| PAPER 1 | Reading and ▶ | Part 1 |
|---------|---------------|--------|
|         | Use of English | Part 2 |
| PAPER 2 | Writing       | Part 3 |
|         |               | Part 4 |
| PAPER 3 | Listening     | Part 5 |
|         |               | Part 6 |
| PAPER 4 | Speaking      | Part 7 |
|         |               | **Part 8** |

You are going to read an article in which four composers write about their own favourite modern composers. For questions **47–56**, choose from the composer (**A–D**). The writers may be chosen more than once.

Mark your answers **on the separate answer sheet**.

## Which writer says the following about their favourite composer?

| | |
|---|---|
| He works closely with the people who interpret his music. | **47** |
| All his compositions have a dramatic quality to them. | **48** |
| He composes music with specific locations in mind. | **49** |
| He creates music that defies analysis. | **50** |
| He may not be the ideal teacher. | **51** |
| His compositions tend to be difficult to play. | **52** |
| His artistic output will outlive that of many of his contemporaries. | **53** |
| His compositions vary considerably in style. | **54** |
| His compositions seem to be ahead of their time. | **55** |
| The music he composes is instantly recognisable as his. | **56** |

# Modern composers

## A  Mark-Anthony Turnage on Louis Andriessen

I marvel at the extreme individualism of Louis Andriessen. Every time you hear a piece of his music, you know it's by him. When I first heard his composition *De Staat*, I was struck by the fact that although it was minimalist music, it was so much more harmonically interesting and hard-edged than most works in that genre. He's influenced a lot by Stravinsky, who is probably my idol, and he has in turn greatly influenced me in his directness, bold colours and harmonic language. He has an emotional depth and a sense of magic that a lot of modern music lacks. A big part of me regrets not studying with him, although he's such an overwhelming figure I might have become merely a bad copy. Andriessen's rigour would have been good for me because he is a master of structure and planning, which I struggle with. He is one of the few composers working today whose music will survive, whereas many of the current big names will sink without trace.

## B  Michael Berkeley on Harrison Birtwistle

I like several modern composers, but the one who, for me, seems to build inexorably on his own intensely personal vision with consistent integrity, is Harrison Birtwistle. Take a piece such as *The Triumph of Time*, seemingly hewn from stone, yet a simple little melodic motif rises up and soon takes on a haunting and unforgettable quality, like the cry of some ancient creature. I seized the opportunity to create a cantata (*Love Cries*) based on the love music from Birtwistle's opera, *The Second Mrs Kong*, because I knew that in compiling it I would learn so much. And I did – Harry moves ideas around like children's building bricks. 'Try that passage upside-down,' he would say. A sense of theatre permeates not only the operas, but even chamber works such as *Ritual Fragment* and *Secret Theatre*. Ultimately, though, it's what I cannot quantify that transfixes me – as Pierre Boulez said of him: 'Where does it come from, this music?'

## C  Sally Beamish on Peter Maxwell Davies

What I love about Max is that he is constantly surprising – from the intense complexity of *Eight Songs For a Mad King*, to the unaffected simplicity of *Farewell to Stromness*, which I recently heard played by guitarist Allan Neave. His opera *Taverner* was my first introduction to the world of 'contemporary' music, at 16, and I was fascinated by it. I then discovered *St Thomas Wake*: the toughness of the musical language thrown into relief by foxtrots. I finally met Max in person when I joined the Scottish Chamber Orchestra as a viola player, and he was conducting. I was on the brink of taking the plunge as a composer, and he encouraged and advised me, inviting me to be his assistant on his composers' course. I felt unequal to the job and wished profoundly I had simply applied as a participant, but I learnt an immense amount, things I have never forgotten. His works still enthral me; every new piece brings fresh surprises and is always an interaction with his performers, and often with the community in Orkney, the Scottish island where he lives.

## D  David Sawer on Benedict Mason

Benedict Mason's pieces always seem to walk the tightrope between perfection and total chaos. They are fresh, playful and ridiculous, and usually of such impossible complexity that they threaten to self-destruct. *Animals* and *The Origins of Dance*, a sequence of 12 dance movements, each precisely 90 seconds long, has the ensemble playing jitterbugs and bossa novas at up to 12 different tempi, coordinated by 12 different click tracks. *Hinterstoisser Traverse* is a 12-minute piece based on one note. The series of pieces *Music for Concert Halls* plays with the acoustical properties of the venues for which they were written. They are more like installations for orchestra, elegantly evoking space and distance through the choreographed movements of the musicians in and around the whole building, while the audience remain in their seats. His experiments are extreme and uncompromising, but entirely logical. The pieces push at the boundaries and point to future possibilities for the concert-going experience.

PAPER 1  Reading and
         Use of English

PAPER 2  Writing ▶  Part 1
                     Part 2

PAPER 3  Listening

PAPER 4  Speaking

You **must** answer this question. Write your answer in **220–260** words in an appropriate style on the separate answer sheet.

---

**1**  You attended a public lecture given by a visiting professor of economics who proposed that early retirement (age 55) be made compulsory in all EU countries. You have made the notes below.

> **A case for compulsory retirement at age 55**
>
> - Younger people can't enter the workforce if older people stay too long in their jobs – unfair.
> - Older people do not have the same energy they once did – younger workers will increase productivity.
> - Older people would be happier without the stress of a long working week, which would be better for them and better for society.

> **These opinions were expressed after the public lecture:**
>
> "With life expectancy over 80 now, how would people support themselves during such a long retirement?"
>
> "For many people, their career gives meaning to their life. If you take this away, what will become of them?"
>
> "Older workers have invaluable experience and skills, which benefits both companies and the national economy."

Write an essay for your own economics lecturer discussing **two** of the points from your notes. You should **explain whether you think the proposition is realistic** and **provide reasons** to support your opinions.

You may, if you wish, make use of the opinions expressed in the lecture, but you should use your own words as far as possible.

PAPER 1  Reading and
           Use of English

PAPER 2  Writing          ▶    Part 1

PAPER 3  Listening              Part 2

PAPER 4  Speaking

Write an answer to **one** of the questions **2–4** in this part. Write your answer in **220–260** words in an appropriate style on the separate answer sheet. Put the question number in the box at the top of the page.

2   The 12-year-old daughter of a family friend has written to you asking for advice about studying English. Your reply should address these questions:

• I'm embarrassed because my accent is strong when I speak English. What can I do to change this?
• I hate English grammar. Can't I just skip it and focus on the other skills?
• I want to be fluent by next year. How many hours a day should I spend studying English?

Write your **letter**.

3   You see this notice in your university library:

> As part of a new information pack for students beginning their first year at Quarry College, we have decided to include some recommendations for the laptops or other electronic devices which are the most suitable for student purposes. We would like to hear your recommendations. Please submit a report covering the following points:
>
> item, brand and model
> how it meets student needs
> cost / value for money
> any disadvantages

Write your **report**.

4   On a radio arts programme, you hear the presenter say how bored he is with novels he reads and promptly forgets. He issues a challenge for listeners to submit a written review of a book that had a major impact on them, and why.

Write your **review**.

PAPER 1  Reading and
         Use of English

PAPER 2  Writing

PAPER 3  Listening  ▶  Part 1
                        Part 2
                        Part 3
                        Part 4

PAPER 4  Speaking

Track 13

You will hear three different extracts. For questions **1–6**, choose the answer (**A**, **B** or **C**) which fits best according to what you hear. There are two questions for each extract.

**Extract One**

You hear two people discussing electronic book readers.

**1**  Why did the man get an e-reader?
  **A**  He wanted it for travelling.
  **B**  It was given to him as a gift.
  **C**  He needed it for his job.

**2**  What does the man believe about the future of printed books?
  **A**  They will definitely be replaced by e-books.
  **B**  They will never be replaced by e-books.
  **C**  They will continue to exist alongside e-books.

**Extract Two**

You hear two colleagues discussing how they get to the office.

**3**  What is the man's reaction when the woman discovers that he drives to work?
  **A**  He is embarrassed about it.
  **B**  He thinks it's quite funny.
  **C**  He doesn't particularly care.

**4**  What does the woman suggest to the man?
  **A**  She challenges him to try taking the bus again.
  **B**  She advises him to start walking to the office.
  **C**  She recommends that he go to work by bicycle.

**Extract Three**

You hear two friends discussing an essay for college.

**5**  When the man arrives the woman is
  **A**  in tears.
  **B**  in control.
  **C**  in a panic.

**6**  What does the man offer to help the woman with?
  **A**  writing her essay
  **B**  planning her essay
  **C**  researching her essay

PAPER 1 Reading and
Use of English

PAPER 2 Writing

**PAPER 3 Listening** ▶
    Part 1
    **Part 2**
    Part 3
    Part 4

PAPER 4 Speaking

**Track 14**

You will hear a student giving a class presentation on citizen journalism. For questions **7–14**, complete the sentences with a word or short phrase.

# CITIZEN JOURNALISM

The student points out that professional journalists have traditionally included comments from local people to (**7**) ........................................................ and make it more meaningful to others.

It was when Web 2.0 tools were developed that citizen journalism really started to (**8**) ........................................................ .

The speaker explains how internet-enabled mobile phones with (**9**) ........................................................ have made it easy and common for people to post material online.

While citizen journalism wasn't widely accepted at first, it has now (**10**) ........................................................ as a very useful tool.

Citizen journalism provides the rest of the world with almost instant access to photos and stories (**11**) ........................................................ online by locals.

A great advantage of citizen journalism is that it can give us (**12**) ........................................................ into how the lives of people are affected during major political crises.

The authorities have also been able to (**13**) ........................................................ faster thanks to the collaboration of citizen journalists.

These days the (**14**) ........................................................ and video reports made by citizen journalists are often used in professional news stories and documentaries.

PAPER 1 Reading and
Use of English

PAPER 2 Writing

**PAPER 3 Listening** ▶

PAPER 4 Speaking

Part 1
Part 2
**Part 3**
Part 4

🎧 **Track 15**

You will hear a conversation between the director of a national charity, Brandon Tate, and a psychologist, Dr Joan Wells, who is also an expert on the issue of unemployment. For questions 15–20, choose the answer (**A**, **B**, **C** or **D**) which fits best according to what you hear.

15 What is Dr Wells referring to when she says 'It's incorrect and it's unhelpful.'?
    **A** the difficulty unemployed people have in coming to terms with their situation
    **B** the pressure put on unemployed people by their friends and family members
    **C** the notion some people hold that unemployment is solely a financial problem
    **D** the negative impact upon the outlook of people dealing with unemployment

16 Mr Tate says that a contributing factor to an unemployed person's sense of hopelessness is the fact that
    **A** their essential nature changes.
    **B** finding a job is such a struggle.
    **C** they eventually decide to give up.
    **D** they know there are too few jobs.

17 Dr Wells compares the range of emotions experienced by an unemployed person to
    **A** the process of regaining control.
    **B** dealing with the death of a loved one.
    **C** reluctant acceptance of a bad situation.
    **D** developing a strategy for moving on.

18 In terms of practical advice, what does Dr Wells say is essential for unemployed people to do?
    **A** remember that it's not personal
    **B** ensure they do not get depressed
    **C** set goals daily and keep moving
    **D** get enough sleep and eat well

19 According to Mr Tate, financial support may be available for
    **A** taking a skills course.
    **B** applying for new jobs.
    **C** doing volunteer work.
    **D** relocating to a new city.

20 In their closing remarks, what do both speakers emphasise?
    **A** relying on friends and family members
    **B** improving application and interview skills
    **C** treating unemployment like a full-time job
    **D** having an action plan and keeping spirits up

PAPER 1   Reading and
             Use of English

PAPER 2   Writing

**PAPER 3   Listening**          Part 1
                                  Part 2
                                  Part 3
                                  **Part 4**

PAPER 4   Speaking

🎧 **Track 16**

You will hear five short extracts in which people talk about travel.

**While you listen you must complete both tasks.**

**TASK ONE**

For questions **21–25**, choose from the list (**A–H**) what each speaker says about their main experience of travelling.

**A**   came late to travelling

**B**   had a career as a diplomat                    Speaker 1 ☐ **21**

**C**   has to travel for a living                    Speaker 2 ☐ **22**

**D**   never travelled anywhere                      Speaker 3 ☐ **23**

**E**   went on trips with friends                    Speaker 4 ☐ **24**

**F**   has a major fear of flying                    Speaker 5 ☐ **25**

**G**   was brought up travelling

**H**   had bad holiday experiences

**TASK TWO**

For questions **26–30**, choose from the list (**A–H**) how each speaker feels about travel now.

**A**   likes how dramatic it is

**B**   disrupts the home life                        Speaker 1 ☐ **26**

**C**   thinks of it as glamorous                     Speaker 2 ☐ **27**

**D**   it's enriching and exciting                   Speaker 3 ☐ **28**

**E**   considers it a privilege                      Speaker 4 ☐ **29**

**F**   feels uneasy about it                         Speaker 5 ☐ **30**

**G**   finds travel terrifying

**H**   can take it or leave it

PAPER 1 Reading and
Use of English

PAPER 2 Writing

PAPER 3 Listening

PAPER 4 Speaking

### Part 1 (2 minutes)

The examiner will ask you a few questions about yourself and about a general topic. For example, the examiner may ask you:

- **Do you prefer the mountains or the sea? Why?**
- **What is your favourite dish from your country?**
- **How might your best friend describe you?**

### Part 2 (4 minutes)

You will each be asked to talk on your own for about a minute. You will each be given three different pictures to talk about. After your partner has finished speaking, you will be asked a brief question connected with your partner's photographs.

> **Choice of drink** (compare, contrast and speculate)

Turn to pictures 1–3 on page **178**, which show people having different drinks.

(*Candidate A*), it's your turn first. Here are your pictures. They show **three women choosing three different drinks.**

I'd like you to compare **two** of the pictures and say **what type of person each one is and what their lifestyle is probably like.**

(*Candidate B*), **which of these drinks would you be most likely to choose? Why?**

> **Waiting** (compare, contrast and speculate)

Turn to pictures 1–3 on page **179**, which show people waiting.

Now, (*Candidate B*), here are your pictures. They show **people waiting.**

I'd like you to compare **two** of the pictures and say **what you imagine the circumstances are in each picture and how these people might be feeling.**

(*Candidate A*), **are you someone who finds waiting difficult? Why (not)?**

### Part 3 (4 minutes)

Look at page **180**, which shows some aspects of social-networking.

**Social-networking sites** (discuss, evaluate and negotiate)

**Here are some ways in which social-networking sites have an impact on our lives,** and a question for you to discuss.

First, you have some time to look at the task.

(*Pause 15 seconds*)

Now talk to each other about **how relevant you think these points are, and whether social-networking sites are really improving our lives.**

Now you have a minute to decide on **the most important benefit of social-networking sites.**

### Part 4 (5 minutes)

The examiner will encourage you to develop the topic of your discussion in Part 3 by asking questions such as:

- There is now a big presence of advertisements and marketing campaigns on social-networking sites. Do you think this is a good or bad thing? Why?
- How do you feel about issues of privacy with regard to social-networking sites?
- Some people believe that the use of social-networking sites in the workplace is reducing productivity. Do you think this is true?

| PAPER 1 | Reading and | ▶ | Part 1 |
| | Use of English | | Part 2 |
| PAPER 2 | Writing | | Part 3 |
| | | | Part 4 |
| PAPER 3 | Listening | | Part 5 |
| PAPER 4 | Speaking | | Part 6 |
| | | | Part 7 |
| | | | Part 8 |

For questions **1–8**, read the text below and decide which answer (**A**, **B**, **C** or **D**) best fits each gap. There is an example at the beginning (**0**).

Mark your answers **on the separate answer sheet**.

**Example:**

**0**   **A**   meditation   **B**   perception   **C**   sensation   **D**   comprehension

| 0 | A | B | C | D |
|---|---|---|---|---|
| | ⸣ | **▬** | ⸣ | ⸣ |

# Teenagers and digital technology

In many countries, there is a widespread (**0**) …….. that teenagers' lives nowadays are (**1**) …….. by technology. However, information (**2**) …….. in a recent study of Australian teenagers' use of and attitudes towards technology suggests that this view doesn't (**3**) …….. the reality of their everyday existence. The research by academics from the University of Canberra in Australia found that, while most teenagers had ready access to home computers, mobile phones and other electronic devices, they generally spent more time on traditional (**4**) …….. such as talking to family and friends, doing homework, and enjoying hobbies and sports than on using technology. Accessing social media and playing computer games (**5**) …….. as low as ninth and tenth (**6**) …….. among the ten most common after-school activities.

Fifteen-year-old Laura Edmonds is one of the teenagers surveyed. She admits to being very (**7**) …….. to her smartphone and makes full use of various apps, but if she needs to (**8**) …….. after a hard day at school, she tends to 'hang out with my friends, listen to music or chat with my mum and dad'.

| 1 | **A** mastered | **B** dominated | **C** prevailed | **D** commanded |
|---|---|---|---|---|
| 2 | **A** amounted | **B** gained | **C** achieved | **D** gathered |
| 3 | **A** repeat | **B** reproduce | **C** reflect | **D** recreate |
| 4 | **A** pursuits | **B** events | **C** operations | **D** processes |
| 5 | **A** classed | **B** ranked | **C** valued | **D** graded |
| 6 | **A** subsequently | **B** separately | **C** correspondingly | **D** respectively |
| 7 | **A** related | **B** attached | **C** absorbed | **D** fastened |
| 8 | **A** unwind | **B** unfold | **C** unload | **D** unbend |

| PAPER 1 | Reading and Use of English ▶ | Part 1 |
| | | Part 2 |
| PAPER 2 | Writing | Part 3 |
| | | Part 4 |
| PAPER 3 | Listening | Part 5 |
| PAPER 4 | Speaking | Part 6 |
| | | Part 7 |
| | | Part 8 |

For questions **9–16**, read the text below and think of the word which best fits each gap. Use only one word in each gap. There is an example at the beginning (**0**).

Write your answers **IN CAPITAL LETTERS on the separate answer sheet**.

**Example:** | 0 | I | N |

# Animals that migrate

Animal migration comes (**0**) ........ many different forms – long or short, seasonal or daily, predictable or seemingly random. But (**9**) ........ one thing unites all migratory species, it is the fight to survive. (**10**) ........ this means looking for food, finding mates or laying eggs, survival is the fundamental motivation. But how do animals travel huge distances to precise destinations (**11**) ........ a map or GPS? (**12**) ........ single answer to this is available. Monarch butterflies, for example, are believed to use the sun to navigate from North America to Mexico. Leatherback turtles, on the other (**13**) ........, which can migrate 20,000 kilometres across the ocean, are thought to be guided by the earth's magnetic field. A seabird called the sooty shearwater flies (**14**) ........ average of 64,000 kilometres yearly over the Pacific Ocean. In (**15**) ........ so, it executes a figure-of-eight between New Zealand, where it breeds, and stopovers in Japan, Alaska and California. This bird seemingly has a variety of tools (**16**) ........ its disposal, using the earth's magnetic field, the sun and the stars, and even sight and smell when flying over familiar territory.

| PAPER 1 | Reading and ▶ | Part 1 |
| | Use of English | Part 2 |
| PAPER 2 | Writing | **Part 3** |
| | | Part 4 |
| PAPER 3 | Listening | Part 5 |
| | | Part 6 |
| PAPER 4 | Speaking | Part 7 |
| | | Part 8 |

For questions **17–24**, read the text below. Use the word given in capitals at the end of some of the lines to form a word that fits in the gap **in the same line**. There is an example at the beginning (**0**).

Write your answers **IN CAPITAL LETTERS on the separate answer sheet.**

**Example:** | 0 | S | U | C | C | E | S | S | | | | | | | | | | | |

# Note taking

| | |
|---|---|
| Of all the skills you need to make a (**0**) …….. of your college or | **SUCCEED** |
| university studies, note taking is still one of the most important, | |
| even in this digital age. Whether you do it by hand or on a laptop, | |
| taking good notes will (**17**) …….. things greatly when you come | **SIMPLE** |
| to do revision and write (**18**) …….. | **ASSIGN** |
| | |
| Nowadays, lecture slides and handouts are often uploaded | |
| onto the college or university intranet. The (**19**) …….. of this | **SIDE** |
| guaranteed availability is that there can be a (**20**) …….. to stop | **TEMPT** |
| listening carefully to the lecturer. The advantage, however, is that | |
| you can focus on the difficult parts of what is said. Taking notes | |
| can aid concentration, but you need to do it (**21**) ……….., recording | **SELECT** |
| only what is most useful to you. | |
| | |
| Lecturers often cover a lot of material swiftly, and to (**22**) ………. | **SURE** |
| that you record everything you need, some form of shorthand | |
| will help. Use abbreviations (e.g.) and symbols (→), and you | |
| can (**23**) ………. certain words ('btwn' for 'between'). It is also | **SHORT** |
| important to be systematic in recording information like sources | |
| of quotes and other (**24**) ………. details. | **BIBLIOGRAPHY** |

| PAPER 1 | Reading and | ▶ | Part 1 |
| | Use of English | | Part 2 |
| PAPER 2 | Writing | | Part 3 |
| PAPER 3 | Listening | | **Part 4** |
| PAPER 4 | Speaking | | Part 5 |
| | | | Part 6 |
| | | | Part 7 |
| | | | Part 8 |

For questions **25–30**, complete the second sentence so that it has a similar meaning to the first sentence, using the word given. **Do not change the word given.** You must use between **three** and **six** words, including the word given. Here is an example (**0**).

**Example:**

**0**  Chloe would only eat a pizza if she could have a mushroom topping.

   **ON**

   Chloe ........................................... a mushroom topping when she had a pizza.

The gap can be filled with the words 'insisted on having', so you write:

**Example:** | **0** | INSISTED ON HAVING |

Write **only** the missing words **IN CAPITAL LETTERS on the separate answer sheet.**

---

**25**  I'm sorry now that we didn't save a bit more money for the holidays.

   **SET**

   I wish ........................................... a bit more money for the holidays.

**26**  When people treated Emily like a child, she didn't like it.

   **RESENTED**

   Emily ........................................... she was a child.

**27**  Reducing the time we spend on boring paperwork would be good for all of us.

   **INTEREST**

   It would be in ........................................... on the time we spend on boring paperwork.

**28**  My cousins, Joe and Ben, are identical twins and when they were small my dad could never work out who was who.

   **DIFFERENCE**

   My cousins, Joe and Ben, are identical twins and when they were small my dad could never ........................................... of them.

**29**  Stefano thought that no one had done much to prepare for Alicia's farewell party.

   **THAT**

   Stefano was under ........................................... done to prepare for Alicia's farewell party..

**30**  People usually need specific qualifications to get onto the nursing course, but they said they would treat Maria differently because of her practical experience.

   **EXCEPTION**

   People usually need specific qualifications to get onto the nursing course, but they agreed ........................................... case because of her practical experience.

PAPER 1 Reading and ▶ Part 1
Use of English      Part 2
PAPER 2 Writing      Part 3
Part 4
PAPER 3 Listening      **Part 5**
PAPER 4 Speaking      Part 6
Part 7
Part 8

You are going to read a magazine article. For questions **31–36**, choose the answer (**A**, **B**, **C** or **D**) which you think fits best according to the text.

Mark your answers **on the separate answer sheet**.

# Artificial reefs

*Rocks under the sea attract lots of marine life. The best-known of these reefs are the spectacular coral reefs, but artificial, man-made reefs are also significant, as Stephen Harrigan reports.*

When the 160-metre-long Vandenberg was deliberately sunk in May 2009, it joined many other shipwrecks in the Gulf of Mexico, off the coast of Florida in the USA. People around the world have long known that shipwrecks are prime fishing sites, and in modern times reefs have been created out of all sorts of objects including old refrigerators, cars, train carriages and oil drilling rigs.

The process of how a man-made hulk like the Vandenberg becomes an undersea garden is governed by variables such as depth, water temperature, currents and the composition of the seabed. But most artificial reefs attract marine life in a more or less predictable sequence of events. First, water currents deposit plankton to provide a reliable feeding spot for small fish, which then draw in bigger predators like blue fin tuna and sharks. Next come the creatures seeking protection from the ocean's lethal openness – hole and crevice dwellers like eels. Opportunistic predators such as jack and barracuda are also quick to come, waiting for their prey to show themselves. In time – maybe months, maybe years, maybe a decade, depending on the ocean's moods – the steel will be encrusted with algae, hard and soft corals, sponges and other forms of sea life.

For decades, oil and gas platforms in the Gulf of Mexico have been prime sites for recreational fishing, since many species of fish seek shelter in their underwater structures. Michael Miglini, the captain of a charter boat called Orion that takes fishermen and divers out to rigs off Port Aransas – an area blessedly spared from the oil that spilled into the Gulf after the Deepwater Horizon catastrophe in 2010 – knows the attraction of artificial reefs for water sports enthusiasts, and the revenue and jobs thereby generated. He says: 'Creating habitat is akin to creating oases in the desert. An artificial reef is a way of boosting the ocean's capacity to create fish, to increase the life of the Gulf.' Biologists suggest, however, that artificial reefs may simply attract fish from natural reefs and become killing zones for certain species, such as red snapper, one of the Gulf's most sought-after game fish.

'When it comes to red snappers, artificial reefs are bait,' says James Cowan, a professor of oceanography and coastal sciences. 'If success is judged solely by an increase in harvest, then artificial reefs are pretty successful. But if those structures – usually deployed in shallow waters to make them more accessible to fishing – are pulling fish off natural reefs farther from the coast, they may actually be increasing the overfishing of species that are already under stress.'

Some artificial reefs have become hazards to navigation and a toxic threat to the waters in which they rest. The danger of pollution is the reason almost 70% of the Vandenberg's $8.4 million sinking budget went to clean-up efforts, including the removal of more than ten tons of asbestos and more than 250,000 metres of electrical wire. And for every metre of wire there was a metre of red tape, since artificial reefs must now be created in strict accordance with the US government's National Artificial Reef Plan.

Even scrupulously planned wrecks can go very wrong. When the Spiegel Grove went down in 2002, the ship landed upside down with one corner of her stern on the bottom and part of her bow above the waterline, ready to serve as a can opener to unsuspecting vessels using the marine sanctuary. It took a massive effort to get her over on her side and fully underwater, and it wasn't until three years later that Hurricane Dennis finally gave her the intended upright – and harmless to traffic – profile.

The notorious Osborne Tire Reef project off the Florida coast was initially thought to be a good idea in the early 1970s, a win-win scheme that would liberate the nation's landfills of up to two million discarded tires to create a thriving marine habitat. But it turned out that vulcanized rubber is actually a poor base for coral growth, and the bundled tires, instead of helping to augment two adjacent natural reefs, ended up smothering and bashing into their fragile organisms. When the bundles broke apart, the tires washed up on beaches. The hopeful Osborne Tire Reef initiative has now given way to its expensive remedy, the Osborne Reef Waste Tire Removal Project.

**31** The main purpose of the second paragraph is to

    **A** highlight the length of time required for an artificial reef to work.

    **B** outline the different stages through which an artificial reef develops.

    **C** emphasise the range of sea creatures that are attracted to artificial reefs.

    **D** explain the diverse factors that determine how successful an artificial reef is.

**32** What point does the writer make about artificial reefs in the third paragraph?

    **A** They can stimulate economic growth in coastal areas.

    **B** Their impact is appreciated by scientists and fishermen alike.

    **C** Their primary function is to improve the marine environment.

    **D** They have helped the Gulf of Mexico recover from an oil disaster.

**33** What does James Cowan suggest about artificial reefs?

    **A** Certain species of fish are driven away by them.

    **B** People excited by fishing from them may move on to natural reefs.

    **C** They should be established in parts of the ocean that are very deep.

    **D** Consideration should be given to the criteria used to assess their value.

**34** Which aspect of artificial reefs does the writer seek to underline with the words 'for every metre of wire there was a metre of red tape'?

    **A** the various dangers they can pose

    **B** the regulations governing their creation

    **C** the costs incurred in putting them in place

    **D** the laws determining what they should look like

**35** What point does the writer make about the Spiegel Grove?

    **A** Boats and ships have to carefully avoid the sunken ship.

    **B** Extreme weather conditions caused the ship to sink.

    **C** The ship is an unsuitable shape to serve as a reef.

    **D** The ship initially settled in an unhelpful position.

**36** What does the writer say about the Osborne Tire Reef?

    **A** It would have worked better in a different location.

    **B** It has provided the inspiration for a similar scheme.

    **C** It was meant to benefit the environment in two ways.

    **D** It shows how little people cared about the ocean in the past.

| PAPER 1 Reading and Use of English | ▶ | Part 1 |
| | | Part 2 |
| | | Part 3 |
| PAPER 2 Writing | | Part 4 |
| | | Part 5 |
| PAPER 3 Listening | | **Part 6** |
| PAPER 4 Speaking | | Part 7 |
| | | Part 8 |

You are going to read four comments in an online discussion about reality TV. For questions **37–40**, choose from the comments **A–D**. The comments may be chosen more than once.

Mark your answers **on the separate answer sheet**.

# Reality TV

*Reality TV programmes such as* Big Brother, Survivor *and* X Factor *have come to dominate the schedules of many television stations in the past decade. Four social commentators offer their thoughts on the phenomenon.*

**A**

The bottom line is that reality TV programmes attract audiences of all ages and types. Viewers want to be entertained, but, at the same time, are often happy to learn something – from a show set in a restaurant kitchen or a fitness camp, for example. Criticisms that particular combinations of people are selected and placed in unrealistic settings, and so reality TV is not real, miss the point. Audiences know that shows like *Big Brother* do not replicate real life, but they do offer us opportunities to observe how people like us, or not like us, interact and deal with challenges. In these unusual situations the participants' behaviour may at times be strange, ill-considered or even offensive, but society is imperfect and audiences know this. People generally watch reality TV shows in an analytical, critical spirit, making judgements about what they see rather than simply wanting to copy it.

**B**

There are many different types of reality TV programmes, of course. Lots of them focus obsessively on appearance, consumerism and celebrity status, and imply that anyone can become famous without working hard or displaying a particular talent. The concern is that impressionable viewers, taking what they see to be real life, may absorb the message uncritically, overlooking the fact that the narrative is invariably manipulated by clever programme makers. Other programmes, however, are more positive and even instructive. One show, *Jamie's Kitchen*, offered jobless youngsters the chance to train as chefs and lead a campaign to improve the quality of school meals. The programme was a valuable learning experience for audiences and participants, and even had an impact on government policy. More programmes like *Jamie's Kitchen* would be welcome. The fact is, however, that the quality as well as the sheer quantity of reality programmes shown on our television screens reflects market demand.

**C**

There seems to be a huge appetite for reality TV, and it is hard to argue with programme makers who claim they are just producing shows their audiences want. The unfortunate thing is that most reality TV is of very poor quality. Not only is it fundamentally dishonest in pretending to show 'reality', when in fact it is a strange mix of fiction and fact, distorted to suit the programme makers' requirements, but it so often relies on humiliation and conflict to create excitement, sending a message that crude, self-centred, empty-headed behaviour is the norm and that celebrity is a worthy aspiration. There are a few reality shows which purport to do good by showing us something we can learn from, some insight perhaps into human behaviour, but even in these cases a straightforward documentary format would be far more informative and trustworthy than these odd fabricated social experiments.

**D**

The most interesting thing about reality TV is that it is not what its label implies and perhaps what many believe it to be. Typically, a group of people are filmed in unusual situations over a period of time – not reality for most us. Occasionally, some 'reality shows' are supposed to reveal something new about people – how they interact, change or deal with a problem, for example – but such revelations invariably turn out to be utterly banal. What is sometimes forgotten is that reality TV is a cheap means to ensure there is always something on TV in this age of multiple channels and 24-hour programming. The fact that it fills the gaps does not mean that audiences want it, however. In fact, many reality shows have extremely low viewing figures, and some TV stations, like the Italian state broadcaster RAI, have decided to remove all reality shows from their schedules.

## Which comment

shares B's opinion regarding the educational content of some reality TV?

37 [ ]

has a different opinion from the others about the authenticity of reality TV?

38 [ ]

expresses a different view from the others about the popularity of reality TV?

39 [ ]

takes a similar view to C regarding the values represented in many reality TV shows?

40 [ ]

PAPER 1 Reading and ▸ | Part 1
Use of English | Part 2

PAPER 2 Writing | Part 3
| Part 4
PAPER 3 Listening | Part 5
| Part 6
PAPER 4 Speaking | Part 7
| Part 8

You are going to read a newspaper article about the history of art. Six paragraphs have been removed from the article. Choose from the paragraphs **A–G** the one which fits each gap (**41–46**). There is one extra paragraph which you do not need to use.

Mark your answers **on the separate answer sheet**.

# Studying art history

In many countries, doing a degree in the history of art is considered something of a minority choice. While no one would deny that art is a fascinating subject with a longer and more diverse history than, say, literature, history of art tends to exist on the margins at most universities, the preserve of a few dedicated students.

**41**

As Janice Burton, a former student at the Courtauld Institute, a specialist university in the UK that focuses entirely on the subject, explains: 'History of art is more than simply the study of creativity and aesthetics. It incorporates all aspects of history, as well as philosophy, anthropology, politics and religion. Art represents an insight into the spirit of a particular period, as well as supplying some of history's most fascinating protagonists.'

**42**

So it's clearly a very interesting subject to study, covering a huge slice of the human experience, but what can you do with it? History of art lecturer Natalia Mellor believes her subject is crucial for the development of public culture. 'Our degree courses produce the museum directors of the future,' she says.

**43**

Not everyone who attains a degree in history of art is forced into the art world, however. Jerome Hasler, for instance, now works for a crisis management consultancy. 'It's not a directly vocational position,' he admits, but history of art has still been very beneficial. 'It taught me to be creative, to research thoroughly and

to appreciate that many factors can contribute to a final product, things I use and value every day in my job.'

**44**

There is a perception, perhaps, that history of art is an elitist subject. Professor Joanna Woodall, who teaches at the Courtauld, is at pains to disagree. 'People often think of art history as elitist, but it's a subject in which everyone has something to contribute. People notice different things and ask different questions,' she says. When considering applications from potential students wanting to take her courses, she is interested in people who clearly have a passion for art and art history, rather than those who have traditional qualifications.

**45**

And what, in practical terms, does studying history of art entail? How is the programme organised, particularly for newcomers to the subject as an academic discipline? Rebecca Murphy, who graduated from the Courtauld last year, enjoyed every minute of it.

**46**

'As you progress,' she says, 'you cover all the different aspects of theory, and every term you get to learn about a different period. In the first couple of years you get to build up this knowledge and then in the third you get the opportunity to tackle more specialist topics of your choice.' Like many of her peers, she is convinced it was worth it. 'The degree enabled me to acquire a lot of knowledge about important subjects, some good transferrable skills and a great bunch of friends too.'

**A** Burton concurs: 'Had I wanted to work in an auction house, curate or write for an art magazine, then I would have been very well placed, especially if I'd continued on with a master's degree, and there were some tempting options at the Courtauld, such as art restoration. But history of art led me into writing, specifically journalism, and achieving a good degree from a prestigious university did my job prospects no harm at all.'

**B** However absorbing or enriching history of art may be, this view of it as being accessible to and useful for only a small and probably privileged group of people can deter many with a genuine interest in it.

**C** Although it has a limited following, it is anything but insignificant in scope or academic rigour, however. It's about art, of course, but it's by no means confined to staring at paintings and stroking one's chin.

**D** 'If you've never formally studied the subject before, you start with a leveller course,' she says. This introduction provides an overall perspective on the degree. 'You then move on to a more in-depth look, and the chance to learn about things you're personally interested in.'

**E** In fact, anyone who wants to be seriously involved in museum and gallery curation needs to ensure they have a solid academic grounding in the subject. You don't get to run a major gallery without a deep knowledge of the art world as a whole – one you can't just get from avidly attending exhibitions.

**F** Another recent history of art graduate agrees: 'It gave me the opportunity to explore the stories within works of art, addressing social, political or personal reasons behind their particular appearance or fame.'

**G** 'We try to look for someone who shows a demonstrable interest in the subject – but that doesn't mean they have to know reams about art history. Those coming to history of art from other disciplines bring something different and enliven the discipline for everyone.'

| | |
|---|---|
| PAPER 1 Reading and Use of English ▶ | Part 1 |
| | Part 2 |
| PAPER 2 Writing | Part 3 |
| | Part 4 |
| PAPER 3 Listening | Part 5 |
| | Part 6 |
| PAPER 4 Speaking | Part 7 |
| | **Part 8** |

You are going to read an article about people who work in museums. For questions **47–56**, choose from the people (**A–D**). The people may be chosen more than once.

Mark your answers **on the separate answer sheet.**

## Which person

| | |
|---|---|
| mentions the difficulty of keeping her professional knowledge up to date? | 47 |
| points out the advantage of specialising in a particular type of work? | 48 |
| is reluctant to take on a managerial role? | 49 |
| claims that people in her field are realistic about their career prospects? | 50 |
| mentions a misconception about the field she is in? | 51 |
| is grateful for the skills she acquired in a previous, different career? | 52 |
| points out that her responsibilities differ from those of other people in similar jobs? | 53 |
| emphasises the importance of talking to a wide range of people in her work? | 54 |
| regrets the range of duties she has to undertake? | 55 |
| regrets the lack of formal training available for her job? | 56 |

# Museum work

## A

Melanie Kershaw works as a museum curator in Scotland. Her typical day might involve working on the museum's computer documentation system, packing up an exhibition of local artists, dealing with security issues or taking guided tours round the galleries. 'It'd be nice if I could focus on the natural history collection, where I have real expertise,' she says. 'But it's only a small museum so I get roped into all sorts of things. We do lots of work with local children and I give talks to geology societies in the area.' Melanie took her first degree in biology and then went into teaching. 'Dealing with school kids for a few years taught me how to communicate with groups, which serves me well here.' She left teaching after doing a part-time museum studies course and has been in her current post for four years now. She feels no real desire to climb the career ladder. 'What appeals to me is researching, documenting and displaying objects, not being in charge of other people, but I'll probably move to a bigger museum eventually.'

## B

There's no traditional route into fundraising for museums and galleries, according to Angela Garcia, the head of development for a museum of culture in the north of Spain. 'You figure things out as you go along. It's not ideal, but that's how it is,' says Angela. 'Lots of my colleagues have come to it in an ad hoc way through an arts degree, some voluntary work, maybe some marketing and then into fundraising.' She manages a team of two development officers and an assistant, oversees a corporate patrons' scheme, administers a development trust and raises other sponsorship for exhibitions throughout the year. 'Networking is crucial,' she says. 'Not just with potential donors, but also with museum visitors, the press and colleagues from my museum and other institutions – it's good to keep up with what's happening elsewhere.' She says the work is challenging with only average financial rewards, but it's far from dull. 'For some people, the idea of museum work still conjures up images of geeks in dusty archives detached from the real world,' she says. 'If they only knew!'

## C

As registrar for a regional museum service, Laura Johansson is responsible for all information relating to the objects kept in eight public museums. 'It could be information about what the object is and where it's come from, or it could be movement records.' says Laura. 'I'm involved with things such as documentation procedures and collections management policies. And unlike some registrars, I'm in charge of the information management system.' With advances in digital technology, it is a fast-moving field. 'That makes it exciting,' she says. 'But I don't really have the time or resources to stay abreast of all the developments in the way I should.' Like many people working in museums and galleries, Laura's career path has not been wholly predictable. After graduating in history, she managed a clothes store for five years, before realising she wanted something different. She completed a diploma in heritage studies and then documented items in a toy museum for three years. That led to her current post.

## D

Yasmin Kumar is a sculpture conservator. 'You've got to know what an object's made from, how long it's been in its environment, the aesthetics of it, and be able to work on it,' she explains. She started by volunteering in museums to get practical experience, but she also has a degree in fine art and an MA in historic artefacts conservation. She is now one of four permanent staff who restore objects and get them ready for display and for going out on loan. 'It's quite narrow,' she says. 'And it can be hard to switch to anything else – we're all aware of that. On the other hand, there aren't many people with our expertise, so we're in demand. I'm often away for several days at a time, travelling with objects or going to work on artefacts in other countries.' Yasmin feels fulfilled, despite the uninspiring pay scales. 'I'd like the chance to earn more, of course,' she says. 'But, like everyone who works in this sector, I know it's not going to happen.'

PAPER 1 Reading and
Use of English

**PAPER 2 Writing** ▶ Part 1
Part 2

PAPER 3 Listening

PAPER 4 Speaking

You **must** answer this question. Write your answer in **220–260** words in an appropriate style on the separate answer sheet.

1 You attended a philosophy seminar in which the tutor suggested that all exams in schools and colleges be abolished. You have made the notes below.

---

**Abolish exams**

- Students are denied the enriching experience of learning because they are under too much pressure to pass the exam.
- Exams are not very effective because they test memory rather than intelligence.
- It's not a fair process; exam stress affects some students more than others. Not everyone performs well in exams.

---

**Other students in the seminar expressed their opinions:**

"But working towards the final exam often gives us the motivation we need in order to study."

"Exam-based assessment is a good way of figuring out whether a student has really understood what they have been taught."

"Taking exams at school and university is actually a good life skill because it trains us to plan, prepare and deliver."

---

Write an essay for your tutor discussing **two** of the points from your notes. You should **explain whether you think abolishing exams is a good idea** and **provide reasons** to support your opinions.

You may, if you wish, make use of the opinions expressed in the lecture, but you should use your own words as far as possible.

PAPER 1 Reading and
         Use of English

**PAPER 2 Writing**      ▶  Part 1

PAPER 3 Listening           Part 2

PAPER 4 Speaking

Write an answer to **one** of the questions **2–4** in this part. Write your answer in **220–260** words in an appropriate style on the separate answer sheet. Put the question number in the box at the top of the page.

**2**  You see this advertisement in a local newspaper.

> Here at Blackshaw Books we have a vacancy for a part-time sales assistant. If you love books and would like to join our small team, please send a letter of application to the manager, Eileen James. The ideal candidate will be organised, reliable and available to work flexible hours.

Write your **letter.**

**3**  You see this notice inside the main door of the apartment complex where you live.

> The Management Committee's plan to build a bicycle shed at the back of the property has met with some resistance. Some residents feel it would be better to create a patio area with picnic benches, while others have requested a small playground for their children. You are invited to send the Management Committee a proposal outlining which of these you would like to see, and explaining why. You may also propose a new idea of your own.

Write your **proposal.**

**4**  You read this advertisement in a technology magazine.

> What mobile phone do you use? With so many models on the market, we are compiling a spreadsheet of mobiles for consumer comparison. We want to publish reviews that highlight the best and worst features and benefits of each phone. Send in a review describing your mobile and explaining why you would recommend it, or not.

Write your **review.**

PAPER 1  Reading and
          Use of English

PAPER 2  Writing

**PAPER 3  Listening**  ▶  Part 1

PAPER 4  Speaking
                        Part 2
                        Part 3
                        Part 4

**Track 17**

You will hear three different extracts. For questions **1–6**, choose the answer (**A, B** or **C**) which fits best according to what you hear. There are two questions for each extract.

**Extract One**

You hear two friends discussing plans for another friend's birthday.

1  Why does the woman not agree with any of the man's ideas?
   A  They would be too difficult to organise.
   B  They would cost too much money.
   C  They wouldn't be appropriate for Ken.

2  The joke between the man and woman at the end was because their friend, Ken, doesn't
   A  like birthday cake.
   B  want any fuss.
   C  get embarrassed.

**Extract Two**

You hear two college friends discussing their classmate, Phil.

3  The man thinks their classmate, Phil, is
   A  strange.
   B  self-important.
   C  unhappy.

4  Why does the woman defend Phil's behaviour?
   A  She's known him a long time; he's a close friend.
   B  She knows about some problems he's been having.
   C  She thinks he could be having some personal difficulty.

**Extract Three**

You hear a man telling his friend about some good news regarding his job.

5  What made the man so happy?
   A  He secured a large order.
   B  He got a salary increase.
   C  He got a bonus.

6  Does he believe he'll get a promotion?
   A  No, it's not company policy.
   B  He thinks it's possible.
   C  He's already been promoted.

PAPER 1 Reading and
          Use of English

PAPER 2 Writing

**PAPER 3 Listening** ▶

PAPER 4 Speaking

Part 1
**Part 2**
Part 3
Part 4

◯ **Track 18**

You will hear a young woman called Louise sharing her views with a group of schoolchildren about the impact of the internet on the music industry. For questions **7–14**, complete the sentences with a short word or phrase.

# THE INTERNET AND THE MUSIC INDUSTRY

The speaker feels that her friend's view that the music industry has been destroyed by the internet is a **(7)** ........................................................ .

Louise acknowledges how stopping people from copying CDs to their computers **(8)** ........................................................ at the time.

She points out that **(9)** ........................................................ became a significant issue once people started using MP3 players.

The consequences, if caught, usually involved **(10)** ........................................................ .

Louise likes being able to buy **(11)** ........................................................ rather than entire albums.

The way music is distributed now **(12)** ........................................................ the role of the big executives.

Louise is encouraged to see that the music industry is still **(13)** ........................................................ .

She likes the fact that musicians can **(14)** ........................................................ their work and reach new fans.

PAPER 1 Reading and
         Use of English

PAPER 2 Writing

PAPER 3 Listening ▶

PAPER 4 Speaking

Part 1
Part 2
**Part 3**
Part 4

◯ **Track 19**

You will hear a radio programme, *Wednesday Weekly*, in which blogging is the topic of discussion. For questions **15–20**, choose the answer (**A**, **B**, **C** or **D**) which fits best according to what you hear.

15  What type of programme is *Wednesday Weekly*?
    **A**  a news show
    **B**  a game show
    **C**  a chat show
    **D**  a tech show

16  Do the guests, Sophie and Joe, agree with Ann's general definition of blogging?
    **A**  They think she's completely wrong.
    **B**  They think she's more or less right.
    **C**  They think she's completely right.
    **D**  They think she only knows a little.

17  What does Joe refer to as the *blogosphere*?
    **A**  the world of blogs
    **B**  the first bloggers
    **C**  personal bloggers
    **D**  random blogs

18  What point is Sophie enthusiastic about?
    **A**  that good blogging is now getting recognition
    **B**  that the quality of bloggers' writing has improved
    **C**  that everyone can now publish their own blog
    **D**  that she has won several awards for her blog

19  According to Joe, who is getting an income from blogging?
    **A**  all, or most, bloggers
    **B**  some guest speakers
    **C**  sellers of e-books
    **D**  only the best bloggers

20  What does new research indicate about live-blogging?
    **A**  that all news stories are now being live-blogged
    **B**  that people prefer live blogs to traditional articles
    **C**  that live-blogging is replacing sports reporting
    **D**  that bloggers have now become more dynamic

PAPER 1  Reading and
         Use of English

PAPER 2  Writing

**PAPER 3  Listening** ▶

PAPER 4  Speaking

    Part 1
    Part 2
    Part 3
    **Part 4**

🎧 **Track 20**

You will hear five short extracts in which people talk about giving money to charity.

**While you listen you must complete both tasks.**

---

**TASK ONE**

For questions **21–25**, choose from the list (**A–H**) what kind of charity, if any, each speaker supports.

| | | |
|---|---|---|
| **A** | an animal shelter | |
| **B** | human rights | Speaker 1 ⬚ **21** |
| **C** | doesn't donate at all | Speaker 2 ⬚ **22** |
| **D** | homeless people | Speaker 3 ⬚ **23** |
| **E** | a local charity | Speaker 4 ⬚ **24** |
| **F** | overseas aid | Speaker 5 ⬚ **25** |
| **G** | medical research | |
| **H** | the environment | |

**TASK TWO**

For questions **26–30**, choose from the list (**A–H**) what each speaker says about the reason for their choice.

| | | |
|---|---|---|
| **A** | sees it as the government's role | |
| **B** | improves others' job prospects | Speaker 1 ⬚ **26** |
| **C** | also had a learning disability | Speaker 2 ⬚ **27** |
| **D** | because of widespread corruption | Speaker 3 ⬚ **28** |
| **E** | considers it a responsibility | Speaker 4 ⬚ **29** |
| **F** | because of a family member | Speaker 5 ⬚ **30** |
| **G** | has plenty of money to spare | |
| **H** | feels a personal duty to help | |

PAPER 1 Reading and
Use of English

PAPER 2 Writing

PAPER 3 Listening

**PAPER 4 Speaking**

## Part 1 (2 minutes)

The examiner will ask you a few questions about yourself and about a general topic. For example, the examiner may ask you:

- **Where are you from?**
- **What do you like and dislike about your hometown?**
- **Who do you admire, living or dead, more than anyone else? Why?**

## Part 2 (4 minutes)

You will each be asked to talk on your own for about a minute. You will each be given three different pictures to talk about. After your partner has finished speaking, you will be asked a brief question connected with your partner's photographs.

> **People and their pets** (compare, contrast and speculate)

Turn to pictures 1–3 on page **181**, which show people with different pets.

(*Candidate A*), it's your turn first. Here are your pictures. They show **three different people with their pets.**

I'd like you to compare **two** of the pictures and say **what kind of personality each of the people probably has and how you imagine their pet affects their life.**

(*Candidate B*), **which of these pets would you be most likely to have? Why?**

> **Extreme sports** (compare, contrast and speculate)

Turn to pictures 1–3 on page **182**, which show people doing extreme sports.

Now, (*Candidate B*), here are your pictures. They show **people doing various extreme sports.**

I'd like you to compare **two** of the pictures and say **why you think people do extreme sports and what kind of person might choose to do sports like these.**

(*Candidate A*), **is the risk associated with these sports worth it? Why (not)?**

## Part 3 (4 minutes)

Look at page **183**, which shows some advantages and disadvantages of renting or buying a home.

> **Renting versus buying** (discuss, evaluate and negotiate)

**Here are some advantages and disadvantages to renting a home and buying a home** and a question for you to discuss.

First you have some time to look at the task.

(*Pause 15 seconds*)

Now talk to each other about **whether you think it's better to rent or to buy.**

Now you have a minute to decide **on the biggest disadvantage to renting and to owning a property.**

## Part 4 (5 minutes)

The examiner will encourage you to develop the topic of your discussion in Part 3 by asking questions such as:

- Do you believe that life is less complicated for people who rent their home? How?
- Some people say that buying a home is more of a burden than an investment? Do you agree?
- Do you think there is too much pressure on people to buy property nowadays?

| PAPER 1 | Reading and Use of English | ▶ | Part 1 |
| | | | Part 2 |
| PAPER 2 | Writing | | Part 3 |
| | | | Part 4 |
| PAPER 3 | Listening | | Part 5 |
| | | | Part 6 |
| PAPER 4 | Speaking | | Part 7 |
| | | | Part 8 |

For questions **1–8**, read the text below and decide which answer (**A, B, C** or **D**) best fits each gap. There is an example at the beginning (**0**).

Mark your answers **on the separate answer sheet**.

**Example:**

**0**   **A**   result        **B**   impact        **C**   difference        **D**   consequence

| 0 | A | B | C | D |
|---|---|---|---|---|
|   | ⎁ | ⎁ | ⎁ | ⎁ |

# The importance of a name

Have you ever thought about the (**0**) …….. your name has on the way others perceive you? A recent study by Dr Simon Laham from the University of Melbourne and Dr Adam Alter from New York University Stern Business School reveals that people with 'easy-to-pronounce' names tend to be (**1**) …….. more positively than those with 'difficult-to-pronounce' names. The researchers found that people with more easily pronounceable names were more likely to be (**2**) …….. upon favourably for political office, and that lawyers with easier sounding names made their way up the career (**3**) …….. faster. Surnames from a wide range of nationalities were used in the study, and researchers stressed that preferences were not (**4**) …….. due to the length of a name or how unusual it was, but rather how easy it was to say.

Dr Laham believes the research highlights the kind of (**5**) …….. that our everyday thinking is (**6**) …….. to. The wider (**7**) …….. is that our decisions are often shaped by preferences that are both trivial and subtle. An appreciation of this may lead to more impartial, fairer thinking and (**8**) …….. of other people.

| | | | | | | | |
|---|---|---|---|---|---|---|---|
| **1** | **A** evaluated | **B** reckoned | **C** figured | **D** determined |
| **2** | **A** put | **B** looked | **C** called | **D** come |
| **3** | **A** order | **B** stairs | **C** scale | **D** ladder |
| **4** | **A** barely | **B** hardly | **C** plainly | **D** merely |
| **5** | **A** angles | **B** biases | **C** weights | **D** turns |
| **6** | **A** subject | **B** obliged | **C** conditioned | **D** obedient |
| **7** | **A** connotation | **B** association | **C** implication | **D** manifestation |
| **8** | **A** attention | **B** regard | **C** treatment | **D** notice |

| PAPER 1 | Reading and ▶ | Part 1 |
| | Use of English | Part 2 |
| PAPER 2 | Writing | Part 3 |
| | | Part 4 |
| PAPER 3 | Listening | Part 5 |
| PAPER 4 | Speaking | Part 6 |
| | | Part 7 |
| | | Part 8 |

For questions **9–16**, read the text below and think of the word which best fits each gap. Use only one word in each gap. There is an example at the beginning (**0**).

Write your answers **IN CAPITAL LETTERS on the separate answer sheet**.

**Example:** | 0 | N O T |

## A bird that can dance in time to music

It is (**0**) ........ often that a video posted online of a funny pet sparks a scientific breakthrough. Yet that is (**9**) ........ happened when scientist Aniruddh Patel saw a clip of a cockatoo called Snowball moving his body in time to a pop song. Scientists used to believe that no species (**10**) ........ from human beings could dance in time to music. Our closest cousins, chimpanzees, can't and (**11**) ........ can cats or dogs, in (**12**) ........ of the fact that they have lived alongside us for millennia.

Dr Patel contacted Snowball's owner and carried out various experiments with the bird, all of (**13**) ........ supported the notion that the cockatoo could genuinely follow different rhythms. Further studies have found that other species of songbird can do the same. (**14**) ........ to Dr Patel, something these birds and humans have in common, but most species don't, is that our brains are wired to hear and reproduce complex sounds. Dance, it is thought, emerged (**15**) ........ a by-product of our ability to imitate sound, and (**16**) ........ vocal imitation we wouldn't be able to keep a beat.

| PAPER 1 | Reading and Use of English | ▶ | Part 1 |
|---|---|---|---|
| | | | Part 2 |
| | | | **Part 3** |
| PAPER 2 | Writing | | Part 4 |
| | | | Part 5 |
| PAPER 3 | Listening | | Part 6 |
| | | | Part 7 |
| PAPER 4 | Speaking | | Part 8 |

For questions **17–24**, read the text below. Use the word given in capitals at the end of some of the lines to form a word that fits in the gap **in the same line.** There is an example at the beginning (**0**).

Write your answers **IN CAPITAL LETTERS on the separate answer sheet.**

**Example:** 0 W O R L D W I D E

## Manchester – city of many languages

The city of Manchester in the north of England is famous
(**0**) ........ for its industries, its rock bands and its football teams.    **WORLD**
But now Manchester has another claim to fame as one of the
world's most (**17**) ........ varied cities. Researchers from the    **LINGUIST**
University of Manchester have discovered that at least 153
different languages are spoken among the city's half a million
(**18**) ......... The researchers say that Manchester's language    **INHABIT**
(**19**) ........ is greater than that of many countries.    **DIVERSE**

The city has been home to many ethnic (**20**) ........ for a long time,    **MINOR**
but there has been a (**21**) ........ change in the make-up of the    **NOTICE**
population in the last two decades, and with continuing
(**22**) ........ into the city from various parts of the world and the    **IMMIGRATE**
arrival of many (**23**) ........ students to study at Manchester's    **SEA**
colleges and universities, the number of languages is likely to
increase.

Currently, two-thirds of the city's schoolchildren are bilingual,
a very significant figure, and an indication that Manchester will
continue to be (**24**) ........ by its great mix of languages and    **RICH**
cultures.

| PAPER 1 | Reading and Use of English ▶ | Part 1 |
| | | Part 2 |
| | | Part 3 |
| | | **Part 4** |
| PAPER 2 | Writing | Part 5 |
| | | Part 6 |
| PAPER 3 | Listening | Part 7 |
| PAPER 4 | Speaking | Part 8 |

For questions **25–30**, complete the second sentence so that it has a similar meaning to the first sentence, using the word given. **Do not change the word given.** You must use between **three** and **six** words, including the word given. Here is an example (**0**).

**Example:**

**0**   Chloe would only eat a pizza if she could have a mushroom topping.

   **ON**

   Chloe ........................................... a mushroom topping when she had a pizza.

The gap can be filled with the words 'insisted on having', so you write:

**Example:**  | **0** |INSISTED ON HAVING |

Write **only** the missing words **IN CAPITAL LETTERS on the separate answer sheet.**

---

**25**   Enrico doesn't cook for himself in the evenings because he's too lazy.

   **BOTHERED**

   Enrico ........................................................ for himself in the evenings.

**26**   When questioned by journalists, the company director said he had never had any involvement in discussions about a merger with another organisation.

   **BEING**

   When questioned by journalists, the company director ........................................................ discussions about a merger with another organisation.

**27**   Why ever did it never occur to me to ask my grandmother if she knew when the picture had been taken?

   **EARTH**

   Why ........................................................ of asking my grandmother if she knew when the picture had been taken?

**28**   I'm sure that facing such an experienced opponent as Maria Suarez wasn't easy, but Ellie played very well.

   **COME**

   It can't ........................................................ against such an experienced opponent as Maria Suarez, but Ellie played very well.

**29**   'Please do whatever you can to persuade your colleagues to bring the date of the meeting forward,' Selina said to David.

   **UTMOST**

   Selina urged ........................................................ persuade his colleagues to bring the date of the meeting forward.

**30**   The new square has made the town centre nicer, but public transport could still be improved a lot.

   **ROOM**

   The new square has made the town centre nicer, but there's still plenty ........................................................ as public transport is concerned.

PAPER 1 Reading and ▸    Part 1
         Use of English    Part 2

PAPER 2 Writing    Part 3
     Part 4

PAPER 3 Listening    **Part 5**
     Part 6

PAPER 4 Speaking    Part 7
     Part 8

You are going to read a magazine article in which a psychologist describes a course he went on to learn how to be a comedian. For questions **31–36**, choose the answer (**A**, **B**, **C** or **D**) which you think fits best according to the text.

Mark your answers **on the separate answer sheet**.

# Comedy and psychology

*As an academic psychologist, Jamie Peters has investigated and written about humour. With the aim of exploring comedy from the perspective of a comedian, he attended a comedy course, as he describes here.*

Earlier this year I did a part-time comedy course. The 18-strong class included people from many different walks of life and was taught by Ryan, a professional stand-up comedian. Of all of the participants, I think I'd probably gigged the most. For the last three years, I've performed a mind-reading show at an arts festival. It wasn't originally meant to be a comedy show – I thought I would cut a commanding, mysterious figure onstage, but on my debut, the audience laughed at my first joke, then continued to laugh throughout all the routines that were meant to be serious. Thankfully, they weren't laughing at me. Well, sometimes they were, but mostly they were with me. So it was the audience who told me I'm funny, but I haven't always understood why, or how to craft and control the comic moments. So, I joined the course to learn. And although, as a psychologist, I've published articles and books about humour, there was hardly a single joke in any of them, so I still felt like a beginner.

'Turn off your internal editor that makes you say the right thing. Find your inner idiot. Remember how to be a child,' explained Ryan. 'Don't try to be clever. Don't try too hard to be funny … and knowing all about the theory of humour is unlikely to help you much. Just muck around. That's what people want to see on stage.' So we did. Ryan would help us loosen up by saying things like: 'Wander around talking to others in the room, but make sure that you're the lowest status person here.' Not to be outdone, I found myself conversing with others whilst lying prostrate on the floor.

I'd say that understanding the psychology of humour has actually helped a little. It was only last year that I stumbled across the book *Inside Jokes: Using Humor to Reverse-Engineer the Mind*, by Hurley, Dennett and Adams. As I read the introduction, I couldn't have grinned much wider if I'd put a coat hanger in my mouth. Past efforts to explain humour had never really cut it for me. For example, those theorists who simply thought that humour was a way of expressing anger, or of social control, or of proving intellect, or of attracting others seemed to have only explained some, incomplete, aspects of motivation, not the mechanics of humour. Here, finally was what felt like a true, unifying theory.

The crux of their thesis is that any self-directed intelligent system will need to correct its own bugs. Think of it in terms of the human mind running software to understand the world around it. As it makes sense of things, there's a risk that the occasional error will be made (a bug), which will have to be debugged before long. Now if this was tedious or onerous, we'd be less inclined to do it. However, evolution has conspired to make the process fun.

In more concrete terms, here's a joke cited in the book: Two fish are in a tank. One says to the other, 'Do you know how to drive this thing?' It works on the principle that we have started to imagine one thing – that the tank is the typical container people keep fish in – and, just in time, the punch-line tells us that our first assumption was wrong – it's the military vehicle. For correctly figuring out the contradiction (or bug), we are rewarded with a pleasurable feeling. The joke is an efficient way of stimulating this natural reaction, and comics have become experts in tickling this mental funny-bone in order to make us laugh.

So, was Ryan right when he said that knowing the theory of humour wouldn't help us that much as a stand up? I think he was. So much of what made our group laugh over our eight weeks of life-affirming mucking around would be very hard to script. During one exercise, four of us were told to perform an improvised opera. Whilst Susan and Caroline sang earnestly on either side of the stage, I spontaneously brought Henry to the floor, where we wrestled each other like out-of-control teenagers. The rest of the group, sitting in the audience, were in uncontrollable fits of laughter. As this moment was lost to the ether, and as a performer, I couldn't be an observer, I'll never appreciate just why it seemed so funny. But the point is, I would never have written this into a script. It was a joyous, found moment.

**31** What does the writer say about himself in the first paragraph?

    **A** He was worried about how other people on the comedy course would find him.

    **B** He wanted to see how theories he had about comedy worked in practice.

    **C** He's had some unpleasant experiences when performing comedy.

    **D** He discovered by chance that he had some aptitude for comedy.

**32** In one part of the course, the writer lay 'prostrate on the floor' because he wanted to

    **A** do what others in the group were doing.

    **B** show defiance of his tutor's instructions.

    **C** try to behave in a more playful manner.

    **D** make himself feel more comfortable.

**33** The writer says 'I couldn't have grinned much wider if I'd put a coat hanger in my mouth' when reading the introduction to the book in order to

    **A** show his pleasure at discovering how it confirmed his own views.

    **B** underline his appreciation of the ideas expressed in it.

    **C** illustrate his sense of confusion at its contents.

    **D** emphasise how humorous he found it.

**34** What does the word 'process' in line 26 refer to?

    **A** understanding the world

    **B** dealing with bugs

    **C** running software

    **D** making errors

**35** What is the main purpose of the fifth paragraph?

    **A** to show why some people are funnier than others

    **B** to give an example of humour present in the book

    **C** to elaborate further on a theory about humour

    **D** to explain the point of a particular joke

**36** What view does the writer put forward in the final paragraph?

    **A** What people find funny is often unpredictable.

    **B** Visual humour is what appeals to people most.

    **C** Theories explaining humour tend to be mistaken.

    **D** Observing comedy is a good way of learning comic skills.

PAPER 1 Reading and ▶ Part 1
Use of English ▶ Part 2

PAPER 2 Writing — Part 3
Part 4

PAPER 3 Listening — Part 5

PAPER 4 Speaking — **Part 6**
Part 7
Part 8

You are going to read four contributions to a debate about proposals to reintroduce wolves into Scotland. For questions **37–40**, choose from the contributions **A–D**. The contributions may be chosen more than once.

Mark your answers **on the separate answer sheet**.

# Reintroducing wolves into Scotland

*Wolves were last seen in the wild in Scotland in the seventeenth century but in recent times there have been proposals to reintroduce the animal to more remote highland areas of the country. Four scientists give their views on the idea.*

### A

The idea of reintroducing wolves into Scotland three centuries after they were eradicated has a romantic appeal, and if, as wolf reintroduction schemes in parts of the USA like Montana suggest would happen, they reduced red deer numbers and consequently stimulated greater biodiversity, this would be very positive. This potential ecological benefit is undeniable but comparisons with the USA are deceptive. Scotland is a small country and keeping wolves away from its many livestock farms would be difficult. Scotland also has limited economic resources, and the funds required to introduce and manage packs of wolves would be far better spent on maintaining and enhancing native species already present in the country. The few opinion polls that have been carried out on the subject reveal that most Scottish people, while attracted by the idea of wolves in their limited remaining wilderness areas, question the sense in pursuing the idea in the foreseeable future.

### B

Scientists largely agree about reintroducing wolves into wilderness areas: by preying on deer and other vegetation-destroying animals, wolves help create conditions for various tree and plant species to prosper, which then attracts a greater variety of wildlife. All this happens at little expense. Even the cost of monitoring the wolves and compensating farmers for any livestock killed can be offset by growth in revenue from tourism as visitors are attracted by the opportunity to observe wolves in their wild habitat. The fact is, however, that Scotland is not ready for wolves. It is a relatively small country with many sheep farmers horrified by the idea that their flocks could be vulnerable to wolf attacks. The Scottish countryside is also heavily used by recreational walkers, climbers and fishing enthusiasts, most of whom would surely feel uncomfortable at the thought of carrying out their hobbies in the company of wolves.

### C

Scotland is currently home to large numbers of red deer which over-graze and prevent native trees and other plants from growing. Each year, many deer have to be culled, but wolves, if re-introduced, would keep the deer population down naturally, leading to reforestation and greater biodiversity. We know this because of wolf reintroduction programmes in the USA. Comparative studies suggest that similar schemes would be eminently feasible in parts of Scotland. Monitoring wolf packs to ensure they were not a threat to farms and the general public would, of course, require funding, but there would almost certainly be a rise in tourism in areas with wolves, which would probably mean a net economic gain. Realistically, we will not see wolves reintroduced into Scotland any time soon, largely because of opposition from the powerful Scottish farming lobby, but surveys indicate a majority of Scottish citizens would actually be in favour.

### D

The impression is sometimes given that wolves are a natural feature of the Scottish landscape and if reintroduced would restore the environment to some original, ideal condition. The fact is, however, that there have been no wolves in Scotland for 300 years and in that time, the country's ecosystem has been transformed. To introduce wolves would effectively mean bringing in an alien species. It is always difficult to know precisely what impact non-native species will have on a particular ecosystem, but in many instances – rats are a classic example in many parts of the world – huge damage has been caused, with considerable economic consequences. Why take a risk in Scotland where the farming sector is going through hard times as it is? It would be far more sensible to focus on looking after species we already have than to get involved in an over-ambitious project involving a potentially dangerous, though glamorous, animal.

## Which writer

| | | |
|---|---|---|
| has a different opinion from the others about the environmental impact of reintroducing wolves? | **37** | |
| takes a similar view to A regarding public attitudes to the idea of reintroducing wolves? | **38** | |
| shares D's opinion about the economic implications of reintroducing wolves? | **39** | |
| takes a different view from the others regarding Scotland's suitability as a place for reintroducing wolves? | **40** | |

| PAPER 1 Reading and ▶ | Part 1 |
| Use of English | Part 2 |
| | Part 3 |
| PAPER 2 Writing | Part 4 |
| PAPER 3 Listening | Part 5 |
| | Part 6 |
| PAPER 4 Speaking | **Part 7** |
| | Part 8 |

You are going to read a magazine article about one of the largest trees in the world. Six paragraphs have been removed from the article. Choose from the paragraphs **A–G** the one which fits each gap (**41–46**). There is one extra paragraph which you do not need to use.

Mark your answers **on the separate answer sheet**.

# A giant tree

*Sequoia National Park in southern California in the USA is the home of some of the largest trees in the world.*

On a gentle slope in Sequoia National Park, over 2,000 metres above sea level, looms a very big tree. Its trunk is rusty red, thickened with deep layers of bark, and 8.25 metres in diameter at the base. It has a name, The President, bestowed about 90 years ago by admirers. This giant sequoia is one of several surviving species of redwoods. Recent research by scientist Steve Sillett of Humboldt State University and his colleagues has confirmed that The President ranks as the second largest among all big trees that have ever been measured.

**41** [ ]

Trees grow tall and wide-topped as a means of competing with other trees, racing upward, reaching outward for sunlight and water. And a tree doesn't stop getting larger – as a land mammal does, or a bird, their size constrained by gravity – once it's mature. A tree too is constrained by gravity, but not in the same way as a giraffe or a condor.

**42** [ ]

They achieve this longevity because they have survived all the threats that could have killed them. They're too strong to be knocked over by wind. Their heartwood and bark are infused with acids and other chemicals that protect against fungal rot. Wood-boring insects hardly bother them. Their thick bark is flame resistant.

**43** [ ]

Another factor that can end the lives of big trees, of course, is logging. Many giant sequoias fell to the axe during the late nineteenth and early twentieth

centuries. But the wood of the old giants was so brittle that trunks often shattered when they hit the ground, and what remained had little value as timber for construction work. It went into fence posts, stakes to support plants, and other scrappy products.

**44** [ ]

Among the striking discoveries made by Sillett's team is that even the rate of growth of a big tree, not just its height or total volume, can increase during old age. An elderly monster like The President actually lays down more new wood per year than a robust young tree. It puts that wood around the trunk, which grows wider, and into the limbs and the branches, which grow thicker.

**45** [ ]

They were given National Park Service permission to do this as part of a larger, long-term monitoring project on giant sequoias and coast redwoods called the Redwoods and Climate Change Initiative. Sillett's group put a line over The President's crown, rigged climbing ropes into position, donned harnesses and helmets, and started to climb.

**46** [ ]

That's how they came to know that The President contains at least 124,000 cubic metres of wood and bark. And that's how they detected that the old beast, at about the age of 3,200, is still growing quickly. It's still inhaling great breaths of carbon dioxide and converting the carbon in a growing season interrupted by six months of cold and snow. Not bad for an oldster.

**A** As they did so, they measured the trunk at different heights, limbs and branches; they counted cones; they took core samples. Then they fed the numbers through mathematical models informed by additional data from other giant sequoias.

**B** Ground fires, in fact, are good for sequoia populations, burning away competitors, opening sequoia cones and allowing seedlings to get started. Lightning hurts the big adults but usually doesn't kill them. So they grow older and bigger across the millennia.

**C** That's the remarkable thing, Sillett told me. 'Half the year, they're not growing. They're in the snow.' They grow bigger than their biggest cousins, the coast redwoods, even with a shorter growing season.

**D** It doesn't need to move around, unlike them, and fortifies itself by continually adding more wood. Given the constant imperative of seeking resources from the sky and the soil, and with sufficient time, a tree can become huge and keep growing. Giant sequoias are gigantic because they are extremely old.

**E** This finding contradicts a long-held premise in forest ecology – that wood production declines in the latter years of a tree's life. That premise may hold true for some trees, but not for sequoias. Sillett and his team have disproved it by doing something earlier forest ecologists didn't: climbing all over the trees and measuring every centimetre of them.

**F** Given the difficulties of dealing with six-metre-thick logs, broken or unbroken, the trees were hardly worth cutting. Sequoia National Park was established in 1890, and automobile tourism soon showed that giant sequoias were worth more alive.

**G** Sillett's team has surveyed quite a few. It isn't as tall as the tallest of coast redwoods or certain species of eucalyptus in Australia, but height isn't everything; it has greater mass than any coast redwood or eucalyptus. Its dead spire, blasted by lightning, rises to 75 metres. Its four great limbs, each as big as a sizeable tree, elbow outward from the trunk around halfway up, billowing into a thick crown. The President holds nearly two billion leaves.

PAPER 1 Reading and ▶ Use of English

PAPER 2 Writing

PAPER 3 Listening

PAPER 4 Speaking

Part 1
Part 2
Part 3
Part 4
Part 5
Part 6
Part 7
**Part 8**

You are going to read an article in which scientists talk about being inspired to take up science. For questions **47–56**, choose from the scientists (**A–D**). The scientists may be chosen more than once.

Mark your answers **on the separate answer sheet.**

## Which scientist

| | |
|---|---|
| appreciates the respect shown them by teachers? | **47** |
| claims to have studied science for the wrong reasons? | **48** |
| took a long time to understand an important aspect of their subject? | **49** |
| takes inspiration from the history of science? | **50** |
| regrets not having had a good science teacher as a young person? | **51** |
| was attracted by the idea that science can be used to do good? | **52** |
| suggests that learning science can require a lot of imagination? | **53** |
| sees the need to give students something missing in their own early education? | **54** |
| gave up a good job for the sake of scientific interests? | **55** |
| had to overcome disapproval to build a career in science? | **56** |

# Being inspired to take up science

## A  Dominique Laver

As a child, what most appealed to me was finding things out for myself through experimentation and observation. One of the most striking things about science at school, however, was having to suspend my disbelief; science lessons transported me and my friends from the everyday world to that of atoms, molecules, proteins and cells – a world in many ways more fantastical than works of fiction, yet one that could help explain why things are as they are. There's a mental leap to make there, and one I hope schools still inspire pupils to attempt. I qualified and worked as a vet, but, after a few years, I felt compelled to investigate the differences between animal brains and behaviour and those of humans. So, not without certain reservations, I left a thriving practice to pursue these questions. Part of the appeal of what I currently do is the ready access to scientific libraries. The idea that the books surrounding me contain the work of generations of scientists, collectively labouring to produce an ever better understanding of how the world works, fills me with awe and optimism.

## B  Graham Sterne

At primary school, one teacher mentioned the word *science* occasionally, but then at secondary school I studied the standard physics, chemistry and biology and immediately found them fascinating. I was particularly filled with amazement at the incredible complexity of biological systems. Where I came from, you left school at the first opportunity to earn a living, and when it became clear that, encouraged by a teacher who saw something in me, I was set on going to university and wouldn't be contributing to the family budget anytime soon, I faced considerable suspicion and resentment. In those days, science was largely taught as facts, and although I forged a successful career working in the pharmaceutical industry, it was years before something fundamental really sank in – that science is about a method as much as facts. This realisation came to me after an intensive period reading books by such contemporary scientific thinkers as Carl Sagan, Richard Feynman and Charles Medawar.

## C  Omar Said

I grew up in a time when the promise of science and technology was difficult to avoid. It offered a sense of certainty that the world can not only be understood, but also enhanced. Unfortunately, this general sense of optimism seems to have dissipated somewhat. At school, and then at university, I had tutors who treated me as though I could make sense of everything they knew about science – its past, present and future. There was never any sense of being talked down to, for which I am very grateful. The one thing I regret was that practical experimentation seldom featured, certainly at school. It may have been a simple question of resources, but, in my own work in physics, I have always tried to explain things from first principles, in the belief that I am giving people a chance to work physics out for themselves, and the one lesson I really try to get across is that scientific theory is nothing unless backed up by experimental evidence.

## D  Stefan Helder

I took sciences at school, not because I excelled at them, but because I was hopeless at the arts and humanities. Yet despite this rather dim view of my early years and the trigger for what I have ended up doing, I can now see that I was always a systemiser. I loved stripping down my motorbike to see how it worked and I also loved making things. But I did badly at school, – to the disappointment of my parents – didn't go to university and never really thought about science for years. Yet I always felt I could do more with my life than the unconventional series of jobs I found myself doing. Then, via a series of fortuitous events, I landed a research job at a hospital. From there, I eventually fought my way onto a PhD in radiology, and this was when I really began to grasp what science could be. Looking back, I feel that the spur for me going into science, rather than some inspirational educator – if only it had been, my route would have been less circuitous – or TV role model, was probably my own innate traits.

PAPER 1 Reading and
        Use of English

**PAPER 2 Writing** ▶ **Part 1**

Part 2

PAPER 3 Listening

PAPER 4 Speaking

You **must** answer this question. Write your answer in **220–260** words in an appropriate style on the separate answer sheet.

---

**1** During a recent class discussion about the world's worst inventions, the lecturer shared her own opinion with the class. She said that the mobile phone was the worst invention and she provided several reasons for this view. You have made the notes below.

> **The mobile phone: the world's worst invention**
>
> - A sense of courtesy has been lost as people continually conduct loud conversations in public places.
> - People have forgotten how to experience the world and observe what's going on around them as they are constantly staring at their mobile phones.
> - Some studies show that excessive use of mobile phones can be a hazard to our health.

> **Other students expressed these opinions:**
>
> "Mobile phones come in very handy when you're meeting people and need to let them know you'll be late."
>
> "The GPS function on mobiles makes it easy to find your way around new towns and cities."
>
> "The built-in camera allows us to take photos of interesting or important images everywhere we go."

Write an essay for your tutor discussing **two** of the points from your notes. You should **explain whether you think the mobile phone is a good or bad invention** and **provide reasons** to support your opinions.

You may, if you wish, make use of the opinions expressed in the lecture, but you should use your own words as far as possible.

PAPER 1  Reading and
         Use of English

PAPER 2  Writing ▶      Part 1

PAPER 3  Listening      Part 2

PAPER 4  Speaking

Write an answer to **one** of the questions **2–4** in this part. Write your answer in **220–260** words in an appropriate style on the separate answer sheet. Put the question number in the box at the top of the page.

2   The vice president of a local IT firm agreed to show you around the company office. She introduced you to three of the managers, who each explained to you what their department does. The following day you decide to write a letter to the vice president to thank her.

   Write your **letter.**

3   You see this pop-up ad on your local tourist information office website.

   > Here at Happy Trails we are working on a new travel guide for visitors to your area. We need the latest information on all forms of entertainment currently on offer in your town. If you would like to contribute to this chapter, please send a report describing the options available.

   Write your **report.**

4   You went to a new recently-opened restaurant with your family to celebrate your father's 50th birthday. Based on this visit, write a review of the restaurant

   Write your **review.**

PAPER 1  Reading and
         Use of English

PAPER 2  Writing

PAPER 3  Listening ▶   Part 1
                      Part 2
                      Part 3
                      Part 4

PAPER 4  Speaking

🎧 **Track 21**

You will hear three different extracts. For questions **1–6**, choose the answer (**A**, **B** or **C**) which fits best according to what you hear. There are two questions for each extract.

**Extract One**

You hear two friends discussing reality TV.

**1**    Why is the woman surprised that the man is watching reality TV?
    **A**   She feels he should be studying for his psychology exams.
    **B**   She thinks he's too intelligent to bother with reality TV.
    **C**   She knows this reality TV programme gets on his nerves.

**2**    The man thinks that reality TV is
    **A**   ridiculous.
    **B**   irritating.
    **C**   very funny.

**Extract Two**

You hear a conversation between two people who meet at a teachers' conference.

**3**    How long has the woman been a teacher?
    **A**   less than a year
    **B**   a few years
    **C**   one full year

**4**    What difficulty is the woman having?
    **A**   She thinks she may have picked the wrong career.
    **B**   She finds the amount of preparation challenging.
    **C**   She feels there are too many students in her classes.

**Extract Three**

You hear two college students discussing where they prefer to study.

**5**    The man is on his way to
    **A**   the library.
    **B**   meet his flatmates.
    **C**   study at home.

**6**    Why doesn't the woman study at home?
    **A**   She finds it too noisy there.
    **B**   She'd find other things to do.
    **C**   She doesn't trust her flatmates.

PAPER 1  Reading and
          Use of English
PAPER 2  Writing
PAPER 3  Listening  ▶
          Part 1
          **Part 2**
          Part 3
          Part 4
PAPER 4  Speaking

**Track 22**

You will hear a speaker called Terry Carville informing a group of students about the *fair trade* movement. For questions **7–14**, complete the sentences with a word or short phrase.

# THE FAIR TRADE MOVEMENT

The problem for small farmers in poorer countries is that importers can buy goods more cheaply from (**7**) ......................................................... .

The fair trade movement provides a more (**8**) ......................................................... way of life for poor farmers and farm workers.

The speaker reassures the audience that, mostly, fair trade goods and those produced in the UK are not in (**9**) ......................................................... .

When UK (**10**) ......................................................... for a particular item are higher than the local supply, fair trade goods make up the difference.

Terry Carville feels that the percentage of fair trade coffee consumed in the UK is (**11**) ......................................................... .

He brought leaflets for students to pass along to managers of supermarkets and cafés that (**12**) ......................................................... fair trade goods.

Participants in the fair trade university and college project organise campaigns to (**13**) ......................................................... of the movement.

They also put more (**14**) ......................................................... measures in place, such as making sure that fair trade goods can be purchased at their university.

PAPER 1 Reading and
          Use of English

PAPER 2 Writing

PAPER 3 Listening ▶

PAPER 4 Speaking

Part 1
Part 2
**Part 3**
Part 4

🎧 **Track 23**

You will hear a phone conversation between a successful actor called Annabel and a teenager called Maurice, who is considering studying drama. For questions **15–20**, choose the answer (**A**, **B**, **C** or **D**) which fits best according to what you hear.

___

**15** Why is Maurice uncertain about applying to study drama at university?
    **A**   He knows he wants to be very rich and famous.
    **B**   He's not taking his college applications seriously.
    **C**   He's worried about not having a regular income.
    **D**   He's concerned that Annabel will be offended.

**16** Why did Annabel stop studying art?
    **A**   She didn't find it interesting or exciting enough.
    **B**   She wanted to return home to Northern Ireland.
    **C**   She felt very passionate about studying drama.
    **D**   She was determined not to do anything risky.

**17** How did Annabel feel about her application to the Royal Academy of Dramatic Art?
    **A**   She fully expected to be accepted because she believed in herself.
    **B**   She was sure she wouldn't be accepted but decided to try anyway.
    **C**   She felt she had a good chance of being accepted, but wasn't certain.
    **D**   She didn't expect to be accepted, but she was committed to trying.

**18** Annabel says that her favourite kind of work is in
    **A**   television.
    **B**   films.
    **C**   the theatre.
    **D**   schools.

**19** What is Annabel's main message to Maurice?
    **A**   Working in theatre is the best job in the world.
    **B**   Acting is hard work and only barely pays the bills.
    **C**   It's wonderful, but be prepared for difficult times.
    **D**   The career is very uncertain so try something else.

**20** Based on what he says, is it likely that Maurice will apply to do theatre studies?
    **A**   He doesn't say.
    **B**   Yes, it's very likely.
    **C**   It's not that unlikely.
    **D**   He has no idea yet.

PAPER 1  Reading and
            Use of English

PAPER 2  Writing

PAPER 3  Listening  ▶

PAPER 4  Speaking

Part 1
Part 2
Part 3
Part 4

🎧 **Track 24**

You will hear five short extracts in which people talk about their favourite subject when they were at school.

**While you listen you must complete both tasks.**

**TASK ONE**

For questions **21–25**, choose from the list (**A–H**) what each speaker enjoyed about that subject.

| | | |
|---|---|---|
| **A** | the analytical aspect of it | |
| **B** | all of the mysteries in it | Speaker 1    21 |
| **C** | learning about our ancestors | Speaker 2    22 |
| **D** | its creative use of language | Speaker 3    23 |
| **E** | the sense of fun in it | Speaker 4    24 |
| **F** | how reliable the subject is | Speaker 5    25 |
| **G** | how complicated it is | |
| **H** | that it encourages self-expression | |

**TASK TWO**

For questions **26–30**, choose from the list (**A–H**) what each speaker does or plans to do for a living.

| | | |
|---|---|---|
| **A** | secondary school teacher | |
| **B** | researcher | Speaker 1    26 |
| **C** | archaeologist | Speaker 2    27 |
| **D** | accountant | Speaker 3    28 |
| **E** | author | Speaker 4    29 |
| **F** | graphic designer | Speaker 5    30 |
| **G** | professor of poetry | |
| **H** | fashion designer | |

PAPER 1 Reading and
         Use of English

PAPER 2 Writing

PAPER 3 Listening

PAPER 4 Speaking

## Part 1 (2 minutes)

The examiner will ask you a few questions about yourself and about a general topic. For example, the examiner may ask you:

- **Do you like cooking? Why (not)?**
- **What is your favourite kind of food?**
- **What type of climate do you like best? Why?**

## Part 2 (4 minutes)

You will each be asked to talk on your own for about a minute. You will each be given three different pictures to talk about. After your partner has finished speaking, you will be asked a brief question connected with your partner's photographs.

> **Medical traditions** (compare, contrast and speculate)

Turn to pictures 1–3 on page **184**, which show different medical practices.

(*Candidate A*), it's your turn first. Here are your pictures. They show **different kinds of medical practitioners.**

I'd like you to compare **two** of the pictures and say **what kind of medical condition each one might treat and what cultural differences there are between these medical practices.**

(*Candidate B*), **what kind of character traits do you think a medical practitioner needs to have? Why?**

> **Places of learning** (compare, contrast and speculate)

Turn to pictures 1–3 on page **185**, which show different kinds of classrooms.

Now, (*Candidate B*), here are your pictures. They show **different places of learning.**

I'd like you to compare **two** of the pictures and say **how these places of learning are different and what they have in common.**

(*Candidate A*), **do you think people have a better learning experience if they have access to technology? Why (not)?**

## Part 3 (4 minutes)

Look at page **186**, which shows some things people can do to cope with homesickness and culture shock.

> **Coping with homesickness and culture shock** (discuss, evaluate and negotiate)

**Here are some things people can do to cope with homesickness and culture shock.**

First, you have some time to look at the task.

(*Pause 15 seconds*)

Now talk to each other about **how these steps can help to cope with homesickness and culture shock.**

Now you have a minute to decide **what you think is the most effective thing people can do to combat homesickness and culture shock, and why.**

## Part 4 (5 minutes)

The examiner will encourage you to develop the topic of your discussion in Part 3 by asking questions such as:

- Do you think that certain types of people are more likely to experience culture shock and feel homesick, or can anyone be affected by these conditions?
- Does the internet make it any easier to live far from your home country? How?

| PAPER 1 | Reading and ▶ | Part 1 |
| | Use of English | Part 2 |
| PAPER 2 | Writing | Part 3 |
| | | Part 4 |
| PAPER 3 | Listening | Part 5 |
| PAPER 4 | Speaking | Part 6 |
| | | Part 7 |
| | | Part 8 |

For questions **1–8**, read the text below and decide which answer (**A, B, C** or **D**) best fits each gap. There is an example at the beginning (**0**).

Mark your answers **on the separate answer sheet**.

**Example:**

**0**  **A**  desire        **B**  mood        **C**  feel        **D**  condition

```
0 | A   B   C   D
    ‿   ▃   ‿   ‿
```

# Pop music – how does it make you feel?

Are you ever in the (**0**) ........ for a happy, up-tempo pop song? If you're American and happen to hear one on the radio, the (**1**) ........ are it was recorded quite a long time ago, according to a (**2**) ........ study carried out by scientists from universities in Canada and Germany. Glenn Schellenberg and Christian von Scheve (**3**) ........ to examine emotions conveyed by music in the American pop charts between 1965 and 2009. They classified songs according to pace and the key they were composed in.

People generally (**4**) ........ faster songs in a major key with happy feelings, and slower songs in a minor key with darker emotions. (**5**) ........ speaking, in the 1960s, the charts were dominated by upbeat music, but over the next five decades it (**6**) ........ to a more melancholic, complicated sound. Intriguingly, in the last decade, the (**7**) ........ of emotionally ambiguous songs (sad-sounding but fast, or happy-sounding but slow) has significantly increased.

The researchers believe these trends may give interesting (**8**) ........ into more general social changes. They speculate, for instance, that people may now engage with more varied emotions.

| | | | | | | | |
|---|---|---|---|---|---|---|---|
| **1** | **A** prospects | **B** chances | **C** bets | **D** outlooks |
| **2** | **A** mutual | **B** tied | **C** joint | **D** coupled |
| **3** | **A** aimed on | **B** kicked off | **C** took up | **D** set out |
| **4** | **A** associate | **B** fit | **C** attach | **D** correspond |
| **5** | **A** Broadly | **B** Largely | **C** Primarily | **D** Widely |
| **6** | **A** translated | **B** swapped | **C** removed | **D** shifted |
| **7** | **A** degree | **B** proportion | **C** dimension | **D** measure |
| **8** | **A** regards | **B** revelations | **C** visions | **D** insights |

| PAPER 1 | Reading and ▸ | Part 1 |
| | Use of English | **Part 2** |
| PAPER 2 | Writing | Part 3 |
| | | Part 4 |
| PAPER 3 | Listening | Part 5 |
| PAPER 4 | Speaking | Part 6 |
| | | Part 7 |
| | | Part 8 |

For questions **9–16**, read the text below and think of the word which best fits each gap. Use only one word in each gap. There is an example at the beginning (**0**).

Write your answers **IN CAPITAL LETTERS on the separate answer sheet.**

**Example:**  0  W H Y ⬜⬜⬜⬜⬜⬜⬜⬜⬜⬜⬜⬜⬜⬜⬜⬜⬜

# The sound of babies crying

Have you ever wondered (**0**) …….. it is so hard to ignore the sound of a crying baby? (**9**) …….. who has found themselves on a plane or train next to a baby in distress will recognise the feeling. Research by Dr Katie Young and Dr Christine Parsons from Oxford University suggests that our brains are programmed to respond strongly to the sound, no (**10**) …….. how hard we try to block it out.

The researchers subjected 30 people (**11**) …….. recordings of babies and adults crying as well as various animal distress noises, (**12**) …….. them dogs whining and cats mewing, and scanned the listeners' brains. The scans revealed that participants' brains responded quickly to all the noises, but only processed significant amounts of emotion in the (**13**) …….. of the babies' cries. Not a single (**14**) …….. of the participants was a parent, yet they all responded in the same way.

The researchers suggest that this brain activity is highly (**15**) …….. to be 'a fundamental response present in all of us', (**16**) …….. of parental status, something perhaps to consider when you are next trapped with a screaming infant.

| PAPER 1 | Reading and Use of English ▸ | Part 1 |
|---------|------------------------------|--------|
| | | Part 2 |
| PAPER 2 | Writing | **Part 3** |
| | | Part 4 |
| PAPER 3 | Listening | Part 5 |
| | | Part 6 |
| PAPER 4 | Speaking | Part 7 |
| | | Part 8 |

For questions **17–24**, read the text below. Use the word given in capitals at the end of some of the lines to form a word that fits in the gap **in the same line**. There is an example at the beginning (**0**).

Write your answers **IN CAPITAL LETTERS on the separate answer sheet.**

**Example:** | 0 | R | E | A | S | O | N | A | B | L | E | | | | | | | |

# Can roads help nature?

It is (**0**) …….. to assume that roads, generally, are not very
good for nature, and there is good evidence to support
this assumption. Scientists William Laurance and Andrew
Balmford point out, for example, that '95% of (**17**) ……..., fires
and atmospheric carbon (**18**) …….. in the Brazilian Amazon
occur within 50 kilometres of a road.' One hundred thousand
kilometres of roads now criss-cross the Amazon, and road-
building there continues, often (**19**) …….. contravening
environmental laws.

**REASON**

**FOREST**
**EMIT**

**LEGAL**

However, Laurance and Balmford believe that roads can
be environmentally (**20**) …….. . In agricultural areas where
forests have already been cleared, good roads ease access
to markets, which improves the (**21**) …….. and profitability
of farms, and tends to encourage people to stay away from
vulnerable wilderness. Laurance and Balmford propose a
worldwide project to establish which areas should not have
roads and which areas governments should (**22**) …….. for
road improvement. They believe a scheme of this kind could
(**23**) …….. the damage roads cause. It would be challenging,
but, in Laurance and Balmford's view, influencing road
development is (**24**) …….. more practical and cost-effective
than any other measure currently deployed to protect crucial
ecosystems.

**BENEFIT**

**EFFICIENT**

**PRIORITY**

**LESS**

**QUESTIONABLE**

PAPER 1 Reading and ▶ Use of English

Part 1
Part 2
Part 3
**Part 4**
Part 5
Part 6
Part 7
Part 8

PAPER 2 Writing

PAPER 3 Listening

PAPER 4 Speaking

For questions **25–30**, complete the second sentence so that it has a similar meaning to the first sentence, using the word given. **Do not change the word given.** You must use between **three** and **six** words, including the word given. Here is an example (**0**).

**Example:**

**0**  Chloe would only eat a pizza if she could have a mushroom topping.

**ON**

Chloe .......................................... a mushroom topping when she had a pizza.

The gap can be filled with the words 'insisted on having', so you write:

**Example:** | **0** | INSISTED ON HAVING |

Write **only** the missing words **IN CAPITAL LETTERS on the separate answer sheet.**

25   My boss says he has no intention of making anyone redundant, even though the situation is difficult for the company right now.

**DREAM**

My boss says he ........................................... off, even though the situation is difficult for the company right now.

26   They say New York was a rather aggressive city 20 years ago but it feels quite friendly these days.

**SUPPOSED**

New York ........................................... a rather aggressive city 20 years ago but it feels quite friendly these days.

27   Jenny was the person who really didn't want to tidy up after the party.

**OBJECTED**

It ........................................... up after the party.

28   The new software isn't the main point for discussion tomorrow, but should anyone raise the subject by any chance, I'll give my views.

**HAPPENS**

The new software isn't the main point for discussion tomorrow, but if the ........................................... up by anyone, I'll give my views.

29   'As we climb higher, it gets harder to breathe,' our guide warned us at the start of the trek.

**THE**

Our guide warned us that the higher ........................................... get.

30   Only when Yoshi was promoted to his new job did he realise how much he was appreciated by his colleagues.

**UNTIL**

It ........................................... his new job that he realised how much he was appreciated by his colleagues.

PAPER 1   Reading and ▶   Part 1
            Use of English      Part 2
PAPER 2  Writing             Part 3
                             Part 4
PAPER 3  Listening          **Part 5**
PAPER 4  Speaking           Part 6
                             Part 7
                             Part 8

You are going to read an article about music and mathematics. For questions **31–36**, choose the answer (**A**, **B**, **C** or **D**) which you think fits best according to the text.

Mark your answers **on the separate answer sheet**.

# Maths and music

*Mathematician Tim Gowers is also a keen musician.*

An excellent way to kill a conversation is to say you are a mathematician. Tell your interlocutor you are also a musician, however, and they will be hooked. Even people who know nothing about mathematics have heard the counter-intuitive notion that mathematical ability is connected to musical ability. As a mathematician with strong musical interests, I have been asked about this many times. Bad news: although there are some obvious similarities between mathematical and musical activity, there is (as yet) no compelling evidence for the kind of mysterious, magical connection many people seem to believe in.

I'm partly referring here to the 'Mozart effect', where children who have been played Mozart compositions are supposedly more intelligent, including at mathematics, than other children. It is not hard to see why such a theory would be popular: we would all like to become better at maths without putting in any effort. But the actual conclusions of the experiment that originally prompted the belief in the Mozart effect were much more modest and remain grossly exaggerated. If you want your brain to work better, then you clearly have to put in hard graft.

But what about learning to play the piano? That takes effort. Could the rewards for that spill over into other areas of intellectual life? Is there any evidence that people who have worked hard at music are better at maths than people who are unmusical? And conversely, are mathematicians objectively better than average at music?

Firstly, there are plenty of innumerate musicians and tone-deaf mathematicians, so the best one could hope to identify would be a significant positive correlation between aptitudes. Then one would try to establish a statistical connection. So, if you want to show that professional mathematicians are on average better at music than other people, you have to decide quite carefully who those 'other people' are. You might expect that a professional mathematician is much more likely than average to come from a family where music was regarded as important, so for that reason alone one would expect at least some 'background correlation´ between the two. Therefore, not much will be proved if you compare professional mathematicians with the wider population.

But surely a connection is at least plausible. Both mathematics and music deal with abstract structures, so if you become good at one, then it is plausible that you become good at something more general – handling abstract structures – that helps you with the other. If this is correct, then it would show a connection between mathematical and musical ability, though not a mysterious one. It would be more like the connection between abilities at football and tennis. To become better at one of those you need to improve your fitness and coordination. That makes you better at sport and probably helps with the other.

Of course, abstract structures are not confined to mathematics and music. If you are learning a foreign language then you need to understand its grammar and syntax, prime examples of abstract structures. Yet we don't hear people asking about a mysterious connection between mathematical and linguistic ability. My guess is this is because grammar feels mathematical, so it would hardly be surprising to learn that mathematicians were better than average at learning grammar. Music, by contrast, is strongly tied up with emotions and can be enjoyed even by people who know very little about it. As such, it seems very different from mathematics, so any connection between the two is appealingly paradoxical.

To dispel this air of paradox, let's look at how we solve problems of the 'A is to B as C is to D' kind. These appear in intelligence tests (car is to garage as aircraft is to what?) but they are also central to both music and mathematics. Consider, for instance, the opening of Mozart's *Eine Kleine Nachtmusik*. The second phrase is a clear answer to the first. The listener thinks: 'The first phrase goes broadly upwards and uses the notes of a G major chord; what would be the corresponding phrase that goes broadly downwards and uses the notes of a D7?' Music is full of little puzzles like this. If you are good at them, when you listen to music, expectations will constantly be set up in your mind. Some of the best moments in music come when one's expectations are confounded, but we need the expectations in the first place.

**31** What does the writer suggest in the first paragraph?

    **A** Musicians tend to be more popular than mathematicians.

    **B** Mathematicians have a reputation for being uncommunicative.

    **C** The attraction musicians often feel for mathematics is well-known.

    **D** The relationship between music and maths is a frequent source of fascination.

**32** What does the writer say about the experiment referred to in the second paragraph?

    **A** The findings drawn from it have been misinterpreted.

    **B** The way it was carried out has been discredited.

    **C** The objectives set out for it were ill-considered.

    **D** The interest aroused by it was unexpected.

**33** The writer's main intention in the fourth paragraph is to outline how connections between maths and music could be

    **A** exemplified by certain people.

    **B** explored most effectively.

    **C** difficult to demonstrate.

    **D** useful to investigate.

**34** What is the writer emphasising with the reference to football and tennis in the fifth paragraph?

    **A** why the idea that music and maths have something in common is reasonable

    **B** how music and maths both have their practical sides

    **C** what is meant by the notion of abstract structures

    **D** how certain skills are developed through practice

**35** What does the writer suggest in the sixth paragraph?

    **A** The structure of language is easier to understand than the structure of music.

    **B** Mathematicians have been proved to be good at language learning.

    **C** Languages generally hold less of an attraction than music.

    **D** Music may be no closer to maths than language is.

**36** What is the writer's main intention in the seventh paragraph?

    **A** to illustrate how music ultimately differs from maths

    **B** to show how abstract thinking applies to both music and maths

    **C** to explain why Mozart is so highly considered by mathematicians

    **D** to describe the mathematical processes composers may engage in

PAPER 1 Reading and ▶
        Use of English

PAPER 2 Writing

PAPER 3 Listening

PAPER 4 Speaking

Part 1
Part 2
Part 3
Part 4
Part 5
**Part 6**
Part 7
Part 8

You are going to read four reviews of a book about teenagers. For questions **37–40**, choose from the reviews **A–D**. The reviews may be chosen more than once.

Mark your answers **on the separate answer sheet**.

# *Teenagers: A Natural History* by David Bainbridge

*We all go through adolescence. Four reviewers share their thoughts about scientist David Bainbridge's book exploring what goes on at this important stage of our lives, and why it is as it is.*

**A**

To anybody exposed to teenagers swinging between extremes of energy and laziness, there is an obvious appeal in scientific explanations of their behaviour. The finely-judged tone of David Bainbridge's language – neither over-technical nor patronisingly simple – only adds to the attraction. Closer inspection, however, induces misgivings. Bainbridge traces the roots of much modern teenage behaviour to biological and psychological developments thousands of years ago. The notion that speculation about our distant origins can provide answers to questions about personal development and social relationships today is far too simplistic. Bainbridge dismisses the notion that the teenager is a modern social phenomenon, but some attention to the influences that have transformed adolescent experience over recent decades would be far more fruitful than trying to explain people in terms of pre-historic life. Popular psychology can be very worthwhile, but this book tells us little about how to raise young people or deal with their difficulties.

**B**

Humans take much longer to mature than any other animal, and David Bainbridge suggests this may be a crucial distinguishing feature because it gives our brains time to develop. This intriguing idea, together with accounts of how physiology and brain activity change as we go through adolescence, is communicated with enviable lucidity. Unfortunately, Bainbridge undermines the effect by repeatedly invoking hypotheses about pre-historic human development to understand specifics of teenagers today. The plausibility of various notions – for example, that risk-taking is 'built into' adolescence because of the survival requirements 300,000 years ago – relies more on wish-fulfilment than science. There is no attempt either to engage with the broader social, political and philosophical contexts within which teenagers develop; always crucial, surely. Despite such reservations, the insights provided into the chemical and physiological changes adolescents go through should definitely cause adults to think about how to respond to their moods and apparently chaotic behaviour.

**C**

Why will the average 15-year-old grumpily roll out of bed at two o'clock in the afternoon? David Bainbridge offers no-nonsense biological explanations to questions such as these: 'the terrible triangle of laziness, risk-taking and anger' reflects consistent reorganisations in the adolescent brain. What is more, Bainbridge draws on anthropology and psychology to show how many of the changes adolescent bodies and brains go through are the result of developments somewhere between 800,000 and three million years ago. Although Bainbridge can sometimes be irritatingly informal – the subject is inherently interesting and does not need any jazzing up or dumbing down – these explanations are coherent and persuasive. Where the book does fall down is in a failure to explore the external context within which modern teenagers move from childhood to adulthood. He is strangely silent, for example, on the impact on teenagers of new technologies such as computer games and the internet.

**D**

David Bainbridge believes that extended adolescence in humans may have been the spur 250,000 years ago to the final phase in the expansion of the human brain; adolescence gives us time to learn and increase our brain power. This fascinating idea, together with compelling explanations about how we can trace many of the transformations, physical and psychological, that modern teenagers go through back to human development in pre-history, are all delivered in fresh, amusing and intelligible prose. In some ways, it is reassuring to find out that certain patterns of behaviour are largely hardwired in teenagers, rather than determined by the way they are brought up, the relationships they have with the people around them and so on. Anyone who has witnessed how dramatically young people can change as they enter adolescence will appreciate how convincing this idea is, and worried parents should find comfort and inspiration in Bainbridge's central theme that supporting children and teenagers is what adults are really for.

## Which reviewer

expresses a different view from the others about
the importance of social factors for understanding
teenage behaviour?

**37** ▢

shares B's opinion on the use of ideas about ancient
human development to explain modern teenagers?

**38** ▢

has a different opinion from the others about the style
of writing in the book?

**39** ▢

takes a similar view to D regarding the book's value
for people responsible for teenagers?

**40** ▢

| PAPER 1 Reading and | Part 1 |
| Use of English | Part 2 |
| PAPER 2 Writing | Part 3 |
| | Part 4 |
| PAPER 3 Listening | Part 5 |
| PAPER 4 Speaking | Part 6 |
| | **Part 7** |
| | Part 8 |

You are going to read a magazine article about chimpanzees. Six paragraphs have been removed from the article. Choose from the paragraphs **A–G** the one which fits each gap (**41–46**). There is one extra paragraph which you do not need to use.

Mark your answers **on the separate answer sheet.**

# Observing how wild chimpanzees behave

*Joshu Foer visits a project in Congo in Africa where scientists can observe the behaviour of chimpanzees and other great apes which have had little or no contact with humans.*

Dave Morgan and Crickette Sanz run an ape research site in the Goualougo Triangle, a remote jungle region of Congo, virtually untouched by humanity. On a sticky September morning, Morgan, Sanz, and I leave the Goualougo base with our tracker Bosco Mangoussou and head into the forest in search of chimpanzees. Our route regularly slaloms around heaps of rotting fruit, whose pungent aromas permeate the humid air.

| 41 |

Eventually, we spot a half dozen chimps lounging in a tree about 40 metres up. This community is well-known to Morgan and Sanz, who have even named each animal. We watch through binoculars as a young female, Dinah, plays with Owen, a juvenile. Finn, the group's most powerful male, looks on. Then something remarkable happens.

| 42 |

The thumping echoes off the surrounding trees. Then she rips a small twig off a nearby branch, dips it into the hive, and swirls it around. She pulls it out, realises there's no honey on it, throws it away, and starts pounding some more. After repeating the process several times, she finally plunges her finger into a crack and yanks out a bit of honey, which goes straight into her mouth.

| 43 |

The fact that this behaviour hasn't been observed at other sites outside central Africa suggests that it is not innate to the species, but rather is a learned skill that has been culturally transmitted. Part of what makes

Dinah's behaviour so intriguing is that she used a big club and a thin twig in sequence to accomplish her goal.

| 44 |

This is what happens: an older female arrives at the rock-hard structure. She rams a thick twig into a small hole and widens it by jiggling the stick vigorously. Then she grabs a thin, flexible stem, drags the end of it through her teeth to make it wet and frayed, like a paintbrush, and then pulls it through her closed fist to straighten out the bristles. She then threads it into the same hole, pulls it out, and nibbles off a couple of bugs that cling to the frayed edges.

| 45 |

'The Goualougo is probably the only place on earth where humans will ever have the chance to see what chimpanzee culture is really about,' conservationist Michael Fay tells me later. 'Ninety-five per cent of chimps on earth don't live like this because of humans.' Chimp study sites elsewhere are surrounded by people and often affected by logging and hunting.

| 46 |

It is known that even selective logging and casual hunting can throw chimp society into disarray if it pushes groups into conflict or decreases the number of termite mounds where they can fish. Morgan and Sanz have suggested that with fewer mounds and, therefore, fewer opportunities for young chimps to learn tool techniques from their elders, chimp culture may slowly decline, and complex learned behaviours may disappear.

**A** This is a powerful and troubling notion: what if everywhere scientists have thought they were observing chimps in their natural state, they've actually been studying behaviour distorted by the presence of humans?

**B** This is the signal for Finn to make a move, seemingly outraged that a young upstart is enjoying a sugary delicacy in his presence. He lunges at Dinah, who drops her club and flees to another limb.

**C** When wild chimps encounter humans, they typically flee in panic – understandable given that the relationship between our two species has often been one of prey and predator. This reticence is part of what makes wild chimp research so difficult. These ones, however, seem unperturbed by our presence.

**D** It is the immense variety of these more than two dozen edible species, ranging from pumpkin-size Treculia africana to rubbery, soft ball-size Chrysophyllum lacourtiana, that makes the Goualougo such an attractive habitat for chimps.

**E** What's so remarkable about this is not just that some clever chimp figured out it could break a plant and use it to fish for food; it's that some other chimp figured out a way to do it even better. Morgan and Sanz have themselves tried the process with both modified and unmodified sticks and found that they collected ten times more termites with the modified tool.

**F** Noticing a cloud of bees emerging from a hole near the main trunk of the tree, Dinah leaps to her feet and breaks off a branch about the size of a human arm. With the blunt end she begins whacking the bark. She knows that somewhere inside is a hive with honey.

**G** This isn't the only form of serial tool use common in the Goualougo. As we witness the beehive attack, a camera set up near a termite mound a kilometre mile away records another chimp engaging in what may be the most sophisticated form of serial tool use by any non-human animal.

| | |
|---|---|
| **PAPER 1 Reading and Use of English** | Part 1 |
| | Part 2 |
| **PAPER 2 Writing** | Part 3 |
| | Part 4 |
| **PAPER 3 Listening** | Part 5 |
| | Part 6 |
| **PAPER 4 Speaking** | Part 7 |
| | **Part 8** |

You are going to read an article in which student nurses talk about courses they have taken online as part of their training. For questions **47–56**, choose from the people (**A–D**). The nurses may be chosen more than once.

Mark your answers **on the separate answer sheet**.

## Which student nurse

gained a better understanding of an aspect of healthcare she had always disliked?  `47`

liked the way a complicated subject was made comprehensible?  `48`

was impressed by the varied approach on the course?  `49`

appreciated being encouraged to come up with new ideas?  `50`

was initially concerned about how much the course aimed to cover?  `51`

had been worried she might be too inexperienced for the course she was taking?  `52`

was helped to reflect on aspects of her performance as a nurse?  `53`

felt inspired by the course to take a practical initiative when on a work placement?  `54`

felt reassured about aspects of her nursing work she had concerns about?  `55`

feels the course she followed fulfilled its stated objectives?  `56`

# Student nurses

*Four student nurses talk about courses they have done online as part of their degrees.*

## A  Alicia Denby

I'm in the second year of my nursing course and I recently took a module called *Leadership in Healthcare*. It was all done online, so an interesting contrast with my normal lectures, seminars and work placements. I was advised to do it by one of my lecturers, but I must admit I was initially apprehensive about it as the idea of leadership seemed more for people already in positions of responsibility and authority, rather than a student nurse. It turned out to be relevant to people across the health service, however. It was well designed with a range of activities including analysis scenarios in which leadership may play a key role; viewing short, interesting films which provided relief from the challenging reading; and regularly exchanging ideas, via different digital media, with other participants. I came away feeling much better equipped for dealing with work issues. In fact, the module gave me an idea for solving a real problem in the ward where I'm now doing a six-week practice stint.

## B  Maria dos Santos

The module I studied was called *Patient Safety* and it focused on procedural errors in the profession – why they occur and what strategies can be employed to avoid them. Impressively, the module manages to achieve its aims; it really does what it says on the tin! What I found particularly helpful was the understanding it brought about that while mistakes may be made by individuals, only the system as a whole can foster an environment where they are less likely to happen. It's precisely this environment that necessitates the number of policies and procedures that abound in the profession, which, in turn, results in the amount of dreaded paperwork we have to deal with – a need I hadn't really comprehended before. Now I approach all the documentation in a very different way. When I read the module overview, I was overwhelmed at first by the potential for problems to arise in healthcare, but by the end of the course I felt reassured that systems are in place to support staff and to provide patients with the safest healthcare possible.

## C  Maya Farsani

The module I did – *Introduction to the Culture of Safety* – explores real issues that new nurses are likely to come across. There are plenty of safety and professional guidelines we have to learn, but I'm not sure we know how to uphold them all in practice. As a third-year nursing student with several work placements under my belt, it made me consider the way I had worked and what my duty of care to the patient really is. I would hope that the attitudes of psychological safety, fairness and transparency dealt with on this course are acknowledged as standard across the clinical setting – and if they aren't, I would want to know why not. I would definitely recommend this course to any other healthcare students! The notion of a culture of safety is quite new in some ways and there's a lot to it, but I never had any sense of having to battle to get to grips with it, and I think that boils down to the quality of the module.

## D  Krystyna Blazek

I'm coming to the end of my degree now and I think what I did on the module *Quality Control in Healthcare* should prove very useful when I'm in my first proper nursing job. It highlighted the fact that the health service is a system, with many variables that affect patient outcomes, so that when an error happens, whether harm occurs or not, blame cannot be placed on an individual but is down to a failure of the system as a whole. This doesn't mean you can just pass the buck and ignore errors, but as a young nurse you have vulnerable people's well-being in your hands, and it is good to know that you're not on your own, that there is a system to monitor and support you. Apart from this, I think the course is also relevant because it shows you the importance of thinking out of the box and not becoming blinkered into believing there is only one way to do something, particularly if things are going wrong.

PAPER 1  Reading and
          Use of English

PAPER 2  Writing          ▶  Part 1
                              Part 2
PAPER 3  Listening

PAPER 4  Speaking

You **must** answer this question. Write your answer in **220–260** words in an appropriate style on the separate answer sheet.

---

**1**  During a college seminar one of your fellow students stated that the sciences are more important than the arts. You have made the notes below.

> **Science more important than art**
>
> - The creative arts are OK as a pastime, just for fun, but they are not necessary.
> - Scientific developments enable us to understand the world we live in.
> - Without the sciences we wouldn't have the knowledge required to treat medical conditions and cure diseases.

> **Other students in the seminar expressed these opinions:**
>
> "Artistic expression is what separates us from animals. Human beings have a talent and a need for art."
>
> "Through art we learn about ourselves in a way that doesn't feature in science."
>
> "Life can be stressful and difficult, but the beauty of art provides something special and vital."

Write an essay for your tutor discussing **two** of the points from your notes. You should **explain whether you think the sciences are more important** than the arts and **provide reasons** to support your opinions.

You may, if you wish, make use of the opinions expressed in the seminar, but you should use your own words as far as possible.

PAPER 1   Reading and
             Use of English

**PAPER 2   Writing**   ▶   Part 1

PAPER 3   Listening      Part 2

PAPER 4   Speaking

Write an answer to **one** of the questions **2–4** in this part. Write your answer in **220–260** words in an appropriate style on the separate answer sheet. Put the question number in the box at the top of the page.

2   You are spending the summer abroad. While you are away, your best friend from home emails you with some bad news. He has just learned that his application to the university he wanted to attend was not accepted. He is feeling very demotivated and unsure about what he will do instead. Write an encouraging and supportive email back to him.

Write your **email.**

3   A former colleague has set up her own catering business and has asked for your help in improving her website. Choose two or three points for improvement, focusing on design, ease of use and organisation. Write a proposal explaining how your recommended changes will make the website more attractive as well as easier for customers to navigate.

Write your **proposal.**

4   A history teacher at a local secondary school would like to show his students a film about an important historical event. He has invited people to send in reviews of films they feel would be appropriate for his final-year students. Write a review and include reasons for your choice of film.

Write your **review.**

PAPER 1  Reading and
         Use of English

PAPER 2  Writing

PAPER 3  Listening ▶

PAPER 4  Speaking

Part 1
Part 2
Part 3
Part 4

 **Track 25**

You will hear three different extracts. For questions **1–6**, choose the answer (**A**, **B** or **C**) which fits best according to what you hear. There are two questions for each extract.

**Extract One**

You hear two people discussing the royal family.

**1**  Why does the woman say she supports the royal family?
   **A**  She likes the romantic idea of royalty.
   **B**  Because she was born in Great Britain.
   **C**  She feels that it's part of her identity.

**2**  At the end, do the man and woman agree?
   **A**  Yes, they completely agree.
   **B**  No, they don't agree at all.
   **C**  They agree on some points.

**Extract Two**

You hear a conversation between two friends about a person called Paul.

**3**  The real reason the woman changes her mind about going to the beach is that
   **A**  the weather looks uncertain.
   **B**  she's actually extremely busy.
   **C**  someone she doesn't like is going.

**4**  What does the man explain about Paul?
   **A**  He actually doesn't have much confidence.
   **B**  He's just someone with a lot of confidence.
   **C**  The truth is that he has no confidence at all.

**Extract Three**

You hear a man and woman discussing the woman's younger brother.

**5**  The woman's principal concern is that her brother
   **A**  is unable to cope with his exams.
   **B**  is not focussing on his education.
   **C**  is going to play football professionally.

**6**  How is the man's attitude to the situation best described?
   **A**  He believes that the brother doesn't need an education.
   **B**  He fully expects the brother to be a professional footballer.
   **C**  He thinks the brother is going through a normal phase.

PAPER 1 Reading and
         Use of English
PAPER 2 Writing
PAPER 3 Listening ▶   Part 1
                      Part 2
                      Part 3
                      Part 4
PAPER 4 Speaking

🎧 **Track 26**

You will hear a woman talking about a personality test called the *Myers-Briggs Type Indicator*. For questions **7–14**, complete the sentences with a word or short phrase.

# THE MYERS-BRIGGS TYPE INDICATOR

During World War II Myers and Briggs first began developing the personality test,
which (**7**) ........................................................ Carl Jung's work.

Intuition, as defined by the speaker, is a way of reaching an understanding of things
that doesn't rely on (**8**) ........................................................ them.

The test is supposed to reveal whether you typically rely on your judgement or your
perception of things, and it categorises people as being either reserved or
(**9**) ........................................................ .

Overall, the speaker doesn't object to the (**10**) ........................................................ of
the Myers-Briggs test, but she doesn't really take it seriously.

She is concerned about having to take the Myers-Briggs test as part of her job
application because of its (**11**) ........................................................ .

Part of her problem with the test is that it fails to
(**12**) ........................................................ situations in which a person doesn't fit into
one category or the other, but somewhere between the two.

Eventually, the speaker contacted the Human Resources manager because she was
(**13**) ........................................................ about having to take the Myers-Briggs test.

The manager at the company put her mind at ease by explaining that they just use
the test as a loose (**14**) ........................................................ .

PAPER 1  Reading and
         Use of English

PAPER 2  Writing

PAPER 3  Listening ▶
                        Part 1
                        Part 2
                        **Part 3**
                        Part 4

PAPER 4  Speaking

**Track 27**

You will hear an interview with a successful novelist called Hilton Sims. For questions **15–20**, choose the answer (**A**, **B**, **C** or **D**) which fits best according to what you hear.

15  How long ago was Hilton Sims' first novel published?
   **A**  two years
   **B**  ten years
   **C**  six years
   **D**  20 years

16  The author has a background in
   **A**  literature.
   **B**  psychology.
   **C**  social work.
   **D**  film-making.

17  When asked about genre, what does the author say about his novels?
   **A**  They don't fit into a single category.
   **B**  He says they're psychological thrillers.
   **C**  They're best described as crime fiction.
   **D**  He refuses to categorise his books.

18  How did Hilton Sims meet the agent who published his first novel?
   **A**  It happened through contacting dozens of publishers.
   **B**  His friends contacted the agent on his behalf.
   **C**  They happened to meet through Hilton's day job.
   **D**  The meeting was just a lucky coincidence.

19  According to the author, what is the main reason for the popularity of crime fiction?
   **A**  People have always been fascinated by the 'good versus evil' battle.
   **B**  Readers enjoy the challenge of trying to figure out what happened.
   **C**  The sophisticated nature of criminal minds has great popular appeal.
   **D**  Science and technology have made solving crimes more interesting.

20  When the author finds it difficult to write, he
   **A**  goes out jogging.
   **B**  breaks for lunch.
   **C**  always sticks with it.
   **D**  writes somewhere else.

PAPER 1 Reading and
        Use of English

PAPER 2 Writing

PAPER 3 Listening

PAPER 4 Speaking

Part 1
Part 2
Part 3
Part 4

**Track 28**

You will hear five short extracts in which people talk about what they do to keep fit.

**While you listen you must complete both tasks.**

**TASK ONE**

For questions **21–25**, choose from the list (**A–H**) what brought each speaker to this form of exercise.

| | | | |
|---|---|---|---|
| **A** | living overseas | | |
| **B** | gym membership | Speaker 1 | 21 |
| **C** | their partner | Speaker 2 | 22 |
| **D** | co-workers | Speaker 3 | 23 |
| **E** | a hospital stay | Speaker 4 | 24 |
| **F** | their partner's friend | Speaker 5 | 25 |
| **G** | a childhood activity | | |
| **H** | a charity event | | |

**TASK TWO**

For questions **26–30**, choose from the list (**A–H**) what effect each speaker says this form of exercise has on them.

| | | | |
|---|---|---|---|
| **A** | becomes very competitive | | |
| **B** | has a sense of balance in life | Speaker 1 | 26 |
| **C** | enjoys being close to nature | Speaker 2 | 27 |
| **D** | likes feeling out of control | Speaker 3 | 28 |
| **E** | feels grateful for good health | Speaker 4 | 29 |
| **F** | is keen to live in the country | Speaker 5 | 30 |
| **G** | loves how thrilling it is | | |
| **H** | brings on a good mood | | |

PAPER 1  Reading and
         Use of English

PAPER 2  Writing

PAPER 3  Listening

PAPER 4  Speaking

## Part 1 (2 minutes)

The examiner will ask you a few questions about yourself and about a general topic. For example, the examiner may ask you:

- **What would be your ideal job? Why?**
- **Who has had the greatest influence on you?**
- **Which world problem are you the most concerned about? Why?**

## Part 2 (4 minutes)

You will each be asked to talk on your own for about a minute. You will each be given three different pictures to talk about. After your partner has finished speaking, you will be asked a brief question connected with your partner's photographs.

> **Modern inconveniences** (compare, contrast and speculate)

Turn to pictures 1–3 on page **187**, which show some modern stresses.

(*Candidate A*), it's your turn first. Here are your pictures. They show **different types of stress** which did not exist 100 years ago.

I'd like you to compare **two** of the pictures and say **what kind of impact each situation generally has on people and whether these situations can be avoided.**

(*Candidate B*), **do you think these are a necessary part of modern life? Why (not)?**

> **Professional occupations and gender** (compare, contrast and speculate)

Turn to pictures 1–3 on page **188**, which show three different occupations.

Now, (*Candidate B*), here are your pictures. They show **different occupations which, traditionally, might be considered to belong to one gender or the other.**

I'd like you to compare **two** of the pictures and say **what kinds of skills are needed to do each of these jobs well and whether men or women are better suited** to each occupation shown.

(*Candidate A*), do you think **society has changed enough to accept men and women working in whatever occupation they wish? Does this vary from culture to culture?**

## Part 3 (4 minutes)

Look at page **189**, which shows what graduates can do to improve their employability.

> **Ways of improving employability** (discuss, evaluate and negotiate)

**Here are some things graduates can do to improve their employability** and a question for you to discuss. First, you have some time to look at the task.

(*Pause 15 seconds*)

Now talk to each other about **how useful these steps might be in improving a new graduate's chances of being hired.**

Now you have a minute to decide **which step would have the most positive impact on a new graduate's employability, and why.**

## Part 4 (5 minutes)

The examiner will encourage you to develop the topic of your discussion in Part 3 by asking questions such as:

- What might make it difficult for a new graduate to be hired?

- Do you believe that a person's attitude is more important to employers than their education and experience? Why (not)?

- Does luck play a part in whether or not a person is hired? What do you think?

PAPER 1 Reading and ▶ Part 1
Use of English Part 2
Part 3
PAPER 2 Writing Part 4
Part 5
PAPER 3 Listening Part 6
Part 7
PAPER 4 Speaking Part 8

For questions **1–8**, read the text below and decide which answer (**A**, **B**, **C** or **D**) best fits each gap. There is an example at the beginning (**0**).

Mark your answers **on the separate answer sheet**.

**Example:**

**0**  **A**  hang          **B**  stick          **C**  fix          **D**  insist

| 0 | A | B | C | D |
|---|---|---|---|---|

# Do we really want variety in life?

Do you seek variety or do you (**0**) …….. with what you know? Research by behavioural scientist Daniel Read suggests we generally think variety is good, but we are (**1**) …….. to avoid it when we actually consume things. In one experiment over several weeks, volunteers were asked to either (**2**) …….. up on snacks (chocolate, fruit and crisps) at the start or select a snack each week. The former went for variety, but those selecting on a weekly (**3**) …….. prior to eating invariably picked the same snack. Moreover, if allowed to rethink, those who had gone for variety often (**4**) …….. to a single snack type.

Professor Read believes we display this 'diversification bias' in many (**5**) …….. of life. A weekly trip to the supermarket, for instance, is likely to (**6**) …….. us to buy a variety of items, some of which are likely to remain uneaten. (**7**) …….., financial managers will spread their investments, even though focusing on certain markets would probably be more profitable. Professor Read himself tries to (**8**) …….. his discoveries into practice: he is now 'more willing to buy ten of the same thing.'

| | | | | | | | |
|---|---|---|---|---|---|---|---|
| **1** | **A** liable | **B** prone | **C** feasible | **D** vulnerable |
| **2** | **A** store | **B** save | **C** shop | **D** stock |
| **3** | **A** norm | **B** pattern | **C** rule | **D** basis |
| **4** | **A** reverted | **B** resumed | **C** recurred | **D** revolved |
| **5** | **A** quarters | **B** circles | **C** spheres | **D** zones |
| **6** | **A** affect | **B** lead | **C** produce | **D** guide |
| **7** | **A** Closely | **B** Comparatively | **C** Correspondingly | **D** Similarly |
| **8** | **A** set | **B** put | **C** fit | **D** get |

| PAPER 1 | Reading and Use of English ▸ | Part 1 |
| | | Part 2 |
| PAPER 2 | Writing | Part 3 |
| | | Part 4 |
| PAPER 3 | Listening | Part 5 |
| PAPER 4 | Speaking | Part 6 |
| | | Part 7 |
| | | Part 8 |

For questions **9–16**, read the text below and think of the word which best fits each gap. Use only one word in each gap. There is an example at the beginning (**0**).

Write your answers **IN CAPITAL LETTERS on the separate answer sheet**.

**Example:** | 0 | T H R O U G H |

## Internships

In many countries going (**0**) …….. difficult economic times, job openings for new graduates can be few and (**9**) …….. between. In this competitive environment, relevant work experience can help job seekers stand (**10**) …….. from the crowd, and many organisations now offer temporary placements, called internships. The problem with (**11**) …….. great many internships, however, is that they are unpaid, and this often puts young people (**12**) …….. applying for them.

Employers and interns sometimes come to mutually beneficial arrangements, however. Dinesh Pathan, applying for an internship with an IT company, negotiated a deal in (**13**) …….. he would be given travel expenses only for two weeks, and then, as (**14**) …….. as he could show his marketing work was adding value, he would be paid a wage. The arrangement worked well: Dinesh had an incentive to work hard, and he ended up feeling 'not so (**15**) …….. an intern as a temporary staffer.' HR consultant Denise Baker says similar arrangements are common. What is more, 'if interns do well, employers would often (**16**) …….. make them full employees than recruit people they don't know'.

| PAPER 1 Reading and Use of English | Part 1 |
| --- | --- |
| | Part 2 |
| | **Part 3** |
| PAPER 2 Writing | Part 4 |
| | Part 5 |
| PAPER 3 Listening | Part 6 |
| PAPER 4 Speaking | Part 7 |
| | Part 8 |

For questions **17–24**, read the text below. Use the word given in capitals at the end of some of the lines to form a word that fits in the gap **in the same line**. There is an example at the beginning (**0**).

Write your answers **IN CAPITAL LETTERS on the separate answer sheet**.

Example: 0 G L O B A L

## Environmental psychology

Most scientists now agree that human behaviour is
causing (**0**) …….. climate change and a disastrous                    **GLOBE**
(**17**) …….. of biodiversity. In order to deal with these problems      **LOSE**
which, in the long term, threaten devastation on a scale which
is (**18**) ……….., we need to find ways to change behaviour. This is   **THINK**
where environmental psychologists come in. 'As we know a lot
about human behaviour, we can help figure out how to motivate
people to do (**19**) …….. things,' says psychologist Amara Brook.     **SUSTAIN**

While jobs (**20**) …….. for environmental psychologists are still      **SPECIFIC**
fairly unusual, psychologists are very much involved in such
disciplines as urban (**21**) …….., conservation and environmental     **PLAN**
health. Using their knowledge of behaviour, psychologists have
helped design (**22**) …….. messages on signs and notices to           **PERSUADE**
encourage environmentally friendly behaviour in nature reserves
and parks. Others have investigated the effects of sunlight
and access to parks and gardens on employee (**23**) …….. and          **PRODUCE**
on children's academic performance. Clinical psychologists
with environmental (**24**) …….. are also in demand because            **EXPERT**
environmental concerns can cause great anxiety. As environmental
issues become ever more significant, psychologists working in this
field will surely become increasingly prominent.

| PAPER 1 Reading and ▸ | Part 1 |
| Use of English | Part 2 |
| PAPER 2 Writing | Part 3 |
| | **Part 4** |
| PAPER 3 Listening | Part 5 |
| PAPER 4 Speaking | Part 6 |
| | Part 7 |
| | Part 8 |

For questions **25–30**, complete the second sentence so that it has a similar meaning to the first sentence, using the word given. **Do not change the word given.** You must use between **three** and **six** words, including the word given. Here is an example (**0**).

**Example:**

**0**  Chloe would only eat a pizza if she could have a mushroom topping.

**ON**

Chloe ........................................... a mushroom topping when she had a pizza.

The gap can be filled with the words 'insisted on having', so you write:

**Example:** | **0** | INSISTED ON HAVING

Write **only** the missing words **IN CAPITAL LETTERS on the separate answer sheet.**

---

**25**  Make sure you know what the time is, otherwise you'll miss the start of the play.

**TRACK**

Make sure you ........................................... as not to miss the start of the play.

**26**  It didn't take Steven long to show his true character.

**MATTER**

It was ........................................... Steven showed his true character.

**27**  If we take everything into account, the street party was a great success in the end.

**CONSIDERED**

All ........................................... out to be a great success in the end.

**28**  Everyone was horrified when the new manager dropped Ripley from the first team and picked Conway instead.

**LEFT**

To ........................................... of the first team by the new manager and he picked Conway instead.

**29**  The company's owners are quite radical because they've got rid of a whole layer of managers, and they've introduced flexible working time.

**DONE**

The company's owners are quite radical because not ........................................... with a whole layer of managers, but they've also introduced flexible working time.

**30**  The police apologised a great deal for having completely failed to recognise the seriousness of the situation.

**COMPLETE**

The police were very ........................................... to recognise the seriousness of the situation.

PAPER 1  Reading and
            Use of English
PAPER 2  Writing
PAPER 3  Listening
PAPER 4  Speaking

Part 1
Part 2
Part 3
Part 4
**Part 5**
Part 6
Part 7
Part 8

You are going to read a review of a book written by an author named Nicholas Carr, about the internet. For questions **31–36**, choose the answer (**A**, **B**, **C** or **D**) which you think fits best according to the text.

Mark your answers **on the separate answer sheet**.

# Review of *The Shallows* by Nicholas Carr

***Internet use may be changing our brains for good, but is this all bad?***
***David Cox reviews Nicholas Carr's investigation of how the internet is affecting us.***

In their early days, as they challenged the established medium of communication, newspapers, cinema and broadcasting, like writing, libraries and printing before them, all provoked anguish. Would the upstart medium replace what was good with what was bad? The internet was bound to ignite the same kind of disquiet. It has indeed, yet according to Nicholas Carr in his intriguing and controversial book *The Shallows*, it is not the change in what our minds consume that should most bother us. It is the change that is being wrought upon our brains.

He tells us he can no longer read a book without getting fidgety and losing the thread. Constant searching and surfing online have made him expect a scurrying stream of particles and this means that the only way he absorbs information is in quick, small doses. The internet has really done his head in and, what is more, his friends fear they have the same syndrome.

Carr describes research which suggests this is no mere metaphor. Studies show that web use alters brain cells, creating new neural pathways and weakening old ones. The brain of a newcomer to the internet starts rewiring itself after just six days of surfing the web. Because of this, according to Carr, our powers of concentration are atrophying. 'As we come to rely on computers to mediate our understanding of the world,' he writes, 'it is our own intelligence that flattens into artificial intelligence.'

His account is plausible but far from surprising. Our grey matter constantly reshapes itself in the face of changing demands and circumstances. About 2,400 years ago, the Greek philosopher Socrates feared that the spread of writing would change the way brains worked: by focusing them on outer symbols (words written down) rather than inner recollection (in the mind), it would undermine memory and trivialise thought, thereby jeopardising wisdom and happiness. There was probably some truth in what he said. Once people could jot down a laundry list, say, the relevant sections of their brains doubtless decommissioned redundant storage capacity. At the same time, however, they learned to process a much richer body of data.

Carr acknowledges that the reshaping of our brains by digital media is in some ways improving them. He accepts that they are growing better at focusing attention, analysing data, multi-tasking and making instant decisions. Yet, for him, these benefits come at too high a price: the ability to attend patiently to lengthy narratives and long arguments is very much more valuable. However, this claim is debateable, to say the least.

Instead of reading the 256 pages in which Carr sets out his case, you could pretty much get his point by looking at one of the many summaries available, like this one, or indeed those to be found in various locations on the internet. This is not to say that Carr's book is poorly written or uninteresting – far from it – but if you take this course, you will be able to use the time saved to absorb the gist of a lot of other ideas as well as his. This might well be the more productive option.

People used to read three-volume novels largely because there wasn't much else to do. If our brains, through internet use, are now being reprogrammed to trawl the shallows broadly rather than narrowly plumb the depths, we may end up, on balance, better off. If we do not, in due course we shall doubtless notice, because we tend to notice these things, and remedial action will be available. An organ that has managed to unravel centuries of conditioning in a mere six days ought to be able to reverse the feat. Either way it will be up to us.

Carr's punchline is: 'We are welcoming the frenziedness into our souls.' Exactly. We are welcoming it, just as we welcomed the ability to read, in spite of the damage it would inflict on our memories. Now our brains are adapting once again to our new-found desires. We ourselves, not our media, are determining the kind of creatures we want to be; and our wits will remain our servants, not our masters.

**31** What point does the reviewer make in the first paragraph?
- **A** Carr's views closely echo those of people in earlier times.
- **B** Concerns about the impact of the internet are inevitable.
- **C** The content of all new media tends to be of dubious quality.
- **D** The internet can effectively take over from all other forms of media.

**32** Which is the 'metaphor' referred to in line 10?
- **A** The internet has really done his head in.
- **B** His friends fear they have the same syndrome.
- **C** He can no longer read a book without getting fidgety.
- **D** The only way he absorbs information is in quick, small doses.

**33** What point is made about the spread of writing in the fourth paragraph?
- **A** It made people reconsider the value of acquiring knowledge.
- **B** It led to life in ancient times becoming more complicated.
- **C** It weakened Socrates' position as a respected thinker.
- **D** It relieved people's minds of certain mental burdens.

**34** What is the reviewer's main intention in the sixth paragraph?
- **A** to suggest how Carr's use of the internet could be more effective
- **B** to explain how Carr's ideas have been stimulated by the internet
- **C** to illustrate why an aspect of Carr's thinking may be misguided
- **D** to criticise the way Carr's book is constructed

**35** What point does the reviewer make in the seventh paragraph?
- **A** People are already careful about how they use the internet.
- **B** Human beings are good at adapting to new circumstances.
- **C** Reading long works of fiction is a waste of time these days.
- **D** It may be too late to worry about the impact of the internet.

**36** What does the reviewer suggest in the final paragraph?
- **A** People are responsible for the internet rather than the other way round.
- **B** The impact the internet is having on us is similar to that of reading.
- **C** Our enthusiasm for the internet is ultimately beyond our control.
- **D** Carr's sense of unease about the internet has some justification.

PAPER 1 Reading and ▶
         Use of English

PAPER 2 Writing

PAPER 3 Listening

PAPER 4 Speaking

Part 1
Part 2
Part 3
Part 4
Part 5
**Part 6**
Part 7
Part 8

You are going to read four contributions made by students to a debate about whether university education should be free of charge. For questions **37–40**, choose from the contributions **A–D**. The contributions may be chosen more than once.

Mark your answers **on the separate answer sheet**.

# Should university education be free of charge?

*In most countries, students have to pay fees to study at university, but there are some countries where the state guarantees a free higher education to all citizens with appropriate qualifications. Should free university education be a universal right? Four students give their views.*

### A

Free university education should be a universal right, but it makes sense for other reasons too. It gives talented people, irrespective of background, the opportunity to gain the knowledge, skills and qualifications that countries need citizens to have if they are to compete in the modern global economy. It enables the less affluent to break out of the class they are born into, and keeps society dynamic and aspirational. The state funding that allows free access also lets universities focus on what they do best, research and teaching, rather than administering fee payment and searching for private sponsorship. Claims that governments are no longer able to pay for free higher education because of competing demands on public finances conveniently ignore the fact that universities are free in some successful countries. Any government with the will to do so – and surveys suggest they would be supported by the wider population – could shift spending away from unproductive sectors like defence and into higher education.

### B

There is little doubt that degree programmes benefit from the level of state funding that is necessary to make higher education free for all. Where universities are largely self-financing, inordinate time, energy and talent is invested in attracting fee-paying students and research-supporting corporate investors. The fact that a number of countries around the world offer free university education of a very high standard proves that it is still a viable proposition, but it would undoubtedly be difficult for a country to change to such a system. Free higher education is ultimately paid for by taxes, and, in this day and age, taxpayers are generally unwilling to pay more, particularly if it is to enable young people, mostly from well-off backgrounds, to qualify for lucrative employment. The idea that free higher education benefits anyone apart from those who would attend fee-paying degree courses anyway is largely illusory.

### C

State-funded, free university education is a fine idea in principle. Besides giving all individuals the opportunity to become more knowledgeable and cultured, it also frees universities from the messy, distracting business of having to find ways to finance their work and allows them to focus on enhancing the student experience and carrying out research. The reality, however, is that the cost of paying for higher education is ruinously high for the state. Public-sector debt in many countries is astronomical, and governments have no choice but to prioritise spending. Unfortunately, higher education comes low down on the list of priorities. Also, the evidence suggests that people who want to go to university will generally find a way to finance themselves, whatever their class or background. Fee-paying does not particularly encourage underprivileged youngsters into higher education but neither does free university access.

### D

In most modern economies, free university education is an illusion. Governments find it hard to provide adequate funds for healthcare, let alone a non-essential service like universities, and trying to convince people they should pay more taxes to finance university students is doomed to failure. States need university-educated citizens, but graduates can afford to pay for themselves, either up-front because of family background or retrospectively by paying off loans. Fee-paying makes no substantial difference to the number of people attending universities, and the figures suggest that people from particular socio-economic backgrounds are neither put off university by having to pay for it nor motivated to attend by having free access. In those countries where university fees have recently been introduced, the impact on universities themselves has been striking. Free of state influence, they have realised that they will only stay in business if they provide an excellent service to their clients, the students.

## Which expert

takes a similar view to A about whether the state
can afford to finance free higher education?

| 37 | |

has a different opinion from the others about how
state funding might affect the quality of university education?

| 38 | |

has a different view from the others regarding the
implications of free university education for social mobility?

| 39 | |

shares D's opinion about public attitudes regarding
free university education?

| 40 | |

| PAPER 1 Reading and ▸ | Part 1 |
| Use of English | Part 2 |
| | Part 3 |
| PAPER 2 Writing | Part 4 |
| | Part 5 |
| PAPER 3 Listening | Part 6 |
| | **Part 7** |
| PAPER 4 Speaking | Part 8 |

You are going to read a magazine article about emotional intelligence and work. Six paragraphs have been removed from the article. Choose from the paragraphs **A–G** the one which fits each gap (**41–46**). There is one extra paragraph which you do not need to use.

Mark your answers **on the separate answer sheet**.

# Emotional intelligence: thinking and feeling at work

*Psychologists say 'emotional intelligence' can help manage our thinking and improve our behaviour at work and in our personal lives. Jill Insley reports.*

If you work in an economy which is going through difficulties, the chances are you're calling on your emotional intelligence (EI) less than you might like, according to research which shows that the art of identifying, understanding and managing your emotions to improve your performance appears to decline in tough economic times. A team of occupational psychologists led by John Cooper studied 12,400 workers, mainly from the UK managerial population between 2001 and 2010, and found that use of emotional intelligence increased steadily during the economically strong years of 2001 to 2007, but dropped sharply between 2008 and 2010 during a banking crisis and recession.

| **41** | |

The term 'emotional intelligence' was first used in psychology in 1966, and although several different interpretations have developed since then it is still a relatively new field. Cooper's report describes it as an 'innate human attribute' which, if understood and used well, can help us manage our thinking and feeling to improve our behaviour and relationships.

| **42** | |

Emotional intelligence is divided into two main areas: personal intelligence and interpersonal intelligence. These, in turn, are split into 16 measurable scales including self-regard and regard for others, self-awareness and awareness of others, emotional resilience, flexibility, trust and emotional expression.

| **43** | |

Measuring emotional intelligence can also identify areas of development for employees in specific positions. An awareness of where you sit on each scale can help determine whether you need extra training, or will excel in a particular industry or sector. Self-employed people score higher than any other occupational group, possibly because there is a greater need to be emotionally intelligent if you are mostly dependent upon yourself for your success.

| **44** | |

The study found that senior managers and directors tend to score highly in all aspects, but especially in self-belief, emotional resilience, positive outlook, going after goals, conflict handling and independence. Low scores on some of these scales, however, can have a negative impact on others, especially if the low scorer holds a senior position.

| **45** | |

Another executive, by contrast, approached a colleague about the performance of a manager he was responsible for with the words, 'I think I've put him into the wrong position because he is very good, but he's not thriving. What's your opinion?' This showed humility and openness, features of good emotional intelligence.

| **46** | |

The consequence of this appears to be that employees feel liked, competent and significant, and the business has become more productive and profitable. The implication to be drawn from this would seem to be that unlike personality traits and IQ, emotional intelligence can be changed and developed, which, in turn, can have a positive impact on work and economic activity.

**A** Having observed both approaches, one senior manager decided his own firm would benefit from the incorporation of emotional intelligence into management methods. Training to this end was accordingly organised.

**B** Results for other work sectors also proved interesting. People with jobs in health, for example, scored significantly lower in self-regard, which may result in them putting the needs of others first, while those in the sales sector scored strongly on self-assuredness, not being easily put off and being able to connect with people without being overly caring.

**C** 'If we liken the mind to a high-performance engine,' it goes on to say, then this 'would be the oil that enables us to maintain and manage ourselves to perform to our full potential.'

**D** Despite this, those who feel their effectiveness generally – but especially at work – isn't up to scratch, need not despair. Emotional intelligence is not fixed and can be enhanced. In order to do this, however, you need to know what your EI rating is.

**E** Using these categories, the study came up with results which seem to confirm some commonly held presumptions. For instance, while there is no significant difference between men and women in overall scores, men have a more critical mindset with higher self-esteem and lower estimation of others. Women, by contrast, tend to have lower self-esteem and higher valuation of others. Also, emotional intelligence improves with age, as we develop a more balanced outlook and become less dependent on, but more trusting of, others.

**F** In an example of this, six managers were asked by a company director to present their views of why a particular problem had emerged in the business. After the first person had outlined what he thought the problem was, the director shouted, 'So you've been lying to me for a year.' Who around that table would now say what they thought the problem was?

**G** The likelihood is that when facing uncertainty people may feel threatened and switch into 'survival mode' to try to protect what they have. Moreover, 'this can make things worse as workers become less adaptive and responsive to change, and may miss business or personal opportunities.'

| PAPER 1 | Reading and Use of English | ▶ | Part 1 |
| | | | Part 2 |
| PAPER 2 | Writing | | Part 3 |
| | | | Part 4 |
| PAPER 3 | Listening | | Part 5 |
| | | | Part 6 |
| PAPER 4 | Speaking | | Part 7 |
| | | | **Part 8** |

You are going to read an article in which critics talk about crime writers that they like. For questions **47–56**, choose from the critics (**A–D**). The critics may be chosen more than once.

Mark your answers **on the separate answer sheet**.

## Which crime writer is described as

| | |
|---|---|
| having discovered a way of staying fresh as a crime novelist? | **47** |
| appearing to mix different genres at times? | **48** |
| using personal experience to good effect ? | **49** |
| using the genre to explore wider social issues? | **50** |
| expressing authentic feelings through their writing? | **51** |
| possessing great command of conventional crime fiction techniques? | **52** |
| exploring a particular geographical setting in an interesting way? | **53** |
| having substantially raised the calibre of their work at a certain point? | **54** |
| being prepared to take artistic risks? | **55** |
| writing in a concise style? | **56** |

# Critics' choice of crime writers

## A  Peter Temple

I started reading Peter Temple's books about ten years ago, and at the time it was fairly orthodox crime fiction set in Australia, much of it involving horse-racing. Then suddenly, with *The Broken Shore*, he hit something quite different and moved up several notches. Since then he has been writing the kind of novels many authors spend a lifetime striving for. He comes out of a line of taut, tough crime fiction that starts with Dashiell Hammett, writing in America in the 1920s and 30s, and goes through the Swedish authors Sjöwall and Wahlöö to William McIlvanney in Scotland over the last 40 years. Crime fiction with them is not just about the story; it's also a vehicle for saying something about the contexts within which the action happens. Frequently using dialogue instead of description, and providing an object lesson in how to say a lot without unnecessary verbiage, Temple absolutely nails the connections between politics, the police and the media. If you want to know anything about the media invasion of privacy, say, it's there.

## B  Liza Cody

There is a lot of good, slick writing out there that turns me off because it's unfelt. If, like me, you look for writers with a gift for language and storytelling, and who possess a willingness to do the hard work of digging into the nitty-gritty of emotional life, Liza Cody is likely to appeal. She doesn't just do the easy thing to be recognised in the marketplace; she goes where the story and her curiosity take her. For instance, she had to self-publish one book, *Ballad of a Dead Nobody*, because no one in the industry was willing to. She had a successful series with a private eye called Anna Lee but she branched out and did some unusual books about a woman wrestler. These days, genre writers are told to create a brand or a series, a recognisable hook. Cody will often turn her back on that and focus on what her inner voice is telling her, which requires courage.

## C  Michael Connelly

The first Connelly book I read was *The Poet*, his first stand-alone novel and a big breakthrough for him. By then, he had written four books in his Harry Bosch series, which I went back to read. Connelly has maintained a level of quality through a long-running series – an incredibly difficult thing to pull off. He does it by stepping away for a while and writing books such as *The Poet* and *Blood Work*, and then he comes back to it fired up with renewed vitality. People talk about how you create suspense and use cliffhangers, reveals and so on, and Connelly is an admirable exponent of all that, but the real secret is to create characters that readers care about. Bosch, a detective in the Los Angeles Police Department, is a character who has grown and changed, who you come to know and empathise with. All that aside, he is a fantastic storyteller. I think his days as a crime reporter on *The Los Angeles Times* stood him in good stead because he never forgets the story.

## D  Johan Theorin

I read Theorin's novel, *Echoes from the Dead*, when judging a competition for a crime fiction prize. It's the first of a quartet of stories, all of which take place on an island in the Baltic Sea. They are very atmospheric. They have this interesting detective who is elderly and lives in a sheltered housing complex, so he can't be out there doing car chases. Theorin is very good on the unspoken secrets of small communities. The first book takes place in the summer and the second, *The Darkest Room*, in the winter. It's about this crumbling house by the shore and there seems to be a supernatural thread running through it. It's as if the narrative switches into the realms of fantasy now and then. It has the most wonderful climax, but Theorin is ready to take his time over the telling of the story, which is unusual these days. If you look at the bestsellers, they are quite pacey and macho. There is nothing wrong with that, but Theorin writes in a much more textured, literary way.

PAPER 1 Reading and
          Use of English

**PAPER 2 Writing** ▶ Part 1
                      Part 2

PAPER 3 Listening

PAPER 4 Speaking

You **must** answer this question. Write your answer in **220–260** words in an appropriate style on the separate answer sheet.

---

**1**   You are doing a Marketing course. As part of the module on advertising strategies, your tutor asks whether advertising is typically designed to exploit or inform, and opens it to a class debate. You have made the notes below.

> **Advertising: Exploitation or Information?**
>
> - Of course it's information-based, how else will consumers learn about the product?
> - Most companies care too much about their reputation to risk false or unclear advertising.
> - There's information *and* persuasion; intelligent people know the difference.

> **Other opinions expressed included:**
>
> "Advertising exploits; it makes people feel bad for not buying things they don't even need."
>
> "It deliberately targets children and vulnerable people, who are less able to discriminate."
>
> "It exaggerates certain things and makes misleading claims."

Write an essay for your tutor discussing **two** of the points from your notes. You should **explain whether you think advertising is typically designed to exploit or inform** and **provide reasons** to support your opinions.

You may, if you wish, make use of the opinions expressed in the seminar, but you should use your own words as far as possible.

PAPER 1  Reading and
           Use of English

PAPER 2  Writing ▶           Part 1

PAPER 3  Listening           Part 2

PAPER 4  Speaking

Write an answer to **one** of the questions **2–4** in this part. Write your answer in **220–260** words in an appropriate style on the separate answer sheet. Put the question number in the box at the top of the page.

2  You see a poster at the train station announcing the arrival of a large circus in your town. As you are opposed to wild animals being kept in captivity, especially being confined and constantly transported, you decide to state your objections and lobby your local council to have the event cancelled.

   Write your **letter.**

3  In recent months, the cafeteria at the company where you work has been consistently losing money. Fewer and fewer members of staff are choosing to have their lunch there, and the chances of the cafeteria closing down are high. The office manager has sent a company-wide email inviting employees to submit a report detailing the existing issues and making suggestions for improvements.

   Write your **report.**

4  You see this notice on an events website based in your area.

---

**WE NEED YOUR HELP**

Here at the Riverfront Theatre we'd like to add to our database of event reviews. If you were at last night's concert given by the student band, *Atmosphere*, we'd love to hear from you. Please send your review of the concert to the email address below.

---

   Write your **review.**

PAPER 1  Reading and
          Use of English

PAPER 2  Writing

PAPER 3  Listening    ▶    Part 1
                            Part 2
                            Part 3
PAPER 4  Speaking           Part 4

**Track 29**

You will hear three different extracts. For questions **1–6**, choose the answer (**A**, **B** or **C**) which fits best according to what you hear. There are two questions for each extract.

**Extract One**

You hear two friends discussing studying.

1   What fundamental point does the man disagree with?
    **A**   having to spend so much time studying
    **B**   having to value doing unpleasant things
    **C**   having to enjoy the present moment

2   What point does the woman clarify?
    **A**   that people needn't seek out difficult tasks
    **B**   that no one can escape their responsibilities
    **C**   that the magazine article was a reliable source

**Extract Two**

You hear a woman admitting that she told a lie.

3   What was the problem with Brooke's choice of song?
    **A**   It wasn't a good tune.
    **B**   It was a sad love song.
    **C**   It didn't suit her voice.

4   The woman lied because
    **A**   she and Brooke are not very close friends.
    **B**   Brooke is passionate about music.
    **C**   she wanted to protect Brooke's feelings.

**Extract Three**

You hear two people discussing Facebook.

5   Which statement best describes the woman's attitude?
    **A**   The neighbour's opinion is correct.
    **B**   The neighbour is entitled to his opinion.
    **C**   The neighbour's opinion is not correct.

6   The man is irritated because his neighbour
    **A**   laughed at his attempts to explain Facebook.
    **B**   dismissed Facebook without having tried it.
    **C**   easily won the argument about Facebook.

PAPER 1  Reading and
         Use of English

PAPER 2  Writing

PAPER 3  Listening  ▶  Part 1
                        **Part 2**
                        Part 3
                        Part 4

PAPER 4  Speaking

🎧 **Track 30**

You will hear a man talking about genetically-modified (GM) foods. For questions **7–14**, complete the sentences with a word or short phrase.

# GENETICALLY-MODIFIED FOODS

The objective of genetically-modified foods is to (**7**) ......................................................
crops and plants so that they perform better.

The speaker says his father feels sorry for UK farmers and their

(**8**) ...................................................... against climate change.

One effect of failed crops due to weather conditions is

(**9**) ...................................................... for some farmers.

The speaker's mother objects to genetic engineering and feels it is dangerous to

(**10**) ...................................................... with how plants naturally grow.

The speaker himself feels that GM foods should not be entirely

(**11**) ...................................................... by governments in Europe and the UK.

His view is that we should be careful not to declare GM foods safe until

(**12**) ...................................................... have been carried out.

His father feels that it shouldn't be a complicated matter to ensure that the correct
labelling of foodstuffs is (**13**) ...................................................... .

The speaker concludes that his own family is a good

(**14**) ...................................................... of public opinion on the GM debate.

PAPER 1 Reading and
Use of English

PAPER 2 Writing

PAPER 3 Listening ▶

PAPER 4 Speaking

Part 1
Part 2
**Part 3**
Part 4

🎧 **Track 31**

You will hear three members of an interview panel discussing the two candidates, John and Rebecca, who are finalists for the job. For questions **15–20**, choose the answer (**A**, **B**, **C** or **D**) which fits best according to what you hear.

15 Based on the discussion, what kind of job do you think the candidates have applied for?
   **A** marketing
   **B** sales
   **C** research
   **D** design

16 What point does the man mention in Rebecca's favour?
   **A** She seems like someone with good ideas.
   **B** She is much more of an introvert than John.
   **C** She made an effort to learn about the company.
   **D** Her professional background might be useful.

17 What concern was expressed about how John described his weak points?
   **A** his lack of consideration
   **B** his lack of confidence
   **C** his lack of responsibility
   **D** his lack of communication

18 Based on the comments from the panel, as an employee Rebecca would probably be very
   **A** dynamic.
   **B** self-conscious.
   **C** pushy.
   **D** conscientious.

19 Based on the comments from the panel, as an employee John would probably
   **A** make a good impression.
   **B** not cope under pressure.
   **C** excel in the role.
   **D** trust his own instincts.

20 By the end of the discussion, the panel members seem to be
   **A** clear on who they will vote for.
   **B** unanimous about Rebecca.
   **C** unanimous about John.
   **D** undecided on who they'll vote for.

PAPER 1  Reading and
                 Use of English

PAPER 2  Writing

**PAPER 3  Listening**  ▶
               Part 1
               Part 2
PAPER 4  Speaking
               Part 3
               **Part 4**

**Track 32**

You will hear five short extracts in which people talk about a challenging experience they have had.

**While you listen you must complete both tasks.**

**TASK ONE**

For questions **21–25**, choose from the list (**A–H**) how the incident affected each speaker when it happened.

| | | | |
|---|---|---|---|
| **A** | started having nightmares | | |
| **B** | got quite depressed | Speaker 1 | 21 |
| **C** | wouldn't go outside | Speaker 2 | 22 |
| **D** | lost all self-confidence | Speaker 3 | 23 |
| **E** | stopped feeling safe | Speaker 4 | 24 |
| **F** | developed a fear of dying | Speaker 5 | 25 |
| **G** | experienced anxiety | | |
| **H** | became a little hysterical | | |

**TASK TWO**

For questions **26–30**, choose from the list (**A–H**) how each speaker feels about the experience now.

| | | | |
|---|---|---|---|
| **A** | has become quite obsessive | | |
| **B** | no longer has any patience | Speaker 1 | 26 |
| **C** | is still trying to get over it | Speaker 2 | 27 |
| **D** | is embarrassed about it | Speaker 3 | 28 |
| **E** | exercises increased awareness | Speaker 4 | 29 |
| **F** | has a more optimistic outlook | Speaker 5 | 30 |
| **G** | doesn't ever think about it | | |
| **H** | has put it into perspective | | |

PAPER 1 Reading and
         Use of English

PAPER 2 Writing

PAPER 3 Listening

PAPER 4 Speaking

### Part 1 (2 minutes)

The examiner will ask you a few questions about yourself and about a general topic. For example, the examiner may ask you:

• **What's your favourite thing about where you are from?**
• **What's the biggest change you've experienced in your life so far?**
• **Are you a 'morning person'? Explain why (not)**

### Part 2 (4 minutes)

You will each be asked to talk on your own for about a minute. You will each be given three different pictures to talk about. After your partner has finished speaking, you will be asked a brief question connected with your partner's photographs.

> **In the spotlight** (compare, contrast and speculate)

Turn to pictures 1–3 on page **190**, which show people in the spotlight.

(*Candidate A*), it's your turn first. Here are your pictures. They show **situations in which people are in the spotlight.**

I'd like you to compare **two** of the pictures and say **what is happening in these photos and how you think the people might be feeling.**

(*Candidate B*), **do you enjoy being in the spotlight? Why (not)?**

> **Less than happy** (compare, contrast and speculate)

Turn to pictures 1–3 on page **191**, which show people who appear to be unhappy.

Now, (*Candidate B*), here are your pictures. They show **people who appear to be unhappy.** I'd like you to compare **two** of the pictures and say **which emotions each person is probably feeling and what probably made them feel this way.**

(*Candidate A*), **do you think that people have a responsibility to be happy in life? Why (not)?**

### Part 3 (4 minutes)

Look at page **192**, which shows some things people can do to go green.

> **Ways of going green** (discuss, evaluate and negotiate)

**Here are some things people can do to go green and help the planet.**

First you have some time to look at the task.

(*Pause 15 seconds*)

Now talk to each other about **which of these things most people are likely to do, and why.**

Now you have a minute to decide **which step you feel people would have the most difficulty adopting,** and **what could be done to change that.**

### Part 4 (5 minutes)

The examiner will encourage you to develop the topic of your discussion in Part 3 by asking questions such as:

• Generally speaking, do you feel most people are willing to sacrifice certain things for the greater good of the planet? Why (not)?

• Some people claim that experts have exaggerated climate change and that reports on global warming are mostly propaganda? What's your view on this?

• What would you say is the single biggest obstacle to making the earth greener?

**CAMBRIDGE ENGLISH**
Language Assessment
Part of the University of Cambridge

Do not write in this box

**Candidate Name**
If not already printed, write name
in CAPITALS and complete the
Candidate No. grid (in pencil).

**Candidate Signature**

SAMPLE

**Examination Title**

**Centre**

Supervisor:

If the candidate is ABSENT or has WITHDRAWN shade here ▭

Centre No.

Candidate No.

Examination
Details

| 0 | 0 | 0 | 0 |
|---|---|---|---|
| 1 | 1 | 1 | 1 |
| 2 | 2 | 2 | 2 |
| 3 | 3 | 3 | 3 |
| 4 | 4 | 4 | 4 |
| 5 | 5 | 5 | 5 |
| 6 | 6 | 6 | 6 |
| 7 | 7 | 7 | 7 |
| 8 | 8 | 8 | 8 |
| 9 | 9 | 9 | 9 |

## Candidate Answer Sheet

### Instructions

Use a PENCIL (B or HB). Rub out any answer you wish to change using an eraser.

**Parts 1 and 5-8:** Mark ONE letter for each question.

For example, if you think **B** is the right
answer to the question, mark your
answer sheet like this:

0  A  B  C  D

**Parts 2, 3** and **4:** Write your answer clearly
in CAPITAL LETTERS.

For Parts 2 and 3 write one letter
in each box. For example:

0  E X A M P L E

### Part 1

| | | | | |
|---|---|---|---|---|
| 1 | A | B | C | D |
| 2 | A | B | C | D |
| 3 | A | B | C | D |
| 4 | A | B | C | D |
| 5 | A | B | C | D |
| 6 | A | B | C | D |
| 7 | A | B | C | D |
| 8 | A | B | C | D |

### Part 2

Do not write
below here

| 9 | | 9 1 0 u |
| 10 | | 10 1 0 u |
| 11 | | 11 1 0 u |
| 12 | | 12 1 0 u |
| 13 | | 13 1 0 u |
| 14 | | 14 1 0 u |
| 15 | | 15 1 0 u |
| 16 | | 16 1 0 u |

**Continues over** ➡

## Part 3

| | | | | | | | | | | | | | | | | | | | | | | | | Do not write below here |
|---|---|---|---|---|---|---|---|---|---|---|---|---|---|---|---|---|---|---|---|---|---|---|---|---|
| **17** | | | | | | | | | | | | | | | | | | | | | | | | 17 1 0 u |
| **18** | | | | | | | | | | | | | | | | | | | | | | | | 18 1 0 u |
| **19** | | | | | | | | | | | | | | | | | | | | | | | | 19 1 0 u |
| **20** | | | | | | | | | | | | | | | | | | | | | | | | 20 1 0 u |
| **21** | | | | | | | | | | | | | | | | | | | | | | | | 21 1 0 u |
| **22** | | | | | | | | | | | | | | | | | | | | | | | | 22 1 0 u |
| **23** | | | | | | | | | | | | | | | | | | | | | | | | 23 1 0 u |
| **24** | | | | | | | | | | | | | | | | | | | | | | | | 24 1 0 u |

## Part 4

| | Do not write below here |
|---|---|
| **25** | 25 1 0 u |
| **26** | 26 1 0 u |
| **27** | 27 1 0 u |
| **28** | 28 1 0 u |
| **29** | 29 1 0 u |
| **30** | 30 1 0 u |

## Part 5

| 31 | A B C D |
|---|---|
| 32 | A B C D |
| 33 | A B C D |
| 34 | A B C D |
| 35 | A B C D |
| 36 | A B C D |

## Part 6

| 37 | A B C D |
|---|---|
| 38 | A B C D |
| 39 | A B C D |
| 40 | A B C D |

## Part 7

| 41 | A B C D E F G |
|---|---|
| 42 | A B C D E F G |
| 43 | A B C D E F G |
| 44 | A B C D E F G |
| 45 | A B C D E F G |
| 46 | A B C D E F G |

## Part 8

| 47 | A B C D E |
|---|---|
| 48 | A B C D E |
| 49 | A B C D E |
| 50 | A B C D E |
| 51 | A B C D E |
| 52 | A B C D E |
| 53 | A B C D E |
| 54 | A B C D E |
| 55 | A B C D E |
| 56 | A B C D E |

Paper 3 Listening

## TEST 1

▶▶ PART 2
   Candidate A

- **What kind of event are the people attending?**
- **How are they responding to the event?**

## Language bank

These people are likely …

They seem to be paying close attention.

They appear to be completely absorbed in what they are seeing and hearing.

This audience is probably …

The people in this picture look like they're being highly entertained.

I'm quite sure they're enjoying themselves.

I'd say these people are …

I'm not certain, but I think …

By the looks of things here …

There's a sense of anticipation in this picture.

In this one, however, there is clearly a great deal of tension.

The spectators look quite nervous here.

They can't bear to watch the match.

By contrast …

amused
anxious
auditorium
edge of their seat
entertainment
fascinated
football match
football supporters
lecture
listening intently
nervous
night out
presentation
screen
seminar
serious
sports event

▶ 1

▶ 2

▶ 3

▶▶ **PART 2**

**Candidate B**

- **What kind of person would choose this job?**
- **What kind of challenges might the job present?**

# Language bank

This looks like …

I imagine this is …

This person is almost certainly friendly and outgoing.

They would need to have …

They'd have to be …

This would be the sort of person who can work independently.

This role requires focus and attention to detail.

In this job, however …

This job needs a lot of patience.

As the picture shows, …

On the other hand, …

But in this role, …

It could be that …

attention to detail
department store
driving instructor
engaging
explain things clearly ·
hardware engineer
intense
keep the customer satisfied
patient
PC repair
people skills
personable
personal shopper
put people at their ease
sales assistant
technical skills
technician
unflappable
work alone

▶ **1**

▶ **2**

▶ **3**

▸▸ **PART 3**
**Candidates A and B**

# Language bank

Yes, I would definitely say it's important, and my main reason for that is …

I'm not completely against it; I just don't think it's all that important. What's your view?

While there certainly are some benefits, such as …

Don't you think teenagers are a little young to be burdened with saving?

At the same time, however …

Being prepared for emergencies is very important. Would you agree?

Do you really feel that saving money would make teenagers feel good about themselves? I'm not so sure.

The way I see it, saving brings a kind of independence, which can only be a good thing.

I'm a little concerned about the idea of teenagers having to worry about later life.

I must say, the idea that saving money will make their dreams come true is quite misleading; wouldn't you agree?

What would you say about the benefit of establishing financial security early?

| | |
|---|---|
| avoid debt | pay into |
| bank statements | put towards |
| cash flow | run out |
| current account | save for a rainy day |
| deposit | save up |
| generate interest | set financial goals |
| learn the value of money | track your spending |
| make ends meet | (a) waste of money |

setting and managing budgets

**Is it important for teenagers to learn how to save money? What are the benefits?**

feeling good about themselves

making their dreams come true

demonstrating responsibility

starting to save for later life

▶▶ **PART 2**

**Candidate A**

# Language bank

This one appears to be a nice corner café.

It's possibly in a university town.

It may be frequented by students.

It's clear that this one is more exclusive.

These restaurants are quite different …

By contrast, this one is …

Here, you'll notice …

I'm fairly sure that …

If you look at the furniture …

It seems a safe bet that this is a fast-food restaurant.

I can tell that …

I would say that this one …

Here, however …

affordable
casual dining
complex dishes
expensive
fine dining
inexpensive
junk food
moderately priced
pavement patio
popular
relaxed atmosphere
simple fare
special occasion
top of the line
unhealthy options
unusual ingredients
wealthy clientele

- **What kinds of dishes are probably served in each restaurant?**
- **Who would typically dine here?**

▶▶ **PART 2**

**Candidate B**

# Language bank

You could reasonably guess that ...

This might be ...

My assumption is ...

This collector is almost certainly an older person.

I suppose you could say ...

While it's important to avoid stereotypes ...

They would need to have an interest in music.

It's just a guess, but ...

I imagine that ...

They'd have to be ...

But it's also possible that ...

This would probably be the sort of person who ...

ambitious
an eye for pretty objects
ceramics
(a) collectible
comfortably off
delicate
desirable
for personal pleasure
hand-painted
(an) investment
middle aged
music fan
obsessed with
outward appearance
passionate about
pottery
rare
recognise quality
retired person
serious collector
sought-after
teapots
vast collection
vintage cars
vinyl / LPs
worth a fortune

- **What kind of person would collect these items?**
- **Why do people collect things?**

▶ 1

▶ 2

▶ 3

▶▶ **PART 3**
**Candidates A and B**

# Language bank

From my point of view, online learning has more benefits than traditional classroom learning.

We've clearly seen real benefits for students since e-learning became popular. Do you agree?

Let's not forget some of the key disadvantages, however.

I see what you're saying, but I think you have to look at the overall picture.

Yes, I know what you mean. That is a concern.

At the end of the day, it's hard to see how a computer program can ever replace a real teacher.

But don't you think that this is simply the way of the future?

I feel it really depends on the individual student. What about you?

To be honest, I think the benefits for both types of learning are about equal.

access any time
case-by-case basis
chat rooms
consider all angles
dynamic
engaging
focus on your own needs
gives the learner more independence
immediate feedback
lack the confidence to work alone
online forums
online support
peer review
prefer a classroom setting
regular interaction
risk falling behind
study in a familiar environment
too much responsibility for some students
when you take into account ...

- How do these people appear to be feeling, and why?
- What kind of negative emotions do you think they might be feeling?

# Language bank

By all appearances, these people are thrilled.

You can tell that they're incredibly happy.

The look on her face is pure delight.

Their happiness really shines through.

They're clearly overjoyed, and probably quite proud too.

Their delight is obvious.

It's possible that they also feel a little nervous.

They may be experiencing some anxiety as well.

These are big steps which can be quite overwhelming.

Deep down they could feel just a bit uneasy too.

best day of their lives
bride and groom
bundle of joy
celebration
deeply in love
first-time home-buyers
get on the property ladder
hand in hand
happy and healthy new baby
home is where the heart is
home sweet home
marital bliss
mortgage
parental responsibility
patter of tiny feet
place to call their own
tie the knot
wedding reception

ADVANCED

**TEST 3**

▶▶ PART 2

**Candidate B**

- How do these shopping experiences differ?
- Is each method of shopping suited to a different type of person? Why?

# Language bank

This one appears to be quite an expensive shop.

The woman shopping here is presumably very wealthy.

You can tell from the interior that it's quite an exclusive place.

Here we have an outdoor market with various stalls.

This one appears to be a more casual shopping experience.

All kinds of people enjoy browsing at markets like these.

You can find everything from antiques to junk.

You can shop online in the comfort of your own home.

Online shopping has become extremely popular.

I think this is probably the most convenient way to shop.

You can find some real bargains online.

at the touch of a button
bohemian
bric-a-brac
click of the mouse
crafts
credit card fraud
delivered to your door
designer goods
e-commerce
flea market
haggle
high-end store
interesting artefacts
opulence
personal service
quick and easy
shipping costs
something might catch your eye
street vendors

▶ 1

▶ 2

▶ 3

# Language bank

When you're in a salaried job you have the benefit of a team environment, which is a good thing, I think.

That's true; you have the support of a manager and also of your colleagues.

It seems to me that employees have a more structured work day.

You can count on receiving a regular salary when you work for a company, can't you?

It's a valid point, and it helps with financial planning.

On the other hand, if you're self-employed you have much more flexibility.

Don't you think it's a lot of responsibility to stay on top of things?

But if it's your own business I imagine you would be motivated to run it well.

I expect it must get lonely sometimes, being self-employed.

Some people probably would feel lonely, but not necessarily everyone.

People who work for themselves can go out to lunch and do other social things.

| | |
|---|---|
| be left to your own devices | freelancer |
| be your own boss | get burned out |
| bite off more than you can chew | goal-oriented |
| bureaucracy | independent |
| cash-flow problems | lack of commuter stress |
| climb the corporate ladder | manage all aspects of the business |
| common goals | management style |
| company policy | nine to five |
| corporate environment | office politics |
| disciplined | rat race |
| dress code | team player |
| driven | team spirit |
| endless meetings | toe the line |
| focus on what you enjoy | work to your strengths |

▸▸ **PART 2**

**Candidate A**

- **What type of person do you think each woman is?**
- **Does their choice of beverage say anything about their lifestyle?**

# Language bank

It seems reasonable to assume that …

Looking at this, I would imagine …

My guess is that this person enjoys good coffee.

She probably likes relaxing with a coffee.

Her lifestyle could be a busy one, and coffee keeps her going.

This woman has gone with the healthy option.

Clearly, she has made an effort to blend fruit for a healthy drink.

She might be a fitness instructor, or a dance teacher.

It's possible that she's on a diet.

It looks like the young woman is enjoying a fizzy drink.

She may be enjoying a cold drink on a warm day.

Drinks like these often have a high sugar content and are quite unhealthy.

She seems quite relaxed and easy-going.

artificial sweetener
bubbly personality
caffeine fix
carbonated
chilling out
coffee addict
coffee break
detox
down-time
keep-fit enthusiast
milkshake
probably caffeinated
smoothie
soft drink
sugar high
super foods

▸ **1**

▸ **2**

▸ **3**

▸▸ **PART 2**

**Candidate B**

• **What do you imagine are the circumstances in each picture?**
• **How might these people be feeling?**

# Language bank

This man is obviously on a train platform.

He may have missed his train.

He could be there to meet his girlfriend off the train.

Who knows; maybe he just enjoys looking at trains!

He doesn't look very happy, but perhaps he's feeling pensive.

Maybe he's just arrived somewhere new.

He looks like a man with things on his mind.

This appears to be the waiting room at a dentist or doctor's office.

Some of the people could be there with a friend or partner.

It's likely that they're feeling unwell or apprehensive.

One of them seems to be quite preoccupied.

They could be at the clinic to get a vaccination, for example, a flu shot.

She's wearing a business suit. This could be a sales meeting for her job.

She might be attending a business meeting.

I would definitely say that she's there for an interview.

Her body language makes me think that she probably feels quite relaxed.

But she could be feeling quite anxious.

anticipation
apprehension
business clothes
fearing the worst
outside the meeting room
reception area
straight posture
the screech of brakes
time passes slowly
train timetable
trying to pass the time
waiting in vain
waiting to be called
watching the clock

▸ **1**

▸ **2**

▸ **3**

▶▶ **PART 3**

**Candidates A and B**

# Language bank

Well, whichever way you look at it, I think social-networking sites are here to stay.

I accept that these sites have certain disadvantages but, overall, I feel our lives are improved by them. And, don't forget, they're fun!

To tell you the truth, I think they're the worst thing that ever happened. They create a false sense of friendship.

I must say, I agree with that point. People are forgetting how to socialise normally.

On balance, though, it depends on how you use them. What do you think?

That's a fair point. Too much of anything is a bad thing!

I've noticed that people can be more cruel online than in person and this worries me.

Sometimes you hear amazing stories about how long-lost friends, and even family members, have reconnected through social-networking sites. I think that's wonderful.

My concern is that people don't seem to know where to draw the line and they share too much personal information.

I suppose we're still learning how to exist in the online world and in social-networking sites.

| | |
|---|---|
| activity log | online chat |
| block friends | post comments |
| comments thread | privacy settings |
| deactivate your account | private message |
| direct message | professional recommendation |
| endorsement | profile picture |
| follow (celebrities and others) | registered user |
| followers | secret group |
| friend request | set up an event |
| game applications | share photos |
| hashtag | status update |
| microblogging | tweet |
| newsfeed | |

**new friendships form / old friends reconnect**

**Are social-networking sites improving our lives?**

**less face-to-face communication makes people more isolated**

**more opportunities to express thoughts and share news**

**cyber-bullying has become a serious problem**

**professional networking sites improve job prospects**

▶▶ **PART 2**

**Candidate A**

- **What kind of personality do you think each of the people has?**
- **How do you imagine their pet affects their life?**

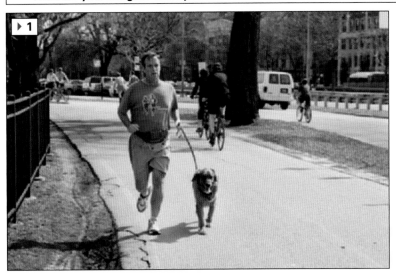

▶ 1

# Language bank

You could guess that the man is quite sporty.

He seems like an outdoor type.

This man might be …

The old lady appears to be very content.

I imagine she's very sweet and loving, and probably a grandmother.

You could probably say …

This boy obviously has a gentle disposition.

He must be quite a brave boy. Not all children like snakes!

He appears to be …

People say they find having a pet very rewarding.

Owning a pet is a lot of responsibility; you have to take good care of them.

Most pets are good companions.

People feel less lonely when they have a pet.

Pets can be a lot of work, but they can also be a lot of fun.

Animals can be fascinating, we can learn a lot from them.

animal kingdom
canine
cold-blooded
feeding time
feline friend
high maintenance
independent traits
indoor cat
intelligent creature
loyal companion
man's best friend
non-poisonous
outdoor lifestyle
reptile
vet's bills
walk the dog

▶ 2

▶ 3

- Why do you think people do extreme sports?
- What kind of person might choose to do sports like these?

# Language bank

I suppose people like the excitement.

There's a big thrill associated with these sports.

The sense of adventure is probably what draws most people.

I think it's all about the speed!

While these sports can be dangerous, they all have safety mechanisms.

They say that people become addicted to the rush of it all.

This looks like a huge adrenalin rush.

Arguably, all sports contain an element of danger.

It's probably a release for anger or stress.

To me, this one looks terrifying!

I imagine they feel a great sense of accomplishment.

It's about challenging yourself, isn't it?

Some people want to push themselves to the limit.

I think they're having enormous fun.

adrenalin junkie
daredevil
determined to succeed
exhausting
fearless
feeling the elements
going the distance
letting off steam
overcoming fears
physical exertion
ready for action
taking a chance
thrill-seeker
trusting
working together

▸▸ **PART 3**
Candidates A and B

# Language bank

It seems to me that renting is fine for a temporary period, but buying is better in the long term.

Many people rent on a long-term basis. I don't see anything wrong in that.

In many countries it's simply not affordable for most people to buy a home.

Exactly. It's a choice that can vary from culture to culture.

Personally, I think you have a lot more freedom when you rent.

Money isn't the only consideration in buying a house. What about the stress?

There's more security in buying a property than renting one.

OK, that's true, but it's only an advantage if you actually like the home you've purchased.

Buying means having to pay property taxes, but this doesn't apply to renting.

| | |
|---|---|
| borrower | lease |
| building society | lender |
| deposit | long-term loan |
| depreciation | maintenance |
| financing | mortgage |
| fixed rates | mortgage broker |
| guarantor | property ladder |
| hidden costs | property rules |
| home owner | property tax |
| interest rates | tenancy agreement |
| landlord / landlady | tenant |

relocating easier when you rent

Is it better to rent or to own your home? What are the advantages and disadvantages?

owning a home is an excellent investment

painting and decorating may not be permitted in a rented property

necessary repairs taken care of when renting

possible decrease in value of a bought home while there's still a mortgage

▶▶ PART 2

Candidate A

• **What kind of medical condition might each of these practitioners treat?**
• **What are the cultural differences between these medical practices?**

# Language bank

In this picture we see a doctor doing his rounds in a hospital.

People go to hospital for complaints from diseases to broken bones.

This one seems to be a more traditional kind of medical practitioner, perhaps in herbal medicine.

She might help local people with stomach complaints, skin problems and other issues.

Here, there appears to be a psychiatrist with a patient.

This could also be a psychologist.

People suffering from depression or anxiety might visit a psychiatrist.

Sometimes people go to counselling if they are finding life difficult to cope with.

Hospitals and mental health professionals are common in most countries.

Various forms of alternative medicine are becoming more popular in western countries.

I don't know very much about this ...

Some people are very sceptical about this form of medicine.

bedside manner
behavioural problems
clinical psychology
conventional medicine
counselling / counsellor
diagnose / diagnosis
healer
healing properties of plants
herbal remedies
herbalist
hospital ward
medical advice
medical chart
mental health issues
personality disorders
prescribe / prescription
ritual
stethoscope
study of the mind
therapist / therapy
traditional medical practitioner
visiting time

▶ 1

▶ 2

▶ 3

▸▸ **PART 2**

**Candidate B**

- How are these places of learning different?
- What do they have in common?

## Language bank

This one shows a modern, brightly lit lecture theatre.

It's probably a university; they look like college students.

Several students are taking notes on their laptops.

On the other hand, these appear to be primary school children.

It looks as though they're having a lesson under the shade of a tree.

My guess is that this is a hot country.

It might be a poor country without proper classroom facilities.

It's possible they just decided to have a class outside to enjoy the nice weather.

By contrast, this is a cookery class.

I'd say it's an adult education course.

It might be at a local community centre.

In all these cases, we can see people learning.

There is one instructor in each picture.

The students are listening or observing.

They all appear to be paying close attention.

blackboard
continuing education
degree course
demonstration
diploma
evening class
learning for pleasure
learning the basics
lecture theatre
lifelong learning
module
outdoor classroom
Powerpoint presentation
rudimentary
tertiary education
training programme
vocational college

▸ **1**

▸ **2**

▸ **3**

▶▶ **PART 3**
**Candidates A and B**

# Language bank

People should be aware that it's normal to feel homesick when you're away from home.

That's a good point.

In some ways, knowing what to expect is half the battle.

Exactly, and remembering that it takes time is important too, wouldn't you say?

Being as positive as possible will also make a big difference.

In principle, getting involved in the local community is a good idea, but it might not be practical.

Yes, there could be a language barrier, for one thing.

I see what you mean. Perhaps the suggestion to make new friends is a better one.

Learning about the other culture is vital, I think. What's your view?

Oh, absolutely. When there's less mystery, there's less difficulty.

Having someone to talk to is an excellent idea. It's important to express your feelings and it also helps you to feel less isolated.

| | |
|---|---|
| a different climate | new environment |
| assumptions and beliefs | regional accents |
| cultural differences | rules of behaviour |
| different values | separation anxiety |
| emotional state | snap judgements |
| etiquette | social norms |
| frustration | stereotyping |
| language barrier | take comfort in familiar things |
| local cuisine | take up a new hobby |
| loneliness and isolation | try to integrate |
| longing for home | unfamiliar surroundings |
| mood swings | well-being |

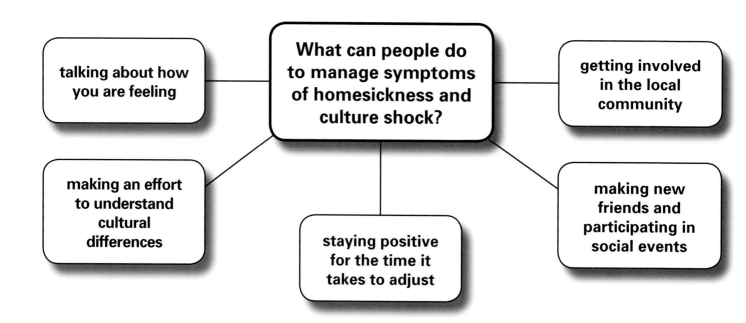

talking about how you are feeling

What can people do to manage symptoms of homesickness and culture shock?

getting involved in the local community

making an effort to understand cultural differences

staying positive for the time it takes to adjust

making new friends and participating in social events

▶▶ **PART 2**

**Candidate A**

- **What kind of impact does each situation have on people?**
- **Can these situations be avoided or not?**

## Language bank

The impact of these situations can vary.

In the modern world, having to wait can bring about stress.

Traffic jams can sometimes be avoided by travelling on quieter roads.

If a traffic jam is caused by an accident, there isn't really any way to avoid it.

We can't see the people but it's likely that they're feeling stressed by the delays.

If you're flying, airport security is simply unavoidable.

People sometimes feel edgy and nervous going through airport security.

Getting frustrated doesn't help the situation.

The more organised people are, the quicker the process goes.

Identity theft can have a devastating impact, both financially and emotionally.

No one likes it when their privacy is violated.

These days, whether we like it or not, computer hackers and viruses are a fact of life.

We should install anti-virus software on our computers.

People should be careful about what information they share online.

backed up for miles
bumper to bumper
carry-on luggage
firewall
frayed nerves
hackers
high anxiety levels
highly stressful
identity theft
malware
metal detector
online security
password protection
permitted items
phishing
privacy settings
security guards
serious congestion
spyware
stuck in traffic
take the necessary precautions
total gridlock
traffic is at a standstill
virus writers
x-ray screening

▶ **1**

▶ **2**

▶ **3**

http://www.l

Virus Alert!

Warning! Threat detected!

A malicious item has been detected!

▶▶ **PART 2**

**Candidate B**

- **What kinds of skills are needed to do each of these jobs well?**
- **Are men or women better suited to each occupation?**

# Language bank

People who work in construction need to be very aware of safety.

They also need stamina as the work can be heavy, and they have to be outside in all weathers.

I think it's becoming a more common career choice for women than it used to be.

To be a nurse or carer, a person needs to be reliable and patient.

It's a care profession, so it's important to have compassion and empathy too.

It's usually viewed as 'women's work' but the stereotype is changing and more men are choosing this profession.

Working as a plumber requires training and official qualifications.

As you work with the public, you also need to be personable.

There's been a huge increase in the number of women training in trades such as plumbing.

These days people are freer to choose whatever profession they want.

Personally, I don't believe that men are better suited to some roles and women to others.

From my point of view it's more about personality. Your character makes you more suited to one role or another, not your gender.

blockage
boiler repair
carer
construction site
dripping taps
efficient
fixing leaks
high-visibility jacket
nursing profession
pneumatic drill
safety equipment
scrubs
sensitive
sympathetic to a patient's needs
tool box

▶ 1

▶ 2

▶ 3

# Language bank

There's no doubt that new graduates need to find ways of setting themselves apart from other candidates.

Learning a second language shows that you have discipline and determination.

I believe that doing work placements demonstrates commitment and provides experience.

As far as I'm concerned, a second language is always a plus, no matter what field you go into.

I also feel that making your CV stand out is vital because it's the first thing a prospective employer sees.

For most people, interviews are often nerve-wracking, so practising techniques and strategies can be very helpful.

In many ways, you're no one if you're not visible on the internet. Graduates should make sure that their posts on social networking sites don't show them in a bad light.

As a matter of fact, I think having a positive online presence is the most useful thing you can do. Employers can learn about you before they've even met you.

| | |
|---|---|
| accomplishments | provide references |
| adaptability | qualifications and skills applicable to the job |
| being innovative | reach the interview stage |
| dress the part | recruitment |
| highlight your strengths | set apart |
| how you come across | showing initiative |
| improve your prospects | stand out |
| make an impression | team spirit |
| make the shortlist | transferable skills |
| objectives | willingness to learn |

▶▶ **PART 2**

**Candidate A**

• **What do you think is happening in these pictures?**
• **How do you think these people might be feeling?**

# Language bank

This picture shows a happy occasion, a birthday. The woman looks surprised and delighted, perhaps her friends surprised her with this birthday cake.

I imagine she's feeling loved and very grateful to have her friends around her.

This man is giving a speech. Judging by the number of microphones, it seems to be an important occasion.

He might be a politician giving a public address.

Perhaps this is an awards ceremony and the person is making an acceptance speech.

I suppose it's possible that he feels a little nervous, but I doubt that. He looks exhilarated.

He might be introducing another speaker.

In this picture, by contrast, the woman has dropped her groceries, which is unfortunate.

She's probably annoyed because she's lost some of her shopping.

People passing by can see what's happened, so she could also be feeling embarrassed.

annoyed
awkward
captivates the audience
centre of attention
comfortable with public speaking
cuts an important figure
doing too many things at once
elated, joyful
embarrassed
everyday accident
expression of love
group celebration
high-level businessman / politician
in control
in his element
in the limelight
in the public eye
in the spotlight
inconvenient
influential person
marking the occasion
multitasking
running errands
shared moment
unexpected treat

▶▶ PART 2

**Candidate B**

# Language bank

The woman in this picture looks distinctly fed up.

Personally, I don't blame her; the person she's at the restaurant with is speaking on his mobile phone. That's just rude.

She's probably feeling neglected and upset. Maybe he makes a habit of ignoring her.

Then again, maybe it's just a quick call. Perhaps she's being unreasonable.

By all appearances, this businessman is very cross. He looks furious.

My guess is that a situation at the office has made him angry.

Maybe he has just lost a lot of money.

Perhaps someone made a mistake that has big consequences for the company.

He could be under a lot of pressure.

This child is crying; he looks so sad.

I'm guessing that his parents have been strict with him; they possibly refused to give him something.

Maybe a sibling, or one of his friends, was mean to him.

There could be any reason, really. Perhaps he's just fallen over.

agitated
blow a fuse
demanding
distressed
don't jump to conclusions
exasperated
finger-pointing
fuming
hard to please
incensed
indignant
over the top
overreaction
petulant
short-tempered
sulky
take a step back
tearful
there are two sides to every story
things are not always what they seem
throw a tantrum

- Which emotions are these people probably feeling?
- What situation might have made them feel this way?

▶▶ **PART 3**

**Candidates A and B**

# Language bank

For the most part, I think these steps are easy enough for the general public to take on board.

It just means making relatively small changes in most cases, such as remembering to carry bags with you.

Awareness is an important aspect too. People need to be informed about where to recycle batteries and electronic goods, for example.

I would agree with that. It's really a question of changing the mindset, isn't it?

To be fair, not driving is simply not an option in some situations. It really depends on where you live, doesn't it?

It's basically about getting into the habit of doing – or not doing – certain things, like having quicker showers to save water, or stopping to think before you buy bottled water.

Maybe something can be done … neighbours carpooling for the school run, for example.

Sometimes I think people are too quick to take the convenient route without thinking about creative solutions.

| | |
|---|---|
| alternative energy | environmentally friendly |
| biodegradable | global warming |
| biofuels | greenhouse gases |
| carbon footprint | organic |
| clean energy | pollution |
| climate change | recycling |
| conservationist | renewable energy |
| eco-tourism | social responsibility |
| energy efficient | sustainable |
| environmentalist | waste management |

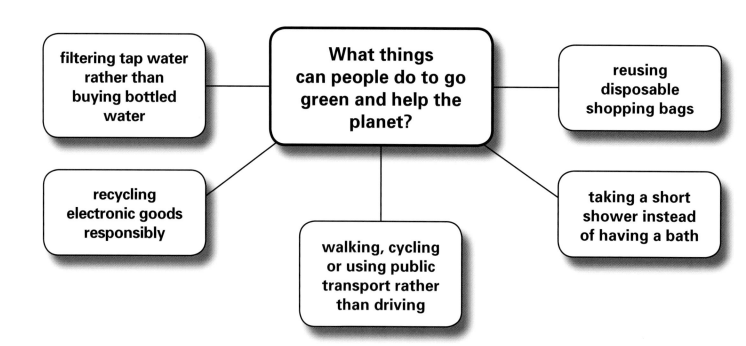

filtering tap water rather than buying bottled water

recycling electronic goods responsibly

**What things can people do to go green and help the planet?**

reusing disposable shopping bags

taking a short shower instead of having a bath

walking, cycling or using public transport rather than driving

## Preparing, planning and checking

### ▸▸ Preparing for the Writing paper

Producing a piece of writing that fulfils a certain function is a difficult task for anybody, even in their native language. To prepare for the Writing paper, it goes without saying that you need to have read widely. Then, you need to have studied all the basic text types you may be asked to produce, and understood the basic features that characterise them: layout, organisation, style and register. You should also practise completing writing tasks in the time allowed in the exam. Remember the criteria the examiners will use in awarding marks:

● Has the candidate achieved the purpose stated in the instructions?
● Does the text have a positive general effect on the target reader?
● Does the text cover all the content points?
● Is the text well organised and are ideas linked appropriately?
● Has language been used accurately?
● Does the text exhibit a good range of vocabulary and grammatical structures?
● Is the register appropriate for the task?
● Is the layout appropriate?

Ideally, the pieces of writing you produce should be checked by an experienced teacher who can provide useful feedback. Such feedback can help you compile a list of useful expressions, such as the useful phrases you find with the model answers in this section. You can also learn what sort of mistakes you make habitually so you can avoid them. For instance, if you find that you frequently make mistakes with a certain tense, you should consult a good grammar guide to clear up your confusion.

### ▸▸ Planning your answer

Perhaps the most useful lesson that experienced writers learn is the importance of planning what to write before they actually begin writing. Most good writers usually write several drafts of a text before they are satisfied with the result. Unfortunately, in the exam you do not have

time to produce several drafts, and it would be a serious mistake to try: you only have time for a single draft. But you do have time to make a plan.

Always read the question carefully and make sure you understand the following:

● Who are you writing for?
● What are the points you must include in your answer?
● Does the text type have any particular layout requirements?
● Do you have the necessary vocabulary to answer the question?

Then prepare a plan or outline of what you are going to write. Its purpose is to help you, so it doesn't matter if you change it or cross things out – nobody else is going to read it. But it has to show clearly the different sections of your writing and what points you must include in which section. When you look at the plan closely, you might want to change it; for instance, something might be better in a different paragraph, or you might realise you will be repeating yourself. When you are satisfied with your outline, you will find it much easier to write your text. Planning takes time, so allow a minimum of 15 minutes for it.

### ▸▸ Checking

Most people make more mistakes than normal under exam conditions, so always allow at least ten minutes at the end to read through your work. Think of your task here as having two parts. First, check that you have answered the question correctly and that you have included all the information that was required. Secondly, check for mistakes in grammar, spelling, punctuation, etc. You should by now have had enough experience to know where you often make mistakes – the spelling of certain words, for instance, or a particular type of punctuation.

If you need to correct something, make the correction neatly and legibly. If you need to cross out something you have written, just put one line through the word or words.

## 1 Essay

▶▶ **Exam task – Part 1**

You attended a philosophy seminar in which the tutor suggested that all exams in schools and colleges be abolished. You have made the notes below.

---

### Abolish exams

- Students are denied the enriching experience of learning because they are under too much pressure to pass the exam.

- Exams are not very effective because they test memory rather than intelligence.

- It's not a fair process; exam stress affects some students more than others. Not everyone performs well in exams.

---

**Other students in the seminar expressed their opinions:**

"But working towards the final exam often gives us the motivation we need in order to study."

"Exam-based assessment is a good way of figuring out whether a student has really understood what they have been taught."

"Taking exams at school and university is actually a good life skill because it trains us to plan, prepare and deliver."

---

Write an essay for your tutor discussing **two** of the points from your notes. You should **explain whether you think abolishing exams is a good idea** and **provide reasons** to support your opinions.

You may, if you wish, make use of the opinions expressed in the lecture, but you should use your own words as far as possible.

▶▶ **Approach**

▶ Pay careful attention to the structure you use for your essay. You can follow these guidelines:

**Title:** Always choose an appropriate title. A good essay title should leave the reader in no doubt as to the topic of the essay. The title should be relevant and, importantly, it should be concise.

**Introduction:** Your opening paragraph is your introduction. Begin by clearly stating the topic, then provide a brief outline letting the reader know what will be covered in the essay. Don't reveal your own opinions in the introduction; wait until the main body of your essay.

**Main body:** Remember, your task in this part of the exam is to discuss two of the points provided. You can certainly add to this as long as you do not exceed the limit of 260 words, but don't submit an essay with fewer than two points discussed. Depending on how many key points you wish to include, the main body of your essay can comprise two or three paragraphs but, ideally, not more. Dedicate one paragraph to each point.

**Conclusion:** Your final paragraph is your conclusion. This is where you should set out a balanced summary of the points you have made. In the essay, it's optional to present your own views on the topic, but this is where you should state or restate your opinions if you do decide to include them.

▶ The tone you adopt is important. Typically for an essay, it should be formal. An informal register is not appropriate for this part of the exam.

▶ Avoid losing focus in the pressurised environment of the exam by organising your thoughts before you begin writing. Having a plan in advance will ensure clarity and readability. Always keep the reader in mind as you write your essay.

Decide on a relevant and obvious title for your essay.

### Should exams be abolished?

The idea that exams should be abolished in schools and colleges is not a new one. In this essay, I will present some of the arguments for and against this suggestion, which regularly arises in education reviews, and consider the implications of each one.

Your opening sentence should clearly spell out the topic.

In the introduction, establish the context of the essay and state what the reader can expect.

First and foremost, many people feel that exams set learners at an unfair disadvantage. This is because some students – including excellent students – get very nervous and find it difficult to cope with the pressures of the exam situation. Their anxiety causes them to perform so poorly that the test is not a fair measure of their knowledge and hard work. In spite of this, it is generally agreed that exams are an important preparation for life, and we all need to manage stress.

Feature a strong topic sentence early in each new paragraph.

Support your key points with examples or additional explanations.

People also question the value of exams as an accurate measure of intelligence. It is argued that simply memorising information does not prove that a learner has meaningfully engaged with a subject. 'A monkey can be trained to memorise things,' is a sentiment often voiced. While this may be true, the question is what could effectively replace exams. The most common option put forward is that of continuous assessment based on coursework submitted throughout the year.

Use passive reporting structures such as *It is thought/agreed/ argued that ...* for general opinions.

If possible, include statistics or quotes to bring your essay to life.

It's a good idea to offer counterpoints for balance.

All in all, opinions are still divided about the value of exams as a form of assessment, but the majority opinion is in favour of retaining exams in schools and colleges. While the exam system certainly has flaws, summarily abolishing it is not a viable option.

Use your concluding paragraph to briefly summarise the essay and to record an outcome.

# Useful phrases

### Introduction

Imagine if ... (all exams were abolished)

This essay will explore the idea of ...

In this essay, I am going to discuss whether ...

### Main body

First of all, ...

The most important issue to consider is ...

In order to decide whether ...

Let us begin by ...

To begin with ...

This is illustrated by ...

A key point to note is ...

On the other hand ...

Another important point is ...

In contrast to this ...

However, it is also true to say ...

### Conclusion

To sum up ...

Summing up ...

In conclusion, we have seen that ...

It seems clear that ...

As I have shown, ...

## 2 Formal letter

▶ ▶ **Exam task – Part 2**

You recently took a domestic flight which was badly delayed, and service from the crew was poor. Write a letter to the customer services manager and include the following information:

- plane sat on the runway for over two hours with no information from the crew

- one member of staff was particularly rude when two passengers asked if they could switch seats

- after take-off, it was announced that no food or drinks would be served, not even mineral water.

Write your **letter**.

▶ ▶ **Approach**

▶ Make sure you know how to structure a formal letter, e.g. a letter asking for information or a letter of complaint. You can follow these guidelines for a letter of complaint:

**Opening:** Use an appropriate salutation (greeting).

**Main body:** First paragraph: state what your complaint is about.

Second paragraph: explain exactly what happened, including where and when.

Next paragraph(s): mention any additional details and say how the problem affected you.

Final paragraph: state how you expect the problem to be resolved.

**Closing:** Use an appropriate ending.

▶ You should always write a formal letter in a formal register.

▶ Although the person writing the complaint letter may be unhappy, or even angry, it's very important to maintain a polite tone throughout.

# Useful phrases

**Opening**

Dear Mr (or Mrs, Ms, Miss, etc.) Surname,

Dear Sir or Madam, (if you don't know their name or gender)

**Main body**

I am writing to complain about …

I would like to express my dissatisfaction with …

I wish to complain in the strongest terms about …

On (date) I purchased (product or service).

I was appalled to discover …

And as if that weren't bad enough, …

To add insult to injury, …

The experience was very distressing …

In the circumstances, I think a full refund is in order.

I expect to be fully compensated for …

Please let me know how you propose to rectify the situation.

I trust there will be a prompt resolution of …

I look forward to receiving your explanation of …

**Closing**

Yours sincerely, (if you have named the person in your opening greeting)

Yours faithfully, (if you have not named the person in your opening greeting)

### ▶ ▶ Model answer

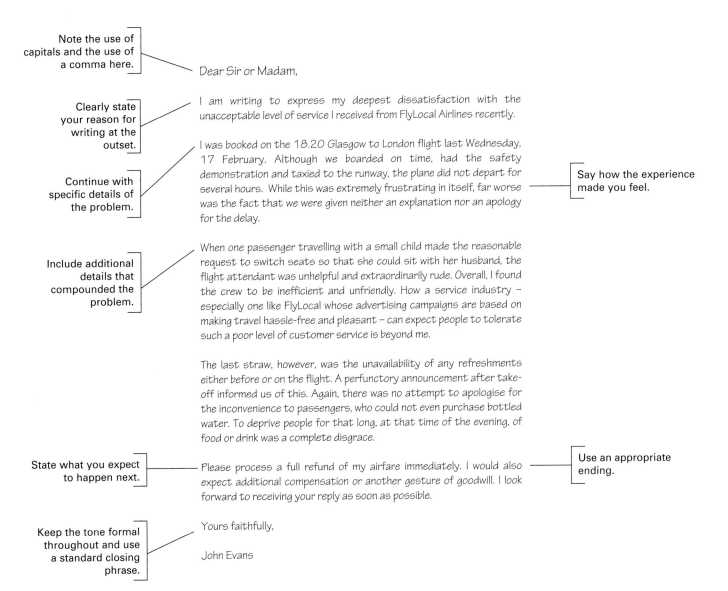

**Note the use of capitals and the use of a comma here.**

Dear Sir or Madam,

**Clearly state your reason for writing at the outset.**

I am writing to express my deepest dissatisfaction with the unacceptable level of service I received from FlyLocal Airlines recently.

**Continue with specific details of the problem.**

I was booked on the 18.20 Glasgow to London flight last Wednesday, 17 February. Although we boarded on time, had the safety demonstration and taxied to the runway, the plane did not depart for several hours. While this was extremely frustrating in itself, far worse was the fact that we were given neither an explanation nor an apology for the delay.

**Say how the experience made you feel.**

**Include additional details that compounded the problem.**

When one passenger travelling with a small child made the reasonable request to switch seats so that she could sit with her husband, the flight attendant was unhelpful and extraordinarily rude. Overall, I found the crew to be inefficient and unfriendly. How a service industry – especially one like FlyLocal whose advertising campaigns are based on making travel hassle-free and pleasant – can expect people to tolerate such a poor level of customer service is beyond me.

The last straw, however, was the unavailability of any refreshments either before or on the flight. A perfunctory announcement after take-off informed us of this. Again, there was no attempt to apologise for the inconvenience to passengers, who could not even purchase bottled water. To deprive people for that long, at that time of the evening, of food or drink was a complete disgrace.

**State what you expect to happen next.**

Please process a full refund of my airfare immediately. I would also expect additional compensation or another gesture of goodwill. I look forward to receiving your reply as soon as possible.

**Use an appropriate ending.**

**Keep the tone formal throughout and use a standard closing phrase.**

Yours faithfully,

John Evans

### 3 Informal letter/email

▶ ▶ **Exam task – Part 2**

A couple of years ago you did a Volunteering Abroad programme in South Africa. Your 17-year-old cousin, Dan, is thinking of doing the same thing and has written to you asking about it.

Read the extract from Dan's email.

> The animal conservation work you did sounds interesting – can you tell me a bit more about it, for example, which animals did you work with? I definitely hope to do a lot of travelling while I'm there too. Can you suggest anywhere I can visit? I suppose what I'm wondering more than anything is whether you think I'll enjoy it.
>
> Thanks, Paul!
> Dan

▶ ▶ **Approach**

▶ The structure of an informal email is less prescribed than a formal email or letter. See the *Useful phrases* section below for appropriate opening and closing expressions. The main body of your email can be structured as you choose, but keep related points together, include linking words and phrases and use paragraphs to break up the text.

▶ Pay close attention to the points made in the input text as you will be expected to address each one in your reply.

▶ Since the question only shows an extract from Dan's email, you also have the option of 'inventing' additional points he may have addressed. However, make sure you don't exceed the permitted 260 word limit.

▶ As this is an informal communication your tone should be friendly and you can use contractions and colloquial expressions, but don't be tempted to slip into slang or text-speak; you are still expected to produce grammatically correct English. A good practice is to follow the tone used in the input text.

## Useful phrases

Opening

Hi [first name],

Hello [first name],

Thanks for your email.

Great to hear from you!

I was delighted to get your email.

I was so glad to hear from you.

It sounds like things are going well.

**Connectors**

By the way, ...

Oh, and one more thing, ...

As I was saying earlier, ...

To tell you the truth, ...

Actually, ...

About your question ...

As far as [X] is concerned ...

To your point about ...

**Closing**

All the best,

Speak soon,

Take care,

Well, that's it for now ...

Cheers,

Have to run,

Drop me a line soon.

## ▶▶ Model answer

Use a casual, informal opening greeting. — Hi Dan,

Acknowledge the email you're replying to. — Thanks for your email; it was really great to hear from you yesterday! I'm so glad you're thinking about going to South Africa. I've just been reading through the travel diary I kept when I did that Volunteering Abroad programme and so many memories came flooding back.

Address the specific points you've been asked about. — Right, you wanted to know about the animal conservation work that I was involved in, so I'll start with that. I requested a placement on a lion reserve in the east of the country because I specifically wanted to work with lions. It was tough, but incredibly rewarding too. I worked with a brilliant team who tracked the animals in the bush. I was given thorough training in animal identification and data collection using the research equipment. Honestly, Dan, it's absolutely amazing to see these magnificent animals in their natural habitat. I really loved it, and I think you would too.

— Include details that will help to paint a clear picture of the experience.

— Using intensifying adverbs will make your email sound more authentic.

Don't be afraid to elaborate on what you've been asked; just keep an eye on your word count. — If you'd like to try the same project, let me know and I'll send you more details. The accommodation is shared and pretty basic, but it's fine. You'll have plenty of opportunities to travel and have fun. I can recommend the spectacular Drakensberg Mountains, which are nearby, and the Blyde River Canyon and beautiful Sodwana Bay. One of my friends even travelled to Mozambique. You should do it!

Bring the email to an end in a friendly way. — OK, I'll leave it at that for now. Drop me a line if you have any more questions or want any more information. Give my love to your Mum and Dad!

— Make the offer to follow up with additional information, if needed.

Use an appropriate closing expression. — Cheers, Dan,

Paul

## 4 Proposal

▸ ▸ **Exam task – Part 2**

A former colleague has set up her own catering business and has asked for your help in improving her website. Choose two or three points for improvement, focussing on design, ease of use and organisation. Write a proposal explaining how your recommended changes will make the website more attractive as well as easier for customers to navigate.

Write your **proposal**.

▸ ▸ **Approach**

▸ A proposal is usually written in a formal register. Depending on the circumstances – in the scenario we are using here, for example – the tone could also be semi-formal because the people concerned know each other personally. A proposal would not typically be informal. Maintain a consistent tone throughout the proposal.

▸ In structure, a proposal should have a logical title, an introduction which provides some background, a main body made up of the suggestions you are proposing and a conclusion which summarises what you have already said. The main body can be structured any number of ways, using headings or bulleted lists, for example. You can always adapt the layout to suit the needs of a given proposal as long as your points are clearly separated, organised and easy for the reader to follow.

▸ A proposal is similar to a report but it is generally created in response to a problem, prompting action or further discussion. Its function is usually to convince somebody of something rather than just reporting facts and statistics. For this reason, make an effort to incorporate persuasive language into your report. It's also a good idea to have some business vocabulary to draw from in case the proposal is business-based.

▸ Even if you think of lots of ideas and suggestions for the proposal in the exam, resist the temptation to include too many. It's better to present a few well-developed suggestions than a long list of ideas.

▸ To make your proposal more effective, expound a little on your suggestions. Mention, for example, how they can be implemented and what they will accomplish.

▸ In some cases, you may wish to discuss finances and budgetary requirements in your proposal. This is optional unless expressly stated in the question.

## Useful phrases

**Introduction**

This proposal will discuss …

As requested, I am submitting this proposal on …

The aim of this proposal is to …

In this proposal I will outline …

**Main body**

Based on this issue, I would suggest …

In terms of …

What I propose here is …

It would be advisable to …

The following steps need to be taken …

One way to counter this problem is to …

This issue could be resolved by …

The benefit of making this change would be …

I would strongly recommend …

**Conclusion**

In conclusion, the way forward appears to be …

Taking all these points into consideration, …

Having assessed the situation, I believe …

I trust you will give this proposal careful consideration.

**▶ ▶ Model answer**

The title should make the subject of the proposal obvious.

Use concise headings for clarity.

Explain what the issue is and how it can be addressed.

## Proposal for improvements to the *Orderin* website

### Introduction
As requested, I am submitting the following proposal to improve the website of your *Orderin* catering business.

Give a basic overview in your introduction.

### Design
The existing design is adequate, but not compelling. The colour scheme is dull and would benefit from some brighter tones. It is also text heavy, which I suggest breaking up with various eye-catching images. I recommend including some shots of the dishes and platters you offer, and photos of catered events showing happy guests.

Make sure your suggestions and recommendations are easy for the reader to follow.

### Ease of use
The whole point about ease of use is that every visitor to your site should have a positive user experience, and there are some basic steps you can take in this regard. For example, set the main menu across the top of the page; people do not enjoy scrolling down too far. The rule of thumb here is 'keep it simple'.

### Organisation
Good organisation allows potential customers to find what they need quickly. Currently, the site lacks a clear structure; it is too cluttered and has too many tabs presented in no logical order. Making a list of the most important topics and deciding on a hierarchy for them will ensure that your key content is obvious at a glance. My advice would be to choose the most popular event types, such as weddings, parties, corporate events.

Tie the points of the proposal together in your conclusion.

### Conclusion
To sum up, the issues with the site can be resolved by following the steps I have outlined above, all of which can be easily and inexpensively implemented.

## 5 Report

▶ ▶ **Exam task – Part 2**

You see this pop-up ad on your local tourist information office website.

> Here at Happy Trails we are working on a new travel guide for visitors to your area. We need the latest information on all forms of entertainment currently on offer in your town. If you would like to contribute to this chapter, please send a report describing the options available.

Write your **report**.

▶ ▶ **Approach**

▶ Reports are typically written in a formal or semi-formal register. Pay attention to the input text and keep the reader in mind as you create your report.

▶ Unlike a proposal, the purpose of a report is to inform rather than persuade. Information in a report should be presented in an organised format, making it easy for the reader to identify the facts. Use impersonal structures to present information, for example *It seems/appears that …, There seems to be …, It has been noted/suggested that …*

▶ The structure should feature a title, introduction, main body and conclusion. You are free to choose any style of layout for the main body but your goal should always be clarity.

▶ In your report, you can invent statistics, incidents, examples, place names and so on to support your ideas. Try to stick to plausible data so that the report does not sound too unrealistic.

▶ Most reports are entirely neutral, but some also feature the writer's opinion. Check the input text to see if it might be appropriate to include your own opinions.

## Useful phrases

**Introduction**
The purpose of this report is to …
This report is based on …
Further to your request for a report on …
This report looks at …

**Main body**
With regard to …
Among the events on offer …
There appears to be widespread agreement that …
It has been noted that …
Moving on to …
It seems widely accepted that …

Opinions vary on the subject of …
As for …
What seems clear is that …
There seems to be a growing demand for …
… has proved to be extremely popular.
Due to the fact that …

**Conclusion**
It can therefore be concluded that …
The obvious conclusion to be drawn from this report …
For the reasons provided …
I trust this report will receive due consideration.

▶ ▶ **Model answer**

Think of a relevant
and concise title.

**Visitor attractions in Oldtown**

**Introduction**
The aim of this report is to illustrate the wide variety of
entertainment available in the Oldtown area for inclusion in a new
travel guide published by Happy Trails.

Break the report into
clear sections with
obvious headings.

**Getting here**
As location is a key consideration for tourists, the convenience of
Oldtown is a great advantage. A domestic airport is situated just
30 kilometres away and the train station connects with several major
routes.

**What's on offer**
Oldtown is a refreshing mix of old and new, combining sites of historical
interest with exciting new events. It has something for everyone, and
here are just some of the options.

Sub-headings help to
categorise different
types of information.

Culture and heritage
- Visit the castle on the outskirts of town for a stunning example of
  medieval architecture.

- Spend an afternoon in the museum on New Street which also
  features an award-winning range of exhibitions for children.

- Enjoy a leisurely river walk, stopping for a picnic in the botanic
  gardens. Thirty-minute walking tours depart from the town hall
  every two hours. A fascinating literary tour is now on offer too.

Bulleted lists draw the
reader's eye to your
key points.

Nightlife
- The Oldtown Theatre runs a compelling programme of plays
  showcasing local talent as well as visiting productions.

- Check out the line-up of bands playing at the Waterfront Hall; always
  book in advance for weekend performances.

- Laughter abounds at the comedy club on Oak Road, open to the
  public on Thursday and Friday nights.

A brief conclusion
summarises the
report.

**Conclusion**
From the information provided in this report, it is clear that Oldtown
is worthy of a dedicated chapter in the new travel guide.

---

## 6 Review

▶ ▶ **Exam task – Part 2**

You see this notice on an events website based in your area.

---

### WE NEED YOUR HELP

Here at the Riverfront Theatre we'd like to add to our database of event reviews. If you were at last night's concert given by the student band, *Atmosphere*, we'd love to hear from you. Please send your review of the concert to the email address below.

---

Write your **review**.

▶ ▶ **Approach**

▶ Reviews are published to describe something, such as a book, film or performance, to the public and to indicate the quality of this product or event. Although a review is an opinion piece, it's a good idea to try to offer a balanced view rather than entirely positive or entirely negative comments.

▶ As always in the Writing paper, study the question and the input text carefully in order to establish exactly what you are being asked to produce and to decide which register you should use. Noting the audience here, an informal or semi-formal tone seems appropriate in this case.

▶ In structure, you can use headings and other formatting styles if you wish. You might decide to first describe the concert and then follow this with your opinions, or you could introduce your views in tandem with the points in your description. State the subject of the review at the beginning and make sure your opinion is stated (or restated) in the concluding paragraph.

▶ Use descriptive language. Include colourful adjectives and adverbs to really convey to the reader what the event was like.

▶ Be careful not to submit a basic list of criticisms and praise. It's important to develop your ideas and to support your points with examples in the review. In other words, don't simply comment that it was good or bad, say *why* it was good or bad.

## Useful phrases

This event took place at …

What made it a success was …

Where it fell down was …

In my opinion, …

I found it rather …

Unfortunately, …

A particular weakness was …

Slightly disappointing was …

It was an incredible performance.

It seems to me that …

You might think …

… something of a let-down.

While I understand this criticism, I also feel …

It's worth mentioning that …

This would appeal to …

What I particularly appreciated …

However, overall …

I highly recommend …

On balance, …

## ▶ ▶ **Model answer**

Choose a suitable title. Don't spend too long trying to think of something clever.

State early on exactly what it is that you are reviewing.

### Enjoy the *Atmosphere*!

The Riverfront Theatre was the place to be last Thursday evening. Up-and-coming band, *Atmosphere*, played their hearts out for 95 electrifying minutes, at once delighting their already solid fan base while also gaining a multitude of new fans.

Try to open with a sentence that will immediately grab the reader's attention.

*Atmosphere* have been around for about a year now. Consisting of four permanent band members, they keep their sound fresh by regularly working with guest performers who contribute a variety of instruments and harmonies to the mix. Their main genre is high-energy rock, which is occasionally softened by pop beats and catchy lyrics.

Ideally, provide a little background to give the reader some context.

What made Thursday's concert such a resounding success was the choice of venue. Clearly this type of platform suits them best … a band with a big sound needs a big venue. Unfortunately, the sound quality was poor at the beginning of their set but this was quickly rectified.

Explain each point you make.

Like any good front man, lead singer Adam Elliott has a powerful stage presence. He connects with the crowd instantly, drawing them in through ballads and conducting them in several rousing choruses.

What *Atmosphere* might need to focus on a little more is rehearsal time. Some of the songs weren't as tight as they should have been and the bass player came in late a few times. Still, this did nothing to spoil the overall experience.

Try to balance your positive and negative comments.

Aim for a strong conclusion and make sure it represents your opinion of the event.

Your really should go and see this band at the first opportunity. They are destined for great things, no question, and I fully intend to catch them again the next time I have the chance.

## TEST **1**

PAPER 1 Reading and Use of English

▶▶ **PART 1**

**eatery** (n) informal word for a restaurant or café

**Paleolithic** (adj) from the early Stone Ages (2.6 million to 10,000 years ago)

**hunter-gatherer** (n) person whose food comes from wild plants and hunted animals, not agriculture

▶▶ **PART 2**

**scepticism** (n) being sceptical or doubting that something claimed to be true is really true

▶▶ **PART 3**

**reside** (v) to live in a particular place

**truck in** (phr v) to transport somewhere by truck or lorry

**arid** (adj) very dry

**moist** (adj) slightly wet

**droplet** (n) small drop of liquid

**desertification** (n) process of becoming a desert

▶▶ **PART 5**

**lengthy** (adj) continuing for a long time

**guillemot** (n) black and white seabird

**symmetry** (n) when two halves or sides of something are an exact match in size, shape, appearance, etc.

**disprove** (v) to show that something is wrong or false

**nibble** (v) to take small bites

**cliché** (n) idea that is used so often it becomes boring and loses meaning

**preen** (v) to spend a lot of time making yourself look attractive

**steer clear of** (phr) to stay away from

**deviate** (v) to do something differently from what is usually expected

**hard-nosed** (adj) not affected by feelings

**incubate** (v) to sit on eggs to keep them warm until they hatch (of birds)

**fraught (with)** (adj) filled with something difficult

**physiology** (n) all the processes and functions of a living organism (also the study of how living organisms function)

**neurobiology** (n) biology of the nervous system (also the study of the biology of the nervous system)

**framework** (n) set of beliefs and ideas used as the basis for making judgements and decisions

**sensory** (adj) connected with physical senses such as sight and smell

**proportioned** (adj) having parts that relate in size and shape to other parts

**peacock** (n) large bird with long blue and green tail feathers that open out in the shape of a fan

**starling** (n) common bird with dark, shiny feathers and loud call

▶▶ **PART 6**

**implication** (n) likely result of something

**prosperity** (n) economic success

**spurn** (v) to reject or refuse

**subsidise** (v) to give money to help pay for something

**demographic** (n) part of the population

**perturbed** (adj) worried

**complacent** (adj) too satisfied with the current situation and not making any effort to change

**unenterprising** (adj) uninterested in starting new projects

▶▶ **PART 7**

**plague** (n) serious contagious disease which kills a lot of people

**boom** (n) period of economic success

**bust** (n) economic collapse, often used in contrast to 'boom'

**pandemic** (n) disease that spreads across many regions or countries

**stalagmite** (n) rock pointing upwards from the floor of a cave, formed over a long period from drops of water containing minerals

**proliferate** (v) to grow fast in number

**surge** (n) rapid rise

**anomaly** (n) something different from what is normal or expected

**pendulum** (n) rod with weight at the end that swings from side to side, found in traditional clocks. 'The pendulum swings' is used as an image to describe something changing from one condition to another, and then back again.

**drought** (n) period with no rain and extreme dryness

**conquistador** (n) Spanish conquerors of the native populations of Central and South America in the sixteenth century

**deforestation** (n) destruction of forests

**moisture** (n) small drops of water

**catastrophe** (n) disaster

**shape** (v) to influence

**sprout** (v) to appear suddenly and in significant numbers

**hallmark** (n) typical feature

**misconception** (n) wrong belief or idea, often based on incorrect information

**ride high** (phr) to be successful

**dire** (adj) very bad

**cautionary tale** (phr) example that provides a warning

**befall** (v) when something unpleasant happens

**divine** (adj) coming from or connected to a god

**commission** (v) to pay for someone to create

**intertwine** (v) to connect closely

▸▸ **PART 8**

**acknowledge** (v) to accept to be true

**precedent** (n) action or decision that is used as an example for something similar to follow

**exceed** (v) to be more than

**entrepreneur** (n) someone who starts a new business

**enterprising** (adj) showing the ability to think of new ideas for projects, especially in business, and to carry them out

**envisage** (v) to imagine will happen

**origami** (n) Japanese art of folding paper to create shapes

**cater (for)** (v) to provide what is wanted

**juggle** (v) to do several things at the same time

**dissertation** (n) long essay as part of a university course

**chance upon** (phr v) to meet or find by chance

**mentor** (n) experienced person who gives advice and help

**keep on track** (phr) to keep doing the right thing

**stand someone in good stead** (phr) to be useful for the future

**prototype** (n) first design of something

**file a patent** (phr) to apply for the official right to be the only person legally entitled to make and sell a product

**TEST 2**

PAPER 1 Reading and Use of English

▸▸ **PART 1**

**word of mouth** (phr) informal spoken communication

**viral** (adj) something that circulates rapidly on the internet

▸▸ **PART 2**

**coral** (n) hard, colourful substance formed from the bones of very small sea creatures and found at the bottom of the sea

**fjord** (n) long, narrow strip of sea between high cliffs

**numb** (adj) without any feeling

▸▸ **PART 3**

**expertise** (n) expert knowledge

▸▸ **PART 5**

**ADHD** (abbrev) Attention Deficit Hyperactivity Disorder: a disorder, mainly affecting children, which makes it hard for them to be still and concentrate, and can affect their ability to learn.

**deprive someone of something** (v) to prevent someone from having something

**Parkinson's disease** (n) disease of the nervous system that gets progressively worse and causes the muscles to become weak and to shake

**stationary** (adj) not moving

**incorporate** (v) to become part of

**life-enhancing** (adj) life-improving

**neurologist** (n) doctor who studies and treats diseases of the nerves

**induce** (v) to cause something to happen

**state of meditation** (n) profound mental calmness

**preceding** (adj) previous

**blissful** (adj) very happy

**blur** (n) something you cannot see or remember clearly

**grey matter** (n) the brain, often referring to intelligence

**jostle** (v) to push roughly for position

**Ritalin** (n) medication used to treat disorders of the nervous system such as ADHD

**aerobic** (adj) exercising the heart and lungs

**tandem** (n) bicycle for two people

**incrementally** (adv) a little more each time and steadily

**hop** (v) to jump

**discrepancy** (n) difference between things that should be the same

**rotate** (v) to go round and round

**cue** (n) signal

**hyperactive** (adj) too active

**notwithstanding** (adv) in spite of

▸▸ **PART 6**

**captivity** (n) the state of being enclosed and not free

**habitat** (n) natural environment of an animal or plant

**intervention** (n) becoming involved to deal with a problem

**enclosure** (n) area of land surrounded by a fence or wall, where zoo animals are kept

**primate** (n) group of mammals including humans, apes and monkeys

**odds** (n) probability

**revive** (v) to bring back to life

**endeavour** (n) attempt to do something difficult

**dissemination** (n) spreading of information

**divert** (v) to entertain

**acknowledge** (v) to accept to be true

**stave off** (phr v) to prevent

**replicate** (v) to copy exactly

**bear fruit** (phr) to be successful

**confinement** (n) state of being enclosed and not free

**enlighten** (v) to help understand better

▶▶ **PART 7**

**scatter** (v) to throw to the ground in different directions

**surge** (v) to move quickly

**thrive** (v) to do very well

**tranquility** (n) peace and calm

**peer** (n) someone of the same age and position

**therapeutic** (adj) helping to treat an illness

**sceptical** (adj) doubting that something is true or useful

**wholesome** (adj) healthy

**coriander** (n) plant whose leaves and seeds are used in cooking

▶▶ **PART 8**

**determine** (v) to decide on

**of note** (phr) of importance

**whimsical** (adj) unusual and not serious

**cute** (adj) pretty

**tome** (n) book

**heavy-hitting** (adj) significant

**stream of consciousness** (n) continuous flow of ideas and feelings as they are experienced by someone

**tidbit** (n) small but interesting piece of information

**creepy** (adj) scary

**harbour** (v) to hide and protect

**impetus** (n) motivation or force that causes something to happen

**hard-hitting** (adj) very critical

**muddled** (adj) confused, unclear

**monstrosity** (n) something very ugly

**refute** (v) to reject

**prose** (n) style of writing

**digestible** (adj) easy to absorb

**unearth** (v) to discover

**gem** (n) something beautiful and precious

**epoch** (n) historical period

**canonical** (adj) belonging to a generally accepted list of the best work in its field

**distilled** (adj) summarised

**caricature** (n) a simplified exaggeration of something

**put the record straight** (phr) to establish the truth

**quibble** (v) to argue or complain about a small matter

# TEST 3

PAPER 1 Reading and Use of English

▶▶ **PART 1**

**biodiversity** (n) large number of different types of animals and plants in a particular environment

**catfish** (n) large fish with long hairs around its mouth which look like cats' whiskers

**intervene** (v) to become involved in a situation in order to improve it or to stop something happening

**spine** (n) sharp, pointed feature, usually to protect an animal

**predator** (n) animal that attacks and eats other animals

**classify** (v) to put things in groups according to type, size, etc.

▶▶ **PART 2**

**organ** (n) part of a human or other animal with a specific purpose, e.g. heart, lungs, liver

**invariably** (adv) always

▶▶ **PART 3**

**adorn** (v) to make someone or something attractive through the use of decorations

**drought** (n) period with no rain and extreme dryness

**fuel** (v) to stimulate or help something to develop

▶▶ **PART 5**

**illustrate** (v) to give information or examples to explain something

**enhance** (v) to improve

**plausibly** (adv) easily believed to be true

**immersion** (n) being completely involved in something

**legacy** (n) something that exists now because of what happened in the past

**crew** (v) to work on a boat

**overlap** (n) where two things cover the same area or subject

**manuscript** (n) the author's copy of a book before it is published

**cut corners** (phr) to do something in the easiest way by leaving something out

**infantile** (adj) like a small child

**petulance** (n) bad-tempered, unreasonable behaviour because you can't have what you want

**remorse** (n) feeling of regret for something wrong or bad that you have done

**poignant** (adj) having a strong impact on your feelings, usually to make you feel sad or moved

**enlightening** (adj) giving information to provide a better understanding

**defy** (v) to resist or obstruct

**reservation** (n) doubt

**prose** (n) style of writing

**showily** (adv) in an exaggerated way designed to attract attention (used to show disapproval)

**tricksy** (adj) cunning and intended to deceive

**device** (n) method designed to get a particular result

**abound with** (phr v) to have large quantities of

**pompous** (adj) formal in an exaggerated way and designed to show superiority

**turn of phrase** (phr) particular way of describing something

### ▶▶ PART 6

**chronological** (adj) in the order in which they happened in time

**cartography** (n) the process of making maps

**(a) wealth of** (n) large amount

**painstaking** (adj) very detailed and careful

**rigorous** (adj) well thought through and supported by detail

**guiding principle** (n) main idea which influences the overall way something is dealt with

**pretension** (n) ambition

**enthralled** (adj) fascinated

**erroneous** (adj) incorrect

**GPS** (n) (Global Positioning System) satellite-based navigation system

**round off** (phr v) to complete

**anecdote** (n) interesting personal story

**trivia** (n) unimportant information

**gloss over** (phr v) to avoid talking about something difficult by only briefly referring to it

**compressed** (adj) squeezed together into a smaller space

**decipher** (v) to interpret and understand

**skip** (v) to avoid or leave out

**sample** (v) to experience a small part of something

**cram in** (phr v) to force many things into a small space

### ▶▶ PART 7

**recreational** (adj) as a hobby or form of entertainment

**treadmill** (n) running machine found in gyms

**puff** (v) to breathe hard

**disconcerting** (adj) confusing

**carb** (n) carbohydrate

**cognitive** (adj) connected with metal processes

**leap** (v) to jump

**duck** (v) to move your head down quickly

**sustain** (v) to make something continue

**treacle** (n) thick, sticky liquid made by melting sugar

**screen** (v) to check or examine

**implausible** (adj) very unlikely to be true

**cutting edge** (phr) very modern and advanced

**genome** (n) complete set of genes in a living thing

**hurdle** (n) obstacle or challenge to deal with

**lactic acid** (n) acid produced in muscles during hard exercise

**gradient** (n) slope

### ▶▶ PART 8

**record label** (n) company which produces recorded music

**innovative** (adj) new and not used before

**entail** (v) to involve

**delegate** (v) to give responsibility for something to someone else

**what makes someone tick** (phr) what makes someone behave the way they normally do

**bemoan** (v) to complain about

**flop** (v) to fail

**burn-out** (n) being extremely tired as a result of having worked too much

**perspective** (n) the ability to think about problems in a reasonable way

**lucrative** (adj) producing lots of money

**feel compelled to do something** (phr) to feel you have to do something

**enamoured** (adj) in love with

**outsourcing** (n) business arrangement in which an outside individual or company does work for an organisation

**let alone** (phr) used to emphasise that one thing is even more impossible than the first thing mentioned

**old-school** (adj) traditional

**break the mould** (phr) to do something dramatically new

**pioneer** (n) one of the first people to do something

**all-consuming** (adj) total

**blur** (v) to become less clear

**merchandising** (n) selling goods

 **TEST 4**

### PAPER 1 Reading and Use of English

▶▶ **PART 1**

**fragment** (n) small, broken piece

**marrow** (n) soft substance inside bones

**dweller** (n) someone who lives in a particular place

▶▶ **PART 2**

**whir** (v) to make the noise of a machine

**harness** (v) to control and use something

▶▶ **PART 3**

**anagram** (n) puzzle in which the letters of a word or phrase are arranged in a different order

▶▶ **PART 5**

**megafauna** (n) large animals

**characterise** (v) to describe

**fossil** (n) remains of an animal or plant which have become hard and turned into rock

**spasm** (n) sudden, violent event

**spill ink** (phr) to write about – an idiom which is not very common

**blitzkrieg** (n) a German word that means a sudden violent attack

**hypothesis** (n) theory to explain something

**havoc** (n) destruction

**annihilate** (v) to destroy completely

**bison** (n) large hairy wild animal of the cow family, native to North America

**moose** (n) large deer native to North America

**baffling** (adj) difficult to understand

**paleontological** (adj) relating to paleontology, which is the study of fossils from prehistoric times

**indigenous** (adj) native to a particular place

**parched** (adj) extremely dry

**denuded** (adj) bare

**water cycle** (n) journey water takes as it circulates from land to the sky and back again

**predator** (n) animal that attacks and eats other animals

**be prone to do something** (adj) to have a tendency to do something

**analog** (n) something that is similar

**pivot on** (phr v) to centre or depend on

**sediment** (n) sand, stones and other substances that settle at the bottom of a lake, river or sea

**refuge** (n) a place of safety

**blurry** (adj) unclear

**inconclusive** (adj) not leading to a definite conclusion

**ominous** (adj) worrying

**scenario** (n) description of how things might have happened

**incremental** (adj) gradual or bit by bit

**discern** (v) to recognise or understand something that is not very obvious

▶▶ **PART 6**

**viability** (n) the possibility that something will succeed in future

**terminal decline** (phr) when something is certain to get worse and come to an end

**speculative** (adj) based on guessing or giving an opinion without having factual evidence

**the bottom line** (phr) the most important point

**obsolete** (adj) no longer in use

**perish** (v) to die

**ephemeral** (adj) lasting only for a short period of time

**demise** (n) the end or death of something

▶▶ **PART 7**

**graze** (v) to eat grass

**ranger** (n) person whose job is to look after a park, nature reserve or area of countryside

**exceed** (v) to be more than

**donor** (n) someone that gives money to a person or organisation that needs help

**livestock** (n) farm animals

**arable** (farming) (adj) growing crops like corn and wheat

**proximity** (n) being close to

**pierce** (v) to be suddenly heard

**tick the box** (phr) to put a mark on a list to show that something has been done

**warthog** (n) African wild pig

**exhilarating** (adj) very exciting

**elusive** (adj) difficult to find

**serenity** (n) calmness

**poacher** (n) person who illegally hunts animals

**scrub** (n) land in Africa covered with small bushes and trees

**jackal** (n) wild African animal similar to a dog

**hyena** (n) wild dog-like animal which has a cry that sounds like a human laugh

**trim** (v) to shorten

**enticing** (adj) attractive

#### ▶▶ PART 8

**defy** (v) to make something impossible

**output** (n) production

**contemporary** (n) people living in the same period of time

**minimalist** (adj) made up of simple ideas and sounds

**overwhelming** (adj) extremely powerful

**rigour** (n) disciplined approach

**integrity** (n) honesty and being true to one's principles

**motif** (n) idea or phrase that is repeated

**cantata** (n) short piece of classical music for singers

**permeate** (v) to be present everywhere

**chamber work** (n) classical music for small group of instruments

**quantify** (v) to analyse

**transfix** (v) to capture someone's attention completely

**throw into relief** (phr) to make something more noticeable

**foxtrot** (n) music for a formal type of dance

**take the plunge** (phr) to decide to do something new and difficult

**walk the tightrope** (phr) to have to balance carefully

**jitterbug** (n) music for a fast style of dance

**bossa nova** (n) Brazilian style of music

**tempi** (n) plural of *tempo* – the speed at which music is played

**acoustical** (adj) relating to sound

**property** (n) quality or characteristic

**venue** (n) place where a performance takes place, e.g. a theatre

**choreographed** (adj) directed in the way that dancers' movements are directed

**uncompromising** (adj) sticking strongly to its character

## TEST 5

PAPER 1 Reading and Use of English

#### ▶▶ PART 1

**app** (n) software application, especially for mobile phones

#### ▶▶ PART 2

**migration** (n) when animals or birds move in large numbers from one place to another, usually at particular times of the year

**a figure of eight** (phr) route which in shape is similar to the number 8

#### ▶▶ PART 5

**reef** (n) natural reefs are rocks or sand mounds under the sea, often covered with corals

**incur (costs)** (v) to have to pay money for something done

**shipwreck** (n) ship that has been destroyed and has usually sunk to the bottom of the sea

**oil rig** (n) large structure and equipment used for taking oil from the ground or the seabed

**plankton** (n) very small forms of plant and animal life

**lethal** (adj) able to cause death

**eel** (n) long thin fish that looks like a snake

**opportunistic** (adj) ready to make use of an opportunity (usually used to express disapproval)

**predator** (n) animal that attacks and eats other animals

**prey** (n) animal that is hunted, killed and eaten by another animal

**encrusted** (adj) covered with a thin, hard layer of something

**algae** (n) very simple plants that grow in water

**coral** (n) hard, colourful substance formed from the bones of very small sea creatures and found at the bottom of the sea

**recreational** (adj) as a hobby or form of entertainment

**spared** (adj) saved or protected

**catastrophe** (n) disaster

**akin** (adj) similar

**oasis** (n) area in a desert where there is water and where plants grow

**game fish** (n) fish that people look for in recreational fishing rather than in commercial fishing

**bait** (n) food put on a hook or in nets to attract and catch fish

**asbestos** (n) material used in buildings and ships as protection against fire and to prevent heat loss. It is now known to be toxic and is used much less than in the past.

**scrupulously** (adv) extremely carefully

**stern** (n) back part of a ship

**bow** (n) front part of a ship

**landfill** (n) hole in the ground where waste materials are deposited

**bundled** (adj) tied together

**augment** (v) to add something to

**adjacent** (adj) nearby

**smother** (v) to cover thickly and kill

#### ▶▶ PART 6

**reality TV** (n) television programmes in which ordinary people are continuously filmed, designed to be entertaining rather than informative

**authenticity** (n) how authentic or real something is

**the bottom line** (phr) the most important point

**replicate** (v) to copy exactly

**invariably** (adv) always

**manipulate** (v) to control or influence in a dishonest way

**distort** (v) to change so that something is no longer correct or true

**humiliation** (n) making someone feel ashamed or stupid

**purport** (v) to claim

**banal** (adj) very ordinary and lacking in interest

#### ▶▶ PART 7

**preserve** (n) activity or job thought to be suitable only for one person or type of person

**aesthetics** (n) ideas about what is beautiful, especially in art

**insight** (n) an understanding of what something is like

**protagonist** (n) significant person who changes a situation

**at pains to** (phr) to make a lot of effort to do something

**peer** (n) someone of the same age and position

**concur** (v) to agree

**auction house** (n) company which organises auctions, where things of value are sold to the people who offer most money

**curate** (v) to organise an exhibition of art or other objects

**absorbing** (adj) very interesting

**enriching** (adj) raising the level of your knowledge or experience

**deter** (v) to make someone decide not to do something

**scope** (n) range of things that a subject deals with

**avidly** (adv) very keenly

**enliven** (v) to make more interesting and lively

#### ▶▶ PART 8

**reluctant** (adj) unwilling, not wanting to do something

**misconception** (n) wrong belief or idea, often based on incorrect information

**roped into** (phr) persuaded to do something you don't really want to do

**ad hoc** (adj) not planned in advance

**patron** (n) person or organisation that gives money and support to artists, museums, etc.

**trust** (n) group of people that manages a fund to support a museum, a school, charity, etc.

**networking** (n) deliberately talking to a range of people who may be useful to your work

**donor** (n) person or organisation that gives money as support

**geek** (n) person who is obsessed with something that may seem boring to other people

**archive** (n) place where documents and records are stored

**heritage** (n) historical culture and traditions of a country or society

**conservator** (n) person whose job is to conserve and restore old works of art and other objects

**artefact** (n) object that is made by a person, usually of historical or cultural interest

### ADVANCED TEST 6

#### PAPER 1 Reading and Use of English

#### ▶▶ PART 1

**subtle** (adj) not obvious

**impartial** (adj) unbiased, objective

#### ▶▶ PART 2

**cockatoo** (n) bird belonging to the parrot family

**millennia** (n) thousands of years

**wired** (adj) organised or structured

**keep a beat** (phr) to stay in rhythm with music

#### ▶▶ PART 3

**ethnic** (adj) relating to a particular race

#### ▶▶ PART 5

**aptitude** (n) natural ability

**prostrate** (adj) facing downwards

**defiance** (n) refusal to obey

**grin** (v) to smile widely

**coat hanger** (n) curved piece of wood, plastic or wire with a hook on, used for hanging clothes

**bug** (n) problem in a computer program

**gig** (v) to perform in public

**muck around** (phr v) to behave in a silly way

**outdo** (v) to do better than someone else

**stumble across** (phr v) to find by chance

**cut it** (phr) to be convincing (idiomatic)

**crux** (n) most important part

**onerous** (adj) needing great effort

**be inclined to** (v) to feel like doing something

**punchline** (n) last few words of a joke that make it funny

**script** (v) to write in advance of a performance

**wrestle** (v) to fight someone by holding them and throwing them to the ground

**lost to the ether** (phr) disappeared for ever

## PART 6

**implications** (n) possible consequences

**eradicate** (v) to get rid of completely

**red deer** (n) a type of deer common in Scotland

**deceptive** (adj) misleading

**wilderness** (n) area of land that has never been developed or used for agriculture

**monitor** (v) to watch carefully and record results

**offset** (v) to use one payment to cancel another cost

**flock** (n) group of sheep

**graze** (v) to eat grass

**cull** (v) to kill a number of animals of a group to prevent the group becoming too large

**feasible** (adj) possible to do

**lobby** (n) group of people who try to influence politicians on a particular issue

## PART 7

**bark** (n) hard outside part of a tree

**sequoia** (n) type of tree which is very large and found in North America

**redwood** (n) very large species of trees. The sequoia is part of the redwood family.

**longevity** (n) long life

**fungal rot** (n) process by which wood decays and falls apart as a result of being attacked by fungus

**flame-resistant** (adj) able to survive a fire

**logging** (n) cutting down of trees for commercial purposes

**brittle** (adj) hard but easy to break – like some glass

**shatter** (v) to break into small pieces

**timber** (n) wood for use in building

**robust** (adj) strong and healthy

**limb** (n) large branch on a tree

**crown** (n) rounded top part of a tree

**harness** (n) set of straps attached to ropes to stop someone falling

**cone** (n) hard dry fruit of many species of tree, e.g. of the sequoia

**seedling** (n) young plant that has grown from a seed

**millennia** (n) thousands of years

**premise** (n) idea that forms the basis of an argument or way of thinking

**eucalyptus** (n) a species of tree, particularly common in Australia

**mass** (n) quantity of material that something contains

**spire** (n) tall pointed part at top of tree

**billow** (v) to move up and spread out like a cloud of smoke

## PART 8

**for the sake of** (phr) in order to do something

**disapproval** (n) when someone thinks something is wrong

**suspend your disbelief** (phr) to believe temporarily that something imaginary or invented is real

**reservation** (n) doubt

**awe** (n) feeling of being very impressed

**resentment** (n) feeling of anger or unhappiness about something you think is unfair

**dissipate** (v) to gradually become weaker

**talk down to someone** (phr v) to speak to someone as if they are less important or intelligent

**first principles** (n) the most basic rules

**trigger** (n) original cause of a particular development

**fortuitous** (adj) by chance

**radiology** (n) study of radiation in medicine

**spur** (n) fact or event that makes you want to do something

**innate** (adj) born with

**trait** (n) characteristic

# TEST 7

## PAPER 1 Reading and Use of English

### PART 1

**up-tempo** (adj) with a fast rhythm

**pace** (n) speed

**key** (n) set of related musical notes based on a particular note. Some keys are major and some minor depending on the types of notes they are based on.

**upbeat** (adj) positive and enthusiastic

**melancholic** (adj) sad

**ambiguous** (adj) having more than one possible meaning or feeling

### PART 2

**whine** (v) to complain with an annoying high sound

**mew** (v) to cry with a soft high noise, like a cat

**scan** (v) to use special equipment to take images of something

### PART 3

**contravene** (v) to do something that is not allowed by law

**wilderness** (n) area of land that has never been developed or used for agriculture

## ▸▸ PART 5

**discredit** (v) to make people stop believing something is true

**ill-considered** (adj) badly planned

**abstract** (adj) involving ideas rather than facts

**hooked** (adj) fascinated

**counter-intuitive** (adj) the opposite of what you would probably feel to be true

**graft** (n) work

**innumerate** (adj) very bad at mathematics

**tone-deaf** (adj) unable to hear the difference between musical notes

**correlation** (n) connection between two things in which one thing changes as the other does

**aptitude** (n) natural ability

**plausible** (adj) could be true

**confined** (adj) restricted

**syntax** (n) the way words and phrases are put together to form sentences

**paradoxical** (adj) and **paradox** (n) a paradox is a situation that has two opposite features and therefore seems strange. For example, music is to do with emotions and mathematics is to do with reason and logic, so it might seem paradoxical for someone to be good at both.

**dispel** (v) to get rid of

**confound** (v) to confuse and surprise

## ▸▸ PART 6

**adolescence** (n) time in a person's life when he or she develops from being a child to being an adult

**patronisingly** (adv) if someone is patronising they show you they think they are better than you

**induce** (v) to cause something to happen

**misgiving** (n) feeling of doubt

**speculation** (n) forming opinions about something without having much evidence

**physiology** (n) way a living body functions

**lucidity** (n) in a clear way

**undermine** (v) to make something weaker

**invoke** (v) to mention or refer to

**hypothesis** (n) theory

**plausibility** (n) how likely something is to be true

**wish fulfilment** (n) hoping that an idea is true

**grumpily** (adv) in a bad-tempered way

**inherently** (adv) in itself, naturally

**jazz up** (phr v) to make something seem more exciting

**dumb down** (phr v) to make something seem easier than it really is

**spur** (n) cause of a change

**prose** (n) style of writing

**hardwired** (adj) naturally part of a person's physical development, not caused by external influences

## ▸▸ PART 7

**tracker** (n) person who can find wild animals by following the marks they leave

**pungent** (adj) strong smelling

**thumping** (n) banging noise

**twig** (n) very small, thin branch

**hive** (n) structure where bees live

**pound** (v) to hit hard

**innate** (adj) born with

**jiggle** (v) to make something move up and down or side to side with quick movements

**stem** (n) long, thin, flexible part of a plant

**bristles** (n) short stiff hairs of a brush

**nibble** (v) to take small bites

**cling** (v) to hold on to

**logging** (n) cutting down of trees for commercial purposes

**disarray** (n) extreme confusion

**termite** (n) insect that lives in large groups, found in hot countries, looks similar to white ants

**mound** (n) large pile of earth

**distort** (v) to change so that something is no longer correct or true

**delicacy** (n) nice thing to eat

**lunge** (v) to make a sudden forward movement in order to attack

**prey** (n) animal that is hunted, killed and eaten by another animal

**predator** (n) animal that attacks and eats other animals

**reticence** (n) shyness, unwillingness to show yourself

**whack** (v) to hit hard

## ▸▸ PART 8

**trepidation** (n) worry or fear that something unpleasant will happen

**relief** (n) something different that is easier or more enjoyable than what you have been doing

**proactively** (adv) preparing for problems before they happen

**ward** (n) department in a hospital

**daunted** (adj) anxious, worried

**pitfall** (n) danger or difficulty that might arise, especially one that is hidden or not obvious at first

**averse (to)** (adj) not liking, opposed to

**eradicate** (v) to get rid of completely

**uphold** (v) to apply, follow or support rules

**under my belt** (phr) if you have something under your belt, you have experienced or achieved it

**transparency** (n) when a situation – a policy, for example – can be understood clearly and easily

**get to grips with** (phr) to understand properly

**boil down to** (phr v) to be a result of

**outcome** (n) result of an action or event

**pass the buck** (phr) to make someone else responsible for something

**think out of the box** (phr) to think in a different, unconventional way in order to be creative

**blinkered** (adj) restricted in thinking, narrow-minded

## ADVANCED TEST 8

### PAPER 1 Reading and Use of English

#### ▶▶ PART 1

**prior to** (adj) before

**diversification** (n) development of a wider variety of things

**bias** (n) personal preference for something, not based on logical reasons

#### ▶▶ PART 2

**work placement** (n) temporary job, often part of a course of study, which provides work experience

**HR** (n) Human Resources, i.e. personnel

#### ▶▶ PART 3

**biodiversity** (n) large number of different types of animals and plants in a particular environment

**devastation** (n) serious damage

#### ▶▶ PART 5

**echo** (v) to express similar ideas

**dubious** (adj) uncertain, probably not very good

**metaphor** (n) way of describing something by comparing it with something else

**do your head in** (phr) to make you feel confused, upset, annoyed (informal expression)

**syndrome** (n) set of physical symptoms showing you have a particular medical problem

**fidgety** (adj) unable to remain still or quiet

**relieve** (v) to take something away

**burden** (n) something difficult or unpleasant you have to deal with

**illustrate** (v) to give information or examples to explain something

**misguided** (adj) wrong because you have understood or judged something badly

**unease** (n) feeling of being worried or unhappy

**anguish** (n) extreme unhappiness

**ignite** (v) to make something start or cause something

**disquiet** (n) feelings of worry and unhappiness

**wrought** (v) caused to happen (past and past participle form of *to wreak* – very formal)

**lose the thread** (phr) to no longer follow an argument or story

**scurrying** (adj) moving quickly

**particle** (n) very small piece of something

**neural pathways** (adj + n) connections between different areas of the brain or nervous system

**rewire** (v) to change the connections in the brain

**atrophy** (v) to become weak

**mediate** (v) to help deal with

**grey matter** (n) the brain, often referring to intelligence

**trivialise** (v) to focus on unimportant things

**jeopardise** (v) to put in danger

**decommission** (v) to stop using

**redundant** (adj) no longer needed

**trawl** (v) to search through a large amount of information

**the shallows** (n) here refers to information that does not require serious or deep thought

**plumb the depths** (v) to go deeply into something

**in due course** (phr) at the right time in the future

**remedial** (adj) aimed at solving a problem

**unravel** (v) to take apart, break up

**conditioning** (n) experience that makes people behave the way they do

**feat** (n) action or piece of work that needs skill, strength or effort

**punchline** (n) here refers to the words that express the main point

**frenziedness** (n) involving a lot of activity and strong emotions, and probably out of control

**wits** (n) intelligence

#### ▶▶ PART 6

**irrespective of** (prep) without considering or being influenced by

**aspirational** (adj) wanting to do better

**inordinate** (adj) more than is expected or sensible

**viable** (adj) having the conditions to be successful

**lucrative** (adj) producing lots of money

**illusory** (adj) not real although it might seem to be

**astronomical** (adj) extremely high

**underprivileged** (adj) having less money and fewer opportunities than most people

**illusion** (n) idea that is not true

**doomed** (adj) certain to fail

**retrospectively** (adv) connected with something that happened in the past

▶▶ **PART 7**

**attribute** (n) quality or feature

**resilience** (n) ability to recover from a difficult or unpleasant experience

**humility** (n) quality of not thinking you are better than other people

**trait** (n) characteristic

**IQ** (n) intelligence quotient, a way of assessing intelligence through certain tests which largely focus on problem-solving, reasoning, memory and mathematics

**liken** (v) to compare

**not up to scratch** (phr) not as good as it should be

▶▶ **PART 8**

**calibre** (n) quality

**concise** (adj) using few words

**orthodox** (adj) conventional

**verbiage** (n) use of too many words

**nail** (v) to get exactly right

**slick** (adj) clever and smooth (used to express disapproval)

**the nitty gritty** (n) the basic or most important details

**private eye** (n) private detective

**pull off** (phr v) to be successful at

**cliffhanger** (n) very exciting moment in a story because you cannot guess what will happen next

**reveal** (n) point in a mystery story when you find out the truth

**exponent** (n) person able to perform a particular activity

**empathise** (v) to understand another person's feelings and experiences

**sheltered housing** (n) special housing for old people

**crumbling** (adj) falling down

**pacey** (adj) fast moving

## ADVANCED TEST 1

### ▶▶ PART 1

*You will hear three different extracts. For questions 1–6, choose the answer A, B or C which fits best according to what you hear. There are two questions for each extract.*

**Extract One**

*You overhear two friends discussing an incident that happened with another friend. Now look at questions one and two.*

**Woman:** Well, it wasn't what she said, it was the way she said it.

**Man:** Right. So, what did you do?

**Woman:** I didn't do anything. She knew very well she was out of line, and she knew I was upset. I thought, I'm not going down this road with her. Not again. I'm not playing her game any more. She's forever speaking before she thinks and hurting people's feelings, and then she acts all surprised when you tell her she's offended you. She's what they call passive-aggressive. She makes it look like you're the one being difficult … it's a waste of time.

**Man:** But if you don't stand up to her then she's just going to keep doing it. I think you need to say something, I really do. And, here's the thing, don't bring it up immediately after an incident, but another time, you know … talk about it calmly and in a reasonable way, explain how her behaviour affects you. She'll be disarmed, I guarantee you, and I bet she'll back down. Give it a try!

**Extract Two**

*You hear two people discussing the British winter. Now look at questions three and four.*

**Woman:** Sometimes I feel like it's a strange, genetic error that I'm British. I mean, I should have been born somewhere gorgeous and sunny, somewhere Mediterranean. These long, miserable winters of ours … ugh, I can't bear them! You know, having to get out of bed when it's still pitch black outside and, it's the same when you come home in the evening. I hate it. And, oh, all the layers you have to wear whenever you go outdoors, or you'd catch your death in the freezing temperatures. It's all so tedious.

**Man:** Really? Gosh, I quite like the winter. Most of the time, anyway.

**Woman:** Maybe I have that condition where the weather makes people sad.

**Man:** Yes, I think you might have. I know the weather is awful and we get so little natural light, but I find it a very cosy time. I actually like wearing all those layers! Big woolly jumpers, scarves and hats. And I enjoy cooking hearty soups and stews or sitting by the wood-burning stove reading a good book. By the time I start getting fed up with the winter, it always seems the spring is just beginning. Perfect!

**Extract Three**

*You hear a couple disagreeing about Valentine's Day. Now look at questions five and six.*

**Man:** Look, it isn't that I'm not romantic, and I'm certainly not cheap. I just think the whole thing is such a lie.

**Woman:** You do realise that all our friends are doing something special for Valentine's Day? Even the single ones, for goodness sake!

**Man:** Yes, but they're just buying into the commercialism of it all which, when you think of it, is exploitation, and there's nothing romantic about that. Suddenly the restaurants increase their prices, and the cost of red roses is crazy! Those traders are greedy, and that kind of materialism really bothers me. And, I'm sorry, but you're letting yourself be exploited. Caring that everyone else is having champagne and chocolates, well …

**Woman:** But I *do* mind! And even though I agree that these are very obvious retail strategies to make a profit, I still want to be part of it. I'll be very unhappy if we stay in on Valentine's Night. We don't have to go anywhere fancy but I really would like us to go somewhere. I think it's important to mark occasions like these, even in a small way.

### ▶▶ PART 2

*You will hear a radio producer describing how she got into her career. For questions 7–14, complete the sentences with a word or short phrase.*

**Tara:** Hello, everyone. My name is Tara Blackshaw and I'm a producer at a major UK radio station. I've been invited to speak to you all today about my career path, and I'm very glad to be here with you.

As I'm sure you're aware, you can certainly take a subject like media studies or broadcast journalism at university. Studying for a degree in one of these areas may well stand you in good stead, but I'm afraid I can't really say much about that particular avenue because it's not the route I chose myself. And I'm not actively discouraging you from doing a media-based degree … all I would say is that it's not essential. Here's something you might find interesting: every single producer I know has tertiary level education, but not one of them studied anything remotely related to working in radio!

I actually have a degree in economics and, for reasons I may never fully understand, I went on to do an MBA; that's a master's in business administration. I was an excellent maths student and the advice I got at school and at home was to pursue my strongest subject. Here's the thing, though: while I was good at maths and economics, I was never passionate about either field. If there's one piece of advice I'd like you to take away today, it's to decide what you love doing, and go for it.

When I finished my MBA, I went travelling for a year. I saw some incredible places and met lots of amazing people along the way. I think, somehow, that journey made me realise how much I wanted to work at something that would keep me interested and motivated. When I got back, it just happened that there was a work experience programme at my local radio station, unpaid, of course, but that didn't put me off. The rest, as they say, is history.

From the moment I set foot in the studio, I knew I had found my bliss. It seems strange to say I felt at home there, considering I'd never been in a studio before, but I did. It instantly felt right. I worked very hard, but I was also lucky. One of the full-time producers decided to emigrate with his family, and I ended up getting his job. Then, after five happy years, I moved to London where I was recruited for the job I'm in now. That was almost 15 years ago!

I would say the quality you need above all else if you want to become a producer is organisation; you've *got* to be an organised person. You can be taught how to use all the studio equipment, but if you're not organised by nature, you will definitely struggle in this role. The other massively important thing is being an 'ideas' person. You really do need to be a creative thinker, as well as a quick thinker, and you have to communicate effectively. I know this sounds like a cliché but you also have to be able to work independently and as part of a team. Sometimes you'll put in extremely long hours, but it's a labour of love, and the end result is usually worth it. So … any questions?

### ▶▶ PART 3

*You'll hear two friends, Fiona and Matthew, discussing an interview which featured an American skier and filmmaker called Nick Waggoner. For questions 15–20, choose the answer A, B, C or D which fits best according to what you hear.*

**Fiona:** Hey, Matt? Am I disturbing you?

**Matt:** Oh, hi, Fiona! No, not at all. Why don't you join me? Here, take this seat. Actually, I've just read a really interesting interview in this magazine.

**Fiona:** Great! So, who was being interviewed?

**Matt:** Do you know the filmmaker, Nick Waggoner?

**Fiona:** Um ….

**Matt:** He's a young director. American.

**Fiona:** Has he made anything I would know?

**Matt:** Well, he makes ski films.

**Fiona:** Ski films?

**Matt:** I know, I know, but these are really cool; different from anything else. Honestly, they're amazing.

**Fiona:** Really?

**Matt:** Yes, believe me! The interview was about a ski film he made in South America a few years ago called *Solitaire*.

**Fiona:** OK …

**Matt:** Yeah. I mean, just think of the extreme conditions of the Andes … stunning views, but punishing winds and unpredictable snows. And there was none of the glamour typical of some film sets for these guys; no personal chefs or posh hotels or helicopters. They slept in tents, endured endless, miserable weather and, before first light, they'd routinely hike 5,000 metres just to get the perfect shot.

**Fiona:** Wow. What did Nick Waggoner say about the whole experience?

**Matt:** He said it was incredibly demanding. In addition to hiking, they also travelled by riverboat and on horseback. He said it rained almost constantly. Can you imagine how dedicated you'd have to be to put yourself through all that?

**Fiona:** Unbelievable. But why choose a location with such hostile conditions?

**Matt:** He basically said it was because the views there were so compelling; simple as that. But a truly terrible thing happened while they were there.

**Fiona:** Gosh, what?

**Matt:** Nick Waggoner was planning to meet, for the first time, this brilliant American skier, Arne Backstrom, in Peru. But the day they arrived, Arne was killed in a ski fall.

**Fiona:** Oh, my goodness, that's awful.

**Matt:** I know. Arne was only 29. Nick and his colleague, Zac Ramras, were completely devastated by it.

**Fiona:** Well, of course. It's hard to know how they managed to go on with the project.

**Matt:** Definitely. In fact, he spoke about that in the interview. He said that he and Zac didn't know what to do, they only knew they had to somehow keep moving forward.

**Fiona:** So, what did they do?

**Matt:** He explained that they had a friend who was a paraglider, so they connected with him.

**Fiona:** Paragliding … is that when you jump from a high place and use a special kind of parachute to float back down?

**Matt:** Exactly; you literally fly. And neither of them had ever done it before; Nick said the first day they tried it, they crashed into a wall!

**Fiona:** Oh, no!

**Matt:** Yeah, he was, like, what am I doing! But he said it became their way of getting back to filming, you know? In some way it also helped them to search for meaning after Arne's death. The second time they went paragliding they hiked for 24 hours to launch off a glacier at sunrise – I mean, imagine! – they turn downhill, then they run, and … jump. Nick said you just have to hope you have enough momentum to get you into the air. He said he would never forget that flight.

**Fiona:** No, absolutely. I expect he wouldn't. To tell you the truth, I'm a bit surprised that he didn't just give up.

**Matt:** Ah, but that's the thing, he does mention that he had periods when he started to hate making ski films but – you should read the interview – then he starts describing the impact that the whole process has on him, and the fact that he truly loves the life of skiing and filmmaking. What he says is quite beautiful, actually. He talks about seeing the sun rise after hiking for hours in the dark, and how it feels to look at that first light on the horizon, or watching the clouds and the crazy weather and colours in the sky … he says this kind of stuff really makes him feel alive.

**Fiona:** He genuinely does sound like an interesting person, a man who will suffer for his art.

**Matt:** Well, it's funny you should say that because he mentions that if he has to suffer for two years just to feel completely alive for five minutes, then that's what he'll do. He's *that* kind of person.

**Fiona:** Wow.

**Matt:** My favourite part is when he adds that creating art is the biggest adventure anyone can have. He says it demands everything of you, the good and the bad, you know?

**Fiona:** Yeah … hey, can I borrow the magazine?

## ▶▶ PART 4

*Part 4 consists of two tasks. You will hear five short extracts in which people talk about being in writers' groups. Look at Task 1. For questions 21–25, choose from the list A–H what each speaker says about their own writing. Now look at Task 2. For questions 26–30, choose from the list A–H what each speaker says about their experience of being in the writers' group. While you listen you must complete both tasks.*

**Speaker 1:** I'd been working on my novel for over a year before I joined a writer's group. My only regret is that I didn't join one sooner! I mean, everyone knows that writing is ultimately a solitary activity and, obviously, a novel is a very big undertaking, so it can be quite a lonely practice. I find the writer's group engaging and it keeps me excited about my work. And at various points when I get a little bit stuck regarding my characters or plot, the group members are more than willing to give me feedback on my ideas. For me, it's a very rewarding experience.

**Speaker 2:** I used to write short stories when I was young, but then I got busy with, you know, life … having a family and all the rest of it. When my friend, Helen, suggested we join a writer's group, I really didn't want to at first – I'd been away from writing for decades – but Helen dragged me along, and I'm so glad she did. Now short-story writing provides an excellent creative outlet for me. I'd forgotten how much I enjoyed crafting stories, often not knowing where they're going to take me. The people in the writer's group are wonderful; their comments are always so encouraging. It's the best thing I've done in years.

**Speaker 3:** Poetry has always been important to me; it's a daily practice, like having breakfast. When I'm not writing it, I'm reading it. I think it's the most expressive of all the literary arts. I joined a writer's group recently but, I don't know, I just don't think it's for me. For one thing, the interaction isn't useful or helpful. People say meaningless things, like, 'Oh, that's nice' or I 'liked it.' But, you see, you have to say why something works or doesn't work, you know? I don't think I'll continue with the writer's group, I'm not getting anything out of it.

**Speaker 4:** Several of my plays have already been produced to moderate success. Writing a play really is a lot of work; in addition to characters and plot, there's stage directions and even set design sketches. Sometimes I put it off, you know, find excuses to do other things; it can be difficult to find the discipline to keep the thing moving. The main reason I joined a writer's group – I know this will probably sound silly – is that it gives me a reason to continue. Every week the group members ask what progress I've made and I feel awful if I have nothing to show them.

**Speaker 5:** Have you heard of 'flash fiction'? It basically means a condensed short story. The word count varies … it's typically around 300 words but it can be higher or lower. I reckon I was doing fine until I joined a writer's group. I'm not saying I'm this brilliant writer, but I think the quality is all right; I'm not bad. Some of my flash fiction has been published, actually, but the people in the writer's group, they just tear everything to shreds. Maybe I'm too thin-skinned, I thought I was OK at accepting criticism but these guys are relentless. If I stay in that group I'll completely lose my confidence and never write another word. I wish I'd never joined.

# TEST 2

## ▶▶ PART 1

*You will hear three different extracts. For questions 1–6, choose the answer A, B or C which fits best according to what you hear. There are two questions for each extract.*

### Extract One

*You hear a man making a phone call to deliver some good news. Now look at questions one and two.*

**Mark:** Hi Julie, it's Mark here.

**Julie:** Mark, how are you?

**Mark:** Oh, I'm fine, I'm so glad I caught you; am I catching you at a bad time?

**Julie:** Not really; I'm just finishing a report. What's up?

**Mark:** I have great news! Guess what.

**Julie:** Um … I don't know. You've just won the lottery?

**Mark:** Well, that would be nice but, no, I've just passed my driving test!

**Julie:** Mark, that's fantastic.

**Mark:** Isn't it? Honestly, I was in such a state. My hands were sweating, my legs were shaking, I literally couldn't see straight.

**Julie:** Yes, I remember feeling exactly the same way – I felt sick and I was almost in tears – I think it's the same for everyone the day of the test.

**Mark:** The strange thing is that it's out of character for me. I mean, I'd been taking lessons for a couple of years and I genuinely felt ready for the test. Also, I don't typically get stressed before exams, so I didn't really expect to feel so anxious. But somehow I was able to focus in the end. Luckily.

**Julie:** Congratulations!

### Extract Two

*You hear a woman telling a friend about her experience at a careers fair. Now look at questions three and four.*

**Woman:** I'm just so discouraged by the whole thing.

**Man:** What?

**Woman:** Oh, I was at this careers fair today. It was terrible!

**Man:** Really? Why was it so awful?

**Woman:** Nobody wants to hire someone with a general arts degree. My parents are going to love hearing this; it's what they've been telling me for years.

**Man:** Things aren't that bad. Don't be so defeatist!

**Woman:** Seriously, the entire focus was on people who want to be accountants or work in the sciences. I have no idea what I'm going to do next.

**Man:** Sorry, but I really think you're exaggerating. You can't give up just because you went to one careers fair and all the hiring managers didn't rush to offer you a job. Think carefully about what you want and then come up with a strategy.

**Woman:** Gosh, you're sympathetic.

**Man:** Well, I mean it. You have an honours degree. You need to demonstrate to employers that you're reliable, dedicated and, most of all, enthusiastic.

**Woman:** Yeah, you're right. I'm just having an off day.

### Extract Three

*You hear a woman discussing plans for her cousin's visit with a friend. Now look at questions five and six.*

**Woman:** Hey, could you take a look at this and let me know what you think?

**Man:** Sure, what is it?

**Woman:** It's an itinerary for this weekend. My cousin is visiting from France; he's never been here before.

**Man:** OK, let's see … the gallery of fine art … the history museum … the law courts … the science exhibition … um, is your cousin our age?

**Woman:** Well, a bit younger, he's 21.

**Man:** And you're planning to drag him to all these boring buildings?

**Woman:** What? They're not boring … these are some of the best places we have.

**Man:** Look, if you want my opinion, you're taking the wrong approach. I'm practically certain your cousin would much rather chill out and experience the town in a different way.

**Woman:** Such as?

**Man:** Well, I don't know *exactly*. Maybe go for coffee somewhere cool, invite some of us along. Take a walk through the city centre, have lunch in a park, just relax, you know? Once he's here you can always ask him what kinds of things he's interested in, and take it from there.

**Woman:** Yes, I suppose you're right.

## ▶▶ PART 2

*You will hear a travel writer describing her relationship with sleep. For questions 7–14, complete the sentences with a word or short phrase.*

**Writer:** Ah, sleep, wonderful sleep! Sleeping is one of my deepest travel pleasures, but I don't talk about it very much because I feel a little guilty. When friends share details of their carefully planned trips, in which every second of precious travel time is filled with activities, meals, museums, and mountain treks, I smile encouragingly and don't say much. What would they think if they knew that my own travel itineraries include long empty spaces for late afternoon naps, and lazy mornings cosy under the bed covers?

Improved sleep is one of travel's happy side effects. When I visited Mexico's Yucatán coast in my early 20s, I was shocked by how many hours – more than 12 – I spent sleeping most days. Far from home and from my own bed, surrounded by strange smells and sounds, I could plunge into a sleep that was deeper, more dream-filled and more enjoyable than I imagined possible.

Freed from alarm clocks and responsibilities, sleep flows more easily. But I don't think a simple lack of stress explains why the quality of travel sleep is so dramatically different. My theory is that sleep is actually an extension of our travels, not a pause from them. When travelling, we open ourselves to new sights, sounds, smells, and ways of being. New and unfamiliar stuff pours into us – cultures, music, landscapes, even ways of moving through space. It's when sleeping that we move through this overwhelming river of different influences. No wonder, then, that sleep becomes so much more intense when we are on the road.

Sleep is also an experience that changes rhythm, sometimes dramatically, from place to place. People obsess about jet lag but I suspect that the difficulties I experience recovering from long journeys have more to do with getting used to local and cultural differences than time differences. On the Caribbean island of Trinidad, for example, people wake at dawn to start their day before it gets too hot, they lose energy around 10.00 a.m. when the sun is high and then return to life with the cool evening breezes. Though Trinidad is just one hour ahead of New York, where I live, I still take days to adjust to the island's different patterns of sleeping and waking.

Travel sleep has another wonderful quality: it is more memorable than sleep at home. Separated by distance and culture from my normal sleep routine, I soon find that I delight in the unexpected smells, textures, and sounds that fill my consciousness in a new place. If a commitment to the movement called 'slow travel' is what now distinguishes the modern traveller, well, what is slower than sleep? Maybe I should stop feeling embarrassed by this tendency of mine and admit everything to my ambitious friends, explaining to them that travel sleep is, after all, an activity too. It certainly always has felt that way to me.

▶▶ **PART 3**

*You will hear a radio interview about the challenges which first-year college students often face. For questions 15–20, choose the answer A, B, C or D which fits best according to what you hear.*

**Faye:** Now we'd like to welcome to the radio programme Martin Ferguson, who is the Information and Advice Officer at Stanmere College in London. Welcome, Martin.

**Martin:** Thank you, Faye. I'm very glad to be here.

**Faye:** First of all, could you say a little about what an information and advice officer actually does?

**Martin:** Certainly. In simple terms, I suppose you could say I'm like a customer service representative for the college. My job is to support students by providing any information they may require. This might involve supplying detailed course information or financial advice. Basically, my role is designed to work with prospective students and guide them through the enrolment process. Then, once they start at the university, I'm available to assist them with any problems they might encounter along the way, especially in their first year.

**Faye:** Excellent. Martin, could you explain the kinds of issues that students new to university life typically face?

**Martin:** Definitely striking a balance between study and everything else. For many students it can be a big struggle to get that right. Bear in mind that the shift from secondary school to university is a huge one: the environment is different, the workload is greater, the degree of independence is higher. Students describe how they'd been used to a very structured routine when they lived at home, but now, suddenly, they have to adjust to a completely different situation. The main problem is that they feel the burden of responsibility for figuring out how to schedule everything themselves.

**Faye:** And just to pick up on something you said there, for many students, going to college is their first experience of living away from home.

**Martin:** Exactly. Day-to-day things that might seem like very ordinary life skills to some people, such as doing the laundry or eating healthy meals at regular times, can present a real challenge to others.

**Faye:** So, what should students do? I mean, what do you say to those who come to you because they have difficulty finding the right balance?

**Martin:** The specific details vary from person to person. Overall, I do three things. Above all, I reassure them that what they're going through is completely normal. Many worry that they may seem weak if they're not coping, especially when it appears that most of their friends are doing fine, but the reality is that many students experience difficulties sooner or later, whether they show it or not. Then I sit down with them and together we draw up a clear timetable tailored to their course and their needs. Finally, I schedule a series of follow-up meetings with them to see how they're getting on.

**Faye:** Sometimes we all need a helping hand to make a plan and put it in place.

**Martin:** Mmm, absolutely, and that's what I tell my students all the time. In the same way, managing their own finances for the first time can be tricky for some students and, again, I help them to create a realistic budget. I also provide them with useful suggestions about being economical.

**Faye:** Great. And, Martin, what are some other problems that college students face?

**Martin:** Mmm, well, principally mental health, but general health can take a toll as well, usually due to not eating properly, not getting enough sleep, maybe partying too hard. Then, apart from the stress some feel in terms of keeping up with their studies and getting through their exams, many students experience other kinds of anxiety. They might feel homesick and isolated, they might worry about making new friends and fitting in.

**Faye:** And how do you support those students? What advice do you give them?

**Martin:** Many students benefit from the workshops we offer, including relaxation techniques and dealing with exam stress. But, on the individual front, I would always reinforce how their feelings are totally normal and nothing to be ashamed of. I try to find out a bit more about their areas of interest and then let them know about clubs and societies run by the Students' Union which they might enjoy. If they're not extroverts, there are always study groups they might like to join. But if a student seems to be exceptionally lonely and possibly feeling depressed, I refer them to the university medical centre which has qualified counsellors on staff.

**Faye:** Thank you, Martin.

▶▶ **PART 4**

*Part 4 consists of two tasks. You will hear five short extracts in which people talk about the things they do to reduce stress. Look at Task 1. For questions 21–25, choose from the list A–H what each speaker says about what brought them to this particular practice. Now look at Task 2. For questions 26–30, choose from the list A–H what each speaker says about the effect the practice has on them. While you listen you must complete both tasks.*

**Speaker 1:** Like so many people, I suppose, I make too many commitments. I actually like it that way, to tell you the truth. I live a full life and, in general, I enjoy being busy. But recently I started to feel overwhelmed, and a friend recommended acupuncture to me. It's a Chinese practice thousands of years old and involves putting needles into certain parts of the body to treat various conditions, including stress and anxiety. Some people can't bear the idea of needles, but I don't mind them. I couldn't believe the difference after my first acupuncture session, it was like a weight had been taken off my shoulders. It's amazing.

**Speaker 2:** I'm a pretty easy-going person, most of the time, but things have been extraordinarily stressful lately. My grandmother died last year, and I have my final college exams coming up in a few weeks. I'd been feeling distracted all the time and I knew I was going to have to find a way to overcome my anxiety, so I did some research and learned about 'mindfulness', an ancient Eastern practice that helps you to cope with stress using breathing techniques. It really works for me. Afterwards I just feel so much better, like my head has been emptied of noise and I can focus my attention where I need to.

**Speaker 3:** Last summer my wife and I moved to a new city with our small son. Did you know that moving house is often listed among the ten most stressful things in life? There were just too many things to organise, too many details to remember, it was a nightmare! I was so tense that my wife suggested I take up something like swimming, and I'm so glad she did. This peaceful sensation comes over me when I'm in the pool. I forget my troubles and feel only the movement and the water. After a swim I always feel great.

**Speaker 4:** I'm a landscape gardener for a living; it's a job I absolutely love and I'm never happier than when I'm working outside. So, no stress, you might think. Well, fortunately there's no emotional stress, the problem is that it can be very taxing on my body, so I've started getting massages. Massage is when someone works on your body to help relax your muscles and to reduce pain. I don't know what I'd do without it! It melts away every single ache and leaves my body completely chilled out. I love it.

**Speaker 5:** Doing a master's degree as well as working part time is not easy. I'd like to quit my job at the restaurant but I can't, I badly need the money. My course workload is very heavy and I spend long hours in the library. I didn't have a proper mix of work and relaxation in my life, so I started doing yoga. Actually, I didn't think I'd find time for an additional activity but, as the saying goes, yoga doesn't take time, it gives time, which is so true. Things don't seem to be as chaotic now, plus my posture is better, I sleep better at night and, overall, I feel stronger.

# TEST 3

## ▶▶ PART 1

*You will hear three different extracts. For questions 1–6, choose the answer A, B or C which fits best according to what you hear. There are two questions for each extract.*

### Extract One

*You hear two former college friends who bump into each other in London. Now look at questions one and two.*

**Noel:** Rebecca? I thought it was you! Gosh, I haven't seen you since university. You look great.

**Becky:** Hi, Noel, what a surprise, how lovely to see you. Do you live here in London?

**Noel:** Goodness, no. I'm just here for some meetings today. I can't stand London!

**Becky:** Um, I live in London.

**Noel:** Sorry, I'm always saying the wrong thing, you know what I'm like. London's just not for me, that's all. I lived here for a year after graduation and I hated it … you know how it's so overcrowded, always going, never stops, never takes a breath. I felt exhausted the entire time I was here.

**Becky:** It's funny, that's what I love about the place. I find it fun and fresh and exciting. There's energy in all that movement, there's always something to do. For me, London is endlessly interesting.

**Noel:** Absolutely. And that's brilliant. I suppose I just prefer the quiet life. I'm a boring person.

**Becky:** Oh, don't say that. Everyone's entitled to their own personal preference. I'm a city girl right now, but in a few years I might prefer the countryside, which is not boring by the way.

### Extract Two

*You hear a new employee chatting with a colleague about her first week at the company. Now look at questions three and four.*

**Gavin:** Hello … Suzanne, is it?

**Suzanne:** Yes.

**Gavin:** Hi, I'm Gavin. Can I join you?

**Suzanne:** Sure, have a seat.

**Gavin:** Thanks. So, how's your first week at the office been? Are you settling in OK?

**Suzanne:** It's very kind of you to ask; yes, it's been fine, and everyone's been really nice. I seem to have a lot of meetings, though … I mean, a *lot*! I've been wondering if that's just because I'm new.

**Gavin:** Sorry to say I don't think so, that's just the way things are around here. Everyone complains about it but it never changes.

**Suzanne:** Wow, that's a bit worrying. I'm not sure when I'm actually supposed to do my work if I'm in meeting after meeting.

**Gavin:** I know; it's a challenge but you'll find a way.

**Suzanne:** What do you do?

**Gavin:** I always bring my laptop into meetings and, as I've learned which items don't concern me, I use that time to check my emails and read any important attachments. I also come in about an hour early every morning. I get a lot done when the office is quiet.

**Suzanne:** Really? I must admit I'm very concerned about managing everything.

### Extract Three

*You hear two friends discussing college applications. Now look at questions five and six.*

**Phillipa:** Hi, Marcus, how are you?

**Marcus:** Oh, hi, Phillipa. I'm just looking at college applications. Hey, have you decided where you want to do your degree?

**Phillipa:** I'm working on it. The place with the best reputation for my subject is *really* far away, but I'd quite like to come home at the weekends, so …

**Marcus:** Right. Personally, I don't mind distance; I don't mind being based at the other end of the country, if necessary. My dilemma is whether to aim for a very large, well-known university, or a much smaller one.

**Phillipa:** Mmm, I see.

**Marcus:** I mean, a huge campus is pretty appealing, there'd always be a lot going on, I think there'd be really interesting students there, and a lot of variety. I just think I'd enjoy my time more. Plus, the bigger universities always attract the best lecturers.

**Phillipa:** Hmm, I don't think that last point is strictly true. And don't forget that in smaller universities classes won't be as big. Less crowded lecture theatres and study groups probably mean more individual attention from your tutors.

**Marcus:** Yes, that's a valid point. I'm going to have to give this some careful thought.

## ▶▶ PART 2

*You will hear a community volunteer called Conor McManus talking about how he first got involved in this area, and describing the kind of projects he has worked on. For questions 7–14, complete the sentences with a word or short phrase.*

**Conor:** Hello, my name is Conor McManus and I'm here to talk to you about community involvement. For me, it all started about four years ago when I was encouraged by a friend to join a local group that was working to prevent a famous supermarket chain from building a massive shopping complex in the centre of our town. To tell you the truth, I was a reluctant participant at first, but my friend was extremely persuasive and eventually I gave in. I'm happy to report that the group was successful, and the supermarket chain had to pull out. The whole experience really opened my eyes to what can be accomplished by a dedicated group of people who pull together and fight for what they believe in.

I really hadn't given this kind of thing any thought previously. I didn't come from a particularly political family and, to be honest, I had a slightly negative attitude to activities such as campaigning. I thought these people were all radical and extreme, and I'm not like that at all. But, as I soon learned, I had a narrow outlook on things. Community activism and community awareness are relevant to everyone who cares about where they live. And, if you're lucky enough to live in a democracy, you have a voice. You have the right to express your opinions on what happens in your own community. You have a right to object to policies you don't agree with. Actually, some would say you have a *responsibility* to speak up.

If you feel you might like to get involved, there are many options open to you. You could opt to help with environmental causes. There may be social or political changes that you want to see. You could work on something that will have an economic impact on your community. The point is that people working together can really make a difference. To give you some more specific ideas, the most worthwhile project I've worked on in the past few years was setting up a soup kitchen for the homeless. At the moment I'm on a committee being consulted by a government department on plans for a number of abandoned buildings in a depressed area of the inner city.

A friend of mine worked with another group to create a community garden. She said it was incredibly rewarding once the fruit and vegetables were ripe because local residents could come and take whatever they wanted. And a full-time gardener gave workshops on how to plant things and look after them; it brought the whole community together.

My experiences have been so positive that I strongly recommend you get involved in some community-based activities. Maybe you have a particular skill, such as graphic design, that you can bring to a group project. Alternatively you could simply donate an hour or so a week to a good cause; it doesn't have to be a major commitment but you get to be part of something that matters. And bear in mind – you never know – if you find you really like it, it could end up being your career path in what we call 'the third sector', which means working for charities or non-profit organisations. Any questions, anyone?

## ▶▶ PART 3

*You will hear a public meeting in which Dr Freya Davidson, the Dean of Studies of Caledonia College, is interviewing Malcolm Meade, the Administrative Officer from the Consulate General of Japan about the Japan Exchange and Teaching Programme. For questions 15–20, choose the answer A, B, C or D which fits best according to what you hear.*

**Freya:** Welcome, everyone, and thanks to Mr Malcolm Meade, Administrative Officer at the Consulate-General of Japan. Many thanks for joining us this evening.

**Malcolm:** Thank you, Dr Davidson; I'm looking forward to our conversation.

**Freya:** Wonderful. Well, most of the students here in the audience will be graduating soon and are here to learn about the JET Programme. First of all, what does JET stand for?

**Malcolm:** Japan Exchange and Teaching. So, it's The Japan Exchange and Teaching Programme, and it began in 1987 with just under a thousand participants from four different countries. Since then it's grown significantly: 25 years later it had placed roughly 50,000 participants from over 50 countries in positions throughout Japan.

**Freya:** That *is* impressive. Could you explain what the programme actually does?

**Malcolm:** Certainly. The JET Programme was initially set up to increase mutual understanding between Japanese people and people from other countries. The idea was to bring native speakers of English right into the heart of Japanese communities, typically working in local schools to help improve English language learning, but also to promote cultural integration in the towns and villages. Then, as the programme evolved, non-native speakers of English were also invited to participate and, later, a role for sports advisers was created.

**Freya:** So, these days, what is the main role of JET Programme participants?

**Malcolm:** The vast majority of participants – more than 90 per cent, I believe – are in teaching roles. They are Assistant Language Teachers (ALTs), who are typically employed by Boards of Education and work in local schools. Together with the Japanese teachers of English in those schools, the ALTs assist with preparing teaching materials and teaching classes. We call this 'team teaching'. The ALTs also bring a special dimension to the classroom by sharing cultural information about their home country and they can really help students with specific aspects of English language learning, like pronunciation. Additionally, they get involved outside the classroom by participating in after-school activities, such as sports teams and English clubs.

**Freya:** Excellent. Would students applying to the JET Programme need to have a command of Japanese? And would they need a teaching qualification or previous teaching experience?

**Malcolm:** There is no expectation that ALTs would already speak Japanese, only that they have a willingness to learn it once they arrive in Japan. Certainly showing that you have an interest in the Japanese language and culture would strengthen your application. A background in teaching is not necessary either.

Again, demonstrating any related experience, for example, working with young people (even informally), or doing volunteer work will stand in your favour. What everyone is required to have is a bachelor's degree, and this can be in any subject.

**Freya:** You mentioned that most people on the JET Programme are ALTs. What other roles are available?

**Malcolm:** Ah, there are two other positions, and they're more specialised. For those whose Japanese is decent, there's a role working in local government offices as a Councillor for International Relations, or CIR. Their job involves things like translating documents and providing support for international exchange activities. The other role is as a Sports Exchange Advisor but only seven people are appointed per year and you can't actually apply for it, you have to be a sports professional nominated by your country's government or Olympic Committee. I imagine most of the people here would be interested in applying to be ALTs.

**Freya:** Yes, definitely. Could you tell us how students go about applying for the JET Programme?

**Malcolm:** Absolutely. Here in the UK, applications are accepted throughout October and November. You can get the application form from your local Japanese Embassy. Then, in January and February, interviews are held at the embassy or consulate and those who pass the interview are notified in April. Information packs are sent out in May, and departure to Japan is in July or August. Contracts are for one year, but can be renewed for up to three.

**Freya:** It sounds like a fantastic opportunity but I must ask you, are there any negative aspects?

**Malcolm:** Well, not really. However, I would say that students should think very carefully before they apply. Remember, it's a commitment for one year and adjusting to everyday life in Japan can be difficult for some. Be aware, also, that most of the placements are out in the countryside where some people find they get lonely.

**Freya:** Good advice. Thank you, Mr Meade.

## ▶▶ PART 4

*Part 4 consists of two tasks. You will hear five short extracts in which people talk about their careers. Look at Task 1. For questions 21–25, choose from the list A–H what each speaker says about how they came to be in this career. Now look at Task 2. For questions 26–30, choose from the list A–H what each speaker says about their plans or hopes for the future. While you listen you must complete both tasks.*

**Speaker 1:** I'm the third generation to run our restaurant chain, which was started by my grandfather in 1956. It was always taken for granted that I would take over; it was never really discussed, just understood. Many people might envy that, but the assumption always bothered me. I never felt free to pursue my own interests. I'm sorry to complain because I earn a good living but I'm really not happy. For years it's been my dream to be a book editor, but I feel tied to the restaurants. Maybe one day I'll find a way to do both.

**Speaker 2:** I'd like tell you that I strategically planned this career path, but I'd be lying. I kind of fell into my job as a Research Analyst at a private investment firm. I hold a Masters of Library Science so I certainly didn't expect to end up in the financial industry, but here I am. As I say, it was quite accidental … someone I studied with works at that firm as their library manager. He recommended me as I'm a good researcher, by nature I'm thorough, a very organised person; and they hired me. The salary is excellent and my goal is to stop working by the time I'm 50.

**Speaker 3:** I'm a group-account director at a major advertising agency and I got here via the traditional route: straight after graduating with a marketing degree I took an entry level position at a small, local business. I kept moving to bigger companies, gradually working my way up, until I was hired by a big

London-based agency. I really enjoy the creative aspect of what we do; you have to be an excellent communicator in this line of work. My old university has actually invited me to come back next year and give some lectures, so I'm very excited about that prospect.

**Speaker 4:** I've never been particularly academic. I've always wanted to work with my hands, so when I left secondary school I enrolled at a technical college where I'm studying for the required certification to be a plumber. That's only one part of the process, though. You also need to do practical training with an established plumber. Being a trainee gives you on-the-job experience and, I must say, I genuinely like the work. It'll probably take a total of three years to be fully qualified. If all goes well, I'd eventually like to set up on my own, you know, work for myself.

**Speaker 5:** A career in law is all I've ever wanted; I suppose I'm known for placing a high value on fairness and doing the right thing. I graduated with a law degree last year and now I'm working on the post-graduate diploma in legal practice, which is called the LPC, the Legal Practice Course. Once I get the LPC, I'll need to find a position with a law firm and work there as a trainee, probably on a two-year contract. I'd like to specialise in human rights law and help people. One day, I hope to join a large charitable foundation like Save the Children or Oxfam.

## ADVANCED TEST 4

### ▶▶ PART 1

*You will hear three different extracts. For questions 1–6, choose the answer A, B or C which fits best according to what you hear. There are two questions for each extract.*

### Extract One
*You hear two people discussing electronic book readers. Now look at questions one and two.*

**Woman:** Ah, you have one of those things for reading electronic books … e-books.

**Man:** An e-reader, yes.

**Woman:** If you don't mind my saying, I don't think I'd want one. No offence! It's just that there's nothing like picking up a good book and curling up on the sofa to read for an afternoon. The smell and feel of a book, you know?

**Man:** I know. Don't worry, I'm not offended, I know exactly what you mean. Actually I felt the same way until my parents got me this for my birthday.

**Woman:** And now you like it?

**Man:** I love it! I got used to it so quickly. It's really convenient; great for the train journey to and from work and brilliant to take on business trips. Whenever I went on holiday I used to stuff my suitcase with five novels and a few biographies; they take up so much space and they're so heavy! But now I just take this.

**Woman:** Well, that does sound handy.

**Man:** Look, I adore books as well. I don't see digital books completely taking over from printed books – not in my lifetime, anyway – they'll just be an alternative, side by side.

### Extract Two
*You hear two colleagues discussing how they get to the office. Now look at questions three and four.*

**Man:** Oh, are you also leaving for the day? I'll walk to the car park with you.

**Woman:** The car park? No, I take the bus.

**Man:** Oh, really? OK, I'll give you a lift home if you like.

**Woman:** Thanks. Hey, you don't live too far from the office. Do you often drive in?

**Man:** Um, to tell you the truth, I always drive to work.

**Woman:** You're joking! The number 70 goes right by your front door!

**Man:** I know, I know. Don't give me a hard time! I always *mean* to get the bus but it takes ages, stopping every few minutes, plus it's often late, and crowded, and everyone seems to be in such a bad mood. I prefer my car. I leave the house when I want, leave the office when I want … no waiting in the rain for that awful bus.

**Woman:** Oh, stop it! You could actually walk to the office from your house. Or cycle. You make the bus sound far worse than it really is! Seriously, I take it all the time and it's fine. I dare you to give it another chance!

### Extract Three
*You hear two friends discussing an essay for college. Now look at questions five and six.*

**Jake:** Hiya, how's it going?

**Amy:** Oh, don't ask. I'm *really* struggling with this essay. It's a total mess! I don't know how I'm going to get it done on time.

**Jake:** When's it due?

**Amy:** Friday, 4,000 words, and I haven't even started writing yet.

**Jake:** Haven't you? So, what's all this?

**Amy:** That? Oh, I've been reading secondary sources for weeks now. Those are my notes.

**Jake:** I see … that's a lot of notes! Do you know what aspect of the topic you're going to focus on?

**Amy:** I haven't a clue! It's a disaster – I could cry. And now I'm completely overwhelmed by the whole thing.

**Jake:** OK, calm down, you'll get it sorted. Can I make a suggestion?

**Amy:** Yeah, please do.

**Jake:** Right. My advice is to stop reading now, and stop making notes. Take a step back and decide on an angle for your essay. Then you should work on an outline. I'll help you if you want.

**Amy:** Oh, really, would you? That would be amazing. You don't have some time right now, do you?

**Jake:** I certainly do. Come on, let's get started!

### ▶▶ PART 2

*You will hear a student giving a class presentation on citizen journalism. For questions 7–14, complete the sentences with a word or short phrase.*

**Speaker:** Good afternoon, and thank you for coming to my presentation. Today I will be speaking about *citizen journalism*, which is something you may or may not have already heard about. Either way, I hope you will find the talk interesting and that you'll stay afterwards for our question and answer session.

Citizen journalism, as the name suggests, is journalism by ordinary people, citizens who are not formally trained as journalists. So, what does it mean and why do we have it?

When a member of the public reports – or contributes to a news report – by submitting an eye-witness account of the story, that's an example of citizen journalism. If you're thinking, 'But this isn't anything new', you have a point. For many years, radio, television and newspaper journalists have sought comments from people close to the situation they are reporting on. These comments enhance their story and give it popular appeal by involving real people the rest of us can relate to. But that's not quite what I mean by citizen journalism, which is directly linked to the rise of the internet.

Citizen journalism began to fully emerge with the development of what we call Web 2.0, which is when it became possible for members of the general public to create and share their own content on the World Wide Web. Since most people now have mobile phones with internet access as well as built-in cameras, the process of uploading comments or photos to the internet has become widespread.

So, once individuals and groups had a vehicle for posting reports of their own version of events, citizen journalism grew rapidly. Reactions to it were mixed initially. Some people didn't take it seriously. Others preferred the traditional order of only following news supplied by trained and qualified journalists. These days, however, citizen journalism has proved itself to be an extraordinarily helpful resource and, indeed, the way of the future.

News organisations in recent years have increasingly relied on citizen journalism to fill in the gaps. During big international news events, locals have promptly published stories online describing what they observed with their own eyes, or they've posted photos of what they have seen. During times of serious political difficulty in various countries worldwide, citizen journalism has provided us with compelling insights into the day-to-day situation, especially for the ordinary people.

Citizen journalism has also played a significant role in collaborating with law enforcement to solve major crimes. The police have typically been able to use photos, videos and eye-witness accounts provided by the public to identify criminals.

In our digital world, many citizen journalists host their own websites or blogs. However, what seems to be emerging is the relatively common practice of professional journalists and documentary-makers producing their own content and combining it with verified audio and video clips from citizen journalists. Now, does anyone have any questions?

## ▶▶ PART 3

*You will hear a conversation between the director of a national charity, Brandon Tate, and a psychologist, Dr Joan Wells, who is also an expert on the issue of unemployment. For questions 15–20, choose the answer A, B, C or D which fits best according to what you hear.*

**Brandon:** If I may start the conversation, it seems to me that many people think unemployment is purely an issue in terms of finances.

**Dr Wells:** An excellent place to start. That is, indeed, the view held by many and it's completely incorrect. It's incorrect and it's unhelpful because it places an additional burden on unemployed people who not only have to deal with the difficulty of their situation, but also with this mistaken view held by their friends and family members. Worries about money are, of course, an issue – there's no doubt – but unemployment can also have a devastating effect on a person's outlook.

**Brandon:** Yes, I've seen this many times. People who, by nature, were always optimistic and positive begin to lose hope. Their confidence in themselves becomes damaged and they gradually give up. By the way, I'm speaking about both people who lost a job they already had and people who are still trying to find their first job.

**Dr Wells:** That's a very good point. It can be extremely frustrating for people who have just finished their education and are eager to join the workforce but struggle to find a job. It's particularly challenging nowadays because more people are applying for fewer jobs.

**Brandon:** And those who have been made redundant are very aware of this. Unfortunately, it can contribute to their sense of hopelessness. It's an extremely difficult thing to deal with, isn't it?

**Dr Wells:** It most certainly is, yes. And just to add to that point, I'd like to mention that in my professional experience as a psychologist, it's very common for people to go through a range of emotions. You might have heard of the stages of grief in coming to terms with the death of someone we loved. Well, it can be quite similar with unemployment.

**Brandon:** Interesting. And what are those stages for unemployed people?

**Dr Wells:** It can vary but generally it starts with anger, then denial, you know, like a refusal to accept what's happening to them. Over time, that denial slowly changes to a kind of reluctant acceptance. The final stage is acceptance and this is a good stage to reach because the person finally feels a degree of control again. Usually,

at that point, they're ready to deal with the changes in their life and begin the process of working on a strategy.

**Brandon:** Is there some practical advice we can share with people who are searching for a job?

**Dr Wells:** Yes, absolutely. I realise this may be difficult but don't take it personally. I know it's awful but the same thing is happening to millions of others too. Above all, it's vital that you put measures in place to help avoid depression. For example, make a weekly plan with activities mapped out for each day such as doing research, going to the job centre, exercising, etc. Setting goals is important. Take care of your health. Eat well and make sure you're getting enough sleep, but don't be tempted to sleep late every day. Keep moving!

**Brandon:** Exactly. Submitting good applications requires focus and energy. For each application you may need to adapt your CV to show how your strengths and skills match the job description. If you want to develop new skills you could volunteer your time to gain whatever experience you need. You could also consider starting a course to learn any new skills. Government subsidies are available for many courses, so you shouldn't have to worry about the expense.

**Dr Wells:** These ideas are invaluable. Another thing I sometimes suggest to people is taking the time to think, to really think carefully, about what they want. Sometimes people realise that a different location may improve their chances of finding a job in their particular line of work. Some discover that they want to take their career in a different direction, to try something new. Others take the opportunity to set up their own business. Support in drawing up a business plan is available at no cost in the UK and, depending on the business idea, there may be funding available for some of the start-up costs.

**Brandon:** The main thing is to develop a plan of action and to take advantage of the resources available to you including, by the way, the encouragement of the people closest to you. If your application is rejected or you are not successful at interview, don't despair, keep trying.

**Dr Wells:** Some people say that coping with unemployment is like a full-time job because you have to work at it every day, and that's exactly the point we're making. Think about the things we've said today. Make a schedule for every week, then take it one day at a time and don't stop believing in yourself.

## ▶▶ PART 4

*Part 4 consists of two tasks. You'll hear five short extracts in which people talk about travel. Look at Task 1. For questions 21–25, choose from the list A–H what each speaker says about their main experience of travelling. Now look at Task 2. For questions 26–30, choose from the list A–H how each speaker feels about travel now. While you listen you must complete both tasks.*

**Speaker 1:** I've been travelling since I was born. My mother was a diplomat, so our family moved every few years, more or less. By the time I was 12, I'd lived in four different countries and travelled to countless more. Now that I'm an adult I continue to travel as much as I can, I feel restless whenever I stay in one place too long. What I enjoy about travelling is that I'm always learning something new, always having new experiences. It adds value to my life and I find it very stimulating. It's what I know; I suppose you could say it's in my blood.

**Speaker 2:** The world is an amazing place, there's no doubt. I've been lucky enough to see some utterly incredible sights: Machu Picchu in Peru, the pyramids of Egypt, the Great Wall of China, but I'd never describe myself as a truly devoted traveller. I'm a bit lazy about it, to tell you the truth. Mates of mine organised all of those holidays and I happily went along each time. But I have young kids now, so my priorities have changed. I don't mind, you know. I'm content with things the way they are. Travel is wonderful but I'm not too bothered about it, you know?

**Speaker 3:** Honestly I fail to understand what people see in travel; I just don't get it, I really don't. I don't travel at all these days, if

I can help it. <u>In the past, every single trip I ever took – *every* one, without exception – was a nightmare.</u> Twice my luggage was lost. Once I got very sick abroad, another time I was robbed. Then there's being squashed on overcrowded flights and those awful airport queues … I literally cannot think of anything more stressful. <u>Travel is just not for me; the mere thought of it makes me feel nervous and uncomfortable.</u>

**Speaker 4:** <u>It took me longer than most of my friends to discover the joy of travelling. I didn't even have a passport until I was 17</u> and went on my first trip, a European tour, with my brother. We bought rail tickets and travelled by train across nine countries, which took two months, and I absolutely loved every minute of it. From that point, I was completely hooked on travelling. I know it'll sound a bit dramatic, but travel has changed my life. <u>It's a true honour, I mean, I'm fortunate to be able to enjoy the luxury of travel. I'm very lucky.</u>

**Speaker 5:** <u>I work for an international company and I have to travel extensively for my job.</u> I visit our offices in the United States, Latin America, Japan, Australia, and everywhere in between. At first it seemed kind of glamorous, all these hotels and restaurants and taxis … but I really don't like it any more. It's quite a lonely existence, to be honest, and <u>all this travel keeps me away from my family and breaks up the harmony of our home.</u> I can't enjoy going away on holiday any more or even taking weekend trips over the summer months. I'm looking for a new job.

**TEST 5**

▶▶ **PART 1**

*You will hear three different extracts. For questions 1–6, choose the answer A, B or C which fits best according to what you hear. There are two questions for each extract.*

**Extract One**
*You hear two friends discussing plans for another friend's birthday. Now look at questions one and two.*

**Colin:** Amanda, I've been meaning to ask you, are we going to do anything for Ken's birthday?

**Amanda:** Mmm, good question. <u>He says he doesn't like birthdays and doesn't want to do anything special,</u> but it is his 21st …

**Colin:** Well, in that case we have to do something! How about organising a weekend away for everyone? Maybe we could go camping.

**Amanda:** We could … but I was thinking of <u>something a little less complicated, only because Ken won't want us to make a big deal of his birthday.</u>

**Colin:** Got it, yes. Then what about throwing a surprise party at my house?

**Amanda:** That sounds great but I think he might die of embarrassment!

**Colin:** Fair enough. So, what did you have in mind?

**Amanda:** Well, I know it doesn't sound particularly exciting but I think we should just book a restaurant in town and invite his closest friends, keep it quiet.

**Colin:** OK, great, we can order a big cake for him and all sing …

**Amanda:** Colin!

**Colin:** Ha, just kidding!

**Extract Two**
*You hear two college friends discussing their classmate, Phil. Now look at questions three and four.*

**Woman:** That was Phil, you know, that guy I know from college. He asked me for my lecture notes from the past two weeks.

**Man:** The past two weeks? Has he been on holiday somewhere?

**Woman:** No, he just didn't bother coming to lectures. He does that now and again, I'm not sure why.

**Man:** No way! That's kind of strange if you ask me. It's not as though he's a close friend or anything like that, is it? He's got a nerve – asking for your notes because he can't be bothered to go to lectures. You're not going to give him the notes, are you?

**Woman:** I don't see why not. I don't mind helping him out … why do you care?

**Man:** Oh, I don't know what to say. I mean, we all make an effort to show up to class, we listen and make notes. <u>What's so special about Phil that he doesn't take the time and trouble like everyone else? He really thinks he's better than the rest of us.</u>

**Woman:** Come on, that's a bit harsh. <u>Maybe there are things going on behind the scenes that we don't know about.</u> Anyway, he asked me, not you, so just forget it.

**Man:** All right, all right. Fine.

**Extract Three**
*You hear a man telling his friend about some good news regarding his job. Now look at questions five and six.*

**Cara:** Hey, Anton. You look pleased.

**Anton:** Hi Cara. I know, I just had the most amazing day at work! There's this very big client based in London – everyone in the industry knows them – and everyone knows that they do business with our main competitor; they don't seem to order from anyone else. Countless colleagues of mine have tried to lure them over to our side but never successfully.

**Cara:** I think I see where this is going …

**Anton:** Yes! I've been working on this thing for months now, Cara. I just got the call this morning – <u>they've placed a *massive* order with us.</u> I couldn't believe the news when I heard it.

**Cara:** Well, good for you. Are you going to get a rise?

**Anton:** I doubt it, although I'll probably get a bonus later this year when they do our employee reviews.

**Cara:** Well maybe <u>you'll get a promotion?</u>

**Anton:** <u>That's a bit more tricky, actually. But you never know …</u>

▶▶ **PART 2**

*You will hear a young woman called Louise sharing her views with a group of schoolchildren about the impact of the internet on the music industry. For questions 7–14, complete the sentences with a word or short phrase.*

**Louise:** Hi, everyone. So, today, I'm going to share my views regarding the impact of the internet on the music industry. It's a topic that many people feel quite strongly about, for example, my friend, Dean. <u>He's a musician and is part of a group that firmly believes the internet has ruined the music industry. Personally, I think that's a slight exaggeration, to say the least.</u>

My position is that the internet has changed the business of music, but not destroyed it. OK, thinking back on it, I'll admit that people in the industry must have been in a panic when <u>everyone figured out how to make a digital copy of their music collection and save it to the hard drive of their computers. I realise that policing this presented a challenge.</u> Of course we all shared files with each other which, strictly speaking, was against the law: it meant that others were enjoying music they'd never paid for. Look, I'm not trying to say that's not a big deal but, come on, it's not exactly a new state of affairs since the invention of the internet. Long before the internet, before we even had CDs, people 40 years ago were most certainly copying their records of The Rolling Stones and The Beatles onto audio cassettes.

<u>Then, I suppose, the next development was the shift from CD players to MP3 players. Illegal music downloads were a real problem; some people were caught and had to face the music, so to speak. Generally this resulted in paying heavy fines;</u> I remember reading about a case in the United States where a college student had to pay $700,000. Mention MP3 players to my friend, Dean, and he'll call them the killer of the album, but this is exactly where I disagree

with him. I don't think it's a bad thing that we could suddenly buy the individual tracks we liked rather than buying an entire album we didn't particularly want. There's been a switch in how we buy music … it's become a different model, you see, but I just can't agree with Dean that it signals the death of the entire industry.

Dean doesn't like it when I say this but, the way I see it, the days when music executives made ridiculous amounts of money are gone, and I think that's not a bad thing. They were too greedy, in my view. Music distribution is a different game now, and it eliminates any need for those guys.

Let's face it, music is not going away. Look around you, it's thriving! There will always be musicians and there will always be people who love music and don't expect it to be free. We've continued to see rising stars in music in recent years, haven't we? And another thing, the internet has actually made it possible for more bands to upload their songs and gain a following. Independent record labels and independent artists are the way of the future. Concert tours, if they're done well, continue to be profitable. I'm sorry but I just find it difficult to feel sorry for the music industry.

▶▶ **PART 3**

*You will hear a radio programme,* Wednesday Weekly, *in which blogging is the topic of discussion. For questions 15–20, choose the answer A, B, C or D which fits best according to what you hear.*

**Ann:** Hello, I'm Ann Jennings and I'd like to welcome you to *Wednesday Weekly, the show in which we discuss everything from pets to politics.* The first topic today is blogging, and let me be the first to admit that I know very little about blogs or bloggers. However, not to worry, with us in the studio we have my first guests, local experts, Sophie Smith and Joe Peters. Welcome, both.

**Sophie:** Thank you, Ann.

**Joe:** Thanks, Ann.

**Ann:** OK, as a starting point I'm willing to reveal what I know; I'll tell you my understanding of blogging and you can correct me if necessary. Right, it seems to me that a blog is a kind of diary on the internet. People create their blog and then they write entries in it – regularly, I presume – which they publish online. Others can read these blog entries and, I think, comment on them. How am I doing so far?

**Joe:** Well, not bad, but it's not the whole story.

**Sophie:** Pretty close, Ann.

**Ann:** But, if that's basically it, it seems a strange practice … to me, anyway. I mean, why would anyone want to make their diary public? It's kind of a private thing. It all seems a little self-centred, if you don't mind my saying.

**Sophie:** No, that's a fair enough comment, but there's more to it than that. While it's certainly true that bloggers are often accused of trying to grab all the attention they can, not all bloggers fit the description you provided.

**Joe:** Exactly. And, to tell you the truth, the trend of so-called personal bloggers has really changed. In the '90s when blogging first started, it was fairly common for people to just blog about their opinions and random thoughts but, over time, the *blogosphere* – the collective term we use for all blogs – became much more specialised.

**Ann:** Oh, well that's interesting. So, how did the blogosphere change? Could you say more about this, Joe?

**Joe:** Um, for one thing, people became more selective in what they wanted to read. Blogs started to be theme-based …

**Ann:** Sorry, I'm not sure I follow your meaning there.

**Joe:** I'm saying that instead of using their blogs just to talk about themselves, people began to focus on their areas of knowledge, for example, blogs on fashion or cooking or travel or technology, and within each of these areas, some blogs really rose to the top in terms of popularity.

**Ann:** So, if I were, let's see … a keen gardener, I could find popular blogs about gardening?

**Joe:** Exactly.

**Sophie:** You can find blogs on literally everything, a recent study claimed that there are about a hundred million blogs published worldwide! Some are serious in nature, some are just for fun, and others are practical. There are environmental blogs, gossip blogs, political blogs, sports blogs … I could go on and on. What's really good is that blogs are now an accepted form of publishing.

**Ann:** An accepted form of publishing?

**Sophie:** Sorry, I didn't phrase that very well. I mean there are some genuinely talented writers out there and now the quality of their work as well as the value of their blogs is being acknowledged. In fact, there are awards for blogs, and some of these are quite prestigious.

**Ann:** Really? I had no idea.

**Joe:** And if I could just add another point, the top bloggers have actually managed to generate revenue from their blogs. Selling advertising is the main method but selling e-books and other products are also sources. There are other methods too, it varies widely, some bloggers might run other promotions or accept bookings as guest speakers.

**Sophie:** Not forgetting that these days all major online newspapers now also publish blogs in a variety of categories.

**Ann:** Gosh, I'm learning so much today! Is there anything else?

**Sophie:** Well, I was going to mention the relatively recent popularity of live blogging. When big news stories break, articles are published about them in the traditional way, but many news agencies also employ live bloggers to continuously publish updates about the story, like a written form of live broadcasting. Live blogging is also used during major sporting events. Recent studies show that the public is becoming more inclined to view the live blog than to read the conventional article.

**Ann:** This has been a fascinating conversation. I'd like to thank Sophie and Joe for opening my eyes to the wonder of the blogosphere. Now, my next guests are a complete contrast …

▶▶ **PART 4**

*Part 4 consists of two tasks. You will hear five short extracts in which people talk about giving money to charity. Look at Task 1. For questions 21–25, choose from the list A–H what kind of charity, if any, each speaker supports. Now look at Task 2. For questions 26–30, choose from the list A–H what each speaker says about the reason for their choice. While you listen you must complete both tasks.*

**Speaker 1:** For most of my life I hadn't ever given to charity; I'd never really thought about it much. Now I donate to a small organisation that runs a youth centre. I started doing this some years ago when I saw how much damage the economic recession was causing nationally and internationally, but I think the way to make a difference is at the community level. I really feel for our youth who are struggling to find work. At least with the youth centre they have somewhere to go, and the most important thing is that it provides them with free workshops on developing their interview techniques and learning how to write good letters of application, that kind of thing.

**Speaker 2:** My grandmother has Alzheimer's disease and I know there are many other families who are going through the same thing. It's a difficult disease for the person suffering from it, and also for their loved ones. I make monthly donations to a large charity which is working to find a cure. With advances in technology there have been some significant breakthroughs already, but in order to continue their work they need our help. I consider this to be a very worthy cause and, I suppose, it's also my way of honouring my grandmother.

**Speaker 3:** For a long time I've been giving money to a well-known charity dedicated to improving the lives of people in very poor countries abroad. I'd see these advertisements on TV and feel awful for those people and the dreadful conditions they have to endure. I'm not a wealthy man, but I manage OK. Compared to the poverty shown in the ads, I'm very lucky, so I kind of felt obliged to help. I know that you hear stories of corruption in these countries. I've thought about stopping my donations, but if everyone did that, we'd be in a terrible state, and there can't be corruption everywhere, can there?

**Speaker 4:** I don't want to sound like a crazy 'cat woman', but, to be fair, domestic animals have to rely on us for their survival, and that's why I give money to a charity that houses and feeds abandoned pets. These poor creatures are neglected or thrown out by their owners and, honestly, what hope do they have without the support of people like me? A lot of people don't like giving to animal charities so I feel it's my duty to help them; I can't bear to think of dogs and cats suffering needlessly.

**Speaker 5:** Charity? I don't think so. Nobody ever gave me anything, that's for sure. You know the old saying 'charity begins at home'? Well, what little money I have goes to keeping a roof over my head and to feeding my kids. I pay my taxes and that's my contribution to society. I work hard but my salary is low and every month it's a battle to make ends meet. I get so angry when I'm asked to make charitable donations. And what are the politicians doing to provide basic care for people in difficult circumstances? That's where the funds should be coming from, if you ask me.

 **TEST 6**

### ▶▶ PART 1

*You will hear three different extracts. For questions 1–6, choose the answer A, B or C which fits best according to what you hear. There are two questions for each extract.*

### Extract One
*You hear two friends discussing reality TV. Now look at questions one and two.*

**Woman:** Seriously, Alex, you're not still watching that reality TV programme, are you?

**Alex:** This? Oh, I certainly am.

**Woman:** I just don't get it. You're the most intellectual person I know, you got the highest honours in psychology last year and this is how you spend your free time? That show is ridiculous!

**Alex:** Ah, but reality television is an excellent source of psychological observations. You might find it ridiculous, but I get a lot out of it. After all, it involves watching how people behave and interact.

**Woman:** Pretty stupid people, you mean. Sorry, but it's the most irritating thing on TV. How does it not get on your nerves?

**Alex:** I find it hilarious! Sit for a while and watch it with me, you'll see.

**Woman:** I don't think so.

**Alex:** Fine, well, to each their own. I can't say that I find those word puzzles you're forever doing particularly intellectually stimulating …

### Extract Two
*You hear a conversation between two people who meet at a teachers' conference. Now look at questions three and four.*

**Gina:** Hi, I'm Gina, Gina Thomson. This is my first teacher's conference. Have you been teaching a long time?

**Steve:** Hi, I'm Steve. Not really … but long enough! About four years now. And you?

**Gina:** I finished my teacher training last June and I was in my first job by September.

**Steve:** Not quite a year so far then.

**Gina:** And yet it feels like 100 years! The longest year of my life, anyway.

**Steve:** Gosh, you don't seem very happy. I hope it turns out to be the right career for you.

**Gina:** I actually love it. I just find it incredibly tough.

**Steve:** That sounds about normal. If you don't mind my asking, what do you struggle with the most?

**Gina:** Definitely the preparation, there's just so much of it. I work late every night and every weekend and still don't feel fully prepared. What about you?

**Steve:** Class size is pretty challenging; I always think I'd manage better with fewer students. The preparation gets easier over time, by the way.

**Gina:** Phew!

### Extract Three
*You hear two college students discussing where they prefer to study. Now look at questions five and six.*

**Woman:** Hi, Ewan. Finals next week, let me guess, are you on your way to the library?

**Ewan:** Actually, I'm heading home. I prefer to study there.

**Woman:** Oh, right? But doesn't it get kind of noisy with all your flatmates coming and going?

**Ewan:** Not really. My room is at the back of the flat and it's pretty quiet; I'd much prefer to be there. Anyway the library is completely hectic, especially at this time of the year.

**Woman:** Wow, that's interesting. Me, I wouldn't last five minutes studying at home. I'd want to watch TV or call my mom or make a snack in the kitchen … I'd never get any work done.

**Ewan:** It's funny, isn't it? I get completely distracted in the library but I can focus almost instantly once I'm at home …

**Woman:** Whereas for me, it's the opposite. You're lucky. I think it'd be great to study at home but I wouldn't trust myself, I know what I'm like.

**Ewan:** Well, I suppose the main thing is to do whatever suits you best. Speaking of which, I'd better get going.

**Woman:** Of course. Good luck, Ewan!

**Ewan:** See you.

### ▶▶ PART 2

*You will hear a speaker called Terry Carville informing a group of students about the fair trade movement. For questions 7–14, complete the sentences with a word or short phrase.*

**Terry:** Good afternoon, everyone, and thank you for coming. My name is Terry Carville and I'm the Director of Public Engagement at Support Fair Trade, a large UK-based organisation which works to promote the practice of fair trade in Britain. I have been invited by the Students' Union to talk about this today.

First of all, what is fair trade? Basically it's a system designed to ensure that farmers and others who work on small farms in developing countries are paid a fair price for their goods. Obviously, it's common commercial practice for importers to buy goods as cheaply as possible and, usually, this means trading with big suppliers at the expense of smaller producers in poor countries. And so, you see, the concept of fair trade ensures a sustainable living for those small farmers and labourers.

We know that these are difficult economic times here in the UK, and some people feel they should buy local rather than fair trade products. Let's get this straight: the important thing to be aware of is that most fair trade items are not, in fact, produced in the UK, so there is no direct competition. In the instances where certain items are grown or produced locally, fair trade often meets out-of-season needs, or simply increases the supply of a particular item to meet UK demands.

Thousands of products have been licensed for fair trade, but the most popular ones tend to be fresh produce, for example, bananas and oranges. Other fair trade food products also widely available include tea, honey, sugar and rice. The item that has perhaps received the most publicity is fair trade coffee. Here in the UK about 20 per cent of all coffee consumed is fair trade, which is an impressive statistic. In fact, the UK is one of the world's leading fair trade markets.

So, how can you and your university play a part in the fair trade movement? Well, as an individual, you can always make an effort to look out for the fair trade label when you're out for a coffee or buying your groceries. If your local coffee shops and supermarkets do not stock fair trade goods, consider approaching a manager; I have leaflets here which you can pass on to them.

As a university, you might like to join the fair trade university and college project, which a significant number of colleges throughout the UK have already done. The idea is to start a campaign to increase awareness of fair trade among staff and students, you know, make sure everyone's 'on message', and, on a more practical level, to ensure that fair trade goods are available on campus. Some universities participating in the project have organised fun events such as fair trade wine tasting or the sale of fair trade roses on Valentine's Day. Publicise events on your university website, and try to get senior faculty members to endorse your campaign.

Being part of a campaign like this is also a positive addition to your CV, demonstrating commitment as well as organisational skills. I have some sign-up sheets here … what are you waiting for? Get involved!

▶▶ **PART 3**

*You will hear a phone conversation between a successful actor called Annabel and a teenager called Maurice, who is considering studying drama. For questions 15–20, choose the answer A, B, C or D which fits best according to what you hear.*

**Maurice:** Hello, is that Annabel?

**Annabel:** Yes, it is.

**Maurice:** Oh, hi. I'm Maurice Rhodes … Leo's brother.

**Annabel:** Hi, Maurice. Leo said you wanted to speak to me. How can I help?

**Maurice:** Right, yes, well, I'm interested in studying drama, I think.

**Annabel:** You don't sound very sure, Maurice. What are your concerns?

**Maurice:** I guess I'm worried about the lifestyle. It doesn't seem very stable. It's not that I have notions of being rich and famous, but I'd be concerned about paying my bills and, you know, just managing day to day.

**Annabel:** I certainly do know! Look, Maurice, if you've called because you want me to talk you into studying drama, sorry but you've come to the wrong place.

**Maurice:** Of course … that's not it, Annabel. I don't expect you to do that. I know it's ultimately my decision. But I thought it might be helpful to hear a little bit about your experience. Is that OK?

**Annabel:** Oh, absolutely. Why don't I begin by telling you how I started out and we'll take it from there. If you think of any specific questions, by all means, ask. Does that sound all right?

**Maurice:** Definitely. Thanks!

**Annabel:** Well, when I finished school, I went to Leeds to study art but I left at the end of the first year; I just wasn't stimulated by it. I suppose you could say I took a risk then because I moved to Northern Ireland – where I'd never been in my life – and enrolled in a theatre studies degree at a small university. The risk paid off because I absolutely loved the course and that's when I knew for sure I wanted a career in acting. Let me tell you something, Maurice, if you're genuinely passionate about something, you won't care what people think or say about you.

**Maurice:** You just go for it.

**Annabel:** Exactly. When I graduated I went travelling for a year, which I highly recommend. I had some extraordinary experiences but most of all I had time to think about the next steps. I knew the odds were narrow but I had limitless determination and I started working on an application to the Royal Academy of Dramatic Art as soon as I got back.

**Maurice:** RADA?! In London!

**Annabel:** The very one. And by some kind of miracle I was accepted.

**Maurice:** Wow. All the greats went there.

**Annabel:** It's certainly a special place but, make no mistake, it was also a tough course, a lot of work.

**Maurice:** I understand.

**Annabel:** I've been an actor for ten years now and I can't imagine doing anything else. I've done a good deal of television work, and small parts in one or two films, but the theatre is my first love. When you land a good part in a great play, it's the best feeling in the world. I've been in plays that toured the country and visited schools along the way. I've been lucky enough to work with the Royal Shakespeare Company.

**Maurice:** No way! That's amazing.

**Annabel:** But, Maurice, these are the highlights. Between times there are a lot of periods when you don't have work; when you audition for a particular role you really want, but don't get it; when you – as you rightly pointed out – worry about money. You have to be prepared for that, otherwise just get a nine-to-five job and forget about the stage. It can be a difficult lifestyle.

**Maurice:** Hmm, yes, that is an important consideration. Do you ever do any other kinds of work?

**Annabel:** I've recorded a few audio books, actually. Long days in the studio but it's not so bad, and it's money in the bank. I also qualified as a yoga teacher a few years ago. When I have time, I teach some classes at a local gym.

**Maurice:** You've given me a lot to think about, Annabel. Thanks so much for taking the time to speak to me about this. I'm pretty sure I'm going to pursue drama after all.

**Annabel:** Good for you, Maurice. Good luck!

▶▶ **PART 4**

*Part 4 consists of two tasks. You'll hear five short extracts in which people talk about their favourite subject when they were at school. Look at Task 1. For questions 21–25, choose from the list A–H what each speaker enjoyed about that subject. Now look at Task 2. For questions 26–30, choose from the list A–H what each speaker does or plans to do for a living. While you listen you must complete both tasks.*

**Speaker 1:** My favourite subject? Definitely maths. I think of it as a 'clean' subject; I know that may sound like a strange thing to say – what I mean is you can depend on it; it's solid – you know, it's tidy … maths explains everything, there are no loose ends. I distinctly remember the joy of learning to count when I was about three years old. Numbers fascinated me then and they still do. No surprise, of course, that this was my area of study at college, and that I work with figures now. I take care of the finances for individuals and businesses, calculating their profits and the taxes they owe.

**Speaker 2:** I'm a university student of fine art and I feel like the luckiest person in the world to study a subject I absolutely love. When I was in secondary school we only had two hours of art class a week; my favourite two hours of the entire week. The teacher really inspired me to develop my own style. I think it's the only subject that truly lets you express yourself. When I graduate I want to work on exciting new ranges of clothing for some big, well-known label. I've already made some interesting garments for my friends and family members. It's the best feeling in the world.

**Speaker 3:** My friends are always teasing me because I'm so enthusiastic about history. They yawn and say it's boring; they say it's a dead subject. But I don't see it that way at all. History teaches us about ourselves, who we are, where we've come from. I enjoy the analysis we get to do, you know, looking back at points in the past and speculating on why certain decisions were made. I've made a career in research and although my work isn't related to history, I know I developed this skill through my study of history.

**Speaker 4:** For me, it's always been literature; always. Reading is my greatest pleasure. Teaching modern verse to university students means I'm one of those fortunate people who get to do what they love for a living. The subject's innovation is what drew me to it in the first place, the way words are used is special, not the everyday way in which we speak to each other, but in a crafted and clever way. Sometimes you have to work at it and puzzle over the meaning, sometimes you take your own meaning from it. I find it personally enriching.

**Speaker 5:** I was always crazy about science, but as the years went on, my focus shifted to the natural sciences and then to earth science. I specialised in geology for years and then became interested in using it to study human activity in the past. I honestly feel privileged every time I go out on a dig, finding the things people have left behind and discovering what their lives were like is amazing. It's an extraordinary feeling to stand on a site and find evidence of how people lived thousands of years ago. Studying early humans also tells us a lot about the human race and how societies developed.

 **TEST 7**

## ▶▶ PART 1

*You will hear three different extracts. For questions 1–6, choose the answer A, B or C which fits best according to what you hear. There are two questions for each extract.*

### Extract One
*You hear two people discussing the royal family. Now look at questions one and two.*

**Man:** It's not that I have anything against the royal family personally, I just don't agree with the system, or with any monarchy for that matter. It's completely out of date, and it's ridiculous. I mean, on what merit does one family get to have so much privilege?

**Woman:** OK, for one thing, it's historical – their right from birth – they've inherited this privilege. I'm totally in favour of the royal family and other traditions – it's who I am – British and proud of it.

**Man:** But kings and queens belong to a different era entirely. We live in a democracy now, so why not just elect our heads of state?

**Woman:** Our prime minister and our politicians are elected …

**Man:** Exactly, and that's enough. We have a functioning government, we don't need an additional layer, it's totally unnecessary and extremely costly too. And I'm fed up with being accused of being radical or extreme whenever I suggest that we abolish the monarchy. I don't mean to offend you but I honestly think your beliefs are motivated by emotion, a sense of romance about the whole thing, rather than seeing this in a practical way.

**Woman:** Well, we'll just have to agree to differ.

### Extract Two
*You hear a conversation between two friends about a person called Paul. Now look at questions three and four.*

**Woman:** I'm not sure what the forecast says but the beach sounds brilliant. I can be ready in half an hour. So, who else is going?

**Man:** Um, Carmen, Annette, Shane, Avril, Paul …

**Woman:** Ah. Um, maybe I'll give it a miss. I really have a lot of stuff to do today. No, you guys go ahead. Have a great time.

**Man:** Wait a second, I do understand that Paul isn't your favourite person. I know he irritates you, but why not give him another chance? You met him on a bad day and, to be fair, you don't know him well enough to judge him accurately.

**Woman:** Once was more than enough! Seriously, I've never met anyone so pushy in my life. He dominated every conversation with his outrageous views. It's as if he was trying to get my attention by shocking me, which was so tedious. I couldn't stand him. Why does he have to be so over the top?

**Man:** To tell you the truth, I think he's fairly insecure. He was pretty desperate to impress you, you know.

### Extract Three
*You hear a man and a woman discussing the woman's younger brother. Now look at questions five and six.*

**Woman:** So, now my younger brother is saying he doesn't need to bother with his final exams at school because he actually believes he's going to have a career as a professional footballer.

**Man:** No! Mind you, he is very talented. And he did well at the individual football trials last month. I wouldn't be surprised if he were signed by a professional club.

**Woman:** Oh, not you as well! Even if he were lucky enough, he still needs an education. In fact, they should make that a condition for young players. He has a totally unrealistic vision of the future … thinks he's going to be a millionaire by the time he's 21. I can't seem to get it through to him that very, very few people actually make it to that level. And he's certainly not mature enough to cope with a lifestyle like that anyway. What those guys are paid is obscene!

**Man:** OK, OK, calm down … you're talking as if he already had a contract with a professional team! It's very common for young men to have a fantasy to be the next Ronaldo or Messi. He'll do his exams, he'll be fine.

## ▶▶ PART 2

*You will hear a woman talking about a personality test called the Myers-Briggs Type Indicator. For questions 7–14, complete the sentences with a word or short phrase.*

**Speaker:** So, have you heard about this personality test called the *Myers-Briggs Type Indicator*? The idea is that it indicates what type of personality you have based on a series of questions you answer. There's nothing new about the test, it's been around since the 1960s although I believe that work first began on it during the Second World War. It draws on the work of the Swiss psychologist, Carl Jung.

Jung considered the way people respond to the world and categorised them into four main groups: thinking, feeling, intuition and sensation. The developers of the Myers-Briggs test wanted to take Jung's theories and apply them in a practical way, so the questions are designed to see which of these groups you fit into. It's supposed to show, for example, whether you have a preference for thinking or feeling, whether you prefer using intuition – that is, making sense of things without consciously analysing them – or sensation. Myers-Briggs also tests whether you're more inclined to focus on how you perceive things or whether you just judge them, and whether you have a tendency to be an extrovert or introvert.

Look, I'd probably enjoy doing the test like a quiz in a fashion magazine, you know, just for fun. I think the basic principle of it is fine, but the fact is that it's very widely used by companies all over the world. The reason I've become so interested in the Myers-Briggs Type Indicator all of a sudden is that I've been asked to take the test as part of a job application process. I did an interview last week at this big company, which I won't name, and it went very well. I really want the job so I was delighted when they contacted me yesterday and invited me to a second-round interview … the problem is that the next phase consists of a Myers-Briggs test, and I'm feeling very uncomfortable about it.

First of all, I think the test has serious limitations. I don't agree with the way it's structured; I don't like the idea of labelling people as one thing or another. Many of us, myself included, fall somewhere *between* two categories rather than squarely into one or the other, but Myers-Briggs doesn't cater for this possibility. I studied psychology at college and, while I accept that Jung did important work, it's also true to say that many experts are now critical of his theories.

I've been feeling so troubled about taking the Myers-Briggs test that I actually phoned the manager of Human Resources at the company this morning and told her about my concerns. I must say she was very understanding and reassuring. She said it's been company policy for many years to feature the test and that it's really only used as a very general guideline. She encouraged me not to worry and added that I'm a very strong candidate for the position. I still wish I didn't have to take the test but I'm not feeling quite as upset about it now.

▶▶ **PART 3**

*You will hear an interview with a successful novelist called Hilton Sims. For questions 15–20, choose the answer A, B, C or D which fits best according to what you hear.*

**Int:** I'm delighted to welcome today's guest, the multi award-winning author, Hilton Sims, who had a meteoric rise to fame with his initial thriller a decade ago. Since then, Hilton has published six additional novels – all of them bestsellers – two of which were made into Hollywood blockbuster films. Hilton, what I think many people find fascinating about the story of your success is that you have no particular background in fiction.

**Hilton:** Actually, I don't have a literary background at all! It's often reported that I worked as a clinical psychologist and people assume this served as a source for much of the material in my books, which are mainly psychological thrillers, but I've never practised psychology. In actual fact I used to be employed by Social Services in South London. I was part of their Child and Family Support team. The work can be grim and obviously my novels are quite grim … sometimes what you discover can be quite disturbing and child-protection cases often end up in court. Other than that, there's no real connection.

**Int:** You mentioned that you write psychological thrillers but many critics describe your novels as crime fiction. Which genre is more accurate?

**Hilton:** Oh, I don't pay much attention to labels like these and the truth is that there can be overlap, books like mine often belong in more than one genre. I know it matters to publishers for marketing purposes, and librarians and bookshop staff need to know which section to put the books in, but I'm only interested in telling a good story. I don't mind how people categorise my work as long as they read it!

**Int:** OK, Hilton, fair enough. So, I'm curious about how you made the switch to full-time novelist …

**Hilton:** Ah, well now, that was a long journey. Would you believe I wrote my first novel 20 years ago? I showed a few chapters to various friends who thought it was pretty good and said I should get it published, but that's where the encouragement stopped! I sent it to dozens of publishers who all rejected it, every one of them. Luckily I had a day job, as you know, but I continued writing in my spare time, even though I didn't think I'd ever be a successful novelist. Then one day it just so happened that I was introduced to a publishing agent at a friend's party and the rest, as they say, is history.

**Int:** Wonderful! There seems to have been a significant surge in the popularity of crime novels, films and television series in recent years. Why do you think that is?

**Hilton:** Yes, that's a very good question. People have always been drawn to the classic struggle between good and evil, haven't they? And, these days, solving crimes has become more sophisticated thanks to developments in science and technology; I think people find these aspects very appealing. More than anything, though, I believe that readers of crime novels and thrillers like working out how the crime was committed and who did it, literally cracking the case before the detectives do. So the readers want to pit their wits against those of the writer as well as against the greatest criminal minds in literature!

**Int:** Obviously you've produced a very impressive body of writing over the years. Do you have to be terribly strict about how much you write every day? Do you have a specific routine?

**Hilton:** I'm very disciplined about it. I get up around seven every morning and go jogging for 30 minutes or so. I love running, it gives me clarity. I'm usually at my desk by eight. We converted the attic at home and it's now my office; I find it difficult to write anywhere else, to tell you the truth. I write solidly until late afternoon only stopping for a brief lunch. But I believe in treating writing like any other job. Even if I'm having a bad day and the words aren't coming easily, I never give up; I persevere. It's my job, after all.

**Int:** Well, Hilton, thanks for joining us today.

**Hilton:** Thank you.

▶▶ **PART 4**

*Part 4 consists of two tasks. You'll hear five short extracts in which people talk about what they do to keep fit. Look at Task 1. For questions 21–25, choose from the list A–H what brought each speaker to this form of exercise. Now look at Task 2. For questions 26–30, choose from the list A–H what effect each speaker says this form of exercise has on them. While you listen you must complete both tasks.*

**Speaker 1:** I've never been someone who takes 'formal' exercise, I mean, I never go to the gym or anything like that. Instead I've started going on hikes every weekend with a group of people from the office. It's perfect for me because I truly appreciate getting out of the city and hiking through the countryside. It doesn't feel like a mission to keep fit, it's just a very enjoyable walk in the fresh air and in beautiful surroundings. Sometimes we're out there all day, *way* better than a noisy gym if you ask me!

**Speaker 2:** I've been a long-distance runner for about eight years now. Before that, I'd probably never run more than 100 metres to catch the bus! Then one day I surprised myself by agreeing to run a marathon with a local group who wanted to raise funds for a children's hospital in our city. I found the training incredibly tough at first, but it was a worthy cause so I really pushed myself. I never cease to be amazed by what our bodies can do. Every run makes me realise how thankful I am to be strong, to be capable of this.

**Speaker 3:** My boyfriend is a real outdoors type, you know, loves fishing and camping and building a fire on the beach at night, that kind of thing. I'm OK with all that, but he also likes extreme sports and I draw the line there. Last year, though, his best mate somehow persuaded me to try rock climbing and I was hooked right away. It demands endurance, there's no doubt about that, but I discovered that I really enjoy the excitement of doing a potentially dangerous sport; I'm completely stimulated by the whole experience. Can't get enough of it!

**Speaker 4:** In my early twenties, I spent a year teaching English in South Korea. Taekwondo was taught at the school where I worked and I grew curious about it. I started joining the classes and made extraordinary progress in quite a short time; I really took to it. What I like is that it gives you a proper work-out but taekwondo also contains an important aspect of meditation, you become more self-aware, you learn to control your breathing, and so you get the dual benefits of feeling centred and strong. I've continued the practice ever since and would like to teach it one day.

**Speaker 5:** We've always been tennis players in my family; I'm not sure when it started but it goes way back, probably to my great grandparents' time. I've been playing ever since I can remember. The nice thing about a family tradition like this is always having a willing opponent to play against, or a partner for a doubles match. I'm not particularly competitive on the court; I just enjoy the sport for its own sake, it always makes me indescribably happy! And there's great excitement in our house every year when the big tournaments are on television. We love it!

### ▶▶ PART 1

*You will hear three different extracts. For questions 1–6, choose the answer A, B or C which fits best according to what you hear. There are two questions for each extract.*

#### Extract One
*You hear two friends discussing studying. Now look at questions one and two.*

**Boy:** All this studying, ugh, when will it ever end?

**Girl:** Oh, cheer up! It *will* come to an end … but you shouldn't wish the time away, you know. Live in the now! Besides, doing things you don't enjoy is known to be good for you, it makes you a better person, so stop complaining about it.

**Boy:** You are joking, aren't you? OK, it's fair enough to be conscious of the here and now – I get that – but by what logic do you imagine that people actually benefit from doing stuff they hate? That just doesn't make any sense.

**Girl:** I read it in a magazine article. It's supposed to be character-building, it shows a sense of responsibility, and more to the point, it's life! I mean, everyone has to undertake things they don't like doing …

**Boy:** Well, yes, but that doesn't mean you have to go out specifically looking for things you know you won't enjoy doing. That's like some old-fashioned form of self-punishment or something.

**Girl:** Hang on, I never said you should search for them, only that you shouldn't mind so much when you do have to do things you'd rather not do. They're quite different ideas.

**Boy:** Whatever.

#### Extract Two
*You hear a woman admitting that she told a lie. Now look at questions three and four.*

**Tanya:** I feel awful, Victor, I just told a lovely person a huge lie. Even as I was saying it I knew I was wrong to be dishonest but I couldn't help it, she caught me off guard and I just said the first thing that came into my head.

**Viktor:** Wait, what's all this about?

**Tanya:** Oh, you know my friend Brooke? She loves singing and has decided to enter one of those TV talent competitions. She's really got her hopes up. So, she called around earlier to tell me the news and, inevitably, insisted on doing the love song for me, the one she's going to sing in the audition.

**Viktor:** Ah, I think I know where this is going …

**Tanya:** Yep, you guessed it. She's passionate about music but she is not musically gifted. She was completely out of tune, which she didn't seem to realise. I couldn't believe it. And the song was wrong for her, she wasn't able to hit the high notes.

**Viktor:** So, what did you say?

**Tanya:** I told her she sounded great. I know! I'm a terrible friend. But what was the alternative: be brutally honest and crush her dreams?

**Viktor:** Oh, dear …

#### Extract Three
*You hear two people discussing Facebook. Now look at questions five and six.*

**Man:** I've just had a tedious argument with my next-door neighbour. He's a really nice man in his late sixties but he has very fixed ideas about things and is never willing to reconsider his position, which gets on my nerves.

**Woman:** Older people have earnt that right, though, and we can all have different opinions surely. What was the argument about anyway?

**Man:** Facebook, of all things, bearing in mind that he's never even looked at a Facebook page in his life! I'm actually not that active on Facebook myself, but his point of view really annoyed me. Basically he was saying that Facebook is a massive waste of time and he more or less said that only idiots use it. I casually pointed out that it has well over a billion users worldwide, but that just made him laugh. In the 1950s and 60s when television was first becoming popular loads of people objected to it on the same grounds.

**Woman:** Maybe they were right.

**Man:** But the thing is, Facebook – just like television – has good and bad points. It all depends on how you choose to use it. It bothers me that my neighbour's mind is so closed.

**Woman:** Oh, well, there's nothing you can do about it.

### ▶▶ PART 2

*You will hear a man talking about genetically-modified foods. For questions 7–14, complete the sentences with a word or short phrase.*

**Man:** Last night I watched a documentary on television with my parents. It was about genetically-modified foods – or GM foods, as they're often called – you know, crops or other plants that have been altered in a laboratory to improve them in some way. Scientists might, for example, take a particular gene from one plant or organism and inject it into another plant to enhance that plant in some way.

Well, the programme turned our supposedly relaxing evening into a night of heated debate. My dad is fully in favour of GM foods – although they sold all their land about 30 years ago, his family were farmers for many generations. Dad sympathises with the plight of farmers in the UK who are fighting an uphill battle against weather patterns that are completely inconsistent due to climate change. In recent years, we've seen more and more extreme weather conditions in Britain, endless rain, unprecedented snow, unbelievably low temperatures. The net result is that a worrying number of farmers are facing financial ruin as their crops are destroyed season after season.

My mum, on the other hand, is wildly opposed to genetically-modified foods; I had no idea she felt so strongly about the issue. According to her, we should never mess about with the natural order of things and genetic engineering is just asking for trouble. In the main, Mum's point is that we don't know enough about the outcomes, we don't fully understand the risks to human health or the impact on the environment. Apparently, some recent studies have shown that where genetically-modified corn is being grown in the United States, it's proving toxic to an endangered species of butterfly. As for human health, the truth is no one knows what the long-term effects of consuming genetically-engineered food really are, but my mother is convinced that they can't be good.

As for me, I'm somewhere in the middle. I share Mum's concerns, I really do, but I see Dad's point too. Oh, and the documentary also touched on the problems faced by poor people in underdeveloped countries where food shortages are a common cause of death … could genetically-modified foods be the solution there? Governments in the UK and throughout Europe remain sceptical about GM foods but I just don't think they should be ruled out completely. That said, I feel we need to proceed with extreme caution; scientists should do exhaustive tests before we can deem these products to be safe.

Mum feels it's already too late. She says a high percentage of genetically-engineered crops are already grown throughout North and South America and, to make matters worse, products containing GM ingredients are not always clearly labelled, which means that people are not necessarily aware of what they're eating. My father thinks this is simply a matter of making sure that food labels are regulated properly, it wouldn't be too difficult to do, in his view.

It seems to me that my family is a pretty accurate representation of society's attitude to this topic: some people are all for it, some are strenuously against it, and others are somewhere in between. Either way, the debate continues.

## ▶▶ PART 3

*You will hear three members of an interview panel discussing the two candidates, John and Rebecca, who are finalists for the job. For questions 15–20, choose the answer A, B, C or D which fits best according to what you hear.*

**Woman 1:** So, we're unanimous on the two finalists, Rebecca Boyd and John Turner. Now we need to make a decision as to which of them we'll hire. I'll begin, if I may, with my own thoughts. While I think they're both exceptional candidates, I have to say I thought John came across better. He was more personable and he certainly didn't lack enthusiasm … that's the kind of employee you want on your team, in my opinion. I'm afraid I wouldn't have the same confidence in Rebecca. She was a little too reserved, I felt.

**Man:** Hmm, I didn't quite see it that way. John might be more of an extrovert than Rebecca, but her answers seemed a lot more focused to me, and I think that's very important. She also has some marketing experience, which would be a valuable asset in this particular role.

**Woman 1:** To some extent, yes, although I feel Rebecca is more of an ideas person, and that's not necessarily who you want going out to meet your customers every day, you know?

**Woman 2:** Sorry, if I could just jump in here, one thing that surprised me was how little John knew about our company. Rebecca had clearly done her research in advance, which is pretty standard practice coming to any interview, isn't it. I was a little troubled by the fact that John hadn't bothered. The other thing that concerned me was how he handled the question about his weak points.

**Woman 1:** Oh, everyone hates that question!

**Woman 2:** No, but that's all the more reason to provide a considered response. He said he struggled with deadlines which, let's face it, would be a significant obstacle in this job and, as if that weren't bad enough, I didn't feel he took accountability for the problem or demonstrated what he was doing to overcome it. Instead he just seemed to be blaming his manager. That's a worry; that's a red flag if you ask me.

**Man:** I must say, I agree. I'm just checking … I can't find anything in my notes about how Rebecca responded to the same question. Do either of you recall?

**Woman 1:** Yes, I have it here. She said she found it challenging to give big presentations, but she quickly added that she had made great improvements by taking additional courses. In fact she mentioned that she'd had very positive feedback after she presented at her company's annual general meeting. I take that as a good sign.

**Man:** Yes … I liked Rebecca a lot, but I'm sorry to say this, she didn't appear to have a solid career trajectory; no five-year plan and she wasn't completely clear about her goals …

**Woman 2:** Not being goal-oriented would certainly be a strike against her in this role, but it occurred to me that she was trying to tailor her answers to illustrate what she could bring to the company rather than what the company could bring to her.

**Woman 1:** On the other hand, I was very impressed with John's answer. That guy definitely knows what he wants! I admire his spirit.

**Man:** Well, let's not get carried away. He's ambitious, that's for sure, and he's definitely keen, but do we believe that he could actually deliver? I mean, do you really believe he would manage with the day-to-day stresses of being on the road? It's a lot of responsibility. You need to be prepared and pay close attention to detail … speaking of which, I noticed a couple of spelling mistakes on his CV. You also have to rely on your instincts and think on your feet. By my reckoning, Rebecca is someone who would keep a cool head. John? I'm not so sure.

**Woman 2:** Yes, I spotted those typos too … not the way to make a good first impression, to say the least. Look, there's no question that he has some great qualities and I think he's going to do very well in life. I'm just not so sure this is the right position for him at

this time. Hiring him would be a risk that might pay off; he could turn out to be employee of the year! But I don't feel he's ready for a role like this yet, and I don't feel ready to take the chance.

**Woman 1:** I think you're being too conservative. I mean, I do understand your reservations about John. I guess it's just that I've been doing this for a long time and sometimes, you know, you just get a 'feeling' about a candidate? I get that with John. Rebecca did a better interview than him, no doubt, but I think he's the person who would really shine in this position.

**Man:** Well, you're obviously decided and Angela knows who she wants in the position, so I guess that leaves me with the casting vote. OK, so I think we should offer the job to …

## ▶▶ PART 4

*Part 4 consists of two tasks. You'll hear five short extracts in which people talk about a challenging experience they have had. Look at Task 1. For questions 21–25, choose from the list A–H how the incident affected each speaker when it happened. Now look at Task 2. For questions 26–30, choose from the list A–H how each speaker feels about the experience now. While you listen you must complete both tasks.*

**Speaker 1:** We'd had our family cat, George, ever since I was a kid. He was really my cat, a present for my eighth birthday and, when I went to university, George came too. He reached the fine old age of 18 and when he died recently I just couldn't come to terms with it. I was so down, crying all the time, unable to get out of bed for days, and I had to see the doctor for some help. Georgie had such a sweet nature, I just miss him so much. It's been a few months now and I'm not feeling quite as bad as I was, but grief takes a lot of time and patience.

**Speaker 2:** Things were going so well professionally that I decided to buy a house. Six months later, the recession hit. I figured things would improve soon enough, but didn't, and a few months after that I was laid off from my job. The value of my house dropped but my repayments didn't and I went bankrupt. My home was taken and I completely stopped believing in myself. Luckily my family supported me and helped me get through the whole thing. It was certainly a difficult time but not the end of the world. I'm young, I'm healthy, life goes on.

**Speaker 3:** It started out as an ordinary morning rushing around town doing the usual chores and errands. I was just leaving the car park of the supermarket when a white van came around the corner at tremendous speed. I tried to reverse but it was too late. The impact was incredibly powerful … I was shaking all over and I was crying. Someone called an ambulance and I don't remember much after that. In actual fact, I was quite lucky, my injuries were mainly superficial, but I'm excessively cautious now, I really *really* pay attention.

**Speaker 4:** The time I was stuck overseas because of tropical storms was much more upsetting than I ever would have imagined. I hated being stranded there for three additional nights, on my own, in a hotel that had no electricity and was running out of supplies. I know it's irrational but I began to believe I'd never see my family again. I worried constantly. At the time, it really felt like the worst experience of my life but I was very young then. When I think back on it now, I see it as nothing more than an inconvenience rather than a true crisis.

**Speaker 5:**

I liked living alone. I was pretty laid back about it. Then, when my flat was burgled I completely fell apart. It wasn't just the shock of having my belongings stolen, but the horror of a stranger going through my things; I couldn't get that idea out of my head. I felt insecure in my home and I couldn't sleep at night. Eventually I went to a therapist, but I can't say I'm back to normal yet. I check multiple times that all the windows are closed, doors locked and the alarm is on. I know it's unhealthy but I can't help it.

## TEST 1

### PAPER 1 Reading and Use of English

#### ▶▶ PART 1

**1** D  **2** A  **3** C  **4** D  **5** A  **6** B  **7** B  **8** C

#### ▶▶ PART 2

**9** which  **10** what  **11** whether  **12** from  **13** By
**14** enough  **15** after  **16** as

#### ▶▶ PART 3

**17** residents (verb to plural noun)  **18** Historically (noun to adverb)
**19** revitalising (adjective to verb)  **20** coastal (verb to adjective)
**21** moisture (adjective to noun)  **22** storage (verb to noun)
**23** inventive (verb to adjective)  **24** reversal (verb to noun)

#### ▶▶ PART 4

**25** no idea (1) + WHOSE folder it was (1)
**26** Michael to MAKE (1) + a formal complaint (1)
**27** demolition of the stadium (1) + took PLACE (1)
**28** NEARLY as impressive as (1) + those of (1)
**29** long as (1) + everyone/everybody TURNS up (1)
**30** to HAVE had (1) + my car serviced (1)

#### ▶▶ PART 5

**31** A: Incorrect. The writer suggests that asking whether birds have feelings may be wrong, but not that names given to birds are inappropriate.
B: Incorrect. The idea that asking whether birds have feelings may be unscientific and 'subjective', but the writer never states that people are often too subjective about birds.
C: Incorrect. Although the writer suggests that we may not give the sight of lovebirds nibbling each other's necks a second thought, this does not mean that insufficient attention is paid to bird behaviour in general.
D: Correct. The writer says that 'Niko Tinbergen warned fellow ethologists to steer well clear of feelings' and that the majority have followed this approach.

**32** A: Incorrect. The writer watched guillemots for years, but he doesn't say he has personal sympathies for them.
B: Incorrect. His father warned him that he would never make a career out of birdwatching, but he has done.
C: Incorrect. Saying that birdwatching was a boyhood obsession from the writer's adult perspective is not the same as saying that he realised when he was young that he had unusual interests.
D: Correct. The writer says that 'birdwatching is the best possible training for studying animal behaviour; to study birds well, you have to almost think like a bird', and that he 'spent years' doing it.

**33** A: Incorrect. The incident involved guillemots but the writer doesn't say this is what originally attracted him to these birds.
B: Correct. 'The moment eventually inspired me to explore and write about the way birds use vision, hearing, touch, smell, taste and feelings to experience the world' – in other words to investigate birds' senses.
C: Incorrect. The writer was 'perplexed' by the guillemot's greeting – which is a kind of challenge – but this is not why he describes the incident.
D: Incorrect. The writer mentions the guillemot's sophisticated vision and recognition system, but this is not why he describes the incident in this paragraph.

**34** A: Incorrect. The writer mentions that bats are mammals, and that bats and humans share certain features. He also refers to Nagel's view that we cannot know what it is like to be another species. There is no emphasis on differences between birds and mammals, however.
B: Correct. The writer says that the study of bird senses 'has been a minority subject' and also that 'understanding … how a bird feels is fraught with difficulties'. He also says that Nagel's point is that 'because it is impossible to know what it is like to be another person, trying to imagine what non-humans feel is a waste of time'.
C: Incorrect. The writer mentions that Nagel is an 'eminent philosopher', but he doesn't say this to emphasise the importance of his own subject.
D: Incorrect. The writer mentions that Nagel's essay was written in 1974 and science has obviously progressed since then. However, this is not why he refers to Nagel here.

**35** A: Incorrect. Knowledge of animal behaviour has changed but not the way that animals behave.
B: Incorrect. The writer suggests that it has been difficult to 'say something different' in this field of science 'for fear of being labelled unprofessional', but not that the debate has become more competitive.
C: Correct. Knowledge of animal behaviour has increased. Therefore, previous ideas about animals have been proved wrong.
D: Incorrect. The writer says that the behavioural thinking he followed is 'a kind of trap', but he also says it 'served him well', so he doesn't regret it.

**36** A: Correct. Behaviourists had assumed that symmetry was a key factor in the selection of partners, without realising that some birds were unable to recognise symmetry. So, not knowing about birds' senses could lead to false conclusions.
B: Incorrect. Birds generally have better vision than humans, but this is not why the writer refers to the study of symmetry.
C: Incorrect. Theories about the importance of symmetry were found to be based on false assumptions, but the writer does not refer to symmetry to demonstrate that scientific theories are regularly disproved.
D: Incorrect. It may be wrong to think that beauty is a key factor in birds' choice of partners, but this is not why the study of symmetry is discussed here.

#### ▶▶ PART 6

**37** D: On the role of museums in education A says: '… the contribution that museums make in communicating culture, knowledge and inspiration to visitors, particularly younger ones, … pays off handsomely.' D says: 'Museums have a crucial role to play in preserving and transmitting a nation's history and heritage, and in broadening intellectual and cultural horizons, among the younger generation in particular.'

**38** B: With regard to the impact of the cost of entry on tourism, A says: 'This is the clearest possible evidence for the popularity of free museum admission, with both local citizens and tourists. It is no coincidence that the UK saw an impressive growth in tourism…'. C says: 'Free admission to museums and galleries … stimulates growth in the tourist industry.' D says: 'Great museums which have free access also help to boost tourism.' B, however, says: 'It is far from certain that free museum access automatically brings in the tourists.'

**39** B: On the way state funding affects the development of museums C says: 'State-funded museums, free of the need to compete to survive, tend to be complacent and unenterprising.' B says: 'Museums which rely on the state for their funding have little incentive to make their collections more exciting and imaginatively displayed.'

**40** C: On public attitudes towards the cost of entry to museums, A says: 'The clearest possible evidence for the popularity of free museum admission, with both local citizens and tourists.' B says: 'Surveys show most people favour free museum admission.' D says: 'Opinion polls show that most people …favour free access.' C, however, says: 'The majority have little interest in museums, and are resentful when they learn how much they are paying for them.'

## ▶▶ PART 7

**41** D: Link between 'At the beginning of the so-called Classic Maya period, some 60 Maya cities sprang up across much of modern-day Guatemala, Belize and Mexico's Yucatán Peninsula' in the previous paragraph, and 'With their pyramids, squares, ball courts, and government buildings, they were where the urban Maya discussed philosophy …'

**42** G: Link between 'In the nineteenth century, … theorists imagined an immense volcanic eruption or earthquake – or maybe an empire-wide pandemic' in the previous paragraph and the contrast with 'Today, however, scientists generally agree that the Maya collapse has many roots, all intertwined – overpopulation, warfare, famine, drought.'

**43** B: Link between 'The early Classic Maya period was unusually wet,' … And during this time, he says, 'the population proliferated, aided by a surge in agriculture' in the previous paragraph, and 'indeed, it was during the rainiest decades of this era, from AD 440 to 660, that the cities sprouted.'

**44** F: Link between 'repeated and, at times extreme, drought. Agriculture declined and, not coincidentally, social conflict rose' in the previous paragraph, and 'when these divine connections failed to produce rainfall and good harvests, tensions probably developed' in the second sentence.

**45** A: Link between 'vast numbers of trees would have been cut down to make space for cities and farms, and to provide fuel' in the gapped paragraph, and 'this widespread deforestation' in the following paragraph.

**46** E: Link between 'localised drying decreased atmospheric moisture by five to 15% annually. 'Even a ten per cent decrease is considered an environmental catastrophe' in the previous paragraph, and 'add this to the broader trend and the situation becomes dire.'

## ▶▶ PART 8

**47** C: 'She thinks she was fortunate to have chanced upon a mentor, John Martino, an older businessman who kept her on track at times.'

**48** D: 'They say the 'wrapper' will never work. But a gut feeling tells me it'll come good.'

**49** C: 'I don't know why no one else has done it. I worry they might do actually.'

**50** B: 'The three games she's released so far have impressed the university so much that it's now policy to encourage sandwich year entrepreneurship.'

**51** C: 'Alexis admits to having missed classes and deadlines in her hectic lifestyle. "Also, I probably haven't done as much reading as I should've."

**52** A: 'It's happened on a much greater scale than she'd envisaged.'

**53** D: 'It's transformed me. I'm much tougher than I used to be.'

**54** B: 'I'd love to go out at weekends like my course mates do, but I can't afford the time.'

**55** D: 'But a gut feeling tells me it'll come good and I need to stick with it. As a poor student, I've got nothing to lose really, so that's what I'll do.'

**56** A: 'She's also good at managing her time. 'It's something I got used to at school – I did competitive athletics and had to fit it around schoolwork.'

 **TEST 1**

### PAPER 2 Writing

#### ▶▶ PART 1 (suggested answers)
#### Question 1
*Style:* Formal
*Content:* 1 Explain what is being proposed (the building of a road that will bypass your town).
2 Choose *two* of the benefits listed and expand on them. For example, say how the quality of life will improve when noise and pollution are reduced, and point out that better transport links might entice companies to set up and/or do business in the area.
3 To balance the essay, counter the benefits with at least two disadvantages, such as environmental concerns including loss of habitat for local wildlife; a decline in tourism revenue as fewer people pass through the town.
4 Conclude with a brief summary of the issue and the likely outcome.
5 Consider including your own opinion in your concluding paragraph.

#### ▶▶ PART 2 (suggested answers)
#### Question 2
*Style:* Formal or semi-formal
*Content:* 1 State the aim of the proposal and give it a suitable title.
2 In your introduction provide some background, i.e. company/employees' needs.
3 Make your suggestions in the main body. Use headings to organise your points.
4 Justify each recommendation by stating *how* it will benefit employees.
5 Write a brief conclusion giving your main points.

#### Question 3
*Style:* Formal
*Content:* 1 Open with a suitable greeting.
2 Then state what the article was about and where and when it was published.
3 Explain how the article made you feel. What did the article say that was untrue or unfair about students' behaviour? Give at least two points. For balance, concede one additional point from the article. Suggest that the editor publishes a more balanced article on this topic as soon as possible.
4 Use an appropriate closing.
5 Remember to remain polite throughout the letter.

#### Question 4
*Style:* Semi-formal
*Content:* 1 State the purpose of the review in your introduction.
2 Give the title and author of the book you are recommending. (It can be made up.)

3 Dedicate a paragraph each to the following points; use headings if you wish: provide a general overview of the book including the genre and a plot summary. Use descriptive language. Describe the main characters. Explain why you feel this book will appeal to a wide range of readers and try to include at least two specific examples to illustrate these points.

4 Write a brief conclusion reiterating your main points.

## TEST 1

### PAPER 3 Listening

▶▶ **PART 1**

1 B   2 C   3 C   4 A   5 B   6 A

▶▶ **PART 2**

7 career path   8 the route   9 media-based degree
10 take away   11 unpaid   12 set foot   13 was recruited
14 labour of love

▶▶ **PART 3**

15 C   16 D   17 C   18 B   19 D   20 A

▶▶ **PART 4**

21 C   22 F   23 H   24 A   25 D   26 B   27 A   28 G
29 E   30 F

## TEST 2

### PAPER 1 Reading and Use of English

▶▶ **PART 1**

1 C   2 D   3 A   4 C   5 B   6 A   7 D   8 B

▶▶ **PART 2**

9 yet   10 what   11 Until   12 enough   13 not
14 of   15 such   16 all

▶▶ **PART 3**

17 height (adjective to noun)   18 Interestingly (noun to adverb)
   19 characteristics (noun to plural noun with different meaning)
   20 survival (verb to abstract noun)   21 threatening (noun to adjective)   22 volunteers (adjective to plural noun)
   23 lengthen (adjective to verb)   24 irrelevant (adjective to negative form of the adjective)

▶▶ **PART 4**

25 NEVER have watched that film (1) + if (1)
26 to have BEEN (1) + a misunderstanding about (1)
27 STAND a/any chance (1) + of getting (1)
28 NOWHERE near (1) + as talkative as (1)
29 is rumoured/said/thought to (1) + have HANDED in (1)
30 are BOUND to be (1) + objections to (1)

▶▶ **PART 5**

31 A:   Incorrect. The writer gives some personal information about his experiences of cycling, but this is not the point of this paragraph.
   B:   Incorrect. The second paragraph is about having a peaceful and empty mind when cycling; the last sentence of the first paragraph refers to the same thing.

C:   Incorrect. The writer does not give an opinion.
D:   Correct. The writer gives details to explain what he means by 'a state of meditation' – for example, 'I have no recollection of the preceding kilometres … time can pass unnoticed in a blissful blur'.

32 A:   Incorrect. The text says that old people who were most active, including those who cycled, had five per cent more grey matter, but this does not necessarily mean that they lived longer.
   B:   Incorrect. The text says that walking and cycling both helped the schoolchildren, but it does not say that one was better than the other.
   C:   Correct. In terms of 'academic achievement', the pupils 'who cycled or walked did better' than those who went by car or public transport. Also, 'old people who were most active, including those who cycled, had more grey matter than those who were least active'.
   D:   Incorrect. The studies found that exercise benefited both children and old people, but it does not say that old people 'appreciated it more'.

33 A:   Incorrect. The text does not say that the studies found this. The studies were about the children's minds rather than their physical fitness.
   B:   Incorrect. Cycling is described as a 'complex' activity, but it does not suggest that children found it hard to cope with.
   C:   Incorrect. The studies suggest that cycling helped children with ADHD, but the text does not say that a lack of physical exercise was what caused their problems.
   D:   Correct. The students in the German study all did exercise, some including cycling, and they all 'did better than they previously had in concentration tests'.

34 A:   Incorrect. All the patients on stationary bikes improved, and no comparison is made with 'ordinary bikes'.
   B:   Incorrect. Dr Alberts' friend who had Parkinson's improved after riding with Dr Alberts, but there is no reference to relationships being an important factor.
   C:   Correct. The 'tandem' group were pushed harder ... and they improved at a greater rate: 'All patients improved, and the 'tandem' group showed particularly significant increases in connectivity between areas of grey matter responsible for functions such as walking and picking things up.'
   D:   Incorrect. In these studies, 'all patients improved' after cycling.

35 A:   Incorrect. Doctors know how cycling can be used in treatment for Parkinson's.
   B:   Correct. A discrepancy is when something contradicts expectations or two facts seem to contradict each other. This paragraph is about the man with Parkinson's disease who cannot walk, but can cycle with ease – something we would not normally expect.
   C:   Incorrect. There is no mention of the question of why Parkinson's affects some people and not others.
   D:   Incorrect. The previous paragraph mentions Dr Alberts' discovery that his friend with Parkinson's improved as a result of cycling. However, 'this discrepancy' refers to the current paragraph, not the previous one.

36 A:   Incorrect. The writer never says that cycling does more for adults than children.
   B:   Incorrect. Cycling seems to help both hyperactive children and the everyday rider to think more effectively. However, the word *notwithstanding* implies a contradiction, and there is no contradiction in the idea that it helps both types of rider.

C: Correct. The studies with hyperactive children suggest that cycling particularly helps them because it is a 'complex' activity. On the other hand, in the final paragraph, the writer says that the most remarkable thing about it for the everyday rider…, is that it can require no conscious focus at all', so it is mindless. So, the phrase tested here refers to the fact that cycling is good for some people because it is 'complex' and for others because it is 'mindless'.

D: Incorrect. The paragraph starts with 'the science of cycling is evidently incomplete' but 'its effects on hyperactive children notwithstanding' does not refer to this.

## ▶▶ PART 6

37 C: On the role zoos play in educating the public, D says '… how much can visitors really discover about wild animals from seeing them in cages and small enclosures?' C says: 'Most visitors go to zoos to be diverted … rather than to learn. One zoo study found that visitors spent less than eight seconds per snake and one minute per lion. What could possibly be learned from that?'

38 D: On the well-being of animals in zoos, A says '… modern zoos look after animals well.' B says 'Zoo animals today are well-fed and cared for in spacious surroundings.' C says 'Care of wild animals in captivity tends to be much more humane than it was in the past.' So A, B and C say similar things. D, however, says 'Zoo animals are psychologically affected and often display abnormal, even self-destructive, behaviour.'

39 A: On zoos and endangered species, B says ' Zoos' efforts to breed animals that are close to extinction have mostly failed … .' C says 'Most zoo-based attempts to breed species in order to stave off extinction have been strikingly unsuccessful.' D says 'Attempts to use zoos for breeding threatened species are also well-intentioned, but, with rare exceptions, they fail to bear fruit.' So, B, C and D say similar things. A, however, says 'Zoos play an increasingly important role in conservation. Without their intervention, many more of the world's surviving species would become extinct.'

40 B: On zoos as centres of research, A says '… expertise, which is developed through long-term, sustained studies at the zoos themselves, but also in support of field work in the wild.' B says 'Studies of animals in zoos provide information that would be very hard to obtain in the wild … findings of this kind are useful for zoologists in both zoos and the wild.'

## ▶▶ PART 7

41 E: Link between 'I'm not doing that,' says 15-year-old Daniel firmly' in the previous paragraph and 'Sofia, however, who is a good head shorter than her fellow pupil, moves forward, methodically pouring out a dozen small heaps.'

42 G: Link between the information about the young people from the London school in the previous paragraph and 'most of them, they soon tell me, have never been to the countryside before.'

43 B: Link in theme between the therapy for the young people described in the previous paragraph and the training for their teachers described in B.

44 A: Link between the feeling of calm that Aaron describes in the previous paragraph and 'A classmate, Hasan, describes a similar sense of tranquillity.' Also, the last sentence of B states that Hasan 'needs support' and the first sentence of the next paragraph: 'And this is what Fielden aims to provide.'

45 F: Link between the farm's income and the number of children who have attended in the previous paragraph and 'An impressive …' at the start of F.

46 C: Link between 'there are more than 80, and they have their own association called Care Farm UK' in the previous paragraph and 'this expansion of the sector is evident'. Also, link between 'there are differing explanations' in C and 'Whatever the reasons' at the start of the final paragraph.

## ▶▶ PART 8

47 D: 'It suffers from some uncertainty of purpose. Clearly not a guidebook … it's not quite an encyclopedia either.'

48 C: 'Prose that is … not always very digestible.'

49 D: 'It is hard to quibble with any inclusions or exclusions of either people or their constructions.'

50 B: 'His elegant, sharp wit is regularly put to good use.'

51 C: 'Gossels has unearthed a number of unfamiliar gems such as Charlotte Perriand's house in the Savoie mountains of France and the black-painted studio of the Swede, Sigurd Lewerentz.'

52 A: 'It grew from Heathcote's popular series of newspaper columns.'

53 C: 'A favourite fiction about modern architects is that they don't live in their own creations … Peter Gossels' book amply refute(s) this charge.'

54 D: 'The distilled version of modern architecture promoted by Pevsner and others became a useful caricature. … The reality was more complicated, and now the publishers Phaidon have produced this huge book to put the record straight.'

55 A: 'This book is so slim and whimsical-looking you could easily mistake it for 'bookshop candy' … but don't be fooled.'

56 B: 'Justifiably hard-hitting in his treatment of many of the skyscrapers that have gone up in London in the last two decades …'

 **TEST 2**

## PAPER 2 Writing

### ▶▶ PART 1 (suggested answers)

**Question 1**

Style: Formal

Content: 1 Explain what is being proposed and elaborate on two of the reasons mentioned.

2 State your own opinion early in the essay: make at least two points in support of your views and try to include specific examples. If you use any of the opinions expressed in the question, paraphrase them. Remember to reflect the advantages and disadvantages for the *majority* of people.

3 Tie up the main points in your conclusion and reiterate your position.

### ▶▶ PART 2 (suggested answers)

**Question 2**

Style: Informal

Content: 1 Open with an appropriate greeting.

2 First paragraph:
- thank Dan for his email.
- mention that you're pleased he's considering the Volunteering Abroad project.

3 Second paragraph:
- answer his question about the animal conservation work you did.
- include some details about your role and say whether or not you liked it.
- say if you feel he would enjoy the experience.
4 Third paragraph:
- talk about the travel opportunities he would have.
- offer to send him additional information.
5 Briefly sum things up in a concluding paragraph. You could ask after his family.
6 Sign off with a suitable closing.
(See page 199 for a model answer to this question.)

## Question 3
*Style:* Formal or semi-formal
*Content:* 1 Give the report a suitable title.
2 In your introduction, state the purpose of the report.
3 In the main body:
- devote a section to each of the bullet points provided in the question.
- use headings for clarity and group supporting details into numbered or bulleted lists.
- try to make realistic recommendations or suggestions and, if possible, mention how they could be implemented.
4 Summarise the main points in your concluding paragraph.

## Question 4
*Style:* Formal or semi-formal
*Content:* 1 State the purpose of the review in your introduction.
2 Give the title of the film you are recommending. (It doesn't have to be real.)
3 Dedicate a paragraph each to the following points; use headings if you wish:
- provide a general overview of the film including the genre and plot. (Use descriptive language.)
- describe the main characters.
- explain what is socially relevant about this film and why it would be appropriate for a public screening.
4 Conclude by summing up the reasons for your choice.

## TEST 2

### PAPER 3 Listening

#### ▶▶ PART 1
1 C  2 B  3 A  4 C  5 B  6 A

#### ▶▶ PART 2
7 (late afternoon) naps  8 side effect  9 pause  10 intense
11 (local and) cultural  12 memorable  13 slow travel  14 admit

#### ▶▶ PART 3
15 C  16 D  17 B  18 D  19 A  20 C

#### ▶▶ PART 4
21 C  22 E  23 B  24 H  25 G  26 C  27 E  28 A
29 F  30 H

## TEST 3

### PAPER 1 Reading and Use of English

#### ▶▶ PART 1
1 C  2 D  3 A  4 B  5 B  6 A  7 C  8 D

#### ▶▶ PART 2
9 so  10 not  11 only  12 such  13 Having  14 which  15 in
16 far

#### ▶▶ PART 3
17 emergence (verb to noun)  18 innovative / innovatory (verb to adjective)  19 adornment(s) (verb to noun – singular or plural)
20 reconstruction (verb to noun)  21 notably (noun to adverb)
22 findings (verb to plural noun)  23 growth (verb to noun)
24 technologically (noun to adverb)

#### ▶▶ PART 4
25 MUST have been (1) + telling the (1)
26 was not/wasn't LONG before (1) + she took (1)
27 THOUGH (1) + Radford's contribution has/contributions have been (1)
28 be relied on/upon (1) + to STAND up (1)
29 call OFF the meeting / call the meeting OFF (1) + came (1)
30 would HAVE no hesitation (1) + in recommending

#### ▶▶ PART 5
31 B: Correct. The second paragraph indicates how far Hendrickson went: 'he hasn't just interviewed … He has investigated … This total immersion school of – well, biography isn't quite the word.'
32 C: Correct. Hendrickson 'interviewed the latter two, and extensively researched the first, telling their … stories fully and sympathetically in the hope that, in the overlap between them, we'd get somewhere close to Hemingway.' This means aiming for a good understanding of Hemingway.
33 D: Correct. The reviewer gives details of the way the book covers Hemingway's writing and his lifestyle. The sentence 'Not that it cuts corners on the wild, action-man stuff either' implies a balance.
34 A: Correct. 'It defies any attempt to reduce it to a neat outline.'
35 B: Correct. The text says that 'pompous turns of phrase' are 'sometimes clumsily repeated … with at least three chapters containing the words 'Amid so much ruin, still the beauty.'
36 C: Correct. 'This book would have been astonishing without it.' *It* here refers to the style it is written in.

#### ▶▶ PART 6
37 D: On the way the book is organised, C says 'overall, it suffers from a lack of a clear focus. Ironically, for a book about maps, the reader all too easily gets lost in all the vivid detail and anecdotes.' D says 'Harder to accept or rationalise is the apparent lack of a guiding principle.'
38 C: On the quality of writing in the book, A says 'all delivered with the expansive liveliness of an expert story-teller.' B says 'this eminently readable history of map-making.' D says 'Garfield has a talent for communicating a telling detail or a curious turn of events.' So, A, B and D all say positive things but C is more critical: 'One is also distracted by some awkward phrasing and surprisingly imprecise language.'

**39 B:** On the reproduction of maps in the book, A says 'the black-and-white map illustrations that feature throughout are often reduced in scale to an extent that they become virtually illegible.' B says 'Regrettably, the visual presentation of maps – too many compressed, hard to decipher images – fails to match the standard of the text.'

**40 A:** On the way the book's author deals with recent developments in map-making, D says 'His chapter on such achievements as satellite navigation systems and mapping structures in computer games shows an admirably open-minded curiosity.' A says 'Garfield, justifiably, is as enthralled by the beautiful, often factually erroneous drawings of the distant past as he is by today's GPS, video-game landscapes and social-media-based graphics.' Both D and A approve of the author's attitude to recent developments in map-making.

#### ▶▶ PART 7

**41 E:** Link between 'starts by getting my standard physical measurements' in the previous paragraph and '… it turns out I've been kidding myself about my height for years.'

**42 G:** Link between '… running at increasing speed on an ever steeper incline …' in the previous paragraph and 'While I am doing this, Dr Carter records my data … that's when we know to increase the gradient.'

**43 A:** Link between 'cognitive tests to assess my reactions' in the previous paragraph, and the description in A of a task requiring the quick coordination of sight, movement and speech, but not strength or stamina.

**44 D:** Link between 'the longest half minute of my life' in D and 'trying to sustain that power for 30 seconds' in the following paragraph.

**45 F:** Link between 'it hurts' in the previous paragraph and 'So much so that hours later I can still feel the lactic acid, brought on by the extreme pedalling, burning in my legs.'

**46 C:** Link between the idea of screening babies to join a superbreed or an elite training programme, and 'Looking at someone's genome to determine whether they're suited to team sports or individual endurance may be 'accessible in the next decade' in C.

#### ▶▶ PART 8

**47 D:** 'With sales and income falling, as they have been virtually everywhere, the smart thing to do is to try to break the mould. Being a pioneer …'

**48 B:** 'But I ensure that when I'm with family and friends, work is blocked out entirely. Without perspective and space, your judgement can go to pieces.'

**49 A:** 'The costs of producing, manufacturing and promoting music have been reduced, so … there's less to lose these days.'

**50 C:** 'I would consider a partnership with somebody who has strengths in areas where you are weak, and vice-versa. That's worked for me.'

**51 D:** 'Labels will need to get involved in artists' tours, in their merchandising and even publishing – activities they have tended to stay away from.'

**52 B:** 'No two days are the same, whether we're promoting an event, filming a documentary, releasing a record, or checking out a band.'

**53 C:** 'We're associated with distributors around the world that are just great at what they do … We have even given up having an in-house sales team; outsourcing works fine.'

**54 D:** 'No one really knows what the landscape will be in two years' time, let alone 20.'

**55 A:** 'The key to success in this business is putting yourself in the position of the other person involved and anticipating their needs or what makes them tick.'

**56 B:** 'We don't play the game of predicting which artists will fly or flop in the market.'

 **TEST 3**

### PAPER 2 Writing

▶▶ **PART 1** (*suggested answers*)

#### Question 1
*Style:* Formal
*Content:* 1 Give some background to the proposal.
2 Develop two of the points provided in the notes: describe the advantages of each point, preferably including examples. Counter these points with issues they may present, or other disadvantages.
3 State what you feel the government should do:
- agree or disagree with the proposal and say why.
- alternatively, suggest another way forward.
- explain how the approach would work and/or how it could be implemented.
4 Write a brief conclusion summarising your key points.

▶▶ **PART 2** (*suggested answers*)

#### Question 2
*Style:* Formal
*Content:* 1 Open with an appropriate, polite greeting.
2 First paragraph: give the nature of your complaint.
3 Second paragraph: state the main problem, explain exactly what happened and how it affected you.
4 Third paragraph, or third and fourth paragraphs: include additional details from the input text; add more details of your own as long as you do not exceed the word count.
5 Final paragraph: state clearly and politely what you expect of the manager.
6 Sign off with a suitable closing expression.
(See page 197 for a model answer to this question.)

#### Question 3
*Style:* Formal or semi-formal
*Content:* 1 Give the proposal a suitable title.
2 In your introduction, state the aim of the proposal.
3 Then make at least one recommendation for the use of the funds, followed by:
- a more detailed explanation of and justification for your recommendations(s).
- a breakdown of the costs.
- a clear description of how they will benefit the university.
Use headings for clarity.
4 In your conclusion, restate your idea(s) and summarise why you believe in them.

#### Question 4
*Style:* Formal or semi-formal
*Content:* 1 Give the review a suitable title.
2 Introduction: state the event you are reviewing as well as where and when it took place.

3 Main body: give an overall description of the event and an overall opinion of it:
- decide which details to highlight next, for example, focus on particular days or specific events.
- describe each one, pointing out whether or not you feel it was a success, and why.
- consider inventing quotes from others at the festival, such as organisers or members of the public.
- try to offer a balanced review, neither overly positive nor negative.

4 Conclusion: state how successful the overall event was and suggest at least one area for improvement.

## ADVANCED TEST 3

### PAPER 3 Listening

**▶▶ PART 1**

1 A  2 C  3 C  4 B  5 B  6 A

**▶▶ PART 2**

7 shopping complex  8 persuasive  9 radical and extreme
10 outlook  11 the homeless  12 workshops  13 donate
14 career path

**▶▶ PART 3**

15 C  16 C  17 B  18 C  19 B  20 C

**▶▶ PART 4**

21 C  22 F  23 H  24 A  25 D  26 F  27 D  28 B
29 E  30 G

## ADVANCED TEST 4

### PAPER 1 Reading and Use of English

**▶▶ PART 1**

1 D  2 B  3 A  4 C  5 B  6 D  7 C  8 A

**▶▶ PART 2**

9 would  10 as  11 not  12 unlike  13 times  14 Despite
15 neither  16 yet

**▶▶ PART 3**

17 volunteers (adjective to plural noun)  18 participants (verb to plural noun)  19 unknown (verb to adjective)
20 Overwhelmingly (verb to adverb)  21 memorable (noun to adjective)  22 unpredictable (verb to negative adjective)
23 implications (verb to plural noun)  24 underestimate (verb to verb with an added prefix)

**▶▶ PART 4**

25 was the LAST person (1) + I expected (1)
26 to my amazement (1) + John GAVE up (1)
27 difficulty/trouble (in) making ENDS meet (1) + without (1)
28 has not/hasn't got ROUND to (1) + reading (1)
29 be BLAMED for (1) + getting/being/feeling upset (1)
30 gave her WORD that (1) + she would (1)

**▶▶ PART 5**

31 C: 'Given how much ink has been spilled on the extinction of the dinosaurs 65 million years ago, it's a wonder that more hasn't been devoted to the fate of the Pleistocene megafauna.'

32 B: 'But it wasn't comprehensive; North America kept its deer, bears, bison and moose, while South America retained jaguars and llamas.' If various species survived, this means that the 'extinction process' or 'disappearance of megafauna' was not comprehensive.

33 A: 'Flannery says … something dramatic happened to Australia's large creatures … strikingly soon after the invasion of a tool-wielding, intelligent predator. There does appear to be more than mere coincidence here.'

34 C: 'The more basic problem is that nothing has been found to prove that humans killed any megafauna – not one animal skeleton with a spear tip in it, for example.' Just as a murder trial cannot proceed without material evidence, the claim that humans killed megafauna has no supporting material evidence to support it.

35 D: 'This argument relies on the lack of fossil evidence for a prolonged human-megafauna overlap. If, however, we find evidence that human beings and megafauna co-existed for thousands of years, then the role of humans in the extinctions would become blurry at best.'

36 D: 'This brings us to today. "The way we've lived and are living is destroying our future," Flannery says. Yet we're only gradually figuring out how we're changing our world and the extent to which we're harming or even driving to extinction countless species.' The writer relates the question of how megafauna became extinct in Australia to climate change and species extinction in the world today.

**▶▶ PART 6**

37 D: On the physical experience of reading printed newspapers, A says 'people like to touch and hold paper, and newsprint tends to be much easier on the eyes than text on a screen.' B says 'There is something very satisfying about turning the pages of a newspaper … It is a feeling many people miss when accessing news in a digital format.' C says 'newspapers are friendlier objects to handle than electronic gadgets.' So, A, B and C all claim that people like the physical experience of reading printed newspapers, more than they enjoy using digital media. D, however, says 'Technological developments mean that digital devices are as easy to handle and read as newspapers.'

38 A: On the quality of news reporting in printed newspapers as compared with digital media, C says 'The content of newspapers tends to be of greater depth, accuracy and trustworthiness than in any other form of media.' A says 'people generally trust newspapers as sources of reliable, detailed information.'

39 C: On the environmental impact of printed newspapers, B says 'Some people have welcomed the replacement of newspapers with digital media for environmental reasons … but this is not a real issue as most newspapers nowadays are printed on recycled paper.' C says 'Forestry and paper production are no less sustainable as industries than those which manufacture and power digital technology.' Both claim that the environmental impact of the newspaper industry is no worse than that of digital media.

40 A: On the viability of printed newspapers, B says 'printed newspapers represent an increasingly antiquated business model, which is unlikely ever to recover.' C says 'The traditional newspaper is destined to perish sooner or later.' D says 'The printed newspaper … is … now approaching the end of its natural lifespan.' So, B, C and D think the future of the printed newspaper is very limited. A, however, takes a

different position: 'if news organisations work in an intelligent way … the future of news on paper should be assured.'

## ▶▶ PART 7

**41** D: Link between 'Is that a black or white rhino?' … We had seen a white rhino first … casually grazing …That's the first clue.' in the previous paragraph and 'as the animal treated our arrival calmly, we could work out which it was.'

**42** F: Link between 'with a small airstrip a short drive away' in the previous paragraph and 'Joseph came to collect us there … either side of the runway gathered zebra …'

**43** C: Link between the reference to 'illegal hunters' and the black market for rhino horn in the previous paragraph, and 'It's so disturbing it hardly bears thinking about' and the description of how poachers are caught.

**44** A: Link between 'Calum and Sophie' in the previous paragraph and 'They have steadily built a fine base for exploring …'

**45** G: Link between 'striving to create a sustainable project and … revenue from tourism' in the previous paragraph and 'this income diversification'.

**46** E: Link between 'a variety of animal calls that pierced the night' in the previous paragraph and 'the interrupted sleep'.

## ▶▶ PART 8

**47** C: 'Every new piece … is always an interaction with his performers.'

**48** B: 'A sense of theatre permeates not only the operas, but even chamber works.'

**49** D: 'The series of pieces *Music for Concert Halls* play with the acoustical properties of the venues for which they were written.'

**50** B: 'It's what I cannot quantify that transfixes me – as Pierre Boulez said of him: "Where does it come from, this music?"'

**51** A: 'A big part of me regrets not studying with him, although he's such an overwhelming figure I might have become merely a bad copy.'

**52** D: '… usually of such impossible complexity that they threaten to self-destruct.'

**53** A: 'He is one of the few composers working today whose music will survive.'

**54** C: 'From the intense complexity of *Eight Songs For a Mad King*, to the unaffected simplicity of *Farewell to Stromness*.' And: 'I then discovered St Thomas Wake: the toughness of the musical language thrown into relief by foxtrots.''

**55** D: 'The pieces push at the boundaries and point to future possibilities for the concert-going experience.'

**56** A: 'Every time you hear a piece of his music, you know it's by him.'

## ADVANCED TEST 4

### PAPER 2 Writing

#### ▶▶ PART 1 *(suggested answers)*

#### Question 1

Style: Formal

Content: 1 Set a context for the essay. Provide an overview of the public meeting.

2 Explain exactly what the professor was proposing, and why.

3 Develop two of his points, building on the reasoning behind them.

4 Say whether you feel his proposition is realistic, explaining why or why not.

5 Bring in some alternative views; include at least one original idea of your own.

6 Conclude the essay with a brief summary and reiteration of your opinion.

#### ▶▶ PART 2 *(suggested answers)*

#### Question 2

Style: Informal

Content: 1 Open with a friendly greeting.

2 First paragraph:
- thank her for her letter.
- tell her that you're delighted she's taking her English studies seriously.
- perhaps say something about the value of having good English.

3 Next paragraph(s):
- address each of her questions from the input text.
- give her some advice on each one.
- consider sharing some of your own language-learning experiences with her.

4 Final paragraph:
- encourage her, but also caution her about setting her expectations too high.
- wish her well and send your best wishes to her family.

5 Sign off with a suitable closing expression.

#### Question 3

Style: Formal or semi-formal

Content: 1 Give the report an appropriate title.

2 Focus on one device; you can invent the brand and type of item if you wish; it doesn't have to be real.

3 State the aim of the report in your introduction.

4 In the main body:
- dedicate a section to each of the bullet points provided in the question.
- paraphrase the input text to give each section a concise heading.
- make the two sections about the device's suitability for student needs, and its disadvantages, longer than the product description and cost sections.

5 Summarise the main points in your concluding paragraph.

#### Question 4

Style: Semi-formal

Content: 1 Open with the reason you are writing this review.

2 State the title and author of the book you are recommending. (It can be made up.)

3 Dedicate a paragraph each to the following points; use headings if you wish:
- say what the book means to you / when you read it / how it made you feel.
- continue by *illustrating* how the book affected you. Give specific examples along with your overview of the novel (the genre and a plot summary).
- describe how and why the main characters are significant and memorable.
- explain why you have confidence recommending this book to others. What is its universal appeal?

4 Write a brief conclusion reiterating your main points.

## PAPER 3 Listening

▶▶ **PART 1**

1 B   2 C   3 A   4 A   5 C   6 B

▶▶ **PART 2**

7 enhance their story   8 emerge   9 (built-in) cameras
10 proved itself   11 (promptly) published   12 (compelling)
insights   13 solve (major) crimes   14 verified audio

▶▶ **PART 3**

15 C   16 C   17 B   18 B   19 A   20 D

▶▶ **PART 4**

21 G   22 E   23 H   24 A   25 C   26 D   27 H   28 F
29 E   30 B

**TEST 5**

## PAPER 1 Reading and Use of English

▶▶ **PART 1**

1 B   2 D   3 C   4 A   5 B   6 D   7 B   8 A

▶▶ **PART 2**

9 if   10 Whether   11 without   12 No   13 hand   14 an
15 doing   16 at

▶▶ **PART 3**

17 simplify (adjective to verb)   18 assignments (verb to plural
noun)   19 downside (noun to noun) / side-effect (noun to noun)
20 temptation (verb to noun)   21 selectively (verb to adverb)
22 ensure (adjective to verb)   23 shorten (adjective to verb)
24 bibliographical (noun to adjective)

▶▶ **PART 4**

25 we had/we'd (1) + SET aside (1)
26 RESENTED being treated (1) + as if / though (1)
27 everyone's / everybody's INTEREST (1) + to cut down / if we
cut down (1)
28 tell the DIFFERENCE (1) + between the two (1)
29 the impression THAT (1) + little had been (1)
30 to make an EXCEPTION (1) + in Maria's (1)

▶▶ **PART 5**

31 B: '... most artificial reefs attract marine life in a more or less
predictable sequence of events. First, ... Next come ... In
time ...'

32 A: '... knows the attraction of artificial reefs for water sports
enthusiasts, and the revenue and jobs thereby generated.'

33 D: 'If success is judged solely by an increase in harvest, then
artificial reefs are pretty successful. But if those structures ...
are pulling fish off natural reefs farther from the coast, they
may actually be increasing the overfishing of species ...'

34 B: 'And for every metre of wire there was a metre of red
tape, since artificial reefs must now be created in strict
accordance with the US government's National Artificial
Reef Plan.'

35 D: 'The ship landed upside down with one corner of her stern
on the bottom and part of her bow above the waterline,
ready to serve as a can opener to unsuspecting vessels.'

36 C: '... initially thought to be a good idea ... a win-win scheme
that would liberate the nation's landfills of up to two million
discarded tires to create a thriving marine habitat.'

▶▶ **PART 6**

37 A: On the educational content of some reality TV, B says
'Other programmes, however, are more positive and even
instructive. One show, *Jamie's Kitchen*, ... was a valuable
learning experience for audiences and participants.' A says
'Viewers want to be entertained, but, at the same time,
are often happy to learn something – from a show set in a
restaurant kitchen or a fitness camp, for example.'

38 A: On the authenticity of reality TV, B says 'The concern is that
impressionable viewers, taking what they see to be real
life, may absorb the message uncritically, overlooking the
fact that the narrative is invariably manipulated by clever
programme makers.' C says 'Not only is it fundamentally
dishonest in pretending to show 'reality.' D says 'The
most interesting thing about reality TV is that it is not
what its label implies, and perhaps what many believe
it to be.' So, B, C and D all say that reality TV is unreal
and they are critical of this. A says 'Criticisms ... miss the
point. Audiences know that shows like *Big Brother* do not
replicate real life.' So A accepts that reality TV is unreal, but
believes that criticisms of this are misguided.

39 D: On the popularity of reality TV, A says 'The bottom line is
that reality TV programmes attract audiences of all ages
and types.' B says 'The fact is, however, that the quality as
well as the sheer quantity of reality programmes shown
on our television screens reflects market demand.' C says
'There seems to be a huge appetite for reality TV.' So A,
B and C all say that there is a lot of demand for reality TV.
D says 'The fact that it fills the gaps does not mean that
audiences want it, however. In fact, many reality shows
have extremely low viewing figures.' So, D questions the
demand for reality TV.

40 B: On the values represented in many reality TV shows, C
says '... it ... sends a message that crude, self-centred,
empty-headed behaviour is the norm, and that celebrity
is a worthy aspiration.' B says 'Lots of them focus
obsessively on appearance, consumerism and celebrity
status, and imply that anyone can become famous without
working hard or displaying a particular talent.

▶▶ **PART 7**

41 C: Contrastive link between '... history of art tends to exist
on the margins at most universities, the preserve of a
few dedicated students' in the previous paragraph and
'Although it has a limited following, it is anything but
insignificant in scope or academic rigour, however.'

42 F: Link between 'As Janice Burton, a former student at the
Courtauld Institute ... explains' in the previous paragraph
and 'Another recent history of art graduate, agrees ...'

43 E: Link between 'Natalia Mellor believes her subject is crucial
for the development of public culture. "Our degree courses
produce the museum directors of the future"' in the
previous paragraph and 'In fact, anyone who wants to be
seriously involved in museum and gallery curation needs
to ensure they have a solid academic grounding ...'

44 A: Link between 'Jerome Hasler ... now works for a crisis
management consultancy ... but history of art has still been
very beneficial' in the previous paragraph and 'Burton concurs
... "history of art led me into writing, specifically journalism ..."

**45** G: Link between 'she is interested in people who clearly have a passion for art and art history, rather than those who have traditional qualifications' in the previous paragraph and '"We try to look for someone who shows a demonstrable interest in the subject – but that doesn't mean they have to know reams about art history."'

**46** D: Link between 'How is the progamme organised, particularly for newcomers to the subject as an academic discipline?' in the previous paragraph and '"If you've never formally studied the subject before, you start with a leveller course."'

▶▶ **PART 8**

**47** C: 'I don't really have the time or resources to stay abreast of all the developments in the way I should.'

**48** D: 'There aren't many people with our expertise, so we're in demand.'

**49** A: 'She feels no real desire to climb the career ladder.'

**50** D: 'And it can be hard to switch to anything else – we're all aware of that' … 'I'd like the chance to earn more, of course,' she says. 'But, like everyone who works in this sector, I know it's not going to happen.'

**51** B: 'For some people, the idea of museum work still conjures up images of geeks in dusty archives detached from the real world,' she says. 'If they only knew!'

**52** A: 'Dealing with school kids for a few years taught me how to communicate with groups, which serves me well here.'

**53** C: 'Unlike some registrars, I'm in charge of the information management system.'

**54** B: 'Networking is crucial,' she says. 'Not just with potential donors, but also with museum visitors, the press and colleagues from my museum and other institutions.'

**55** A: 'It'd be nice if I could focus on the natural history collection, where I have real expertise,' she says.'

**56** B: 'There's no traditional route into fundraising for museums and galleries … You figure things out as you go along. It's not ideal.'

# TEST 5

## PAPER 2 Writing

▶▶ **PART 1** (*suggested answers*)

### Question 1

Style: Formal

Content: 1 Give the essay a relevant title.

2 State the topic and say what the essay will cover.

3 Choose two of the points provided. Describe them in more detail, giving examples.

4 Say whether or not you agree with these points, providing reasons either way.

5 Introduce some opposing views on abolishing exams.

6 Conclude the essay with a brief summary.

(See page 195 for a model answer to this question.)

▶▶ **PART 2** (*suggested answers*)

### Question 2

Style: Formal

Content: 1 Open the letter with *Dear Ms James,* (note comma).

2 State that you are writing to apply for the sales assistant vacancy.

3 Say where and when you saw it advertised.

4 Explain what makes you suitable for the post (one or two paragraphs):
- emphasise that you are passionate about books.
- mention any relevant work experience you have.
- say that you work well as part of a team, and provide an example or two to illustrate this.
- explain how you are organised and reliable, and demonstrate this with examples.

5 Say that your CV is enclosed and you can supply additional information if required.

6 State where and when you can be reached. Thank Ms James for her time.

7 Sign off with *Yours sincerely,* (name).

### Question 3

Style: Semi-formal

Content: 1 State why you are writing the proposal and give it a suitable title.

2 Provide some background information, for example, describe the available space.

3 Make one or two suggestions for the use of space (original ideas or from the text):
- state what your recommendation is.
- explain why this is a good use of the space.
- give examples of how it will improve the property and benefit most residents.
- use headings and/or lists to organise your points.

4 Make your suggestions in the main body. Use headings to organise your points.

5 Write a brief conclusion reiterating your idea and summarising your main points.

### Question 4

Style: Formal or semi-formal

Content: 1 State the purpose of the review in your introduction.

2 Name the brand and model of mobile phone you are reviewing (real or not).

3 Say whether or not you would recommend this product, and explain why:
- list the key functions of the phone.
- point out its best features, what you like about it.
- talk about who this product would benefit or appeal to and why.
- describe the worst features and any problems you've had with the phone.
- explain how these issues have affected your user experience.

4 To conclude, restate your main points and whether you recommend this product.

# TEST 5

## PAPER 3 Listening

▶▶ **PART 1**

**1** C  **2** B  **3** B  **4** C  **5** A  **6** B

▶▶ **PART 2**

**7** slight exaggeration  **8** presented a challenge  **9** illegal music downloads  **10** (paying) (heavy) fines  **11** individual tracks  **12** eliminates  **13** thriving  **14** upload

**PART 3**

15 C   16 B   17 A   18 A   19 D   20 B

**PART 4**

21 E   22 G   23 F   24 A   25 C   26 B   27 F   28 H   29 E   30 A

ADVANCED
# TEST 6

## PAPER 1 Reading and Use of English

**PART 1**

1 A   2 B   3 D   4 D   5 B   6 A   7 C   8 C

**PART 2**

9 what   10 apart   11 neither/nor   12 spite   13 which
14 According   15 as   16 without

**PART 3**

17 linguistically (noun to adverb)   18 inhabitants (verb to plural noun)   19 diversity (adjective to noun)   20 minorities (adjective to plural noun)   21 noticeable (verb/noun to adjective)   22 immigration (verb to noun)   23 overseas (noun to adjective)   24 enriched (adjective to verb in participle form)

**PART 4**

25 can't be BOTHERED (1) + to cook (1)
26 denied (ever) BEING (1) + involved in (1)
27 on EARTH (1) + did I never/didn't I think (1)
28 have been easy (1) + to COME up (1)
29 David to (1) + do/try his UTMOST to (1)
30 of ROOM for improvement (1) + as far (1)

**PART 5**

31 D: 'It wasn't originally meant to be a comedy show … but on my debut, the audience laughed at my first joke, then continued to laugh … .'
32 C: '"Remember how to be a child," explained Ryan. "… Just muck around …" So we did.'
33 B: 'Here, finally was what felt like a true, unifying theory.'
34 B: 'The crux of their thesis is … will need to correct its own bugs … will have to be debugged …'
35 C: 'In more concrete terms, … For correctly figuring out the contradiction (or bug), we are rewarded with a pleasurable feeling.'
36 A: 'The point is, I would never have written this into a script. It was a joyous, found moment.'

**PART 6**

37 D: On the environmental impact of reintroducing wolves, A says 'if … they reduced red deer numbers and, consequently, stimulated greater biodiversity, this would be very positive. B says 'By preying on deer and other vegetation – destroying animals, wolves help create conditions for various tree and plant species to prosper, which then attracts a greater variety of wildlife.' C says '… wolves, if re-introduced, would keep the deer population down naturally, leading to re-forestation and greater biodiversity.' So, A, B and C all argue that the environmental impact would be positive. D, however, is concerned about what the impact would be: 'It is always difficult to know precisely what impact non-native species will have on a particular ecosystem, but in many instances … huge damage has been caused.'

38 B: On public attitudes to the idea of reintroducing wolves, A says 'Most Scottish people … question the sense in pursuing the idea.' B suggests many people have a similarly negative view: '… many sheep farmers horrified by the idea … recreational walkers, climbers and fishing enthusiasts, most of whom would surely feel uncomfortable …'

39 A: On the economic implications of reintroducing wolves, D says 'in many instances … huge damage has been caused (by alien species), with considerable economic consequences …' A makes a similar point: 'Scotland also has limited economic resources, and the funds required to introduce and manage packs of wolves would be far better spent on maintaining and enhancing native species already present in the country.'

40 C: On Scotland's suitability as a place for reintroducing wolves, A says 'Scotland is a small country and keeping wolves away from its many livestock farms would be difficult. Scotland also has limited economic resources …' B says 'Scotland is not ready for wolves.' D says 'the country's ecosystem has been transformed. To introduce wolves would effectively mean bringing in an alien species … Why take a risk …?' So, A, B and D all argue that Scotland is unsuitable. C, however, takes a different position: 'Comparative studies suggest that similar schemes would be eminently feasible in parts of Scotland.'

**PART 7**

41 G: Link between 'Recent research by scientist Steve Sillett of Humboldt State University and his colleagues has confirmed that The President ranks as the second largest among all big trees that have ever been measured' in the previous paragraph and 'Sillett's team has surveyed quite a few.'

42 D: Link between 'A tree too is constrained by gravity, but not in the same way as a giraffe or a condor' in the previous paragraph and 'It doesn't need to move around, unlike them …'

43. B: Link between 'Their thick bark is flame resistant' in the previous paragraph, and 'Ground fires, in fact, are good for sequoia populations, burning away competitors, …'

44 F: Link between the details about the sequoia wood having little commercial value in the previous paragraph and 'Given the difficulties of dealing with six-metre-thick logs, broken or unbroken, the trees were hardly worth cutting.'

45 E: Link between 'Among the striking discoveries made by Sillett's team is that even the rate of growth of a big tree, not just its height or total volume, can increase during old age' in the previous paragraph and 'This finding contradicts a long-held premise in forest ecology – that wood production declines in the latter years of a tree's life.'

46 A: Link between 'Sillett's group put a line over The President's crown, rigged climbing ropes … started to climb' in the previous paragraph and 'As they did so, they measured the trunk at different heights …'

**PART 8**

47 C: 'I had tutors who treated me as though I could make sense of everything they knew about science … There was never any sense of being talked down to, for which I am very grateful.'

48 D: 'I took sciences at school, not because I excelled at them, but because I was hopeless at the arts and humanities.'

49 B: 'It was years before something fundamental really sank in – that science is about a method as much as facts.'

**50 A:** 'The idea that the books surrounding me contain the work of generations of scientists ... fills me with awe and optimism.'

**51 D:** '... the spur for me going into science, rather than some inspirational educator – if only it had been, my route would have been less circuitous ...'

**52 C:** 'It offered a sense of certainty that the world can not only be understood, but also enhanced.'

**53 A:** 'One of the most striking things about science at school ... was having to suspend my disbelief ... from the everyday world to that of atoms, molecules, proteins and cells – a world in many ways more fantastical than works of fiction.'

**54 C:** 'The one thing I regret was that practical experimentation seldom featured, certainly at school ... scientific theory is nothing, unless backed up by experimental evidence.'

**55 A:** 'I left a thriving practice to pursue these questions.'

**56 B:** 'When it became clear that ... I was set on going to university, and wouldn't be contributing to the family budget anytime soon, I faced considerable suspicion and resentment.'

# TEST 6

## PAPER 2 Writing

▶▶ **PART 1** (*suggested answers*)

### Question 1
*Style:* Formal
*Content:* 1 Decide on an appropriate title for the essay.
2 In your introduction provide some background and an overview of the topic.
3 Develop two of the lecturer's points and include examples where possible.
4 Say whether you think the mobile phone was a good invention and explain why.
5 Provide at least two views counter to the lecturer's and supported by examples.
6 Conclude the essay with a brief summary and restate your own opinion.

▶▶ **PART 2** (*suggested answers*)

### Question 2
*Style:* Formal
*Content:* 1 Open the letter with a formal greeting.
2 First paragraph:
- invent a date for the visit and thank her for having you as a guest.
- say what the visit meant to you.
3 Second paragraph: talk about the three managers you met. Express your gratitude for their time.
4 Third paragraph:
- reiterate how you benefited from the visit.
- say something about the company as a whole and/ or their area of work and why it interests you.
- thank the vice-president one last time.
5 Sign off with *Yours sincerely*, since you have used the person's name.

### Question 3
*Style:* Formal or semi-formal
*Content:* 1 Think of a suitable title for the report. Also make up a name for the town.

2 Explain why you are writing the report.
3 Decide how you want to organise the document, for example:
- general attractions in the town.
- categories of entertainment: art, culture, historical interest, nightlife, etc.
- use appropriate headings for each section and bulleted lists for grouped points.
4 Summarise the main points in your concluding paragraph.
(See page 203 for a model answer to this question.)

### Question 4
*Style:* Formal or semi-formal
*Content:* 1 First of all, invent details about the restaurant:
- what is it called and where is it?
- what type of food does it serve and is it expensive, moderate or inexpensive?
2 Introduction:
- state when you dined there and who with.
- give your overall impression of the place from when your first walked in.
3 Main body:
- make some comments about the menu in general.
- describe some of the dishes you ordered; say what was good and bad about them.
- describe the quality of the service.
- comment on the cost/value for money.
4 Conclusion: say whether or not your experience there was a good one, and state whether or not you would recommend it to others; reiterating why.

# TEST 6

## PAPER 3 Listening

▶▶ **PART 1**
1 B   2 C   3 A   4 B   5 C   6 B

▶▶ **PART 2**
7 big suppliers   8 sustainable   9 direct competition
10 demands   11 impressive   12 do not stock   13 increase awareness   14 practical

▶▶ **PART 3**
15 C   16 A   17 D   18 C   19 C   20 B

▶▶ **PART 4**
21 F   22 H   23 A   24 D   25 C   26 D   27 H   28 B
29 G   30 C

# TEST 7

## PAPER 1 Reading and Use of English

▶▶ **PART 1**
1 B   2 C   3 D   4 A   5 A   6 D   7 B   8 D

▶▶ **PART 2**
9 Anyone/Everyone   10 matter   11 to   12 among
13 case   14 one   15 likely   16 regardless/irrespective

**17** deforestation (concrete noun to process noun)   **18** emission(s) (verb to noun)   **19** illegally (adjective to negative adverb)
**20** beneficial (noun to adjective)   **21** efficiency (adjective to noun)
**22** prioritise (noun to verb)   **23** lessen (adverb to verb)
**24** unquestionably (adjective to negative adverb)

▶▶ **PART 4**

**25** would not/wouldn't DREAM (1) + of laying anyone (1)
**26** is SUPPOSED to (1) have been (1)
**27** was Jenny who (1) + OBJECTED to tidying (1)
**28** subject HAPPENS to (1) + be brought (1)
**29** we climbed/we climb, THE harder (1) + breathing would/will (1)
**30** was not/wasn't UNTIL (1) + Yoshi's promotion to (1)

▶▶ **PART 5**

**31** D: 'Even people who know nothing about mathematics have heard the counter-intuitive notion that mathematical ability is connected to musical ability. As a mathematician with strong musical interests, I have been asked about this many times.'

**32** A: 'The actual conclusions of the experiment … were much more modest and remain grossly exaggerated.'

**33** C: 'The best one could hope to identify would be a significant positive correlation between aptitudes … not much will be proved if you compare professional mathematicians with the wider population.'

**34** A: 'It would show a connection between mathematical and musical ability, though not a mysterious one. It would be more like the connection between abilities at football and tennis. To become better at one of those you need to improve your fitness and coordination.'

**35** D: 'It would hardly be surprising to learn that mathematicians were better than average at learning grammar.'

**36** B: 'Let's look at how we solve problems of the 'A is to B as C is to D' kind. These … are also central to both music and mathematics … Music is full of little puzzles like this.'

▶▶ **PART 6**

**37** D: On social factors influencing teenage behaviour A says 'Bainbridge dismisses the notion that the teenager is a modern social phenomenon, but some attention to the influences that have transformed adolescent experience over recent decades would be far more fruitful.' B says 'There is no attempt either to engage with the broader social, political and philosophical contexts within which teenagers develop; always crucial, surely.' C says 'Where the book does fall down is in a failure to explore the external context within which modern teenagers move from childhood to adulthood.' So, A, B and C all criticise the book for failing to look at social influences. D, however, says 'In some ways, it is reassuring to find out that certain patterns of behaviour are largely hardwired in teenagers, rather than determined by the way they are brought up …'

**38** A: With regard to explaining modern teenagers by referring to the way humans developed in ancient times, B says 'Bainbridge undermines the effect by repeatedly invoking hypotheses about pre-historic human development to understand specifics of teenagers today. The plausibility of various notions … relies more on wish-fulfilment than science.' So, B does not find this approach convincing. A says something similar: 'The notion that speculation about our distant origins can provide answers to questions about personal development and social relationships today is far too simplistic.'

**39** C: On the style of writing, A says 'The finely-judged tone of David Bainbridge's language – neither over-technical nor patronisingly simple.' B says 'communicated with enviable lucidity'. D says 'all delivered in fresh, amusing and intelligible prose'. So A, B and D all praise the writing. C, however, criticises the writing: 'Bainbridge can sometimes be irritatingly informal …'

**40** B: With regard to the book's value for people responsible for teenagers, D says: 'parents should find comfort and inspiration in Bainbridge's central theme that supporting children and teenagers is what adults are really for.' In other words, the book should encourage parents to be sympathetic and supportive. B implies something similar: 'the insights provided … should definitely cause adults to think about how to respond to their moods and apparently chaotic behaviour.'

▶▶ **PART 7**

**41** D: Link between 'rotting fruit, whose pungent aromas permeate the humid air' in the previous paragraph and 'It is the immense variety of these more than two dozen edible species … that makes the Goualougo such an attractive habitat for chimps.'

**42** F: Link between 'Then something remarkable happens' in the previous paragraph and 'Noticing a cloud of bees emerging from a hole near the main trunk of the tree, Dinah leaps to her feet and breaks off a branch …'

**43** B: Link between 'she finally plunges her finger into a crack and yanks out a bit of honey, which goes straight into her mouth' in the previous paragraph, and 'This the signal for Finn to make a move, seemingly outraged that a young upstart is enjoying a sugary delicacy in his presence.'

**44** G: Link between 'what makes Dinah's behavior so intriguing is that she used a big club and a thin twig in sequence' in the previous paragraph and 'This isn't the only form of serial tool use common in the Goualougo.'

**45** E: Link between 'she grabs a thin, flexible stem, drags the end of it through her teeth to make it wet and frayed, like a paintbrush, and then pulls it through her closed fist to straighten out the bristles' in the previous paragraph and 'What's so remarkable about this is not just that some clever chimp figured out it could break a plant and use it …'

**46** A: Link between '"Ninety-five per cent of chimps on earth don't live like this because of humans." Chimp study sites elsewhere are surrounded by people and often affected by logging and hunting' in the previous paragraph and 'This is a powerful and troubling notion …'

▶▶ **PART 8**

**47** B: '… which, in turn, results in the amount of dreaded paperwork we have to deal with – a need I hadn't really comprehended before.'

**48** C: 'I would definitely recommend this course … The notion of a culture of safety is quite new in some ways and there's a lot to it, but I never had any sense of having to battle to get to grips with it, and I think that boils down to the quality of the module.'

**49** A: 'it was well designed with a range of activities including analysis scenarios … viewing short, interesting films … and regularly exchanging ideas.'

**50** D: 'I think the course is also relevant because it shows you the importance of thinking out of the box …'

**51 B:** 'When I read the module overview, I was overwhelmed at first by the potential for problems to arise in healthcare ...'

**52 A:** 'I was initially apprehensive about it as the idea of leadership seemed more for people in positions of responsibility and authority, rather than a student nurse.'

**53 C:** 'As a third-year nursing student with several work placements under my belt, it made me consider the way I had worked.'

**54 A:** 'In fact, the module gave me an idea for solving a real problem in the ward where I'm now doing a six-week practice stint.'

**55 D:** 'As a young nurse you have vulnerable people's well-being in your hands, and it is good to know that you're not on your own, that there is a system to monitor and support you.'

**56 B:** '... the module manages to achieve its aims; it really does what it says on the tin!'

## TEST 7

### PAPER 2 Writing

▶▶ **PART 1** (suggested answers)

#### Question 1

Style: Formal

Content: 1 State the topic of the essay and where the original discussion took place.

2 Develop two of the 'science is more important than art' arguments.

3 Say whether or not you agree with these points and explain why.

4 Include at least two opposing arguments and give your own views on them.

5 Write a brief conclusion summing up the main points and reiterating your position.

▶▶ **PART 2** (suggested answers)

#### Question 2

Style: Informal

Content: 1 Come up with a name for the friend and open with a friendly greeting.

2 First paragraph:
- acknowledge his email.
- sympathise immediately about the news.

3 Second paragraph:
- say that you understand how he must be feeling.
- encourage him to be patient, and remind him that he is likely to get some good offers from his other college applications.

4 Third paragraph:
- tell him again that things will work out, give one or two examples to support this.
- make some suggestions of things he could do to take his mind off his worries.

5 Finish by mentioning when you'll be back and remind him again to cheer up.

6 Sign off with a suitable closing.

#### Question 3

Style: Semi-formal or formal

Content: 1 In your introduction, state the purpose of the proposal and give it a suitable title.

2 Invent a name for the online business (optional).

3 Be sure to focus on two or three of the areas specified in the question.

4 Organise the proposal into sections:
- clearly state what the issues are.
- suggest the improvements that you recommend and explain exactly what they entail.
- point out how these changes will improve the site for customers.

5 Write a brief conclusion summarising your proposal. (See page 201 for a model answer to this question.)

#### Question 4

Style: Formal or semi-formal

Content: 1 State the purpose of the review in your introduction.

2 Give the title of the film you are recommending. (It doesn't have to be real.)

3 Dedicate a short paragraph each to the following points, bearing in mind that the film is intended for students in their late teens:
- state what historical event the film is about and what makes it a good choice for this teacher's needs.
- provide a general overview of the film including the genre and a plot summary. Use descriptive language.
- describe the main characters.

4 In the conclusion, reiterate your choice and sum up your main points.

## TEST 7

### PAPER 3 Listening

▶▶ **PART 1**

**1** C   **2** B   **3** C   **4** A   **5** B   **6** C

▶▶ **PART 2**

**7** draws on   **8** consciously analysing   **9** extrovert   **10** principle   **11** limitations   **12** cater for   **13** troubled   **14** guideline

▶▶ **PART 3**

**15** B   **16** C   **17** A   **18** D   **19** B   **20** C

▶▶ **PART 4**

**21** D   **22** H   **23** F   **24** A   **25** G   **26** C   **27** E   **28** G   **29** B   **30** H

## TEST 8

### PAPER 1 Reading and Use of English

▶▶ **PART 1**

**1** A   **2** D   **3** D   **4** A   **5** C   **6** B   **7** D   **8** B

▶▶ **PART 2**

**9** far   **10** out   **11** a   **12** off   **13** which   **14** long   **15** much   **16** rather

▶▶ **PART 3**

**17** loss (verb to noun)   **18** unthinkable (verb to negative adjective)   **19** sustainable (verb to adjective)   **20** specifically (adjective to adverb)   **21** planning (verb or concrete noun to process noun)   **22** persuasive (verb to adjective)   **23** productivity (verb to noun)   **24** expertise (noun to noun)

## PART 4

**25** keep TRACK of the time (1) + so (1)
**26** only a MATTER of time (1) + before (1)
**27** things CONSIDERED (1) + the street party turned (1)
**28** everyone's horror (1) + Ripley was LEFT out (1)
**29** only have they (1) + DONE away (1)
**30** apologetic about (1) + their COMPLETE failure (1)

## PART 5

**31** B: 'The internet was bound to ignite the same kind of disquiet.'

**32** A: Options B, C and D describe Carr's behaviour in literal terms, and so are not metaphors. 'It's done my head in' is an idiom used when something has seriously confused you or caused a breakdown in your ability to think normally. The third paragraph says that 'studies show web use alters brain cells' so you cannot think in the way you used to. So, in Carr's case, 'the internet has really done his head in' is more than just a metaphor; it describes how he experienced the impact of the internet.

**33** D: 'Once people could jot down a laundry list, say, the relevant sections of their brains doubtless decommissioned redundant storage capacity.'

**34** C: The reviewer suggests that Carr may be wrong when he claims that being able to 'attend patiently to lengthy narratives and long arguments' is more valuable than 'analysing data, multi-tasking and making instant decisions'. In the sixth paragraph the reviewer uses Carr's own book to elaborate on this point, saying that it may be a better use of time to read summaries of Carr's book than the whole book itself.

**35** B: 'We may end up, on balance, better off. If we do not, in due course we shall doubtless notice … and remedial action will be available. An organ that has managed to unravel centuries of conditioning in a mere six days ought to be able to reverse the feat.' This suggests that if we discover that internet use is not in fact good for our brains and for us, we will do something to fix the problem.

**36** A: 'We ourselves, not our media, are determining the kind of creatures we want to be.'

## PART 6

**37** B: On whether the state can afford to finance free higher education, A says 'Claims that governments are no longer able to pay for free higher education … conveniently ignore the fact that universities are free in some successful countries. Any government with the will to do so … could shift spending away from unproductive sectors like defence and into higher education.' B says 'The fact that a number of countries around the world offer free university education of a very high standard proves that it is still a viable proposition.'

**38** D: On how state funding might affect the quality of university education, A says 'The state funding that allows free access also lets universities focus on what they do best, research and teaching … ' B says 'Where universities are largely self-financing, inordinate time, energy and talent is invested in attracting fee-paying students and research-supporting corporate investors.' C says 'It … frees universities from the messy, distracting business of having to find ways to finance their work, and allows them to focus on enhancing the student experience and carrying out research.' So, A, B and C think state funding has a positive effect on the quality of university education. D, however, suggests the removal of state funding enhances the quality of universities: 'Free of state influence, they have realised that they will only stay in business if they provide an excellent service to their clients, the students.'

**39** A: On the implications of free university education for social mobility, B says 'The idea that free higher education benefits anyone apart from those who would attend fee-paying degree courses anyway is largely illusory.' C says '… that people who want to go to university will generally find a way to finance themselves. Fee-paying does not particularly encourage underprivileged youngsters into higher education, but neither does free university access.' D says 'The figures suggest that people from particular socio-economic backgrounds are neither put off university by having to pay for it nor motivated to attend by having free access.' So, B, C and D say that free university education seems to have little impact on social mobility. A, however, says 'Free university education … enables the less affluent to break out of the class they are born into, and keeps society dynamic and aspirational.'

**40** B: On public attitudes regarding free university education, D says 'Trying to convince people they should pay more taxes to finance university students is doomed to failure.' B says '… taxpayers are generally unwilling to pay more, particularly if it is to enable young people, mostly from well-off backgrounds, to qualify for lucrative employment.'

## PART 7

**41** G: Link between 'If you work in an economy which is going through difficulties, the chances are you're calling on your emotional intelligence (EI) less than you might like …' in the previous paragraph and 'The likelihood is that when facing uncertainty people may feel threatened and switch into 'survival mode' to try to protect what they have.'

**42** C: Link between 'Cooper's report describes it as an 'innate human attribute' which, if understood and used well, can help us manage our thinking and feeling to improve our behaviour and relationships' in the previous paragraph and '"If we liken the mind to a high-performance engine," it goes on to say …'

**43** E: Link between 'Emotional intelligence is divided into two main areas, personal intelligence and interpersonal intelligence. These, in turn, are split into 16 measurable scales including …' in the previous paragraph, and 'Using these categories, …'

**44** B: Link between 'Self-employed people score higher than any other occupational group …' in the previous paragraph and 'Results for other work sectors also proved interesting.'

**45** F: Link between 'Low scores on some of these scales, however, can have a negative impact on others, especially if the low scorer holds a senior position' in the previous paragraph and 'In an example of this, six managers were asked by a company director to present their views of why a particular problem had emerged in the business …'

**46** A: Link between 'Another executive, by contrast … this showed humility and openness, features of good emotional intelligence' in the previous paragraph and 'Having observed both approaches, one senior manager …'

## PART 8

**47** C: '… stepping away for a while and writing books such as *The Poet* and *Blood Work*, and then he comes back to it fired up with renewed vitality.'

**48** D: 'There seems to be a supernatural thread running through it. It's as if the narrative switches into the realms of fantasy now and then.'

**49** C: 'I think his days as a crime reporter on the Los Angeles Times stood him in great stead.'

**50** A: 'Crime fiction with them is … also a vehicle for saying something about the contexts within which the action happens … nails the connections between politics, the police and the media.'

**51** B: 'A willingness to do the hard work of digging into the nitty-gritty of emotional life.'

**52** C: 'People talk about how you create suspense and use cliffhangers, reveals and so on, and Connelly is an admirable exponent of all that.'

**53** D: 'A quartet of stories, all of which take place on an island in the Baltic Sea … Theorin is very good on the unspoken secrets of small communities.'

**54** A: 'Then suddenly, with *The Broken Shore*, he hit something quite different and moved up several notches.'

**55** B: 'She doesn't just do the easy thing to be recognised … genre writers are told to create a brand or a series, a recognisable hook. Cody will often turn her back on that and focus on what her inner voice is telling her.'

**56** A: 'Providing an object lesson in how to say a lot without unnecessary verbiage.'

 **TEST 8**

## PAPER 2 Writing

▶▶ **PART 1** (*suggested answers*)

### Question 1
*Style:* Formal
*Content:*  1 Set a context for the essay. Give some background to the topic and class debate.
2 Choose two of the points from the notes and elaborate on them; add examples.
3 Make your own position clear:
  - say whether advertising mainly informs or exploits.
  - remember, you can also choose to have a balanced view of the argument.
  - support your views with reasons and examples.
4 Offer some alternative views on the matter and say whether you agree with them.
5 Write a brief conclusion summing up the main points and reiterating your position.

▶▶ **PART 2** (*suggested answers*)

### Question 2
*Style:* Formal
*Content:*  1 Open with an appropriate greeting such as *Dear Sir or Madam,*.
2 First paragraph: state why you are writing and mention where and when you saw the poster.
3 Second paragraph: describe in detail your objections to the circus, such as the confinement of the animals, and add any original ideas of your own.
4 Third paragraph:
  - state what you expect of the council.
  - reiterate why this issue is important.
  - say that you hope to hear back as soon as possible.
5 Sign off with a polite closing expression.

### Question 3
*Style:* Formal or semi-formal
*Content:*  1 Give the report a suitable title.
2 Introduction: state the purpose of the report and give a little additional background about the situation.
3 Main body:
  - devote a section to each issue with the cafeteria (choose two or three).
  - describe the problem in each case.
  - mention what employees have been saying.
  - make suggestions for improvements.
  If possible, explain how these changes could be implemented.
4 Summarise the main points in your concluding paragraph.

### Question 4
*Style:* Informal or semi-formal
*Content:*  1 Give the review a title.
2 Introduction: try to open this type of review with a strong sentence, and state what you are reviewing: the name of the band, the venue, when it took place and any other relevant details.
3 Main body:
  - provide some background information about the band, for example, how many members, what genre of music they play, etc.
  - single out some positive points about the concert and describe them.
  - balance the review with some negative observations.
  - state whether you enjoyed the concert or not.
4 Conclusion: state whether you would recommend this band to others and say why.
(See page 205 for a model answer to this question.)

**TEST 8**

## PAPER 3 Listening

▶▶ **PART 1**

**1** B  **2** A  **3** C  **4** C  **5** B  **6** B

▶▶ **PART 2**

**7** enhance  **8** uphill battle  **9** financial ruin  **10** mess about
**11** ruled out  **12** exhaustive tests  **13** regulated
**14** representation

▶▶ **PART 3**

**15** B  **16** D  **17** C  **18** D  **19** B  **20** A

▶▶ **PART 4**

**21** B  **22** D  **23** H  **24** G  **25** E  **26** C  **27** F  **28** E
**29** H  **30** A